# RECLAIMING
# OUR ROOTS

# RECLAIMING OUR ROOTS

## AN INCLUSIVE INTRODUCTION TO CHURCH HISTORY

### VOLUME 2
### MARTIN LUTHER TO MARTIN LUTHER KING

## MARK ELLINGSEN

WIPF & STOCK · Eugene, Oregon

Wipf and Stock Publishers
199 W 8th Ave, Suite 3
Eugene, OR 97401

Reclaiming Our Roots, Volume II
An Inclusive Introduction to Church History:
From Martin Luther to Martin Luther King, Jr.
By Ellingsen, Mark
Copyright©1999 by Ellingsen, Mark
ISBN 13: 978-1-62032-082-2
Publication date 3/1/12
Previously published by Trinity Press International, 1999

*To Betsey,*
*one of my first conversation partners,*
*and certainly my favorite,*
*about the Reformation and contemporary theology*

# CONTENTS

# ACKNOWLEDGMENTS

It is hardly surprising that two books in a series would be indebted to the same folks, and so I want to acknowledge some of the same debts that I noted in the first volume. I am an author who does not write alone. The room in which I write is always filled with friends, both literally and figuratively. This book has been written about friends and heroes, about my Christian roots. As was the first volume, this book was occasioned by my responsibilities within a very special part of the Christian community — the Interdenominational Theological Center in Atlanta, Georgia, and the historic African American church it serves. Both volumes have their origins in the lectures I have delivered over the years in the Center's introductory courses on church history. As a result, both books continue to bear the marks of my oral presentations and of the wonderful students whom I have been privileged to teach in this very special institution.

Profound is my debt to the students I have taught over the years. Due to their insightful interventions, I have frequently changed my perspective on material and clarified my thinking. I hope that many of them who read this book will be able to recognize that it is they who wrote a portion of the work. No less than in the first volume, which was dedicated to them and other members of the African American church's largest theological institution, they have been coauthors.

I count my wonderful colleagues from the Center no less my coauthors. Their invaluable support, provocative insights regarding the African American church, and encouragement to explore the implications of the history of the Church for globalizing a theological curriculum have been essential elements in the writing process. Thanks again, my colleagues and friends!

As usual, my family spent the most time with me in the room in which I wrote and edited. An occasional good conversation with my children, my mother, and my wife, Betsey, in the middle of a paragraph that needed more work and further reflection had a way of making the writing process a lot more fun. My mother, Edna, spent many hours helping me with the arduous task of indexing the volume and running off the hard copy from the computer. We too were not alone in the room, as we reminisced about our deceased loved ones and our shared roots while we worked.

As for Betsey, her contribution as conversation partner predates this book. As we talked about some of the Reformers and the contemporary theologians dealt with in this volume, I was reminded of the long and happy history of twenty-eight years in which we have been engaged in these conversations, almost since the beginning of my seminary days at Yale. Of all my conversation partners, some of whom I have known longer than I have known Betsey, none has been involved with me and my work in quite as intimate a way as she has through our long association and subsequent years of marriage. I indicated in volume 1 that she would receive the thanks she deserves this time. Consequently the book you have in your hands is a heartfelt thank you to her for joining me in conversation and in our life together.

## INTRODUCTION

# FORERUNNERS
# OF THE REFORMATION

The study of church history may seem a bit more relevant to those who have worked through the first fifteen centuries of the Church's life than to those who are just starting their study at the brink of the Reformation. Such experienced students, if they no longer think of church history as a mere collection of facts but as an opportunity to engage in conversation with the Church's richly diverse heritage, have also begun to appreciate the relevance of the discipline as a necessary competency for ministry. These students are ready to appreciate the role that church history can play as (1) community builder (teaching the faithful their heritage), (2) safety patrol (sensitizing church leaders to the errors of the past that still must be confronted), (3) instrument of liberation (teaching the ability to look at reality from the perspective of the other, no longer chained to one's own suppositions and cultural biases), and (4) source of theological creativity (providing access to the stimulating insights of the great theological minds of the past). Although this book and its companion volume are unique in offering a truly inclusive presentation of the rich diversity of Christian roots, readers will nevertheless experience a degree of familiarity with this text's subjects. They bring us closer to home, are more modern. Protestants will finally encounter the stories of their own denominations. However, at this point in the story of the Church's life, on the eve of the Reformation, we are still a long way from the modern world that we know.

My concern to initiate a "conversation" between readers and the data of the Church's history is crucial in order to avoid reducing courses in the field to the mere accumulation of facts. The material in this book will only come alive when readers enter into conversation with the great theologians since the fifteenth century — argue with them and/or assess the degree to which the readers' own theological commitments are indebted to these great mentors. Readers need to imagine what life and ministry were like in the centuries covered in this volume to appreciate why the Church took the positions and acted as it did.

1

In order to facilitate this appropriation process of the material covered in this volume, in each chapter the concluding section will frame a question with the intent of prodding readers to come to some conclusion about the issue addressed. Each of these issues is framed with an eye towards helping readers develop their own theological perspective. At other points in the chapters, questions are posed about the events, persons, and movements considered. Rather than determine mastery of historical facts, these questions aim to guide readers in developing their own theological perspective in relation to the material covered. They can help readers reclaim the rich diversity of Christian roots and order its wealth. In keeping with this book's commitment to inclusivity, these questions are deliberately open-ended and do not lend themselves to quick and simple answers. They do not require expertise, but they will require long periods of reflection and a willingness to live with the material. Instructors might use these questions (or formulate their own) as a means of assisting the process of educating students to think theologically about both the tradition and present realities. Sensitivity to these pedagogical matters is one of the distinguishing characteristics of this introduction to church history.

The sort of contemporary dialogue with the past that I suggest presupposes that one has first taken the historical figures and events being considered on their own terms and in their own context. This commitment implies that we have actually read the works of the giants of the Church's past. Study of the primary sources is absolutely essential. To that end, I have prepared texts that facilitate such study. At every point in each chapter when theological commitments are attributed to the persons considered, primary-source documentation is provided. These references provide a starting point for investigating the actual writings of the theologian on the subject in question. As such, this book and its companion volume are invitations and tools for facilitating an actual encounter between readers and the great theologians of the past.

Even when this feature of the textbook in your hands is taken into account, I nevertheless urge a careful and limited use of it. Like every other survey of the rich history of the Church, it shortchanges readers. It can only function adequately as an introduction to church history when its readers are keeping the author and his interpretations "honest" by supplementing the text with ample readings in the primary sources themselves.

In connection with the historian's concern to be "honest" with the sources, it is curious to note that as the twentieth century has proceeded, historians have become increasingly aware of the distortions that can result if the Reformation is regarded as a precursor of modernity. In fact, the Reformers were thoroughly medieval people, who were responding to what were essentially medieval issues. Consequently, before examining the life and work of the sixteenth-century Protestant Reformers, we need to remind ourselves first of the socioreligious dynamics of medieval Western society in its waning stages.

## Life in the Middle Ages

For those living in Western society in the Middle Ages, life was harsh, as it had been in the previous centuries. Human experience was oppressively constricted, with few options. To a great extent, such regimentation was a function of the precariousness of human life. Survival was the name of the game. For both the elite and the masses, a sense of powerlessness was typical. Since the fall of the Roman Empire, even the southern regions of the West had become second-class cultures in comparison to surrounding Greek and Islamic cultures. But life was also harsh for Christians in these regions. The Orthodox Church in Constantinople was threatened with invasion. Islamic rulers governed Coptic Christians. In East Asia, Nestorian Christianity (still rejecting the unity of Christ's person) shrank. Everywhere people were bereft of power to resist the plagues, famines, robbers, and local wars that beset them.

In the fleeting, transitory world that Westerners knew, it is little wonder that the Church and monastic life exerted the important impact that they did. In a world of meaningless change, people yearned for permanence, something eternal, and for deliverance from the crises they faced. The Church alone could offer this to the citizens of medieval Western society.

As thoroughly dependent on the spiritual realm as they were, medieval Westerners were not about to make religion merely a Sunday affair, as characterizes much modern Western life. This was no secular society. The practical meaning of religion, a sense of divine intervention in daily life, a sense of the miraculous, was indelibly imprinted in the medieval Western psyche. Such miracles were everywhere in evidence. They were revealed in religious ceremonies (as bread was daily transformed miraculously into Christ's body in the Eucharist, as taught by the Catholic doctrine of transubstantiation) and evident in saintly lives, healings, and holy relics, which were typically on display. Through these, powerless human beings had something to which to cling: the supernatural was there to protect them from all flux.

This medieval sense of total dependence on God and the loss of a central, uniting governing power in Europe after the fall of Rome (even the great Carolingian Empire created through Charlemagne's military

conquests lasted less than a century) had important sociopolitical consequences. They combined to create a social milieu in which the Church
and the papacy as its head came to play the powerful role as sanctifier of
governments and coordinator of international military operations, such
as the Crusades.

## The Decline of the Middle Ages

Medieval life as heretofore described began to unravel in the late thirteenth and fourteenth centuries. At least three factors account for this:
socioeconomic changes, the corrupting influence of secular power, and
intellectual developments.

### Socioeconomic Changes

One of the major developments during these centuries was the gradual evolution of a capitalist economy, including international trade. The
High Middle Ages, from the time after Charlemagne in the early ninth
century until the fifteenth century, organized itself with a system called
"feudalism." Basically feudalism is an economic system in which (because there is no trade and money is not circulating) wealth is defined
by land ownership. Recall that peasants (called "vassals" in this system) placed themselves under the protection of a lord due to the unruly
circumstances of early medieval society. Gaining such protection was se-
cured contractually. The one who was protected was allowed to stay on
the land that the family had owned and continue to work it. The lord
who offered the protection was ceded ownership of the land and consequently was entitled to a certain percentage of its products. Originally
the contract was binding only during the lifetime of the two parties.
However, in time the system became hereditary. Thus, if a father ceded
his land to a lord, the father's son would also have rights to work the
land after the father's death, but it would still be owned by the heirs of
the lord.

Towards the end of the Middle Ages the system started to break
down. As living conditions worsened, the masses came to recognize how
it exploited them. Capitalism began to emerge, as trade flourished. With
trade, wealth came again to be measured, not in terms of land, but in
terms of accumulated capital and cash. A natural rivalry developed between the bourgeoisie and the feudal lords, thus further undermining
feudalism. Petty royal wars, after all, were bad for business. They stifled
trade. Kings (sovereign rulers of large ethnic groups) whose power had
been markedly reduced during the period of feudalism (for in some cases

lords controlled more land and so more loyal troops than the kings) could now bypass the lords and hire their own troops. These kings also had the support of the rising class of merchants, for strong centralized rule would unite more people in peaceful coexistence, thereby opening larger markets for the emerging capitalists. The end of feudalism marked the beginnings of the creation of strong national states in Europe, such as England, France, and eventually Spain, as we know them today.

The capitalist need for market expansion had other sociopolitical implications. Trade with other continents, especially with the Far East, seemed the answer for the new Western economy's mandate for growth. This quest for new markets in the East, the search for more direct travel lines to the Asian continent, was of course the dynamic that drove the Portuguese to Africa and the Spanish, with Columbus at the helm, to the New World.

A fundamental economic law is that significant alterations of capitalist economies require cheap labor in order to be implemented. Developing capitalism required such cheap labor. Slavery, an institution already indigenous to Africa, especially in Islamic quarters, suggested such a pool of cheap labor. European explorers of the continent, observing its practice of coerced indentured servanthood, eventually evolved the institution of the modern slavery of people of African descent in response to the new economic climate. This linking of slavery and capitalism is one of the marks of the transition from the Middle Ages to modernity. Does capitalism depend on oppression?

### Secular Power Corrupts

A second characteristic of the late Middle Ages that contributed to the disintegration of the age was the corrupting influence that secular power, and the quest for such power, had on the Church, as evidenced in the Church's foreign missions work. The Catholic Church's work in the new mission fields in Asia and Africa was to a great extent linked to colonialism. Generally speaking, the first target of the missions was the European colonists or those indigenous peoples of the region who became Westernized for various reasons. The cultural arrogance of these Roman Catholic outreach efforts is evident not only in the Church's general refusal to provide educational opportunities and the possibility of ordination to converts from the indigenous peoples but also in the decision in the early sixteenth century to undertake a mission to Ethiopia (a nation that already had an established, albeit non-Catholic, church). Perhaps the clearest evidence of colonialism's corruption of the late medieval Catholic missionary work was the papacy's 1434 sanction of the institution of slavery. Eugenius IV claimed that colonization at least rescued the heathen from perdition. A number of priests based in African missions in that century and later are reported to have owned slaves.

On the European continent itself, the Church was clearly corrupted by its leaders' quest for power. A clerical career was seen as an opportunity for social advancement or a way of preserving the social status of one's kin. Nobles or the wealthy often guided their younger sons to the priesthood in order that those who could not inherit the estate might still lead the good life, for at least then their children would have control over substantial property owned by the Church. Given these dynamics, it is hardly surprising that *simony* (the buying and selling of ecclesiastical posts) was widespread. Indeed the system became so corrupt that many held clerical posts, profiting monetarily, but were never on the scene to give pastoral care. Clerical celibacy was frequently violated publicly. Bishops and local priests often flaunted their illegitimate children. Educational requirements for the priesthood were virtually nil. Corruption was even evident in monasteries, which in the late Middle Ages were often little more than houses of pleasure.

Such dynamics in the Church are not really astonishing when we recognize that circumstances were even worse with the papacy. Several cataclysmic events in the thirteenth and fourteenth centuries rocked it and the whole Western church. These included the Hundred Years' War (a series of military actions largely fought between England and France from 1337 to 1453), the bubonic plague (which decimated much of western Europe's citizenry and economy in 1347), and the conquest of Constantinople by Moslem Turks in 1453. Eastern Orthodox Christianity was effectively cut off from further expansion and contact with the West.

When the fourteenth century began, the papacy was in the hands of Boniface VIII (ca. 1234–1303), a shrewd political operator. In the tradition of reforming popes who preceded him in the thirteenth century, Boniface tried to stabilize the political situation. He forced Italian troublemakers into exile and sought to pressure both the French and the English kings to put off conflicts that eventually led to the Hundred Years' War. In these efforts he was only partially successful.

Relations with the French king grew tense. In 1302, Boniface's response was to issue a papal bull entitled *Unam Sanctam*, which claimed that the spiritual authority should judge the temporal authority.[1] The French king, Philip, reacted negatively to Boniface's assertion. The pope explored several options for responding to the king's recalcitrance, fi-

---

1. There had been earlier precedents for such an assertion of ecclesiastical authority, particularly a 1202 papal decree of Innocent III entitled *Sicut universitatis Conditor* and a letter of Gregory VII to the bishop of Metz in 1081.

nally threatening excommunication. Philip responded by capturing the pope. Having lost authority, Boniface died shortly thereafter.

Subsequent popes sought reconciliation with the French. Pope Clement V (1264–1314) was elected by a pro-French party. Never once during his pontificate did he come to Rome. He took up residence in Avignon, France. From 1309 until 1377 it was the papal residence. During this period of the "Avignon papacy," the pope was little more than a tool of French policy. Simony was also widespread at this time, and long episcopal vacancies were encouraged in order that the diocesan funds would be diverted to Avignon to support its lifestyle and military actions.

Calls for the papacy to return to Rome and for an end to papal corruption were heard throughout the Church. The Avignon papacy was demonstrably corrupt. All church resources were put in the service of the French during the Hundred Years' War. These dynamics created a real sense of alienation towards the papacy among France's rivals — England and the Holy Roman Empire. Finally after appeals by the great and internationally renowned mystic Catherine of Siena (1347–80), Pope Gregory XI (1329–78) returned to Rome in 1377.

Gregory's return did not settle the problems, for the same political dynamics continued to exist. In fact, he almost succumbed to pressure to go back to Avignon. With his death, a French pope seemed a shoo-in for election (since in the Avignon period a majority of the cardinals appointed were French). Under pressure from Roman citizens, a reform-minded pope was elected. However, he was too radical in his reforms. Disgruntled cardinals elected a pretender, who took up residence in Avignon. Thus, the Church was divided by what has come to be known as the Great Western Schism.

The schism proceeded to the chagrin of many. In the late fourteenth century, as efforts to bring the rival popes to negotiation failed, the conciliar movement began developing. The movement's core commitment was the belief that a universal council representing the whole Church through the bishops had more authority than the pope. Conciliarists took this position as a way to resolve the papal schism. A council could settle the question of who was the legitimate pope (Council of Constance *Sacrosancta*).

Cardinals of both parties met in Pisa in 1409. With the support of most of the European royalty, they elected a new pope. Unfortunately the two rival popes refused to resign, so now the Church had three popes. Eventually the schism was resolved when the Roman pope resigned after the Council of Constance meeting in 1415 deposed the successor of the pope elected by the earlier Council of Pisa. The cardinals at Constance proceeded to elect Martin V (1368–1431), and the

Avignon pretender lost influence. The schism was thereby resolved. During the next decades, Martin and his successor successfully diffused subsequent councils, and the conciliar movement in general fell into dissolution. From then on, councils of the Roman Catholic Church would ever remain subordinate to the pope.

Following these controversies, popes of the late fifteenth to early sixteenth centuries were heavily influenced by the *Renaissance* (a rebirth of interest in classical Greek and Roman civilization). Some scholars have even concluded that this movement affected pontiffs more than the gospel did. In any case, the prime agenda of the papacy in these years seems to have been to restore the glories of ancient Rome by whatever means it took — bribery, intrigue, war.

Good Renaissance men that they were, these popes were great patrons of the arts, sometimes devoting more attention to beautifying Rome than to the care of souls. The best cases in point are the popes who reigned just before and during Martin Luther's lifetime. They supervised the decoration of the Vatican and the completion of the Vatican's Sistine Chapel and St. Peter's Cathedral. Of course, all this cost money, so they authorized the sale of *indulgences* (the remission by the Church of punishments deserved by the sinner, in effect enabling the believer's more prompt release from purgatory). Outraged about these developments, many committed Christians determined that the shenanigans must stop. Consequently on the eve of the Reformation in the sixteenth century, in the waning stages of the Middle Ages, a yearning for reform was in the air, which sets the stage for considering the intellectual developments that characterized the late Middle Ages.

### Intellectual Developments

*The pre-Reformers.* The desire for reform manifested itself in the work of the pre-Reformers of the late fourteenth to early fifteenth centuries. Foremost among these figures were the British theologian John Wycliffe (ca. 1330–84) and his next generation admirer John Huss (ca. 1372–1415), the Bohemian Catholic. Girolamo Savonarola (1452–98) was another pre-Reformer thorn in the side of the hierarchy. An Italian Dominican, Savonarola was especially critical of the luxury lived by many of the political and ecclesiastical leaders of the day. For a while he kindled the beginnings of an aborted monastic reform but was condemned a heretic and eventually hanged.

John Wycliffe was not only a much-admired professor of theology at England's most prestigious university; his political connections among England's elite were also most impressive. Consequently any reform movement he initiated was sure to gain a hearing. Drawing together followers who became known as the Lollards (a pejorative title derived from the word meaning "mumbles"), Wycliffe argued on behalf of a reform agenda against the exercise of authority by the Church for its own benefit or the exercise of such authority for purely secular purposes. Given the fact that during his lifetime the papacy resided in Avignon, France, totally under the thumb of the French king, it is understandable why this Englishman took such a stand.

In the context of the Great Western Schism — when rival popes made claims to be the true pope — and in the midst of an anticlerical sentiment held by many in the late Middle Ages, Wycliffe began to teach that the true Church is, not the pope and the hierarchy, but the invisible body of the predestined. This Augustinian point would be more fully developed by the Protestant Reformers, especially Luther. Along the same lines, Wycliffe urged putting the Bible back in the hands of the laity.[2] Wycliffe's followers picked up this theme and worked to have the Bible translated into English.

The English pre-Reformer's most controversial position was his rejection of *transubstantiation* (the Roman Catholic belief that the consecrated bread and wine in Communion become the body and blood of Christ and are no longer bread and wine) in favor of the claim that though the body of Christ is present in Communion, his presence does not destroy the bread (*Propositions of Wycliffe condemned* 1–2).[3] Wycliffe's followers, the Lollards, went so far as to deny the value of pilgrimages, indulgences on behalf of the deceased, and even confession. They also condemned the exercise of political authority by the episcopacy (*Lollard Conclusions* 6–9). Since these were attacks at the very heart of medieval Catholicism, it is no wonder Wycliffe and the Lollards were condemned, especially when they started applying the servant model of authority to the way in which the state should exercise authority (*De Haeretico Comburendo*).

Wycliffe died in communion with the Church. His treatment of soteriology as the cooperation of prevenient grace with works of merit was a Catholic position — in the sense of Thomas Aquinas (*On the Pastoral Office* II.12; *De domino divino* 61). Wycliffe's affirmation of prevenient grace took an Augustinian character with his understanding of predestination as an election either to salvation or to reprobation, which is known as "double predestination" (*Sermons* 1.52; 2.24). His views were formally condemned posthumously by the Council of Constance in 1415. In Wycliffe's native England, though his early support from the

---

2. His commitments are suggestive of the characteristic Reformation concept of the priesthood of all believers.

3. This view is most suggestive of the positions taken later by Luther or Calvin on the Eucharist.

nobility gradually began to erode, the Lollard movement became a popular one that exerted much influence on Parliament. Although most of the Lollards among the nobility recanted as the pressure against Wycliffe intensified and as it became evident that the movement jeopardized their own self-interest, the movement went underground. Early in the sixteenth century it enjoyed a revival. Lollard loyalists were an important part of the eventual success of the Reformation in England later in the century.

John Huss was an earnest, albeit second-hand, student of Wycliffe, but was more moderate than his mentor. The overriding concern of this well-known Bohemian Catholic preacher and university professor was to restore sincere practice of the Christian life in the Church, not to alter its doctrines (*On Simony* 10). Huss lived during the period of the Great Western Schism. After a controversy with the Catholic hierarchy over the validity of teaching the works of Wycliffe, Huss began to teach that an unworthy pope ought not to be obeyed. The Bible, he argued, is the final authority by which popes are to be judged (4).[4] Like the Reformers, Huss rejected indulgences.

Huss's followers (largely members of the nobility and the bourgeoisie) joined with a lower-class Bohemian Christian movement, the Taborites, which taught that anything not found in Scripture is an illicit practice. That is, if the Bible does not say anything about a practice, it is to be rejected.[5] The Hussites, by contrast, only condemned what the Bible explicitly condemned. The dispute between these two distinct viewpoints regarding the role of biblical authority has played itself out in a number of distinct forms throughout the Church's history. Consequently readers should try to discern their own positions relative to these options. Despite their differences, the two groups formed a coalition, which made two demands: (1) that Communion be given in both kinds (since during the Middle Ages only bread had been distributed to the laity so that they would not run the risk of desecrating Christ's blood by dribbling it as they drank) and (2) that clergy be deprived of all wealth.

The Council of Constance condemned Huss in 1415, but his followers achieved a compromise that addressed several of their concerns with the Bohemian Church. Those who remained dissatisfied, most of whom were Taborites, left the established church, thus forming the Union of Brethren, who spread to Moravia in present-day Germany. This group eventually evolved in the eighteenth century, under the leadership of Ludwig von Zinzendorf (1700–1760) into the Moravian Church.

---

4. Such arguments clearly prefigured the Reformation affirmation of *sola scriptura*.
5. The Taborites were also an apocalyptic movement.

*Mysticism.* The quest for reform was also evidenced in the growing impact of *mysticism* — a set of beliefs that maintains that through disciplined contemplation one can achieve communion (union) with God. Such commitments have the (sometimes unwitting) effect of undercutting the authority of the Church and its external rites. To the extent that one can have access to God through one's personal experience, it follows at least by implication that such Christians do not require intermediaries.

To be sure, mysticism was no new development in the late Middle Ages. Bernard of Clairvaux (1090–1153) and Francis of Assisi (1181/2–1226) in the High Middle Ages had been prominent mystics. In the late Middle Ages, the big names in mysticism were Meister Eckhart (ca. 1260–1327), Thomas à Kempis (1380–1471), an anonymous German work called *German Theology*, Julian of Norwich (ca. 1342–after 1413), Catherine of Siena (1347–80), and the Brethren of the Common Life — a mystical order founded by Gerhard Groote (1340–84). Some of these mystics, such as Eckhart (*Sermons* 1), were very influenced by the philosophy of Neoplatonism. Others, such as à Kempis, unwittingly endorsed a kind of Semi-Pelagianism (*On the Imitation of Christ* 1.25; 2.1). Such views were very much in the air in the late Middle Ages.

In the work of two women mystics of the period, Catherine of Sienna and Julian of Norwich, we can identify some very significant trends. Along with *German Theology* (2,9), both affirmed unambiguously the unconditional love of God and prevenient grace (Catherine of Siena *Dialogue* 148; Julian of Norwich *Showings* 82,58,11). Besides teaching grace and election (*Dialogue* 134), Catherine also emphasized striving for perfection (47). Julian's contributions are no less significant. As early as the fourteenth century, the Catholic Church countenanced (did not condemn) her references to God as Mother.[6] The second person of the Trinity is God our Mother, she claimed, in the sense that in becoming incarnate God has in the second person taken on our sensuality. Presumably in accord with the cultural suppositions of the era, Julian understood womanhood in terms of sensuality. Julian also regarded God's motherhood as manifest insofar as the second person of the Trinity is identified as Wisdom (Sophia), who created us in our sensuality, and deemed Christ as the Mother of mercy (*Showings* 58). Has Julian solved our modern problem with divine gender?

Late medieval mysticism clearly made significant positive contributions to the Reformation. Besides indirectly undermining the authority of Catholic ecclesiology, mysticism aided in the recovery of the Pauline-Augustinian emphases on sin, unconditional forgiveness, and the char-

---

6. She also spoke of God as Brother and Savior.

acter of Christian life as a constant struggle. These were themes that Martin Luther came to stress.[7] In addition, Erasmus (ca. 1469–1536), the greatest of the Renaissance humanists, was trained in the Brethren of the Common Life schools.

*Renaissance humanism.* The humanism of the Renaissance was a sweeping intellectual development that eventually undermined medieval life. As noted, the Renaissance was a rediscovery of the glories of ancient Greek and Roman cultures and their art, and *humanism* is the term employed to designate the practice of these Renaissance ideals. Tied to the Renaissance agenda was the hope that these new sources and opportunities for learning (the printing press had just been invented) could help reform the Church.

One immediate consequence of the movement was an outburst of significant artistic interest and the creation of some of the West's greatest artistic treasures. The work of famed artists such as Michelangelo (Buonarroti; 1475–1564) and Leonardo da Vinci (1452–1519) come to mind. Both focused much more on extolling human splendor than the glories of heaven, as was typical of the art of earlier medieval centuries. This stylistic shift, then, provided one more indication of the end of the medieval "Age of Faith." Artists and other educated persons were thus freed to begin to consider human beings and reality without reference to God. Though such observations sound normal to our modern ears, they were astounding to the medieval mind-set.

The Renaissance preoccupation with ancient texts eventually led to questions about the authority of the West's Latin translation of the Bible, the Vulgate, which had been Western Christianity's only authoritative Bible since its preparation by Jerome in the fourth century. We see in this agenda the beginning of Western scholarly concern to consider the Bible in its original languages, an agenda that the Reformers and pre-Reformers readily embraced. Already in the Renaissance, then, the stage was set for our modern approach to exegesis.

The greatest Renaissance scholar was the Dutch humanist and illegitimate son of a priest Erasmus, who became the truly international star of Renaissance scholarship. Erasmus sought a reformation of the Church through classical learning. He urged educated Christians to seek a balanced life. In his view, the ethics of Jesus, purged of Scholastic speculation, was the key to such living. Such an ethic closely resembles Stoic philosophy, which Erasmus admired. As Stoicism advocated, Erasmus claimed that the key to a balanced life not swayed by passions was the practice of discipline (*Enchiridion Militis Christiani* I.5;

---

7. In fact, there is much debate among scholars concerning whether much of Luther's theology is not indebted to mysticism.

II). Somewhat in the spirit of Thomas Aquinas and the Scholastic tradition, Erasmus claimed that this ethic is only possible because of divine mercy (*Concerning the Immense Mercy of God*).

In addition to these commitments, Erasmus held that the Church would do well to purge all pomp. He was also critical of monasticism.[8] In Erasmus's view, discipline is more important than doctrine. His thought is marked by a kind of mystical piety, like the one he learned in the schools of the Brethren of the Common Life. Thus, people are to find God through inwardness, not through external ceremony. During the Reformation, Erasmus took an unsurprising middle ground between the Catholics and Reformers in the dispute.

Should a last word on the Renaissance be one of mixed judgment? Its optimism and anthropocentrism were unquestionably harbingers of the modern era. Yet this human-centered movement could not of itself reform the Church.

**Nominalism.** The oldest of the intellectual currents that transformed the Middle Ages, nominalism is rooted in the philosophy of two famed philosophers of the British Isles — John Duns Scotus (ca. 1265–1308), who was really only a forerunner of movement, and William of Ockham (1285–1347), who was its true progenitor. Other late Scholastic, nominalist theologians include Robert Holcot (d. 1349) and Gabriel Biel (d. 1495).

Nominalism was committed to demystifying the use of reason, a philosophical aspect that was highly influential on Martin Luther. The movement's indebtedness to Scotus has its roots in his insistence that reason and faith do not intersect at all points, that some truths of faith are beyond the sphere of reason. Though of course Aquinas had made this point with regard to some truths of faith, Scotus greatly increased the list of revealed truths that a Christian should believe but cannot prove (*On the First Principle; Quodlibeta* 7.23). These commitments were also related to his emphasis on God's sovereign freedom (*Oxford Commentary on the Sentences* I.41), a theological affirmation that also greatly influenced nominalism.

Whereas Scotus still believed in the reality of universals (*Oxford Commentary on the Sentences* I.43), William of Ockham went beyond Scotus's claims by developing a principle that was to be later known as "Ockham's razor:" Explain what is the case in the simplest way (*Reportatio* II,Q.15). He challenged the Aristotelian-Platonic idea that a universal form is more real than the perceived individual thing itself (*Summa totius logicae* I,C.xiv). For example, one need not posit the idea

---

8. At this point we seem to hear heralds of Luther's doctrine of vocation, the belief that all stations in life and legitimate jobs are equally valid opportunities to serve God.

of the universal form of humanity in order to conclude that the students in a class are human beings who really exist. For Ockham, what you see is what you get (*Quodlibeta* I.Q.i).

What are we to make of the nominalist rejection of the reality of universal forms? It has clearly won the day in the Western intellectual tradition. The nominalist emphasis on the reality of the individual physical things and the unique experience of them, not on spiritual-rational entities such as the forms, focused academic inquiry on the truth to be gained though experience of the physical world in a way that made the rise of modern science possible. That may or may not be a good thing.

Setting reason free in this way, as the nominalists did, entailed recognizing its limits. In contrast to most Scholastic theologians, notably Thomas Aquinas, nominalists claimed that reason could not prove the core doctrines of the faith, not even the existence of God (Ockham *Quodlibeta* I.Q.i). There is a wholesome commitment at stake in the insistence on the discontinuity of reason and faith. Virtually all of the nominalists in the tradition of Scotus, especially Ockham, were concerned to affirm God's sovereign will. Nothing is above God; not even reason may judge God. Thus, one should not say God always does good; rather, what God does is good only because God does these things. If God acts, it is good even if the action is evil according to the standards of human reason. By the same token, God did not *need* Jesus to redeem human beings, for however God had decreed to save us would have worked. God's solemn (predestining) will is the final reality (Ockham *Quodlibeta* VI.Q.vi; Duns Scotus *Oxford Commentary on the Sentences* III.19).

Such emphases on the sovereignty of God's Will seem quite Augustinian and suggestive of Luther and Calvin. Their collective concept of faith as, not mere belief, but trust is also most suggestive of themes in Luther and Calvin (Ockham *Quodlibeta* I.Q.i). Also the general turmoil in ecclesiastical institutions of the day led nominalists to skepticism about the authority of church structures like the papacy and councils (Ockham *Brief Statement on the Tyrannical Principate* 3.15). Since reason is always subordinate to God, only one authority was left: an infallible Scripture. Ockham more or less embraced this affirmation (*Dialogue* 1.2.2).

Despite apparent points of agreement, the nominalists and the Reformers also had important differences. These were so significant that one might claim that the Reformers' disagreements with the nominalists may be what the Reformation was all about. For reasons that are unclear (we can only assume it might relate to the preoccupation with reform and the concern about Christian commitment that characterized the thought of many Christian scholars in the late Middle Ages), nominalists modified the characteristic mode of the Scholastics for describing redemption. All Scholastics employed the concept of preparation for grace and human will's responsibility.[9] Human beings must do something, it was taught, in order to prepare themselves to receive God's saving grace when it is given. The great Scholastic theologian and recognized spokesman of the Catholic Church Thomas Aquinas best illustrates how these Scholastic commitments do not necessarily lead to works righteousness. Of course, he insisted that there is a role for the human will in receiving grace, in preparing for grace. However, just as clearly, Aquinas insisted that even that act of preparation by our wills ("the movement of the free will toward God") is an act of God's grace that is infused in the believer (*Summa Theologica* I/II.113). In that sense he affirmed that salvation is *sola gratia* (by grace alone). God does everything. Even our turning to God in preparation is a consequence of God's act. Is there anything inimical to Protestantism in these commitments?

By contrast, the nominalists used the scheme of preparation for grace, but many of them failed to give credit to God's grace as the driving force of the human will in preparing to receive the grace that saves. When humans do their very best, God accepts what they have done of themselves as adequate preparation (Biel *Commentary on the Sentences* II.27–28; Holcot *Super Libros Sapientiae* III.35). In other words, along with Aquinas the nominalists teach that we are saved though cooperation of grace and works. However, unlike Aquinas, they held that the human work of preparation preceded the initial gift of grace.

Although rooted in Scotus's Augustinian commitments to assert the sovereignty of God's Will and a correlated doctrine of predestination not based on merit (Scotus *Quodlibeta* 16.17), Ockham and his followers radically amended these commitments by applying the "razor" to explaining the reality of justification. Committed to viewing the Thomistic concept of prevenient infused grace as extraneous, they prioritized the believer's preparatory work of turning to God in the salvation process, thus amending Scotus's concept of predestination. In their view, God elects on the basis of foreseen good works by the elect (Ockham *Ordinatio* D. XXXVIII, Q.unica; *Predestination and the Foreknowledge of God* 1). These conceptual moves locate human freedom at the beginning and the end of the salvation process, prior to God's election (which is de facto based on human response) and God's acceptance of the sinner (which nominalists posit to be contingent on human response since without such work grace is not merited).

What operates in nominalist thought is, not an outright Pelagianism,

---

9. James 4:8 (NRSV): "Draw near to God, and he will draw near to you."

but a kind of Semi-Pelagianism. God does not act alone in the saving process, for the believer is a kind of junior partner, both cooperating with grace and also meriting grace. It was against such teaching — that humans can contribute to their salvation and even initiate it — that Luther rebelled. As we will note, he and the other Reformers reacted against the teaching of the nominalist theologians and its appropriation by the late medieval Catholic Church. But it is less clear that in so doing the Reformer actually rejected the teaching of Aquinas and the officially endorsed dogma of the Roman Catholic Church.

## Conclusion: Was the Late Medieval Church in Decline, and Was This Decline Merely the Logical Outcome of Seeds Sown by the Roman Catholic Church in Previous Centuries?

Was there something about the Roman Catholic heritage that mandated the sort of (negative) developments we have noted in the late Middle Ages? Of course, one might contend that not all of these developments were negative. In that case, the Reformation was not mandated as a necessary corrective.

It might be true to say that in some aspects of its theology (at least with reference to the question of how we are saved or forgiven), the Semi-Pelagian tendencies of nominalist Catholic theology in the late Middle Ages represent a decline from High Scholasticism. Insofar as nominalism does not represent official Catholic teaching, it seems defensible to argue that the Roman Catholic heritage is not to blame for this distortion. Of course, it could also be argued that the very logic of Scholasticism, as represented by Thomas Aquinas, with its insistence on the faithful's cooperation with grace sowed the seeds for the Semi-Pelagian inclinations of nominalist theology.

As we have observed, corruption permeated ecclesiastical life in this era. Institutionally would the Western church have been less victimized by the political realm and by corruption had it not had an episcopal hierarchy? Of course, it was these same structures and the theology of the Catholic Church that nurtured the reforming instincts of the late Middle Ages. Perhaps Catholicism cannot be cited as a cause in the late medieval Church's decline.

With regard to ethics, it seems defensible to argue that the reforming instincts of the late Middle Ages, save its countenancing of slavery and permissive stance regarding Western cultural imperialism on the mission fields, represent a "harvest" of the best traditions of the medieval

Roman Catholic tradition. On the other hand, some of the data could be deemed so ambiguous as to call this conclusion into question. For example, an inherently sexist bias in Roman Catholicism seems reaffirmed by the fact that women were denied the priesthood in the late Middle Ages, as they have been throughout much of the history of the Catholic tradition. On the other hand, there are some indications of a significant role for women in the late medieval Church. Especially noteworthy in this connection is the significant impact of the female mystics Catherine of Siena and Julian of Norwich. As early as the fourteenth century, the Catholic Church countenanced the "feminist theologian" Julian and her references to God as Mother, which perhaps could be taken as an argument against an essential patriarchal bias in the Roman Catholic heritage.

In Africa, the record of the Roman Catholic tradition was abysmal, particularly concerning its position on slavery during the late Middle Ages. Yet the Church also had some intriguing successes in indigenizing the gospel in some regions during this period and in the decades immediately following. For example, in the mid-sixteenth century Catholic missionaries made an effort to accommodate the gospel to the cultures of China and India (see pp. 126–27 for more details). Even prior to, or at least as early as, the dawn of the Reformation, the Catholic Church exhibited a degree of sensitivity to indigenization on the mission field. In 1518, Pope Leo X (Giovanni de' Medici; 1475–1521) decreed a general approval of ordaining qualified Africans, Ethiopians, and Indians. In the Kongo, where Portuguese missionaries had successfully indigenized the gospel and converted the royal house early in the sixteenth century, the king's brother (or son) Henrique was ordained as the first black Catholic bishop since the fall of the Catholic Church in North Africa in the Islamic invasion of the seventh century. However, though ordained with Vatican approval, indigenous clergy were not uniformly accepted by the Church and were largely treated with hostility on the mission fields. What to make of these ambiguous dynamics in the Church's missionary work is a question that students of the late Middle Ages and of the heritage of the Church universal must answer for themselves. The scholarly community has not reached a consensus on these matters of great ecumenical import.

In determining the significance of the material covered in this introduction for understanding the Reformation and the validity of the continuing existence of Protestantism, the theological issues we have raised seem particularly crucial. Perhaps the greatest failure of the late medieval Church was in the area of theology, in its treatment of the doctrine of justification, with its insistence on a role for the believer, unaided by grace, in the salvation process. But as we have already observed, this is not what the Roman Catholic Church authoritatively teaches. However, should the Scholastic theological traditions of the High Middle Ages, themselves rooted in certain developments of the early Church, not be held responsible for creating a climate in which the questionable nominalist commitments emerged?

These reflections raise a pressing theological-ecclesiastical question for the student of church history: To the degree that Luther and the other Reformers were reacting primarily to a distinct theological strand within the Roman Catholic Church of their time, not to the official theology of the church, what are the implications for the Reformation and the continuing validity of Protestantism? How readers answer this and the foregoing questions will say much about their ecumenical and theological positions.

# CHAPTER 1

# MARTIN LUTHER
## PILGRIMAGE TO REFORMATION

Should the Roman Catholic tradition be blamed for the insidious developments in the late Middle Ages? Perhaps the negative developments in the period were a function of the corruption of Catholic institutions or of heterodox theological commitments that had illicit influence on the Church of the day. If this is so, have Protestants then unfairly blamed the Roman Catholic tradition? This is an important point for assessing whether the Reformation as initiated by Martin Luther (and Protestantism in general) was really necessary.

## Life in the Late Middle Ages

The era of Martin Luther is known as the late Middle Ages. In this period, life in western Europe was a little more modern than in the High Middle Ages. Feudalism was waning. Capitalism and an urban environment were developing. Yet in many ways, life was just as stark and threatening as it had been centuries before. Although the horrible plagues of the Middle Ages were abating somewhat, life was still fragile, easily snuffed out by illness (a syphilis epidemic was underway), starvation, bad weather, and war. Vestiges of pre-Christian western European religions were still in evidence in the popular piety, and common people believed the woods, waters, and caves were populated by elves, sinister spirits, and demons ready to seduce humans to sin and powerlessness. Increasingly, though, a sense of self-reflectiveness such as modern people experience began to spread among the masses.[1] The result of these late medieval dynamics was that life was more confined,

---

1. Modern Western people ask questions about human origins and their own individual happiness and fulfillment. Except for the elite, premodern Europeans had no time for these questions, which are foreign in societies where clan or tribe is more important than the individual. Moreover, such questions are luxuries when survival is threatened, as it was for many western European medieval people.

structured, and regimented than life would be experienced by their heirs or their compatriots in the twentieth century.

People of late-twentieth-century Western society try to control emotion. We do not show our deepest feelings on the job or anywhere else in public. Our jobs or our social standing might be in jeopardy were we fully to reveal ourselves. Except for some Renaissance scholars, ordinary western Europeans of the late Middle Ages knew a different set of manners and way of life. For them, the contrast between suffering and joy, between adversity and happiness, appeared more striking than it does for modern people. All experience had an unrestrained directness and absoluteness for adults, something like the way children experience emotion. Everything one did or felt in this world was expressed in the extreme, often in public. Uncontrollable sobbing at a funeral or when hearing an emotional speech was good manners. Even the consummation of marriage was a public act, with official witnesses. Everywhere there was passion, and it was expressed publicly.

There were no ambiguities in the late medieval world as there are today. What is good and right was absolutely fixed and certain. Justice had to prosecute what is unjust everywhere and to the bitter end, come what may. Retribution and punishment went to the extreme, even to the point of revenge. Perfect justice demanded. it! To the late medieval European mind, there was perhaps nothing like a good execution or some torture of the guilty to get the juices flowing. To be sure, the Church tried to teach gentleness and clemency, yet it too demanded justice. This is what the sacrament of confession was all about. After all, late medieval people had a righteous God who demands justice!

Times were harsh. Life was harsh. Late medieval western Europeans were basically pessimistic people. Consequently they often found themselves oscillating, shifting back and forth, between hatred and goodness, between cruelty and tenderness, between the fear of hell and childlike joy.

## The Role of the Sacrament of Confession in Late Medieval Piety

When one endeavors to reexperience the feelings of late medieval western European people, the Catholic Church's sacrament of penance makes all the more sense. The sacrament's origins are rooted at least as early as the third century with policies instituted by Cyprian of Carthage to deal with how to restore Christians who had lapsed during a persecution. A crucial turning point in the sacrament's development, one with great consequences for Christian piety in the Middle Ages, was the Catholic Church's Fourth Lateran Council's decision in 1215 that "all believers of both sexes who have attained the age of discretion must faithfully confess their sins in person at least once a year to their own priest, and must make the effort to carry out the imposed penance according to their ability" (Fourth Lateran Council *Constitutions* 21). Over the centuries, in view of the comfort the sacrament offered the medieval faithful, its use became even more frequent. When the sacrament of confession is properly understood, it is evident how it reflects the late medieval preoccupation with justice under strictly enforced legal standards.

The precise character of the sacrament — how it works — requires attention. If such attention is not given, confession may be incorrectly deemed, as most Protestants do, to be a manifestation of works righteousness. In fact, however, the medieval Catholic Church and its legacy apparently made all the right qualifications, at least the same kind of qualifications that Thomas Aquinas and most of the other medieval Scholastic theologians did in avoiding Pelagianism. Of course, it would be quite another matter if we conclude that Aquinas, who represents the official teaching of the Catholic Church, failed to avoid Pelagian tendencies. In that case, a similar critique could be made of the Catholic sacrament of confession.

At any rate, on Roman Catholic grounds, the sacrament consists of at least four elements: (1) contrition (truly feeling sorry for one's sins), (2) confession (the actual identification and enumeration of sins), (3) absolution (the priest's proclamation, on behalf of the Church and of God who has given the Church such authority, the priest's proclamation of forgiveness), and (4) penance or satisfaction (assignments in spiritual discipline given by the priest to the one who has confessed, exercises aimed at denying oneself for the good of the soul).

The real purpose of the sacrament of confession and penance is not to change God's mind concerning the believer. God is already determined to save. Confession and its spiritual discipline are occasions for obtaining the proper spiritual disposition to merit forgiveness (Gabriel Biel *Exposition of the Canon of the Mass* 31.C). Forgiveness or eternal life is merited in this schema in the sense that a righteous God can only justify one who has been made worthy of eternal life by the infusion of grace (by God's act of internalizing his grace in the believer). Confession and penance are acts of preparation for receiving the grace that makes one worthy of eternal life. For Catholic theology at its best, even this act of preparation, through confession and penance, is still a work of God through humans (Aquinas *Summa Theologica* I/II.113.2; I/II.114.3).

The late medieval preoccupation with strict enforcement of legal standards is very much in place in the Catholic sacrament of confession. Even God is bound by the legal code in determining who will be saved. One who is saved must be prepared in order to be worthy of meriting salvation. However, what might happen to those who had received grace but died before obtaining sufficient grace to merit eternal life? This problem was solved for the Church by the promulgation of the doctrine of purgatory under the leadership of Pope Gregory I (ca. 540–604) in the late sixth century. In this intermediate state, the remaining sins of the faithful could be purged until eternal life was merited. This doctrine would have most important consequences for the development of the Church's teaching on indulgences.

There are biblical references for the doctrine of purgatory. A passage in 2 Maccabees 12:43–45 refers to Judas Maccabeus as taking up a collection for a sin offering as atonement for the dead "so that they might be delivered from their sin" (NRSV). Matthew 12:32 presumes such a place as purgatory where sins might be forgiven after death. Jesus says, "Whoever speaks a word against the Son of Man will be forgiven, but whoever speaks against the Holy Spirit will not be forgiven, either in this age or in the age to come" (NRSV). Is this sufficient textual evidence to conclude that the Bible teaches purgatory?

The doctrine of purgatory served another useful role in pastoral care for late medieval western European people. Recall the emotionalism of the people of late medieval European society. They were prone to swing back and forth in their emotions, to the extreme. They were petrified of hell. Uncertainty among the devout concerning whether they had been contrite enough to do the good confession all the more intensified the uncertainty.[2] In this context, the doctrine of purgatory could function to give some comfort to alleviate anxiety. Even if one's confession was not perfect, at least in purgatory opportunity would be provided to work off the deficiencies. The only problem is that the Church of the day, like the emotions of its people, tended to swing from one extreme to the other. Sometimes purgatory was portrayed, not merely as a middle ground between heaven and hell where a person could work off sins, but as a place of horrors as hot as hell.

When one keeps in mind the emotional extremes in which people lived in the fifteenth and early sixteenth centuries, it is little wonder that the faithful could not tolerate the Church playing with their emotions this way. Such disillusionment was all the more exacerbated by the general disgust many educated people felt towards the rampant corruption characterizing the Church of their day. The stage was set for a man like Luther who could not handle these extremes any longer.

---

2. Another point introduced by the Catholic Church in this period was that the first step, contrition, needed to be sincere, truly arising from the love of God and not motivated by self-love, the mere desire to avoid hell (Antoninus Pierozzi *Confessional* 1.2.5).

### The Doctrine of Indulgences

The Catholic Church did make another effort to mitigate spiritual terror. The doctrine of indulgences played this role. An official basis for the doctrine was a 1343 papal bull issued by Clement VI (1291–1352). Actually indulgences could boast an older history, having probably originated during the time of the Crusades. Crusaders who fought in battle were given pardon from punishment for any sin committed. Those who did not participate in the Crusades were given the opportunity to purchase an indulgence. The Fourth Lateran Council ratified this policy regarding indulgences. Then in 1300 Pope Boniface VIII declared a year of Jubilee, whereby an indulgence could be procured by making a pilgrimage to Rome (or by purchasing the indulgence). This was the real beginning of the indulgence trade. The Jubilee was so successful that it inspired many more such years. It is little wonder that Pope Clement VI made indulgences official in 1343.

The argument on behalf of indulgences was that Christ had given the Church through Peter the power of forgiveness of sins. Jesus, being perfect, provided more merits than he or the Church could ever need. Biblical precedents could be provided. In Matthew 16:19 and 18:18, Peter was given the power of the keys, which was interpreted to mean that Peter's successor, the pope, has this authority. Given this infinite treasury of merits, it is evident that such merits may be shared with those who avail themselves of them. When these merits are conferred on the faithful, it makes them more meritorious (worthy of eternal life) and so has the effect of reducing the temporal punishments they would have otherwise deserved, either in this life or in purgatory.

The next step in the process of developing the teaching on indulgences was to apply it directly to those who had died in the faith. Loved ones of the deceased who were concerned about the sufferings their loved one might be enduring were a ready market for the indulgence trade. Given the emotional highs and lows that constituted life in western Europe in the late Middle Ages, a pitch to purchase indulgences was a winner. Consequently in western Europe, especially in Germany, the following sales pitch was heard: "As soon as the coin in the coffer rings, the soul from purgatory springs."

## Background of the Indulgence Controversy

In Western Christianity, a storm broke loose over indulgences, particularly over a clever deal worked out in the second decade of the sixteenth century between Pope Leo X and Albert of Brandenburg (also known as

Albert of Mainz; 1490–1545). Albert was a member of the very influential house of Hohenzollern in Germany, a family making a fortune by exploiting the region's resources in collaboration with foreign powers. At the time of the deal, he was a bishop of Halberstadt and Magdeburg, quite a feat since he was not old enough to be a bishop in any diocese.[3] Nevertheless, he and his powerful family wanted more: the too young bishop wanted to be archbishop of Mainz, which would make him primate of all Germany.

Inasmuch as simony was a way of life in the late medieval Church, it took money to get a job like that of archbishop. Consequently the deal to be struck involved paying the pope 10,000 ducats, which Albert could borrow and then repay from funds raised through the sale of indulgences authorized by the pope. The authorization was given on condition that half of the sales' proceeds went directly to the papacy. The pope wanted the money because he was putting the finishing touches on the great basilica of the Vatican, St. Peter's, and needed money to get the job done. Consequently, he cut the deal with the German bishop. These developments yield great irony, for the greatest, perhaps most famous, of all the Catholic churches in the world, St. Peter's, was paid for with money that eventually led to the fragmentation of the Church.

Albert's policies in selling indulgences represented a departure from previous methods of administering them. Most striking of all the innovations was the decision to *sell* the remission of sins. Other related innovations included the development of a precise schedule of rates — the amount to be paid depended on a person's status and wealth. Once a person had obtained the certificate of indulgence, it was said, the graces granted to the living through the indulgence might be bestowed even if the recipient did not make confession or worship. No less scandalous was the directive that an indulgence is valid even if the purchaser is insincere.

Albert procured a good salesman for the job. John (Johann) Tetzel (ca. 1465–1519), a Dominican, had sold indulgences for the papacy since 1504. He had a real flair for promotion, apparently without a sense of business ethics. His characteristic modus operandi when on a sales trip was to meet the local dignitaries outside the town he was entering. Then along with them he would stage a parade led by papal symbolism into the center of town. There the "sales pitch" (sermon) would begin, replete with characteristic lines: indulgences make the sin-

---

3. The episcopacies were "in the family" in the still feudal economy of late medieval Germany. All the property associated with the Church meant that having a bishop among one's kin yielded more land, and so more wealth, to the family's control.

ner "cleaner than when coming out of baptism," and "the cross of the indulgence seller has as much power as the Cross of Christ."

Outrage over this sort of false advertising was widespread among the learned, among the growing number of Renaissance scholars in the German territories at the time.[4] One factor in the negative reaction of the elite to Tetzel's sales pitch was a growing German nationalistic sentiment, which sensed that Tetzel and his episcopal and papal benefactors were fundamentally in the business of exploiting the German people. In Saxony, one of the German principalities, specifically in its main university town of Wittenberg, the most influential protest was launched in 1517 on the eve of All Saints' Day (October 31) by the young Augustinian friar, also a professor at the university, Martin Luther. It is clear that Luther did not intend to start a public controversy and still less to divide the Church or start a new one of his own. He prepared ninety-five theses simply for scholarly debate, attaching them to the door of the city's principal church, in hopes that reform of the Church catholic could be affected from within.

## Early Life of Martin Luther

The young Augustinian friar was born in 1483 in Eisleben, Germany, to a family with peasant roots that was joining the rapidly expanding German middle class. The family had great plans for Luther, regarding him as a brilliant lad who could someday make a good living in the legal profession and support them in their old age. Luther received such training until his 1505 decision to become a member of the Augustinian Order. The decision was the result of a pledge he made in the name of Saint Anne (traditionally thought to be the mother of the Virgin Mary) during a storm. He had vowed that he would devote his life to such a vocation should he be saved from the storm. Though Luther's actions might strike modern readers as odd, they represent commonsense behavior in his own highly emotional late medieval context.

Luther's peasant roots are important for understanding him. Despite all his education, he never really lost touch with those roots. Some people receive a high level of education and can never quite mix with ordinary people again because their tastes are too cultured. Though this was true of other prominent sixteenth-century Reformers, it was not the case with Luther. He remained someone who could go home again.

---

4. Recall that in the sixteenth century and for centuries to come Germany was not a united nation but, largely as a consequence of feudalism, remained divided into numerous local principalities.

Examples abound of Luther's continuing ability to relate to the mass mentality. He was a talented musician, but the music of his greatest hymn, "A Mighty Fortress," was from a tavern. Understanding these class biases in Luther in relation to the other Reformers is crucial. Indeed, such biases reflect in the thought of all the Reformers, and it is tempting to speculate whether their respective class orientations reflect in the sort of constituencies their traditions attract.

## In Quest of a Loving Father?

A number of interpreters (notably the eminent psychologist Erik Erikson) have made much of Luther's allegedly strained relationship with his father as a formative feature in his spiritual pilgrimage. Unable to find a loving relationship with his earthly father, it is argued, Luther sought a loving relationship with his heavenly Father. Such psychologizing of history may be a good example of the wrong way to do history, that is, reading the data in the light of modern values and suppositions. In the case of this increasingly influential reading of Luther, the parenting style of the young Reformer's elders is read in light of Dr. Benjamin Spock and other modern theories of permissive parenting. To do history the right way, one must read the data in light of its contemporaneous cultural context. Granted, Luther endured his share of beatings from stern parents (*Table Talk*, in *Luther's Works* [hereafter cited as *LW*] 54:235). Discipline in his educational environment was also exceedingly strict (457). However, this was characteristic of the educational style of the day.

As for Luther's relationship with his father, one can infer from the Reformer's voluminous writings that a warm affection and appreciation for his father emerged (at least as much affection as a son in a Germanic culture will ever express). Luther does not appear to have been a man searching for another (spiritual) father.[5] Though Luther's father originally disapproved of his son's entering the priesthood (*Table Talk*, in *LW* 54:109; *Letter to Hans Luther* [1521], in *LW* 48:331ff.), they apparently reconciled. Martin wrote pastoral words of comfort to his father while he was dying (*Letter to Hans Luther* [1530], in *LW* 49:267–71), and the father happily received the consolations, claiming emphatically on his deathbed that he'd be a knave not to believe his son's teachings (*Table Talk*, in *LW* 54:27). Even more significantly, in other writings Luther explicitly expresses deep appreciation for "the very kind love he had for me" (*Letter to Philip Melanchthon*, in *LW* 49:318–19) and his

---

5. A search for a spiritual father seems more evident in the life of the Genevan Reformer John Calvin than of Luther.

thankfulness for how his dear father "lovingly and faithfully kept me at the University of Erfurt, by his sweat and labor helping me to get where I am" (*Sermon on Keeping Children in School*, in *LW* 46:250–51). In view of this data, is it not somewhat questionable historiography to try to reduce Luther's spiritual pilgrimage to a quest for a more adequate father figure?

## Luther's Struggle with Angst

Luther clearly experienced despair (*Angst*) in his spiritual life over the question of whether he could be saved. As a monk, even though he regularly availed himself of all the spiritual disciplines available to him in the monastery in Erfurt that he joined, including the sacrament of confession, he found no relief. The monastic vocation and its discipline were offering him little more than more despair.

Such despair, recall, was not the sign of a maladjusted religious fanatic. Indeed, it seems typical of the extreme emotionalism of late medieval western European people. Anxiety about oneself and one's worth is a general human problem that most self-reflective people experience. Furthermore, in Luther's case a preoccupation with salvation and damnation permeated the very cultural air he breathed. For Luther, by his own admission, the despair manifested itself most clearly in his feeling that he had not rendered adequate satisfaction to God, which is presumably a reference to the last stage of the sacrament of confession (*Preface to the Latin Writings*, in *LW* 34:336). The enumeration of sins in the medieval sacrament also caused him anguish, as he lived in fear of failing to confess one (*Exhortation to All Clergy*, in *LW* 34:19). Finally Luther's uncertainty about being adequately contrite about his sins occasioned despair (Ninety-five Theses 30). It seems there was no true contrition for Luther because his confession was not motivated by the love of God. He hated God, he claimed — hated the righteous God who punishes sinners, who is too transcendent in his holiness to be satisfied by works of contrition. In addition, because Luther could not love this God, he concluded that his contrition and his confession of sin must be imperfect (*Preface to the Latin Writings*, in *LW* 34:336–37).

Such hatred of God must have reached high levels of intensity given the nominalist philosophical and theological training Luther had had. Nominalists supposed that confession and penance are something we must do in order to make ourselves worthy of God's grace. This rendered Luther's early picture of God even more demanding than would have been the case had he endorsed Aquinas's view of God's role in the process of preparation for grace. At least then the budding Reformer could have had the comfort that even in his own penitential endeavors to merit God's saving grace for eternal life, he could count on God's cooperation.

A related feature of nominalist philosophy that only exacerbated the situation was its adherents' insistence on the unconditioned character of God's Will, not bound by any rules save those of God's own making. Given such suppositions, God is under no obligation to confer reward on the merits of the faithful. And there was yet another disconcerting incertitude about salvation — the fear that one may not have been elect by God. Such speculations eventually led Luther to join with nominalists along with Augustine in discussions about *double predestination* (the idea that God makes a "double" decision in eternity, electing some to salvation and others to damnation; *Bondage of the Will*, in *LW* 33:190).

In essence, then, Luther's *Angst* was occasioned by his sense of his unworthiness, his failure to merit eternal life before the judgment of a righteous God.[6] An important spiritual pillar for Luther as he grappled with a sense of unworthiness was his primary confessor, the minister general of the Augustinian Order, Johann von Staupitz (d. 1529). As part of the guidance the future Reformer received, for a time he was directed to study mysticism. Although this did not alleviate his *Angst*, mysticism had a considerable impact on his thought. Indirectly Staupitz contributed further to Luther's spiritual struggles when he directed the young monk to undertake a business visit to Rome on behalf of the order. In fact, the pilgrimage distressed Luther, as he witnessed the lethargy of Rome's clergy.

Staupitz's more enduring contribution to Luther's development, perhaps the result of recognizing the future Reformer's considerable academic skills and the Saxon ruler's desire to obtain more faculty at his Wittenberg University, was his advice to Luther, against Luther's wishes, to study for a doctorate in theology, especially in biblical studies. This new assignment led the budding Reformer to disciplined study of the Scriptures, which eventually culminated in an exciting new insight. The insight may itself have been occasioned by Staupitz's own theological preoccupation with the Pauline-Augustinian themes of human sin and the awareness that we are truly unworthy of the salvation that God has worked in us solely by grace (Staupitz *Libellus de executione aeternae praedestinationis* X.68–69).

Luther's exciting new discovery, called the "tower experience" by most scholars, has occasioned much scholarly debate. When the experience took place is not exactly known.[7] More certainty exists about

---

6. An inadequate concept of the "righteousness of God" was certainly a major factor in the soon-to-be Reformer's trials.

7. One strong possibility is that the breakthrough occurred after Luther completed his doctorate and assumed a position on the faculty of Wittenberg University, at a time

the nature of the discovery. The breakthrough for Luther in his struggles came through dealing with the Book of Romans and its references (1:17; 3:5, 21–22) to the "righteousness of God."

In essence, Luther discovered that the "justice," more properly the righteousness, of God does not refer to the punishment of sinners. It is not the equivalent of a divine justice that rewards the faithful according to what they deserve, as medieval theology in the West had characteristically construed the phrase (Aquinas *Summa Theologica* I/2ae, Q.112, Art.3). Rather the righteousness of God is Good News. Consequently, the phrase can only refer to that which is given to those who receive the righteousness of God through faith. This righteousness is a passive righteousness given to the faithful, not because they fulfill the demands of divine justice, but because God gives it to them as a free gift (Rom. 3:21ff.). The faithful have been released from the spiritual burden of having to strive to achieve righteousness, for it is already theirs as a gift.

Ever Augustine's disciple, Luther claimed as the African Father had that the righteousness of God is "not that whereby God is Himself righteous, but that with which He endows man when He justifies the ungodly." Faith and justification are the work of God. Luther's spiritual anguish, though never entirely put aside, would never again haunt him with the crippling anguish it had in earlier years (*Preface to the Latin Writings*, in *LW* 34:337; cf. Augustine *Spirit and the Letter* 9.15). Luther's insight combated his despair. Though sin remains, it does not count against us; thus, there is no need to despair (*Lectures on Romans*, in *LW* 25:258ff.). Such an insight meant that believers can look at themselves in a new light, as people who, despite their shortcomings, have been deemed righteous and affirmed by God. No matter what one's feelings and no matter what negative images society tries to cast on believers, Christ has abolished these negative perceptions. Feeling is opposed to faith, and faith is against feeling (*Easter Sermon*, in *Weimarer Ausgabe* [hereafter cited as *WA*] 10/I:222).

Luther's "new" insight is all about self-esteem for the anguished and is truly the central point of the Reformation. The righteousness of God is not about what God is like and his judgment of sin; rather, it is a phrase that describes what God is doing for those who receive salvation from him. It is the righteousness by which God makes them righteous, reckons or regards them as righteous, and in so doing saves them (*Lectures on Romans* in *LW* 25:258ff.). Long before he began to address abuses associated with indulgences, the young Augustinian monk was gaining supporters for such views on the faculty of his university.

---

between 1515 and 1516 when he was working on a series of lectures on the Book of Romans.

Note that this new (Reformation/Augustinian) insight did not lead Luther to reject the Catholic theological inheritance in toto. In fact, at this early stage in his career, the Reformer Luther at times still described the way to salvation in a manner most consistent with the medieval Scholastic notions of salvation as a process of collaboration between grace and the human will (*Lectures on Romans*, in LW 25:241, 368).[8] That these references predate 1517 suggests that the tower experience occurred not long before the posting of the Ninety-five Theses or that at least it took that long for the Reformer to appreciate the full implications of his breakthrough regarding the righteousness of God.

Armed with new insights regarding the righteousness of God, the passive character of the righteousness that saves us, and the need to affirm that our salvation is totally a gift of God, Luther could not abide the buying and selling of indulgences. The indulgence trade directly contradicted the idea that we are saved *sola gratia*, for the sale of them seemed to indicate that we can *do* something to save ourselves or our loved ones. Given his nominalist training and tendency to interpret the Catholic heritage in light of nominalist suppositions, this was especially problematic for Luther. In his view, Catholic theology mandated interpreting the purchase of indulgences as a preparatory act for receiving grace, as an autonomous act independent of grace. As such, the indulgence trade was fundamentally Pelagian, for it contradicted the belief that our salvation is by grace alone since it presupposed that we can do something autonomously (purchase indulgences) to merit grace. It is this set of assumptions that forms the backdrop for Luther's critique of indulgences in the Ninety-five Theses.

## The Indulgence Controversy Flares

Luther's seemingly innocent invitation to scholarly debate had a shattering popular impact that was totally unforeseen. In many respects, the German Reformer's Ninety-five Theses was a case of having the right voice at the right time. Amid the general disgust with corrupt church practices in the late medieval period was a sense that reform was needed. Luther's theses struck that chord. Also not to be overlooked was the growing sense of nationalistic sentiment in Germany at the time, the revulsion against foreign exploitation that was developing among the masses and their leaders.

---

8. In some cases, Luther's affirmation connotes the nominalist idea that a preparatory act of the will merits grace *de congruo*, that is, receives grace as a result of the believer's autonomous preparatory work unaided by grace (181; *First Lectures on Psalms*, in *LW* 11:396).

When Luther issued his theses, printers immediately began distributing copies of both the original Latin text and a German translation all over the German territories. In addition, the Reformer sent copies to his bishop, Albert of Mainz, apparently unaware of the intricate financial stakes the bishop had riding on the indulgence operation (*Letter to Cardinal Albrecht, Archbishop of Mainz*, in *LW* 48:43–49). The bishop immediately sent the information Luther had shared with him to Rome, asking Pope Leo to intervene. The Holy Roman emperor also sought the pope's intervention.

## The Heidelberg Disputation and the Theology of the Cross

The pope, who had obvious interests in maintaining the indulgence trade, asked Luther's Augustinian Order to handle the matter internally. Luther was called to a chapter meeting of the order held in Heidelberg. The strategy of his mentor Staupitz, the minister general of the order, was to give the pope what he wanted without Luther's putting his foot in his mouth. He thus counseled Luther to debate on a topic other than indulgences, to focus instead on the themes of grace, sin, and free will in relation to his new (Augustinian) theological insights. In preparation for the debate, the budding Reformer prepared theological theses that he more or less designated as the theology of the Cross.[9] Suffice it to say that his theology of the Cross functioned to affirm his commitment to the fact that salvation is by grace alone, only by means of the redeeming work of Christ on the Cross, which meant that we ourselves (and so implicitly through our purchase of indulgences) can contribute nothing to our salvation. Luther claimed that in order to understand this point about Christ's work, all our preconceptions about God and ourselves must be negated. The Cross itself, he argued, is the ultimate paradox that slays our false presumptions about ourselves and what we can contribute to our salvation (*Heidelberg Disputation* 1–4, 13–20, 22–23.26).

The disputation was a great success for Luther. He gained much support from his order, winning a number of its up-and-coming younger members to his cause, most notably Martin Bucer (1491–1551), who eventually led the Reformation in Strasbourg, and Johann Brenz (1499–1570), who later played a similar role in the province of Württemberg.[10] As noted, the disputation concerned issues related to grace, sin, and free will, but it effectively demonstrated how closely linked Luther's version of an Augustinian position was to the indulgence controversy.

---

9. Its basic components will be analyzed in the concluding section of the chapter.

10. Bucer was especially impressed with Luther's knowledge of Scripture, the early Church, and his courtesy in responding to questions.

## The Diet of Augsburg

After the disputation in Heidelberg, Luther returned to Wittenberg with a strengthened power base. Pope Leo next called for a meeting between Luther and the pope's emissary, Cardinal Thomas de Vio Cajetan (1469–1534), at Augsburg at an assembly meeting of all the princes and nobles in the German territories (the Diet of Augsburg). The meeting did not go well, as Luther was lured into challenging papal authority in favor of something like a conciliarist position (*Proceedings at Augsburg*, in *LW* 31:262, 284), which, as we have noted, taught that a universal council of the Church has more authority than a pope and which had been more or less condemned by Pope Leo in 1516 at the Fifth Lateran Council (*Pastor Aeternus*).

Soon after the meeting in Augsburg, Luther returned to Wittenberg and issued a call for a council to settle the dispute. This was published widely, making Luther's cause more and more popular as well as dangerous (*Appeal of Friar Martin Luther to a Council*, in *WA* 2:40). His mentor Staupitz invited him to avoid the turmoil by joining him in his retirement home in Salzburg, Austria, that they "might live and die together" (*Weimarer Ausgabe Briefwechsel* 1:267). The Church and its history would likely have been very different had Luther accepted.

## The Reform Finds Political Allies

Luther was able to move freely to these meetings with relative certainty of protection because he had the support of his regional prince — the elector of Saxony — Frederick III, known as "the Wise" (1463–1525). Though not yet an adherent of Luther's views, Frederick was determined to ensure that his subject got a fair hearing and was strongly committed to ensuring that posterity would call him "wise," a reputation, it seems, he wanted very badly. He also had some baser motives for protecting Luther, for he had not liked Italians meddling in Germany or the financial inroads that Albert of Mainz and his family were trying to make on his territory.[11] As time went on, the guidance of Frederick's trusted chaplain George Spalatin (1484–1545), who was an ally of Luther's, had its impact, and eventually the prince became a "true believer" in the Reformer's cause. Luther's collaboration with political authorities in this way (he did need the elector's support) would have important consequences for the evolution of the Reformer's thought and for subsequent European developments in Lutheranism, such as the creation of

---

11. Of course, Luther himself was not above stroking German national sentiment in gaining support (*To the Christian Nobility of the German Nation*, in *LW* 44:143–44, 208).

state churches. (In Germany, these state-sponsored, officially established church bodies are called *Landeskirchen.*)

The Holy Roman emperor Maximilian I died early in 1519. The pope then had another problem. Who would be the next emperor? Leo preferred one of the German princes: Frederick the Wise looked like a good candidate. However, the front-running candidates were the king of Spain and the king of France. The pope feared both because each had sufficient power to jeopardize the pope's own political influence and might. Of the two, Charles I (1500–1558) of Spain was preferable, for at least then the papacy would not find itself under French domination, as it had been during much of the Middle Ages. Eventually Frederick, realizing the inviability of his own candidacy, supported the pope's second choice (who became Emperor Charles V).

The papacy then needed to keep Frederick happy, which would not happen if tensions over Luther remained. The papal strategy to heal the tensions was to send an emissary to Wittenberg, who happened to be related to Frederick. All parties agreed to a truce in hostilities, each side pledging to end polemics with the other.

## The Leipzig Disputation

John (Johann) Eck (1486–1543), another German Catholic professor and a vehement opponent of Luther, found a way around the compromise by attacking one of Luther's Wittenberg colleagues, Andreas Bodenstein von Karlstadt (also Carlstadt; ca. 1480–1541). The attack was actually a subterfuge to get at Luther. A debate on the issues at stake was planned, the famous Leipzig Disputation. In the debate, Eck shrewdly manipulated Luther to acknowledge that the Church is built, not on Peter, but on Christ, such that the ultimate authority rested with Christ over against the papacy. He also maneuvered Luther to concede that the Council of Constance may have erred in condemning John Huss (ca. 1372–1415).

Eck clearly won the propaganda battle surrounding the debate, as it seemed that Luther had finally tipped his hat as a heretic who supported other condemned heretics. On the other hand, the debate significantly enhanced Luther's renown. Everyone wanted to learn more about him. He was now both a national and an international figure. German nationalists, disgruntled with Rome's interference in the Holy Roman Empire by contributing to the foreign domination of German peoples through the papacy's influence peddling in the election of emperors, found a rallying point in Luther. Internationally, Renaissance humanists were also initially attracted to Luther's reform program.

### The Diet of Worms: The Final Breach

The stage was set for the final breach — the pope's excommunication of the heretic. Since the committed Catholic Charles of Spain was the elected emperor, the pope no longer needed to use finesse. Consequently, following the 1519 Leipzig debate, he issued a *bull* (an official papal decree) ordering the burning of all of Luther's books and demanding he either submit to Roman authority or be excommunicated (*Exsurge Domine*). Luther burned the document. He also wrote three of his most famous treatises that same year.

Reactions to news of the bull varied in different German provinces. Some conducted public book-burnings; others demonstrated full support of Luther. The Reformer's ruler Frederick, more and more convinced that Luther was correct, was still intent on getting a fair hearing for his subject and arranged to have a hearing for Luther before the next meeting of rulers, including the new emperor, at the 1521 Diet of Worms.

In essence, Luther attended the meeting but refused to back down. Before the emperor and all the German rulers, he took his bold stand, a model in courage that has inspired others to this day. With his reputation, his life, on the line, he said:

> Your Imperial Majesty and Your Lordships demand a simple answer. Here it is, plain and unvarnished. Unless I am convinced by the testimony of the Scriptures or by clear reason (since I put no trust in the unsupported authority of Pope or of councils, since it is plain that they have often erred and often contradicted themselves), I am bound by the Scriptures I have quoted and my conscience is captive to the Word of God. I cannot and I will not retract anything, since it is neither safe nor right to go against conscience.
>
> I cannot do otherwise, here I stand. I can do no other. May God help me. Amen. (*LW* 32:112–13)

Anything else one might write about these words of courage would be anticlimactic. Suffice it to say that Luther's work was placed under an imperial ban by the diet. As a convicted heretic, Luther was to receive no shelter. His ruler, though, had made contingency plans, provided a hiding place for him at the castle of Wartburg. Hidden away in safety, Luther undertook the monumental job of translating the Bible into his native German tongue.

In Luther's words of courage in his remarks to the diet, the Reformer seems to appeal to his conscience as of greater authority than the teachings of his ecclesiastical superiors. This has led many, most recently Pope

John Paul II, to conclude that the Reformer was a forerunner of modern thinking and its sometimes anti-institutional individualism. However, it could be argued that Luther was appealing, not so much to the individual's conscience, as to the authority of Scripture.[12] Judgment on this matter is best deferred until the whole of Luther's theology is considered in the next chapter. Was Luther a forerunner of the modern world and its individualism or a thoroughly late medieval man committed to the authority of its institutions?

## Conclusion: Was the Reformation a Tragic Mistake?

Any assessment of the Reformation as a mistake must be conducted in view of all the misunderstandings during the indulgence controversy as well as in view of the New Testament mandate concerning the unity of all Christians (John 17:20–21; 1 Cor. 12:12ff.). Insofar as matters of faith alone are proper causes of division of the Church, a review of the theological issues at stake in occasioning the Reformation needs to be provided.

For Luther, the issue at stake in the Reformation and the indulgence controversy was theology, not merely ecclesiastical corruption. The real problem with the indulgence traffic in his view was that it compromised the new insights he had gained regarding an Augustinian view of the righteousness of God and the centrality of affirming that we are saved by grace alone, not by works (justification by grace through faith). He had not given up on the Catholic Church; he wanted to reform its theology, not leave it. Luther was kicked out of the Catholic Church, but it was not his intention to divide it.

The question is whether the Catholic Church's theology really did compromise the theological commitments of Luther. If not, or at least if Catholicism is today teaching views that do not compromise Luther's version of justification by grace through faith, then was not the Reformation a tragic mistake? Is there any legitimate rationale for the continuation of Protestantism? After all, it was a dispute on this issue that was at the core of the indulgence controversy that occasioned the birth of Protestantism. From the Catholic side, the question is whether Luther's theology really is incompatible with Catholic faith-commitments. If not, the Reformation and the papal excommunication were tragic mistakes.

---

12. Yet an appeal to Scripture and reason, it could also be credibly maintained, ultimately absolutizes the authority of individual interpretation. On the other hand, one should not overlook Luther's loyalties to the Roman Catholic tradition, for it was always his intention to remain within the Catholic Church.

In order to assess the theological issues at stake in the Reformation, it is necessary to review the official Roman Catholic position articulated by Thomas Aquinas and other Scholastic theologians on the role of grace alone in justification in contrast to the nominalist view. Recall that Aquinas and his Scholastic colleagues shared with the nominalists a common belief that the faithful are justified/saved in a process of cooperation of grace and works. For Aquinas and the other Scholastics, the process begins with grace, which is infused as a kind of substance in the faithful, which in turn inspires the works that are done. These works in turn merit more grace. By contrast, for the nominalists, our autonomous works of preparation merit grace. When the "razor" of William of Ockham is applied to this idea of an infused grace that inspires works, to claim that believers by their own free will confess their sins and thus merit grace is shown to be a more obvious and plainer description of the salvation process. This view certainly appears to be Semi-Pelagian in a way that Aquinas and the rest of the Scholastics are not.

There are indications that Luther, trained as he was in nominalism, understood the Scholastics and the Catholic tradition as a whole in light of nominalism. For example, the Reformer suggests that Scholastics compromised the themes of sin and grace by imagining that original sin, like actual sin, is taken away (*Lectures on Romans*, in *LW* 25:260–61). In fact, this is not a fair criticism of Aquinas, who affirms that original sin is a habit (a disordered disposition of nature, resulting from the dissolution of original justice and prior to all actual sins) in all humans, presumably even in those with grace infused (*Summa Theologica* I/II.82.1). In that connection, could it not be argued that Luther's insistence that we are saved by grace alone, that our works do not make us righteous but that righteousness creates works (*LW* 31:55–56), is most compatible with Catholicism's claim, as expressed by Aquinas, that infused grace leads the faithful to works in order that we might receive the grace that saves? Could Luther's problem have been that he did not see this grace orientation in the Scholastics because he was reading them in light of his nominalist teachers? In that case, the Reformation would have been a tragic mistake based on Luther's misunderstanding of the Roman Catholic tradition coupled with corruption in the ecclesiastical structures of his day.[13] To the degree that these problems have been overcome, is the existence of Protestantism still justifiable?

Likewise, Luther claimed that when Christians are concerned to teach good works and how they might be made secure, as the Scholastics

---

13. The misunderstanding was his failure to recognize the anti-Pelagian, grace-oriented elements in Aquinas's theology. It was exacerbated by the unfortunate combination of nominalist dominance of the Catholic theology of Luther's day coupled with the practice of buying and selling indulgences.

had done, it leads to pride and works righteousness (*Lectures on Romans*, in *LW* 25:263). Insofar as this preoccupation with works (habits and virtues) is an overriding concern of much Scholastic theology, has Luther correctly identified the inherent danger of Catholic theology, even when it makes all the proper anti-Pelagian moves Aquinas sought? In that case, insofar as Pietist, Pentecostal, Baptist, and Reformed traditions have a similar preoccupation with nurturing good works, does Luther's critique pertain to them, that they run the risk of nurturing false pride and works righteousness? On the other hand, could it be that when it comes to the core issue of the Reformation, these Protestants ultimately have more in common with Aquinas and the best elements of the Roman Catholic tradition than with Luther? Any attempt to answer these questions must take into account further analysis of Luther's theology at the outset of the Reformation, particularly some of his theological convictions as expressed in the Ninety-five Theses.

## Luther's Theology at the Outset of the Reformation

The very first of Luther's ninety-five theses was his insistence that the whole of Christian life is an act of repentance. In a sense, this affirmation linked his involvement in the indulgence controversy with an Augustinian view of justification by grace through faith. One always needs repentance because Christians always remain in sin (*Lectures on Romans*, in *LW* 25:262–63). Similarly the Reformer seems to have drawn on the kind of paradoxical thinking of his evolving theology of the Cross, which was spelled out later in the disputation at Heidelberg, in his critique of indulgences. He claimed paradoxically that prophets who point to the Cross when there is no Cross are blessed (*Heidelberg Disputation* 93) and that the faithful should be confident of heaven even through suffering (94–95). Note the possible convergencies between Luther's insistence on the need for daily repentance and the Scholastic emphasis on the need for confession and works of preparation for grace (works that are themselves motivated by grace).

To be sure, the German Reformer sought limits on papal authority. For Luther, the power of the pope must only be a human right by consent of the faithful (*Leipzig Disputation*). Suppose the papacy no longer claimed to be a divinely instituted office but asserted its authority on grounds of human convention among Christians (with the argument that inasmuch as every church needs a central office, it might as well for good historic reasons locate the central office in Rome). Luther could endorse a role for the pope in a united church. It is evident again that he was at heart a man of the Roman Catholic Church. The papacy was not, contrary to much popular opinion, the theological issue that occasioned the Reformation.

By no means was the Reformer about the business of a complete repudiation of all papal teachings. At many points Luther was merely calling for reform, with special attention to correcting abuses in the practice of the Catholic Church of his day (*Leipzig Disputation* 26, 38, 50, 91). Given the authority he still granted the pope and his general concern with life and practice, is Luther properly deemed a heretic on Catholic grounds? Was his excommunication a tragic mistake? It is evident that we should speak only of a "conservative Reformation" in his case.

In view of the Reformer's preoccupation with the centrality of the Augustinian formulation of justification by grace through faith (at least a certain [anti-Pelagian] strand of Augustine's thought) and the righteousness of God, an assessment of Luther's condemnation as a heretic must wait until the implications of the great German theologian's views for the doctrines of the Church and sanctification (Christian life) are considered. Luther developed the notion that the Christian is simultaneously saint and sinner (*simul iustus et peccator*). Christians are saints because they have been made righteous by God, yet in fact they remain hopelessly mired in their egocentricity/concupiscence. They are "curved in on themselves" in the sense that even in their good deeds human beings are always seeking to gratify themselves and their desires. From this, it follows that the Church cannot be portrayed as a community of the pure; in fact, it is more like a hospital for the sick (*Lectures on Romans*, in *LW* 25:260, 262–63, 345).

Luther's insistence that the redeemed Christian is ever mired in sin is a necessary consequence of his commitment to the centrality of justification by grace through faith. If we are not always in sin, then there is some aspect of our lives for which we do not require grace and forgiveness. This is clearly a distinction from the best elements of the Catholic tradition. Even with Aquinas's insistence that the whole process of salvation is ultimately moved by grace, he presupposes that there is growth in grace, that as we merit more grace we become less sinful. Are these differences between Luther and him sufficient to divide the Church?

Other differences between Aquinas's and the Reformer's views on justification should be highlighted. For Luther, the righteousness given the believer is passive; for Aquinas, we are not passive in receiving righteousness but active. Likewise, grace for Luther is external; we are counted or declared righteous (*Lectures on Romans*, in *LW* 25:260). For Aquinas, grace is internal; it becomes a habit to make one righteous (*Summa Theologica* I/II.110.1). Finally only Luther declares justification to be the central doctrine, the heart, of Christian faith (*Lectures on Galatians*, in *LW* 26:106). Aquinas does claim, however, that justification is the greatest of God's works (*Summa Theologica* I/II.113.9). Are these differences significant enough to fracture Christian unity?

Luther's theology of the Cross as articulated in the *Heidelberg Disputation*, in which he emphasized the paradoxical character of the Cross and so of Christian faith, needs to be considered in connection with these questions, for it also serves his commitment to affirming the centrality of justification by grace through faith. Certainly the Cross is the ultimate paradox; on it (eternal) life was received through death. Likewise God is revealed in all his glory by becoming an ordinary man in Jesus (*Heidelberg Disputation* 20). It follows, then, that every aspect of Christian faith must be under the paradoxical character of the Cross. As such, all human works and wisdom are called into question by this paradox (Ibid., in *LW* 31:52).

Other implications follow from Luther's theology of the Cross. (1) God is found, not in grand things like rational speculation, but in ordinary, daily things (*LW* 31:39). (2) God's revelation is seen to be most authentic, not in grandiose miracles, but in suffering, just as he suffered on the Cross (20). (3) In a sense, God hides himself even when he reveals himself, which is always in a surprising way. (4) More often than not, God is hidden (*deus absconditus*) rather than visible. And (5) Christian life is itself hidden since we are simultaneously saint and sinner — our righteousness is hidden by our sin (6; *LW* 31:44, 57). The last point accounts for why no talk of abundant life appears in Luther and his tradition; that is, Christians will always endure temptations and doubt; it is part of bearing the Cross (*Large Catechism* 3.106). Also, for Luther, the true Church is invisible, hidden in visible ecclesiastical institutions that are far from perfect. In a point most suggestive of contemporary liberation theology, Luther claimed later in his life that members of the Church are usually drawn from the poor and lowly (*On the Papacy in Rome*, in *LW* 39:70; *Sermons on the Gospel of John*, in *LW* 22:189ff.).

Luther marshaled all these tenets in the service of his overall commitment to the Augustinian view of the righteousness of God and the centrality of the doctrine of justification by grace through faith for Christian life (*Heidelberg Disputation* 1–3, 23, 25–26, 28). His emphasis on the paradoxical character of God's work means that the best of human efforts and wisdom, works done in conformity with the law of God, are of no value and also implies that God's work alone is what brings about the good. In that connection, the Reformer goes so far as to deny free will in the sense that apart from grace one can only sin (13–15).

*Concluding Questions*

Luther's theology of the Cross and positions in the Ninety-five Theses raise important questions for the unity of the Church. His intention was to recover the Augustinian heritage for the Church (*Preface to the Latin Writings*, in *LW* 34:337). Did he succeed? Is there anything in his thought that is ultimately irreconcilable with the Roman Catholic heritage? If not, must we conclude that the Reformation was a tragic mistake?

# CHAPTER 2

# LUTHER'S THEOLOGY AND THE ONGOING CONTROVERSY

After Luther's excommunication and the Diet of Worms in 1521, Frederick the Wise provided a hiding place for the Reformer at the castle of Wartburg, where he began to translate the Bible into German, a work he eventually completed more than a decade later. Its publication was of incalculable importance both for the Reformation and for shaping the German language.[1] Luther, of course, was not to remain in his hideaway forever.

## Luther's Life after Worms

Throughout his life, Luther was kept busy responding to practical needs. (No ivory-tower theologian was he.) The crises that drew him away from Wartburg were a function of actions undertaken by some of his collaborators in Wittenberg in extending the work of the Reformation during his exile. In essence, upon the Reformer's excommunication those in agreement with him had a similar problem. They could no longer find a home in the Roman Catholic Church. As a result, it was necessary to begin to develop their own church. In time, they would come to be called "Lutherans," a pejorative title to suggest that they were followers of Luther, not really Catholic Christians. They much preferred to be known as "Evangelicals," that is, as Catholic Christians who were faithful to the gospel. The idea of a distinct Lutheran Church was not by design; it was an "accident" occasioned by Luther's excommunication. The accidental character of the rise of the Lutheran reform meant that there was no "master plan" for what should be changed and what should be retained. In that sense we may refer to the haphazard character of the Lutheran Reformation.

---

1. Before Luther's translation appeared, each of the German territories had its own dialect. The appearance of Luther's translation effectively rendered his own regional dialect as *the* proper version of German.

41

In the course of extending the work of the Reformation during the Reformer's exile, some of Luther's followers seem to have gone too far and too fast. Luther himself had not implemented any of his proposals prior to his exile (another evidence that his was a "conservative Reformation"). In his absence, a number of monks and nuns left their monastic communities and were married. Not only had Luther's abandonment of his monastic discipline following his excommunication effectively challenged monasticism; his emphasis on justification by grace through faith also issued a similar challenge. Monastic life was seen as the ministry par excellence in which the faithful medieval Catholic could earn merits. The Reformer's teaching now destroyed this motive. Hit especially hard were the mendicant orders, which had relied on the generosity of the laity for their subsistence. Such generosity was motivated by a Catholic soteriology whereby the faithful could merit more grace through this sort of self-denial. Given Luther's view, such generosity would avail nothing before God.

As these events were transpiring, worship came to be held in German for the first time, and Communion was offered in both kinds (both the bread and the wine). The new German service was basically a German translation of the Roman Catholic liturgy. Luther supported continuance of the historic liturgy (*Order of Mass and Communion*, in *LW* 53:19ff.) and approved all of these changes that had been instituted by his primary collaborator, Philip (Philipp) Melanchthon (1497–1560).[2] Then his colleague Andreas Bodenstein von Karlstadt (also Carlstadt; ca. 1480–1541) undertook more sweeping reforms. He preached a fully egalitarian message, claiming that Luther's teaching of the priesthood of all believers — a concept that the Reformer had articulated in one of his famed 1520 treatises (*Freedom of a Christian*, in *LW* 31:353–56; cf. 1 Pet. 2:9) — had obliterated all distinctions of class and position. Karlstadt began tearing down images of saints in the churches of Wittenberg, rejected the use of clerical vestments, and decried the Catholic notion of a physical presence of Christ in the Eucharist. In a sense these reforms represent the first signs of a kind of Puritan, Anabaptist, radical anti-Catholicism that characterizes much of Protestantism.

The situation was further exacerbated by the appearance in Wittenberg of three laymen from a significant trading center to the south, the town of Zwickau. These laymen, the so-called Zwickau Prophets, claimed direct revelation from God, proclaimed the advent of a new age, and called for the abolition of infant baptism and the dissolution of all political authority. Things were in chaos. Melanchthon was unsure how to respond. Luther decided the gospel itself was at stake and

---

2. To this day, Lutheran services follow the same order as the Catholic Mass.

resolved to return from the safety of his exile, risking his life on the journey in order to quell the storm. He preached some powerful sermons, which stemmed the tide (*Eight Sermons at Wittenberg*, in *LW* 51:70–100). His success in dealing with both of these controversies accounts for the present very Roman Catholic character of Lutheranism. Readers need to consider whether this development and Luther's positions on these controversies were in the best interest of his movement and the Church catholic.

The Holy Roman emperor was determined to stamp out the new Lutheran heresy, but each time he had plans in place to undertake military action, conflict broke out on another front demanding his attention and requiring a change of plans. Another problem was that one of the successors of Pope Leo X, Clement VII(1478–1534), was more interested, as Leo had been, in Italian politics and the beautification of Rome than in ecclesiological matters. As a result, Emperor Charles got little encouragement for his military plans to obliterate the German heresy. Charles's aims were further frustrated by the support that Luther began to gain from German knights (vassals), whose fortunes had been declining with the rise of capitalism and wane of feudalism. They perceived their ill fortune to be the fault of foreign domination and were prepared to defend Luther from perceived foreign encroachments.

## The Peasants' Revolt

The next turbulence faced by Luther was stirred up by the German peasants. Periodic rebellions of peasants, as early as 1476, were largely a function of the emergence of capitalism, which, as might be suspected, hit the laborers (in this case, small farmers) hardest. As the value of money rose, they were realizing less and less of a profit for their goods than they had obtained in an economy of trade via exchange of goods. Other more prosperous peasants who had settled in cities yearned for more democracy.

In challenging the authority of the church hierarchy, Luther was perceived as a friend of the peasants. As noted, he never lost touch with his own peasant roots. Problems came when in 1524 the peasants began to invoke the Reformer in support of their economic demands. Luther was very sympathetic to their economic program as such (*Admonition to Peace*, in *LW* 46:19ff.). Indeed, he preferred feudalism to capitalism and advocated fixed lower interest rates (*Temporal Authority: To What Extent It Should Be Obeyed*, in *LW* 45:233ff., esp. 238, 305). Even the Reformer's critique of indulgences was related to his concern for the poor. In the Ninety-five Theses (43, 45) he claimed that it is better to give to the poor than to purchase indulgences.

In 1525 with the peasants under the leadership of Thomas Müntzer (also Münzer; ca. 1490–1525), an actual armed revolt began. An educated former priest, Müntzer became one of the leaders of the Lutheran Reformation in Zwickau until his dismissal in 1521 for being too radical in the reforms he was advocating (somewhat in the spirit of Karlstadt's agenda, including direct criticism of Luther). Luther had a direct hand in his banishment and subsequent failure to find a new permanent position. Even during his Lutheran period, Müntzer worked hard at cultivating the support of peasants. It was these peasants, particularly those surrounding the region of the town of Mühlhausen where Müntzer had served briefly, who initiated a revolution against the establishment and eventually installed Müntzer as their religious leader.

The peasants' socioeconomic agenda to overturn the structures of exploitation linked the rebellion to religion. The new order was to be a Christian society. Of course, the German powers of the day rose up in defense. The princes crushed the revolution, resulting in almost one hundred thousand peasant casualties.

Müntzer claimed to be inspired in a theological sense. The present revelation of the Spirit was more authoritative than the words of Scripture, he insisted. Following the peasants' agenda, he sought to establish a theocratic community in which the Church would rule the state (*Highly Necessary Defense and Answer against the Soft-Living Flesh of Wittenberg*). By contrast, Luther backed the princes in the controversy. The Reformer was especially concerned that the peasants had effectively blasphemed God by committing horrible wartime atrocities in God's name. They had even claimed to be establishing God's kingdom on earth through their revolt. The doctrine of justification seemed compromised by their agenda, for if we can bring in the kingdom of God by our activities, as the peasants claimed, then we are effectively claiming to be able to save ourselves by our works. In response, the Reformer developed his two-kingdom ethic (to be considered below), which repudiated all efforts to legislate the gospel in hopes of establishing the kingdom of God in the political realm.

Luther's response to the peasants was an overreaction. He commanded the princes to "stab, smite, and slay" the peasants, and in so doing the princes, as rightful authority ordained by God, were doing God's Will (*Against the Robbing and Murdering Hordes*, in *LW* 46:54–55). The princes gladly responded, as the thousands of peasants slaughtered attest. The majority of historians, tending to overlook the Reformer's theological rationale for rejecting the peasants, have never quite forgiven him for his support of the establishment of his day. Could his position on the matter have been as much a case of paying his debts to the princes who had been protecting him as it had to do with theology? This question can best be answered and the viability of Luther's theological perspective can be more effectively assessed after considering a more detailed discussion of his two-kingdom ethic (see pp. 54–56).

## Luther's Attitudes towards the Oppressed

In the course of the dispute with the peasants, Luther also went on record as opposing the abolition of private property (*Against the Robbing and Murdering Hordes*, in *LW* 46:51–52). However, the real issue in his unfortunately harsh stand against the peasants was probably not over economics (the Reformer was apparently no blind advocate of capitalism) but over the desire to silence their religious heterodoxy. Of course, eliminating heretics was part of the heritage of the medieval inquisition, and all the Reformers, as we shall see, followed in its traditions.

Such harshness towards alternative religious perspectives surfaced all too unfortunately in Luther's attitudes towards the Jews. Though early in the Reformation he had offered some comfort to them from earlier persecutions (*That Jesus Christ Was Born a Jew*, in *LW* 45:199ff.), later on in his career, after encountering efforts of some liberated Jews to proselytize Christians, he advocated their extermination in harsh terms (*On the Jews and Their Lies*, in *LW* 47:137, 174–76, 268–74).[3] The debate about whether the Reformer was anti-Semitic rages to this day. His record is clearly mixed, though his positive concern for the Jews at some points in his career ought not be overlooked.

The Reformer's record is a little brighter in his attitudes towards Africans. Granted, Luther refused to condemn slavery, particularly when confronted by the peasants. He insisted that Christian freedom is not a completely physical matter (*Admonition to Peace*, in *LW* 46:39). However, in other contexts, he insisted that slaves should be permitted to flee and that a good commonwealth will grant their slaves their life and livelihood (*Lectures on Deuteronomy*, in *LW* 9:232–33).

In the late medieval period, propaganda justifying the exploitation of Africans seems to have already begun filtering down to western European masses. One common saying appears to have been that Africans were filled with (or were children of) the devil. In one of his later lectures, Luther questions this horrible calumny, claiming that the biblical ancestors of Africans (sons of Noah) may have done evil but that does not mean that they were in themselves evil or not redeemable (*Lectures on Genesis*, in *LW* 2:194–95, 197). Other remarks made in the

---

3. Four centuries later, Hitler happily appropriated Luther's language.

same lectures are even more promising. Most suggestive of contemporary Afro-centric modes of analysis, he praised the virtue of ancient Egyptian culture (2:305) and claimed that the ancient Greek philosophers received their ideas from Egypt (1:4). Such an assessment was not novel to Luther. It had been a fairly common assessment of a number of the prominent theologians of the early Church, notably endorsed by Clement of Alexandria (ca. 150–ca. 215; *Exhortation to the Heathen* 6).

Many Afro-centric scholars have sought to identify an African presence in the Bible. Luther also was amenable to this project, as he claimed early in his career (even before the Reformation) that one of the wise men was Ethiopian (*First Lectures on the Psalms*, in *LW* 10:412–13). In addition, the Reformer was aware of and praised the churchly character of the ancient, though still flourishing, Ethiopian Orthodox and Coptic churches (*Proceedings at Augsburg*, in *LW* 31:281). Luther's views on the Jews are surely reprehensible at some points, but do his reflections on Africans, by contrast, offer promising models for developing contemporary models for social justice and multiculturalism?

## The Erasmian Controversy

The turbulence in the German states brought about by the latest round of the Peasants' Revolt precipitated Luther's next controversy. Moderate humanists, notably the famed Erasmus (ca. 1469–1536), lost confidence in Luther's reform. Erasmus and his colleagues had assiduously sought a middle path in advocating reform. Luther's Reformation placed these humanists in an even more difficult situation. Now their critics were claiming that they knew all along that humanism led to heresy. The only thing that Erasmus and his humanist colleagues could do was to distance themselves from Luther, a project the great Dutch humanist sought to undertake.

Erasmus worked carefully in picking the issue on which to attack Luther, who in his view had obviously become too radical in his reforms.[4] The renowned humanist chose to focus on the question of free will in Luther's thought. Given the German Reformer's Augustinian view of the Christian as always a sinner, free will must be denied (Luther *Bondage of the Will*, in *LW* 33:113–15, 247ff.). If free will were not denied, it would mean that we could choose to save ourselves, which would in turn lead to the *Angst* that emerges when we begin to wonder if we have done enough to render ourselves worthy of salvation.

Luther's denial of free will does not mean that he taught *determinism*

---

4. Recall that Erasmus was interested primarily in behavior and institutional, not doctrinal, reform.

(the idea that everything, including the smallest details of life, happens necessarily, predetermined by God), though some of what he wrote against Erasmus could be construed in that way (*Bondage of the Will*, in *LW* 33:36–39).[5] However, the Reformer seems to have believed that humans retain freedom in areas of life that do not relate directly to our relationship with God (242–43; *Lectures on Genesis*, in *LW* 2:350). At least this is the way in which Luther's heritage has been interpreted, notably first by Melanchthon (Augsburg Confession 18). The basic point for Luther is that we have no free will when it comes to avoiding sin. We sin in whatever we do, for we can never escape the egocentricity that underlies everything we undertake. We do have a certain degree of freedom, though, in everyday matters, such as our choice of what clothes we wear on a given day or whether or not to continue reading a book. However, we will inevitably sin when we undertake even these activities and decisions because all are driven by a preoccupation with selfishness and maximizing our pleasure.

For Erasmus, Christian life is a life lived in conformity with the ethics of Jesus (*Enchiridion Militis Christiani* I.5; II); therefore, he insisted on free will not just in these temporal activities but also in spiritual matters of love. For in order to conform to the ethics of Jesus, the believer must be free (albeit in cooperation with grace as the principal cause of action). The humanist thus criticized Luther for his rejection of freedom in that realm (Erasmus *On Free Will*). The Reformer responded by claiming that Erasmus had put us at the heart of the Reformation. Indulgences were merely a peripheral issue compared to free will. It is necessary to take the power of sin more seriously than the humanists had, he argued, for only by God's act alone can we be saved. We can do nothing on our own to contribute to salvation. If, however, we have a free will and can renounce our sin, then we do not need God quite as much. In one response to Erasmus, Luther was so concerned to emphasize this point that he went so far as to endorse something like double predestination (*Bondage of the Will*, in *LW* 33:146, 140).

Luther's affirmation at this point seems related to his use of the theology of the Cross to affirm our justification by grace by proclaiming God's hidden ways. The Reformer claimed that there is a hidden Will of God (not revealed in Christ) that elects in eternity to harden the hearts of some to damnation (*Bondage of the Will*, in *LW* 33:138–47). As such, salvation is always a (surprising) work of grace received by faith (62–63). Though double predestination was wholeheartedly endorsed later in the sixteenth century by the Reformer of Geneva John Calvin

---

5. Some historians believe that Luther did retain a necessitarianism throughout his career.

(*Institutes* 3.21.1; 3.23.1), as Augustine had centuries before, Luther himself moved away from it. In this debate between predestination or Erasmian free will, who is correct?

## Luther and Women

One other aspect of Luther's life worth noting is his 1525 marriage to Katherine von Bora (b. 1499) and his general views about women. Only during the Renaissance had romantic love as an ideal attached to marriage entered Western culture. Romance was not really Luther's agenda in marrying his Katie (*Letter to Nicholas von Amsdorf*, in *LW* 49:117), a feisty much younger ex-nun who announced that other candidates for marriage did not suit her as well as Luther.

Von Bora was one of a significant number of nuns (and monks) who fled their convents after the onset of the Reformation, presumably in order to enjoy the Christian freedom that Luther had extolled. They were also no doubt inclined to renounce their vows in regions that were becoming Lutheran, since such dynamics dried up their sources of support, so necessary especially for the mendicant orders. The Reformer felt a great obligation to ensure the welfare of these nuns and sought to find suitable marriage partners for them, for in this patriarchal context, marriage was the only decent lifestyle available to women who had not taken religious vows.

Luther was not the first of the Reformers to marry, but as the most renown his marriage was a cause célèbre. Not surprisingly it was greeted in some circles as a scandal. Though clearly patriarchal in his relationship with his spouse, Luther sought to practice a gentleness with her that seems not to have been typical of male-female relationships in late medieval Germany (*Lectures on Genesis*, in *LW* 3:354). He also conferred on her significant household responsibilities, including the family business and decision making, as evidenced in his bequeathing the full family estate to her in his will.

Over the years, Luther's love for his wife clearly grew and is reflected in much of his writing (*Letter to Michael Stiffel*, in *LW* 49:154). The warm relationship between the two and the significant responsibilities she came to exercise, which Luther publicly acknowledged, provided a significant role model, especially when combined with Luther's teaching on the priesthood of all believers and *vocation* (the idea that every secular calling, even family work, is a spiritual service; *To the Christian Nobility of the German Nation*, in *LW* 44:130). The model certainly set significant precedents for elevating the status of women in later centuries, especially the status of those devoting their lives to homemaking.

To some extent, Luther and the other Reformers helped remove medieval taboos from sexual impulse, an impulse that of course (in its medieval context) was blamed on women. In his typical earthy fashion, the Reformer celebrated sex. For example, he counseled a woman who did not receive sex from her husband either to run away or have an affair (*Babylonian Captivity of the Church*, in LW 36:103–4; *Estate of Marriage*, in LW 45:20–21). In the same connection and in accord with medieval custom, Luther was willing to sanction premarital sex in the context of a committed relationship among those engaged (*On Marriage Matters*, in LW 46:293). Is this perspective a useful resource for ministry after the sexual revolution?

Luther's general concern about the status of women is evident in his advocacy of education for girls as well as boys (*Ordinance of a Common Chest*, in LW 45:188–89). His interactions with women's issues also took the form of reflections on their role as leaders in the Church. As is typical of the Reformer, we find two distinct perspectives in his thought on this matter. An important characteristic of Luther's theology is its unsystematic, contextual character — in one situation advocating the proclamation of God's Word one way, and in another situation proclaiming a different view. He explicitly acknowledges the viability of doing theology in this manner (*Small Catechism*, pref.; *Table Talk*, in LW 54:138). For example, when dealing with strictly ecclesiastical concerns, the Reformer would exclude women from ordination, apparently on grounds of their distinct nature (*On the Councils and the Church*, in LW 41:154–55). However, in another context, when considering issues related to the actual practice of ministry apart from its relation to church practice, he seemed willing to regard the Church's failure to ordain women as simply a social convention. He would allow women to baptize, even to minister in emergencies (*Concerning the Ministry*, in LW 40:23). Indeed, he even conceded that women may even preach as well as men (*Sermons on I Peter*, in LW 30:135). The ordination of women in the modern Lutheran Church may not be such a departure from tradition after all.

Also noteworthy in connection with Luther's "feminism" is his reflections of the nature of God. He was willing to refer to a female dimension of the Godhead, that is, to speak of God as Mother (*Lectures on Isaiah*, in LW 17:139; *Sermons on the Gospel of John*, in LW 23:325).

### Controversy on the Lord's Supper: The Marburg Colloquy

Luther faced a controversy with a fellow Reformer in the 1520s on the issue of how to understand the status of the consecrated elements in the Lord's Supper. Like many of the earlier Reformers, Luther had rejected the Catholic concept of transubstantiation (*Babylonian Captivity of the Church*, in *LW* 36:28–35). Ever the good Catholic, Luther himself continued to affirm that Christ was really present in the sacrament, though the elements remained bread and wine (*Small Catechism* VI). However, one of his contemporaries, Ulrich Zwingli (1484–1531), the Reformer of Zurich, took the next step and rejected the idea that Christ was present in the sacrament. For him, the consecrated elements were mere symbols that serve only to remind us of Christ (Zwingli *On the Lord's Supper*).

The diverging views of these two prominent Reformers, each with large followings, caused consternation among their political patrons. The disagreement seemed to fracture Protestant unity, which would be crucial in order to fend off the military schemes of the Holy Roman emperor and the other Roman Catholic princes. Consequently, in order to solidify Protestant political unity, one of the Protestant German princes, Philip of Hesse, tried to bring all of the prominent Reformers together to iron out an agreement. This happened in 1529 in the famous Marburg Colloquy. Luther, Melanchthon, and Zwingli were summoned to participate, as well as the Reformers of Strasbourg and Basel, Martin Bucer (1491–1551) and John Oecolampadius (1482–1531), respectively.

The meeting was able to achieve a consensus statement on almost all of the issues.[6] However, participants could not achieve consensus on "whether the Body and Blood of Christ were bodily present in the bread and wine" (*LW* 38:88). Luther displayed a characteristic biblical literalism and insisted on a literal reading of Jesus' words, "This is My Body" (19ff.). Zwingli along with Oecolampadius continued to maintain the symbolic view of the sacrament (20–21, 34, 37–39). Bucer took a kind of middle position between the two contesting parties (71–72).[7]

The dispute among the participants in the colloquy was and remains a crucial point of division in the Reformation. Any hopes of its being a unified movement were forever dashed after Marburg. An analysis of the issues at stake in the disagreement will be provided in the final sections of this chapter and in the next one.

## Political Dynamics

The final issue pertinent to Luther's career as a Reformer is how the churches that resonated to his teachings came to be guaranteed protection. After the Diet of Worms, the key dynamic was the ongoing tensions

---

6. The Augsburg Confession, an authoritative statement of Lutheran doctrine, was likely based on this earlier statement.

7. See pp. 108–9 for a detailed discussion of Bucer's middle position.

between and scattered military actions involving Protestant-oriented and Catholic-oriented princes in the Holy Roman Empire. These dynamics are described in the final section of the chapter in connection with the formulation of the Augsburg Confession and the settlement of these tensions by the Peace of Nuremberg. At this juncture, suffice it to say that Luther's life and his theology were not without important political consequences. Likewise, the institutionalization of the Reformation's insights, both with regard to the establishment of the Lutheran Church and Protestantism as a whole, is not just a function of the power of Luther's theology. Politics was an important factor in these developments. Does that fact speak for or against the Reformation's truth and validity? A critical analysis of Luther's mature theology provides some data for answering these questions.

## Luther's Theology

The rich diversity that characterizes the Reformer's theology was a function of Luther's self-conscious effort to address his context. In different contexts, he would offer different emphases (*Table Talk*, in *LW* 54:404).[8] In the midst of his theological diversity, however, are some constants. One of these is his commitment to the centrality of justification by grace through faith. In his view, it is the main doctrine of Christianity on which everything else depends (*Lectures on Galatians*, in *LW* 26:106). Another constant in his theological reflections is a commitment to the core themes of the theology of the Cross.

In connection with these core themes, it is necessary to clarify at this point that Luther's emphasis on justification should not be construed as meaning that our faith saves us. It is grace, not faith, that saves. Faith is a mere instrument for receiving the gift, nothing more than trust (*Large Catechism* I.1). In fact, insofar as Luther taught predestination, in his view faith itself is a work of God. In justification, the believer is passive (*Commentary on Psalm 51* in *LW* 12:368). Luther's claim that justification is the central or chief article of Christian faith means, for the Reformer and his heritage, that every other doctrine, every other thing a Christian says or does, must be interpreted in light of this doctrine. We will observe the implications of this claim in the rest of Luther's theology.

Luther's claim that the believer is passive in receiving righteousness is a consequence of his insistence on the bondage of the will. Everyone is

---

8. Such is the theological style of most giants of the faith, and we can observe it particularly in the theology of the early Church.

trapped by original sin in his (Augustinian) view; we have no free will in spiritual matters. Even if we do good things in the civic realm — such as studying hard, remaining faithful to a spouse, or earning a good livelihood — we are hopelessly trapped in sin, caught up in our selfishness (*Lectures on Romans*, in *LW* 25:475, 345). Even our best works are indeed marred by sin (*Defense and Explanation of All the Articles*, in *LW* 32:91). Sin traps us. Has Luther not described the human situation as most people experience it? Ultimately are not all actions motivated by the quest for pleasure or ego gratification?

Such an analysis of the human situation suggests why justification by grace apart from works was so central for Luther. Never reaching the point when we are no longer caught in selfishness, we always need to return to grace. Consequently we always need God's forgiveness and must repent daily. This is what Luther meant in the first of his Ninety-five Theses when he asserted that "the whole life of the faithful [is] to be an act of repentance." The insistence that we are continually trapped in sin entails his affirmation that Christians are *simul iustus et peccator.*

### Law-Gospel Dialectic

Attempting to ensure that we never give the impression that our deeds or spiritual commitments save us led Luther and his tradition to insist on distinguishing law and gospel (*Freedom of a Christian*, in *LW* 31:348; *Lectures of Galatians*, in *LW* 26:270, 330, 115). All Scripture (the Word) and other Christian discourse either convey a demand by God and condemn us (law) or unconditionally affirm us with the message of God's forgiving love (gospel).[9]

Law and gospel must be kept distinct at all costs, Luther argues, as distinct as heaven and earth. If they are mixed, justification by grace is compromised because then the gospel is no longer portrayed as unconditional acceptance but is mixed with law (with conditions for being saved). The law-gospel dialectic is a most helpful tool for preaching — challenging preachers to ensure that they have not spoken of God's love in such a way that it has "strings" attached. To achieve this, one must always analyze one's proclamation to see whether the gospel has not been mixed with divine demands and expectations (the law).

Several other tenets, including the dialectical or polar aspect of Luther's thought, follow from the law-gospel dialectic. One consequence previously noted is the concept of the Christian as *simul iustus et peccator*. If the law is to be kept distinct from the gospel, it follows that

---

9. One hears echoes of Augustine's distinction between the letter and the spirit in these remarks (*On the Spirit and the Letter* 7–9).

the faithful person must be made righteous only through grace, never through his or her own goodness (by performing acts of the law). Consequently, the faithful person must still remain a sinner, or else justification would be contingent on that individual's performance of the law to some extent. The perduring character of sin in the life of the Christian, our inability to get away from it, is powerfully articulated by the Reformer's definition of sin as selfishness, as being curved in on oneself (*Lectures on Romans*, in LW 25:475, 345).

## Freedom from the Law

Keeping the law and the gospel distinct means that the Christian is free from the law. The Christian is free in the sense that the law no longer condemns (*Freedom of a Christian*, in LW 31:356; Rom. 3:21–24; 8:1; Gal. 3:10–14). In that sense, Christian life is a radically "new" mode of existence. Even if we have not measured up to what God has commanded (most clearly, though not exclusively, embodied in the Ten Commandments), we are not condemned or rejected by God. Christians are also free from the law in another sense for Luther. They are free in living the Christian life, for they do not need the law when serving God. Indeed, Luther argues, the law just gets in the way, rather like the law would get in the way of a couple loving and serving each other spontaneously (*Treatise on Good Works*, in LW 44:26–27; Gal. 5:1). Do happily married couples need someone to tell them how to love each other?

In a sense, Luther advocates a kind of "situational ethic" at this and other points, expressing an openness to the Christian's disobeying God's commandments if the disobedience serves God's Will (*Lectures on Genesis*, in LW 3:257–62; 5:150–51; *Christian Love and the Command to Love*, in *Luther's Sermons* 7:65–66; WA 36:39f.). However, at some points, particularly when confronting those practicing sloth in the Christian life, not really trying to walk the walk, Luther advocated the use of the law as a measure of Christian living, the so-called third use of the law (*True Piety, the Law and Faith, and Love to Our Neighbor*, in *Luther's Sermons* 2:375; *Lectures on Galatians* in LW 26:378–79, 373; *Second Antinomian Disputation*, in WA 39/I:485).

## Uses of the Law

Freedom from the law in Luther's theology raises the question of the purpose of the law. The Reformation tradition has posited three distinct uses (or purposes) of the law. (1) In the *civil/political use*, the law of God serves as a guideline for just legislation enacted by governments and other secular institutions. If a law or institutional guideline does not conform to the law of God as embodied in the Ten Commandments (in Luther's case those commandments pertaining to the second table of the Decalogue), it is unjust. (2) In the theological use, the law of God functions to condemn sin. (3) In the third use, the law is used as a guide for living Christian life. Though there may be some exceptions, as noted above, Luther largely rejects, never endorses, this view, designating the theological use the principal one (*WA* 39/I:460). By contrast, for Calvin and other Reformers, the third use is the principal one (Calvin *Institutes* 2.7.12; cf. Luther *Sermon on I Tim. 1:8–10*, in *WA* 17/I:122f.; Luther *Law and Its Works*, in *Luther's Sermons* 6:270).

## The Christian Life and Brave Sinning

Luther's strong doctrine of sin means that the best the Christian can do is sin, even in good works. The Christian ethic is to sin bravely (*Letter to Philip Melanchthon*, in *LW* 48:281–82). The "brave sin" is the acknowledgment by Christians that even in their best deeds, they are still sinning.

## The Two-Kingdom Ethic

Luther's law-gospel dialectic has implications for his view of the relationship between church and state, as expressed in his two-kingdom ethic. Essentially Luther is self-consciously appropriating Augustine's views on the two cities at this point (*Commentary on Psalm 101*, in *LW* 13:198; *Temporal Authority: To What Extent It Should Be Obeyed*, in *LW* 45:81–129). Given his commitment to the distinction between the law and gospel, and his Augustinian belief that the state must coerce obedience and justice through the threat of punishment, the Reformer could not abide any view that would suggest that the gospel be legislated by the state or made the law of the land, as the peasants had advocated. Were that to transpire, the gospel would be transformed into the law, thus forfeiting the blessed assurance of justification by grace.

To remedy this possible outcome, Luther insisted that the state should be the realm of the law (its civil use), not of the gospel. Rulers are to follow the law of God (esp. the second table of the Decalogue) and should ensure that the laws of the state conform to it, which is known not just through the Word of God but also through reason (inasmuch as the law of God is embodied in the structures of creation — a conception known as the "natural law"; Rom. 2:14–15). Consequently rulers need not be Christian in order to rule well (*Lectures on Deuteronomy*, in *LW* 9:19). Even Christian rulers, though, are to have no jurisdiction over the Church.

In like manner, though the gospel always has the final word in the Christian life and for the Church, faith is not to impose the gospel on the state, lest the gospel might be distorted into the law and the two become confused. The closest thing to an exception to this ethic emerged in the Reformer's thought after Lutheran state churches were beginning to be established. In this context, he did concede a role for government in protecting the Church and not granting such privileges to adherents of other religious commitments (*Open Letter on the Harsh Book concerning the Peasants*, in *LW* 46:70). Despite his later openness to this role for the state, regarding it as ordained by God (Luther does not envisage it as a purely secular realm), the state is only valid in his view if it aims to achieve justice (*Commentary on Psalm 101*, in *LW* 13:152, 163f.).

Christians live in both realms, in both the state and the Church, just as they are subject to both the law and the gospel. Luther's two-kingdom ethic challenges Christians to base their individual interactions on the principles of the gospel (the kingdom on the right), ever being guided by its forgiving word, while rendering political and institutional judgments (the kingdom on the left) in light of the insights provided by natural reason and the law.

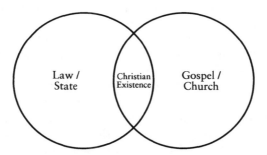

Luther's view might be illustrated by employing two circles that overlap but are not concentric. One circle represents the state, and the other the Church. The Christian lives in the territory between the two, dwelling in both realms. As noted, the state is governed by principles of reason and justice (the natural law or the law of God), and the Church is the realm of the gospel. As distinct spheres, the principles of the gospel are not to be imposed on the state.

It is often alleged that Luther advocated a passive social ethic in view of the policies he advocated in dealing with the Peasants' Revolt. In fact, he was willing to support rebellion when the gospel was imperiled, though not when only justice was at stake (*Lectures on Galatians*, in *LW* 26:98–100). He was even open to nonviolent resistance as a witness against injustice (*Temporal Authority: To What Extent It Should Be Obeyed*, in *LW* 45:124–25). In fact, early in his career, he was apparently willing to countenance the possibility of a Christian rebellion against injustice (*Epilogue to a Pamphlet of Sylvester Prieras*, in *WA* 6:347). Also one should not overlook the somewhat liberal, anticapitalist economic theory that Luther espoused. He staunchly advocated the Church's establishment of economic "safety nets" for the poor (*Ordinance of a Common Chest*, in *LW* 45:169–94).

## Justification and Sanctification

It has been tempting to some critics of Luther to claim that his emphasis on justification apart from works of the law and the Christian's freedom from the law lead to a "do-your-own-thing" Christianity — antinomianism. In part this critique is related to a failure to recognize a richness in his thought concerning the doctrine of justification.

Often Luther spoke of justification forensically, that is, as merely involving being declared righteous. There is no real change in the believer on these grounds (*Lectures on Romans*, in *LW* 25:261; *Lectures on Galatians*, in *LW* 26:130). Often this is the only way that justification is understood by interpreters of Luther, which accounts for the view that he neglects good works. After all, on grounds of the forensic view, the justified Christian is still the same old sinner. Sanctification (holiness and dedicated Christian living) is (sometimes temporally) distinguished from justification.

Yet Luther also described justification another way, one that bears evidence of the influence of mysticism (the idea of the believing soul's internal fellowship with God) on his thought. For Luther, justification is also conformity (union) with Christ. In this model, the dominant image is of Christ and the believer as united in wedded bliss. Thus, what happens when the believer is justified is rather like what happens in any good relationship. The qualities and behavioral patterns of the lover rub off on the loved one. People in a long-term relationship are not the same as they were before that relationship began. Likewise Christ in the believer gives himself over to the faithful, takes on himself all that belongs to the believer (his/her sin), and the believer starts sharing Christ's estate (the promise of salvation and his good qualities (*Freedom of a Christian*, in *LW* 31:351ff.). Christ lives in us, Luther claims, and so we are simultaneously sanctified; his holiness becomes ours. Similarities between this model for describing justification and the Eastern Orthodox idea of salvation as *deification* (becoming like God) are striking. In any case, for Luther this model connotes that we become "Christs" to one another, as by taking on Christ's characteristics we come to serve each other (367–68). Good works spontaneously flow from one filled with Christ and his goodness, as naturally as love flows from one who is in love. There is no justification without sanctification.

Given this model of describing justification, it is clearly evident that Christians gain nothing with regard to salvation by doing good works. Christians are totally free in reference to the works they do. The sole motivation for doing good works is to thank God — a motivation that develops quite spontaneously in virtue of living with Christ (*Freedom of a Christian*, in *LW* 31:360–61). Luther makes a similar point when he claims, "A Christian lives not in himself, but in Christ and his neighbor" (371). Christians are truly free when they are serving God and their neighbors because they have no real self apart from these others. We are most free, most ourselves, when we are wrapped up in the life of Christ and our neighbors. As people who have been made righteous by Christ, we are just "doing our thing" when we serve (364–65). Doing good works is a joyous response. Luther makes another significant related point in this context. Christians are perfectly free lords, subject to none, but at the same time, paradoxically, Christians are also perfectly dutiful servants of all, subject to all (344). We are most free, most ourselves, when we are serving.

Does this notion of justification as conformity to Christ protect Luther from the charge that he is not sufficiently concerned with good works? If not, why not? Of course, sanctification and the practice of the Christian life are not the priority that justification by grace through faith is for him.

### Luther's Mature View of Predestination

The Reformer's emphasis on salvation and good works as God's work and his insistence on the inescapability of sin, which meant the denial of free will in spiritual matters (*Heidelberg Disputation* 13–15; *Bondage of the Will*, in *LW* 33:194–95), mandated his affirmation of predestination. In some contexts, especially when combatting Pelagian tendencies, Luther endorsed double predestination. Yet at other points, with more personal questions about salvation or about how to live the Christian life at stake, rather than more polemical concerns, Luther focused simply on God's election to salvation (*Sermon on Preparing to Die*, in *LW* 42:105–6). Christ (and so love), Luther says, reveals the majesty of God (*Lectures on Genesis*, in *LW* 5:46, 48; *Sermons on the Gospel of John*, in *LW* 22:156–57).

Luther even held out the hope of universal salvation, of a "second chance" for all to come to faith (*Letter to Hans von Rechenberg*, in *LW* 43:54; 1 Pet. 3:19). Other times, in a manner compatible with the later Lutheran concept of single predestination, he spoke of all having the gift, though it was possible some might throw the gift away (*Lectures on Romans*, in *LW* 25:260).[10] Stressing the importance of faith, the Reformer even referred on occasion to the validity of calling faith "a work in its place" (*Disputation concerning Justification*, in *LW* 34:159–60), understanding the salvation process in terms of a divine-human cooperation (albeit with grace driving the process), as did Thomas Aquinas. Aspects of his view of predestination's mystery may be more appropriately articulated in some pastoral contexts than in others.

## View of Scripture

Luther's commitment to the centrality of justification to some extent is reflected in his view of Scripture. At least in certain contexts, the Reformer would not countenance as authoritative those portions of the Bible that failed to give testimony to justification by grace through faith. On this basis he prioritized the most important books of the Bible and threatened to throw James out of the canon (*Licentiate Examination of Heinrich Schmedenstede*, in *LW* 34:317).

Luther's critical approach to Scripture also surfaced in his critical perspective on the Apocrypha (the eleven books of the Roman Catholic Bible between the Old and New Testaments). In this regard, he reflected attitudes characteristic of other scholars of his era. Nevertheless, he finally included most of them (though not all) in his translation of the Bible, with the claim that the books are "not held equal to the Scriptures but are useful and good to read" (*Weimarer Ausgabe Deutsche Bibel* 2:547). Later Reformers and translations were more critical of these books. Puritans in the seventeenth century were the most vehemently opposed to including the Apocrypha in the Bible, which explains the omission of these books from most Protestant Bibles.

A core commitment of Luther's regarding biblical interpretation was his break with allegorical interpretation, which had dominated in much medieval Scholastic theology, in favor of a literal reading (*Lectures on Genesis* in *LW* 1:232–33; *First Lectures on the Psalms*, in *LW* 10:72–73; *Babylonian Captivity of the Church*, in *LW* 36:30). For him, the literal sense referred to the plain meaning of Scriptures interpreted christologically, that is, in light of the message of God's unconditional love

---

10. This view has been called "single predestination" because it posits that God makes only a "single" divine decision in eternity, to elect salvation, inasmuch as damnation, the fault of the unbeliever, is not God's decision.

revealed in Christ (*First Lectures on the Psalms*, in *LW* 10:7, 225; 11:304).

There is no little debate among scholars concerning whether Luther's literalism might embody a kind of premodern Fundamentalism. Though committed to the critical hermeneutic of a plain reading interpreted christologically, the Reformer also spoke of Scripture as testifying sometimes only to material blessings, to straw, in order to reveal Christ (*Preface to the Old Testament*, in *LW* 35:236). It is merely the swaddling clothes and manger into which Christ was wrapped (*Sermon on the Gospel for the Festival of the Epiphany*, in *LW* 52:171). Elsewhere the Reformer claimed that since Christ is Lord of Scripture, he would stand with him (and his word of unconditional love) over against the Scripture (*Lectures on Galatians*, in *LW* 26:295f.).

On the other hand, the Reformer claimed that the words and expressions of Scripture are divine (*Commentari in XV Psalmos graduum*, in *WA* 40/III:254). On at least one occasion, he seems expressly to have affirmed the Bible's inerrancy (*Sermon on John 16:16-23*, in *WA* 34/I:347). Another time he claimed that the apostles were infallible teachers (*Theses concerning Faith and Law 59*). It is claims like these, coupled with the development of seventeenth-century Protestant orthodoxy (see chap. 9 below), that have authorized some Lutheran denominations (most notably the Lutheran Church-Missouri Synod) to adopt a theologically conservative posture right up to the present.

The Reformer proceeded to qualify these affirmations. Knowledge and the mere history of Christ are not sufficient for faith, he claimed (*First Lectures on the Psalms*, in *LW* 10:397). The reader must experience Christ in the text. Through the Word of God in Scripture, one actually *encounters* Christ, does not just receive information about him (*Freedom of a Christian*, in *LW* 31:357). Such claims are related to the Reformer's appropriation of the Pauline spirit-letter distinction (2 Cor. 3:6). Luther developed this point further, claiming that the Bible only comes alive as authoritative when the Spirit uses the letter of the text to speak to the individual (*First Lectures on the Psalms*, in *LW* 10:211-13, 4-5). Related to these claims is the Reformer's characteristic preaching style, in which he tried to ensure that Christ be "for me" by seeking to have hearers identify with the characters in the biblical stories — to see themselves, for example, as the citizens of Bethlehem who have no room for the baby Jesus (*Gospel for Christmas Eve*, in *LW* 52:7ff.).[11]

---

11. Such a style of proclamation bears strong affinities to the hermeneutic of many early Church Fathers who rejected allegory and is not unlike the classical style of African American preaching.

## Trinity and Christology

Luther was a catholic theologian, embracing all elements of the historic creedal formulations. One of the most important and influential of his writings was a text entitled the *Small Catechism*, one constitutionally mandated for study in the Lutheran tradition, which includes study of the creeds. However, Luther endorsed the trinitarian and christological formulas in a unique, creative way.

For the Reformer, the persons of the Trinity are intimately related in that what happens to the Son happens to the Father (*Sermons on the Gospel of John*, in *LW* 22:346; *Sermon on the Gospel for the Main Christmas Service*, in *LW* 52:46). The Father's true essence is revealed in Christ (*Sermons on the Gospel of John*, in *LW* 24:140–41, 115). In that sense, Luther seems to emphasize the unity of the three persons. These beliefs are related to Luther's break with Greek philosophical assumptions (concerning the impassibility of the divine nature) that had undergirded Christian reflections about the doctrine of God since the first centuries. Luther locates time in God, rather than as something external to God and by which God is unaffected. Time is in God in the sense that all time is but an instant to him; God grasps everything in a single moment (*Sermons on II Peter*, in *LW* 30:196). God is thus affected by time; therefore, what happened to the man Jesus affects the whole Godhead.

Regarding Christology, Luther embraced the same orientation that characterized the ancient school of theology of Alexandria, affirming the *communicatio idiomatum* (communication of properties). Whatever happens to Jesus' human nature happens to his divine nature, and vice versa, meaning that as Christ suffered, so God suffered on the Cross. And God suffers when we suffer (*Lectures on Isaiah*, in *LW* 17:358). Such a vision of God is most compatible with modern ideas of God as a God of the oppressed and suffering.

Luther's affirmation of the *communicatio idiomatum* is evident in his reflections on the Lord's Supper, especially in his endorsement of Christ's real presence in the sacrament. To the question of how Christ's body can be present simultaneously in all the various locations where he is said to be present at the times Communion is celebrated, Luther responded by claiming that Christ's human nature shares the properties of the divine nature, its omnipresence (*This Is My Body*, in *LW* 37:59ff.; *Confession concerning Christ's Supper*, in *LW* 37:210, 212). Also compatible with the Alexandrian idea of a God who suffers in Christ is the *classic view* of the atonement (Christ's work understood as a struggle with the forces of evil), which tended to predominate in the early Church. Luther recovered this theme (*Lectures on Galatians*, in *LW* 26:281–82), breaking with the medieval Scholastics who tended more characteristically to emphasize the *satisfaction theory* (Christ's death portrayed as offering recompense to the wrath of God). Still the Reformer at times endorsed this view as well (177). The problem is that Luther never explained how he held the two views together.

## Church and Ministry

Luther's commitment to the centrality of justification by grace through faith as the doctrine that shapes all others is evident in his views of the Church, ministry, and sacraments. In his view the Church is not something we create. Not a holy community, the Church is rather an infirmary for sinners. Since God created new life and grace as a cure for sin, presumably the hospital is the Lord's doing as well. Elsewhere the Reformer identified the Church in terms of the gospel and the sacraments, all of which are God's doing (*On the Papacy in Rome*, in *LW* 39:75; *Lectures on Genesis*, in *LW* 5:224).

Likewise in Luther's view, ministry is a function, not of individual holiness, but of the call of God, a work of God with the pastor as his mask or puppet (*Lectures on Genesis*, in *LW* 4:66). Furthermore, he insisted, all are called to the priesthood through gifts of God — baptism, gospel, and faith (*To the Christian Nobility of the German Nation*, in *LW* 44:127, 129). Luther's recovery of the idea of the priesthood of all believers for the Church means that for him every Christian may baptize or give absolution (128). Likewise Luther viewed every job as having a spiritual dimension. After all, every occupation has the opportunity to be useful to fellow human beings (130).

Luther's views on ministry had obvious implications for undercutting clergy dominance in the late Middle Ages, not to mention their attractiveness for our context. All Christians function as priests, it might be added, insofar as they are to perform sacrifices throughout their lives. Christians are people who sacrifice their lives in service on behalf of the neighbor (*Treatise on the New Testament*, in *LW* 35:99–101). Ordained ministry, then, first and perhaps foremost, merely involves being set apart from the universal priesthood. It is in that sense nothing but a functional office. (One is only an ordained minister as long as one serves in that office; it is not a life-time job.) Likewise, Luther maintained, ordination by a bishop is not required for a valid ministry (*To the Christian Nobility of the German Nation*, in *LW* 44:127–30). This was a helpful point for the Reformer to make in undercutting late medieval clerical authority. However, this is not the whole story of Luther's view of the ordained ministry. In other contexts, he insisted on affirming that the pastor is not a mere employee of the universal priesthood but stands over against the Church in some regards (*Infiltrating and Clandestine Preachers*, in *LW* 40:391–92; *Large Catechism* I.4). The Reformer was also open to maintaining bishops where feasible, as is evident from the numerous letters written to leaders of the young Lutheran Church in various locales, in each case addressing them as "Bishop." To this day, the Lutheran Church in Sweden has even retained apostolic succession.

With regard to the papacy, Luther had harsh things to say about the pope in polemical contexts. For example, he referred to the pope as the anti-Christ (*Why the Books of the Pope and His Followers Were Burned*, in *LW* 31:394; *Smalcald Articles* II.IV). On the other hand, Luther was willing to respect the pope's authority up to a point. In fact, later in his career, he asserted his willingness to accept the pope's authority as long as the pope accepted justification by grace through faith. He put it this way:

> Once this has been established, namely that God alone justifies us solely by His grace through Christ, we are willing to bear the pope aloft on our hands but also to kiss his feet. (*Lectures on Galatians*, in *LW* 26:99)

### Sacraments

Luther seems to undercut Roman Catholic sacramentology. In highly polemical anti-Catholic contexts, he rejected the Roman Catholic claim of seven sacraments (*Babylonian Captivity of the Church*, in *LW* 36:26). Yet in another context, addressing more pastoral, less polemical issues, the Reformer seems to have endorsed the sacramental status of all seven (*On the Councils and the Church*, in *LW* 41:166). At the very least, he was willing to endorse confession as a sacrament in some contexts (*Babylonian Captivity of the Church*, in *LW* 36:86). In many respects, should Luther still be considered a good Catholic?

Concerning baptism, the Reformer advocated infant baptism, making his argument for the practice in an interesting way. It is common to think of Luther as the prime proponent of *sola scriptura*. Yet in this case he appealed, not to Scripture, but to the Church's historic practice to authorize such baptisms, arguing that God would not deceive the Church so long if infant baptism were an illicit practice (*Concerning Rebaptism*, in *LW* 40:241; *Large Catechism* 4). Of course, infant baptism logically fit Luther's commitment to the centrality of justification by grace through faith. What better way to testify to the character of salvation as a gift than for a church to proclaim that the infant is saved before he or she can comprehend what has transpired?

As in the Roman Catholic tradition, Luther insisted that something happens in baptism, that it is not a mere symbol. He identified the sacrament with repentance (*Babylonian Captivity of the Church*, in *LW* 36:58) and elsewhere affirmed a kind of baptismal regeneration (*Small Catechism* IV.3). The Christian is born again in baptism. As such, the sacrament puts a permanent mark on the believer, predisposing the baptized to a life of renouncing sin for Christ's sake (Rom. 6), and it remains valid even when one is not faithful. The Christian life, the Reformer claimed, may be identified as "a daily Baptism, once begun and ever continued" (*Large Catechism* IV).

With regard to the Lord's Supper, Luther insisted, as the Hussites had, on receiving the sacrament in both kinds, a practice suspended by the Catholic Church in the Middle Ages (*Babylonian Captivity of the Church* in *LW* 36:27). He also rejected the Roman Catholic concept of the Mass as a sacrifice if it means that the Eucharistic sacrifice is necessary to further placate God because Christ did not do all it took to save us on Good Friday (35). Yet Luther was open to calling the sacrament a sacrifice in the sense that in it our sins are sacrificed, as we are made people called to sacrifice ourselves in service (*Treatise on the New Testament*, in *LW* 35:98ff.).

Though Luther rejected transubstantiation, significantly he viewed it as a less grievous error than some of the other late medieval sacramental abuses (*Babylonian Captivity of the Church*, in *LW* 36:28–35). Moreover, he soundly rejected a symbolic view of the sacraments, as held by the Anabaptists and Zwingli. Luther also refused to endorse a position that is usually identified with him — *consubstantiation* (Christ and the Communion elements unite, resulting in a kind of hybrid substance).[12] In fact, Luther's position was that Christ's body is in the substance of the consecrated bread as his divine and human natures are one, with each maintaining its own integrity (*Small Catechism* VI). To understand what Luther intended, think of a joyful reunion between spouses. When they greet each other, they physically embrace. However, the embrace conveys another reality — love is "really present" in the physical reality without compromising the true physicality of the embrace. Likewise Christ is really present in the consecrated bread and wine.

Luther presented a less intellectually satisfying explanation of the sacrament than did Zwingli, for its status as a symbol makes much more sense. As will be evident in the next chapter, this was certainly in line with Zwingli's Renaissance humanist agenda. Luther's theology of the Cross, by contrast, was much more content to live with rational paradoxes. Moreover, two issues in particular were at stake for Luther in maintaining this view over against Zwingli's.

---

12. This position was attributed to the Lutheran view by early Reformed theologians.

One issue at stake for Luther in affirming the real presence was his belief that in the sacrament we receive Christ through the mouth (*manducatio oralis; That These Words of Christ, "This Is My Body," Etc., Still Stand Firm*, in *LW* 37:100–101). While from a Zwinglian-rationalist perspective the idea that we eat Christ might seem barbarous, for Luther such an affirmation provided an occasion to break with the dualistic tendencies of Greek philosophy. If we receive Christ through the mouth and receive him in our bodies in the sacrament, we have the assurance that he loves our body, not just our soul.

The second issue at stake for Luther was his affirmation that even unbelievers receive Christ, albeit to their detriment (*manducatio impiorum;* 1 Cor. 11:27; *Large Catechism* V), a belief growing out of the Reformer's commitment to the centrality of justification. What better way to affirm this commitment than to assert that even our lack of faith cannot stop God?

## Eschatology

Though Luther did not engage in speculation about the end times, he clearly believed in an imminent end, that the world was in the end times. He interpreted the restoration of the Holy Roman Empire by the papacy and the pope's increased temporal power in his day as fulfillments of the prophecies of the Book of Revelation (*Prefaces to the New Testament*, in *LW* 35:405–6). This eschatological orientation helps explain the urgency Luther seemed to have felt about his ministry and is reflected in his depiction of the radical newness of the Christian life, which he affirmed in his theology.

The Reformer also broke with medieval convention regarding his view of the status of the believer in death. Luther was not inclined to affirm the medieval Catholic notion that the faithful soul enters Paradise with death or goes to purgatory to serve its time, though on some occasions he does speak this way (*Sermon at the Funeral of the Elector, Duke John of Saxony*, in *LW* 51:234). Luther's more characteristic view, however, was to conceive of death as sleep — as a kind of "soul sleep" (*Letter to Hans Luther*, in *LW* 49:270). The Reformer tried to take into account those New Testament texts suggesting that the dead have an active life with God (Luke 16:22ff.; Rev. 4–5); consequently, he claimed that in the sleep of death the soul experiences visions and the discourses of God. It sleeps in the bosom of Christ, as a mother brings an infant into a crib. The time flies in this sleep, just as an evening passes in an instant as we sleep soundly (*Lectures on Genesis*, in *LW* 4:313).

### Why Is Luther's Theology Not Normative for Protestantism?

First and foremost, Luther offers a theology of justification by grace. In the tradition of Augustine, it is a theology that self-consciously reflects doctrinal diversity, embracing distinct views in different pastoral contexts (*Small Catechism*, pref.) Luther himself affirmed theological diversity as long as a given theological formulation did not compromise the testimony to salvation by grace alone.

In view of the fact that only some Lutheran readers are likely to find themselves in substantial agreement with his views (esp. his emphasis on the centrality of justification by grace through faith), the question to be considered is how he falls short, why the rest of the Protestant world has not made his theology normative. Precisely where do the weaknesses as well as the strengths of his thought lie? Is his emphasis on the unconditional character of God's love and acceptance the word of affirmation and self-esteem required for our sinful condition, or must it be supplemented by a word of Christian responsibility?

## The Augsburg Confession: Faithful Witness to Luther's Theology?

No portrayal of Luther's heritage is complete without mention of the Augsburg Confession, which is important for several reasons. First, from a purely historical standpoint, it is significant because Lutherans drew it up in 1530 at a diet in Augsburg as an attempt to summarize their doctrinal position. This diet had been summoned by the Holy Roman emperor, Charles V, who was also the king of Spain and a staunch Catholic. Charles had been rallying a number of Catholic princes in Germany to his side. In 1529 he had succeeded in convening a second Diet of Spire (Speier) to reaffirm the Edict of Worms, which had been issued at a diet convened in that city in 1521, and to condemn Luther, designating him a criminal. At the diet in 1529, a number of the princes who followed Luther and German nationalists stirred by his resistance to the Catholic hierarchy protested the planned reaffirmation of his condemnation. Thus, the name "Protestant" was first attributed to those followers of Luther who "protested" against the Diet of Spire's reaffirmation of the Edict of Worms.

Luther's primary collaborator, Philip Melanchthon, who was known for his diplomatic skills as well as for his brilliance, was charged with drawing up a document to explain the protesting party's views. Actually the document he authored had a longer history of development, dating back to Luther's controversy with Zwingli. At any rate, when the German princes convened the next year at the Diet of Augsburg, the

Protestant princes signed the document. Enraged, the emperor was ready to take action. The Protestant princes formed a coalition, the Smalcald (Schmalkaldic) League. Then Charles decided to bring matters to a head, marshaling his Spanish resources to march on the German princes and crush the resistance.

Soon after Charles made his decision, the fortunes of the Protestant princes changed. The king of France intimated that he was ready to take on Charles. To the east, the Turks seemed to be gearing up for a war. In these circumstances, Charles needed a united Germany in support of his other war efforts. Consequently, he offered to cut a deal with the Protestant princes, which they took and signed in 1532: the Peace of Nuremberg. The deal was that the German princes and their territories could remain Protestant as long as they did not seek to propagate their faith in other regions. Also the Protestants had to promise not to seek more reforms than what were described in the Augsburg Confession. In exchange, Charles got their support.

Among the effects of this peace treaty was its provision of the stability needed to guarantee Protestants, Lutherans, that their new religious commitments and the churches they had begun would endure. In fact, the treaty notwithstanding, the Lutherans did broaden their sphere of influence into other German territories. The treaty has affected the religious life of Germany to the present. To this day there are some German territories that are Catholic, while others, the majority, are Lutheran. In these, the Lutheran Church is the state church (state supported). In the others, the Catholic Church is the state church.

The establishment of state churches had the effect of deeming Anabaptists unacceptable in these territories. A major reason for the subsequent persecution of Anabaptists was related to their presenting a religious option not covered by the Peace of Nuremberg; thus, it was viewed as subversive. The only legitimate *Protestant* option, both Protestant and Catholic princes agreed at the time, was one whereby the believer could subscribe to the Augsburg Confession, which brings us to another important consequence of the Peace of Nuremberg. It effectively made the Augsburg Confession the definitive statement of Lutheran belief, a status it retains in Lutheran churches all over the world. The teaching of the Lutheran Church is defined and guided by the Augsburg Confession. To be sure, Lutherans affirm *sola scriptura*, but always with the Augsburg Confession in view to act as a check against the improper interpretation of Scripture.

## Theological Commitments of the Confession

Lutherans believe that the Augsburg Confession, though not written by Luther, well summarizes his theology in a nutshell. Does it?

The purpose of the confession was to explain the emerging Lutheran faith to the Catholic princes in such a way that they would recognize the Catholic faith in Lutheran commitments (Augsburg Confession, pref.). Thus, it is an irenic document, containing none of Luther's sometimes bombastic polemical style. One is also hard pressed to find in it anything like the paradoxes of the first Reformer's theology of the Cross.

However, most of Luther's other theological commitments seem to find a place in the confession. For example, justification by grace through faith apart from works of the law is affirmed. Also in the spirit of Luther, the confession clearly asserts that faith does not justify, but God does (IV). Although not identified as the chief article of faith in the article devoted to this doctrine, later in the document "the teaching about faith" is identified as the chief teaching in the Church (XX). The confession affirms, as did Luther, our bondage in sin, the loss of free will in spiritual matters. The only freedom remaining to the sinner is "in the accomplishment of civil righteousness and in the choice of things which are subject to reason" (II, XVIII). "Civil righteousness" refers to actions that merit praise in society as things that good, decent people do, such as maintaining family values, working hard, etc. Even if such good deeds are done, we still sin, for we are trapped in sin.

Although the confession makes clear that we are not saved by our works, it contains no detailed discussion of the law-gospel dialectic or of freedom from the law in the sense of the sort of situational ethic found in some of Luther's writings. In fact, the confession even states (in response to the Catholic charge that Lutherans were forbidding good works) that "it is necessary to do good works" (XX). Whether this remark is a mandate to do good or merely a description of the spontaneity of good works (that believers cannot help themselves but do good works) is a matter of much debate in Lutheran circles. The confession's claim that the Holy Spirit works to renew the hearts of believers certainly suggests the latter. In any case, is this a sufficient affirmation concerning good works to silence critics of Luther and his tradition?

Something like Luther's two-kingdom ethic is sketched in one of the articles (XVI), but its implications for Christian social ethics are not described, save their insistence in response to the position of the later Anabaptists (see pp. 91–95) that Christians may hold civil offices and that all Christians should obey just laws. Although the document, as noted, proclaims the priority of God's act and denies free will, there is no affirmation of predestination.

The confession (XX) endorses Luther's insistence that mere knowledge of the events pertaining to Christ is not faith, that one must also believe in its impact. There is no statement about the authority of Scripture, a fact that has been taken by some Lutherans to mean that in principal the Lutheran Church has an "open canon" (that is, is not limited to the books of the Bible in establishing what is authoritative for theology).

Without as much elaboration or clarification as Luther provided, the Augsburg Confession (I, III) affirms the trinitarian and christological formulations of the Catholic tradition. The document's Roman Catholic commitment is also evident in its stance towards Roman Catholic practices, such as holy days, festivals, the cult of saints, and the like (XV, XXI): permission is given for maintaining these as long as they not burden consciences. Even the sacrament of confession is not abolished (XXV).

The centrality of justification is reflected in the confession's treatment of the Church and ministry. Both are defined in terms of Word and sacrament, as what God does, not what we do (VII, V). The document insists that pastors might only minister when regularly called to a position (XIV) and authorizes the marriage of priests (XXIII). With regard to the sacraments, the Augsburg Confession endorses the rite of confession (IX) as well as infant baptism and the real presence of Christ in the Lord's Supper (IX, X). The same abuses that Luther criticized regarding the Supper are also critiqued (XXII, XXIV).

Is the Augsburg Confession a faithful witness to Luther's theology? Without doubt, the confession has historically plagued the Lutheran tradition. Lutherans have struggled with whether the Augsburg Confession must be critiqued in the interests of doctrinal purity in light of Luther's sharp polemics and cutting-edge paradoxes or whether the authentic Lutheranism is the irenic, ecumenical perspective of the confession. Must a choice be made between the theology of Luther and the Augsburg Confession? If so, which one has it right?

## CHAPTER 3

# ULRICH ZWINGLI, THE SWISS REFORMATION, AND THE ORIGINS OF THE ANABAPTIST MOVEMENT

The Augsburg Confession had its origins as a response to the dispute between Martin Luther and Ulrich Zwingli (1484–1531) over the sacrament of the Lord's Supper. A contemporary of Luther's, Zwingli carried out the Reformation in Zurich, Switzerland. He has become a somewhat forgotten man due to the fact that no modern denomination unambiguously emerged from his theology.[1] Yet he was very influential in the sixteenth century.

It is reported that at the Marburg Colloquy Luther said that the Swiss Reformer was of a "different spirit" (*LW* 38:70–71). There is some truth to the observation. Luther, a man of the people, never lost touch with his peasant background. Zwingli was more the intellectual, a fine and devoted Renaissance humanist. From that perspective, his characterization of Luther as a "bumpkin," presumably a country bumpkin or hick (Zwingli *That These Words, "This Is My Body," Will Always Retain Their Ancient Meaning*) is certainly understandable given the German Reformer's populist propensities.

Born not far from Zurich, in a well-to-do family with a father who had followed his father as chief magistrate of the region, Zwingli received the very best education available at the time. Eventually it would lead this talented scholar to study the Renaissance humanists, notably Erasmus, who became a great influence on him.

Following ordination in the Catholic Church, Zwingli became a parish priest, where his learning gained him notoriety in this period of poor clergy training. A number of events in the budding Reformer's life led him to become critical of the Catholic Church of his day. Indeed, a critical mind-set towards the Church was typical of humanists.

Zwingli's own criticisms came to focus on the mercenary work of

---

1. Reformed churches in Germany as well as the United Church of Christ and the United Church of Canada have some roots in his reform.

Swiss soldiers. The Swiss at that time were in great demand for their military skills, regularly recruited at high prices from the various European courts. Even the papacy turned to the Swiss for military protection.[2] Zwingli came to feel that through these mercenary practices foreigners were exploiting Swiss soldiers and that the entire experience was effectively undermining the moral fiber of the Swiss people. Zwingli's fervent Swiss nationalism was another key influence on his thought and career. Such nationalism, combined with his humanist propensities, no doubt led him to preach against the notion that pilgrimages to holy sites could earn merits.

By 1518, Zwingli had been promoted to serve as a parish priest in Zurich. He soon began raising questions about indulgences, while fiercely insisting that the challenges he raised to the practice were conclusions he had reached independently of Luther.[3] Given his apparently excellent preaching, stimulating teaching, and learning, as well as his commendable devotion, the budding Reformer gained growing support. He may not have been above reproach with regard to morality, a fact that he acknowledged. It is likely that he was engaged in a *clerical marriage* (living out of wedlock) with a widow. Of course, this was not all that unusual in the late Middle Ages, characterized as it was by much corruption. Given the widespread practice of this sin, Zwingli's affair would hardly have been shocking to his parishioners. In any case, he continued to have enough support that when a seller of indulgences arrived in Zurich, Zwingli succeeded in expelling him.

In light of the turbulence going on in Germany at this time, Zwingli came to be linked with Luther in the mind of the public. As the controversy over indulgences developed, Zwingli became more and more radical with regard to worship practices, his view of the sacraments, his reliance on the sole authority of Scripture, and his militant stand against mandated clerical celibacy.[4] At a 1523 meeting of the Zurich Council, after a debate between Zwingli and a bishop's representative left the Reformer's views unchallenged, the council voted to allow him to continue to preach. The decision amounted to Zurich's break with Rome. The Reformation had happened.

The decision precipitated more rapid reform, in part related to Zwingli's belief that all practices with no scriptural support must be rejected.[5] Encouraged by such a theological perspective and the council's support, many priests, monks, and nuns married. Communion in both

---

2. To this day, the pope's bodyguards are members of the Swiss Guard.

3. As early as the late fourteenth century, the Lollards had already condemned indulgences and some of the other issues that preoccupied Zwingli.

4. He eventually married his lover, Anna Reinhard.

5. For all his intellectual sophistication, Zwingli was much more a forerunner of mod-

kinds came to be celebrated. Eucharistic vestments of the clergy and images were banned (for Zwingli was a militant iconoclast), organs were removed from churches, and the singing of hymns was abolished in worship with the argument that there was no biblical authorization for such practices. Only metrical versions of the Psalms accompanied preaching and the reading of Scripture in the worship services of Zurich. The general Protestant rejection of the Catholic liturgy in favor of a "free" form of worship is largely due to Zwingli.

The Zurich Reformer's impact on Protestantism as a whole is also apparent in his reform of the church calendar, trimming almost all of the festivals. The heritage of this reform is readily apparent in the failure of most of the Protestant world to observe commemoration of saints' days or Lent, Epiphany, and the like. Another profound aspect of Zwingli's reform was the promulgation of general education with no class distinctions. The educational program was to be in the style of the core commitments of Renaissance humanism, including a broad general education in the classics and the sciences, with concern about cultivating morality, physical fitness, and social skills (Zwingli *Of the Upbringing and Education of Youth in Good Manners and Christian Discipline*).

In virtually all of these reforms, Zwingli had the total support of the Zurich Council. A kind of theocracy was established in the city. Certainly the church-state cooperation in Zurich was far more intimate than it had been in Saxony in the case of Luther.[6] For example, mandatory worship attendance was legislated and enforced. Such reform procedures spread to many other distinct geographical and political regions in Switzerland.

As was the case in Germany at the time, Switzerland was divided into different regional governments (cantons). Some turned Protestant; others remained Catholic. Armed conflict between both sides began to transpire. In 1531 the Peace of Kappel was signed, granting each region freedom to make its own choices regarding religion. Switzerland's division among Protestant and Catholic cantons continues to this day.

One of the armed conflicts, just before the treaty was signed, involved an attack by five Catholic cantons on Zurich. In the war effort, Zwingli, a longtime army chaplain who loved the men of the military, was killed at the age of forty-seven. Succeeding him was Johann Heinrich Bullinger (1504–75), whose charitable and conciliatory spirit would be of great consequence in preserving Zwingli's insights and in the even-

---

ern Fundamentalism than Luther was, as the German Reformer was quite content to allow traditional church practices to stand as long as they did not contradict Scripture.

6. The Zurich Reformation was more organized and structured than the rather haphazard reforms led by Luther.

tual development of the Reformed tradition. The illegitimate son of a Swiss Catholic priest, who himself had opposed the sale of indulgences, Bullinger became an admirer of Zwingli's theology and was a natural successor. Building bridges to John Calvin, he brought the Genevan and Zurichian strands of the Reformed heritage together.

## Zwingli, Luther, and the Anabaptists

From the time of the outbreak of the Reformation in Zurich until Zwingli's death were two important chapters in his life: his confrontation with Luther and his interactions with the Anabaptists. The Zurich Reformer's confrontation with Luther, particularly at the Marburg Colloquy as well as the political dynamics that occasioned this meeting, were outlined in chapter 2. The underlying theological issues at stake in the conflict will be examined later in this chapter. Despite the importance of what happened at Marburg, perhaps Zwingli's most significant long-term impact lay in his interactions with the budding Anabaptist movement.

Essentially, Zwingli's impact on the Anabaptist movement is traceable to the influential role he played as teacher and inspiration for some in Zurich who would eventually lead an Anabaptist reform. A blend of learned scholar, great preacher, and attractive, forceful personality, Zwingli attracted a number of talented students. Most of them were drawn to study with the Reformer for purposes of a Renaissance education, not so much for religious instruction. However, the Zurich Reformer challenged his students to master not just the Greek classics but also the biblical languages. This opened the door for scholarly study of the Bible, from which Zwingli was able to recruit talented supporters for his reform.

Among the most well known of Zwingli's students, one who eventually broke with him to become leader of a more radical reform was Conrad Grebel (ca. 1498–1526), who was from a prominent and wealthy Swiss family. Grebel's father had served as a member of the Zurich Council. Given his background, it is not surprising that Grebel received the very best humanist education possible.[7] At the time that he first began to study with Zwingli, Grebel was living the life of a vagabond humanist scholar. Other significant peers of Grebel's who became leaders of the Anabaptist movement with him in Zurich included Felix Manz (ca. 1498–1527) and George Blaurock (1491–1529). A na-

---

7. This higher social standing and superior education in comparison to Luther are typical not just of Zwingli but also of the first leaders of the Anabaptist movement.

tive of Zurich, Manz was the illegitimate son of a priest. Like Erasmus, he seems to have enjoyed the educational advantages that were only accessible to the elite classes. The Swiss-born Blaurock did not seem to have the intellectual prowess of his two peers but impressed everyone with his religious zeal.

These three students of Zwingli's, through their study of the Scripture with the master, began to identify with his reform and were among its key advocates. However, further study led them to identify some points with which they felt he had not been sufficiently faithful to the biblical witness. One of the first problems that they identified was Zwingli's propensity to appeal to the Zurich Council to help settle ecclesiastical questions (Conrad Grebel *Letter to Vadian*). This began to create more tensions in Zwingli's relationships with the more radical Reformers. The Radicals proceeded to meet privately to formulate more "biblical" principles of reform for Zurich. One of the suggestions of these "brethren" (as they called themselves) was that since the New Testament church was a community gathered from the world, a contemporary church that consisted only of those who had personally decided for Christ should be established.[8]

These students of Zwingli began to distance themselves further from him. They corresponded with Thomas Müntzer (also Münzer; ca. 1490–1525) and Andreas Bodenstein von Karlstadt (also Carlstadt; ca. 1480–1541).[9] The next crucial insights in their study were the recognition that "the Gospel and its adherents are not to be protected by the sword" (pacifism) and that only believers should be baptized, thus rejecting infant baptism (Grebel *Letter to Thomas Müntzer*).

William Reublin, a pastor in a neighboring village, was the first of those related to the Brethren who actually preached against infant baptism. Grebel's correspondence with Müntzer suggests that the leader of the peasants was at least laying the groundwork for such a view. The crucial developments came in 1525 when the Zurich Council intervened in the dispute between Zwingli and the Brethren, siding with Zwingli and denouncing the Radicals with a choice of either renouncing their views or going into exile. Just a few days later, the Brethren made a decisive response. One of their number, George Blaurock, requested that Conrad Grebel baptize him. After that transpired, Blaurock proceeded to baptize most of the other believers among them.[10] The Anabaptist movement had truly become a reality!

---

8. As a result of calling themselves "brethren," they have come to be known as the Swiss Brethren.

9. It is in this sense, as well with reference to their theological proposals, that we may refer to both men as forerunners of the Anabaptist movement.

10. It is interesting to note that these first Anabaptist baptisms were not by immer-

Grebel and Manz proceeded in the next months to go from house to house in Zurich evangelizing and baptizing in accord with their new insights and practices. They undertook a ministry in the outlying regions with great success. Their work was creating much controversy not only among the proponents of Zwingli's reforms but also among Catholics. Zwingli was able to convince the Zurich Council to repress the Brethren. Grebel and Blaurock were arrested in November of 1525, and a few months later so were Manz and many other Anabaptists. The charges were rather flimsy.

Zwingli accused the Brethren of sedition on grounds that they had allegedly denied the validity of the magistracy. In fact, it seems that all the Brethren denied was that Christians could serve in this capacity (cf. Schleitheim Confession 6.2). Though Grebel was able to escape, he died shortly thereafter. Blaurock was banished from Zurich but died a few years later as a martyr under the auspices of the authorities of Innsbruck. Manz had been executed earlier under the auspices of Zurich authorities. The Anabaptist movement offered many powerful witnesses of the faith. Despite Zwingli's harsh judgment of these "wayward" followers, there is a genuine sense in which the Anabaptists were legitimate heirs of his theological heritage.

## Is Zwingli's Theology Superior to Luther's Version of the Reformation?

Just as Luther had an organizing principle to his theology (justification by grace through faith), from which most of his other theological commitments logically followed, so Zwingli's theology followed logically from his core commitments. Two perduring themes emerge in a study of the Zurich Reformer's life: (1) his concern to dialogue with the insights of Renaissance humanism and (2) his Swiss nationalism, which stemmed from his concern to protect young Swiss soldiers from foreign exploitation. Because of these dual concerns, Zwingli's theology would be framed in such a way as to be in dialogue with Renaissance suppositions, and consequently with classical Greek philosophy (to whose insights Renaissance humanism was programmatically committed), as well as to be of service to the Swiss people. These concerns were linked to Zwingli's other agenda, the one that so appealed to the first leaders of the Anabaptist movement: the commitment to seek to restore biblical faith and practice, which meant cutting through the accretions of tra-

---

sion. Only in the following months did that practice develop as a result of special requests of a few of the converts.

dition that had accumulated over the centuries (Zwingli *Of the Clarity and Certainty or Power of the Word of God*).

Given this biblicistic orientation, Zwingli was far less concerned than Luther with preserving the Catholic heritage. After all, Zwingli's reform involved the self-conscious decision to leave the Catholic Church for something more in touch with the biblical faith. However, unlike the Anabaptists, he did not totally reject all aspects of the Catholic heritage. For example, he expressly continued to affirm the creeds (*Account of the Faith*).

## View of Scripture and Theological Method

In view of the preceding commitments, Zwingli's affirmation of Scripture alone follows logically (*Account of the Faith; On True and False Religion*) and is reflected in his claim that all church practices with no biblical support must be rejected (in contrast to Luther's willingness to retain all traditional uses not in contradiction with the Bible). It was on this basis that Zwingli advocated stripping churches of organs and other Catholic practices (liturgy, clerical garb, images, etc.), which were and still are common in Lutheranism. It would be a mistake, though, to understand Zwingli's commitment to *sola scriptura* as his equating the Word of God with the Bible. In fact, for him the Word of God is not only found in the Scriptures but is God's creative action. To be sure, Scripture contains the gospel. Consequently Zwingli posited the infallibility of the Bible, or at least that the Word would never lead us astray (*Of the Clarity and Certainty or Power of the Word of God*).

Given Zwingli's admiration of Erasmus and the ideals of the Renaissance, it is hardly surprising that the Swiss Reformer approached Scripture with the suppositions of a Renaissance humanist, including reliance on its principles of interpretation. His approach surfaced quite clearly in his debate with Luther over the sacrament of the Lord's Supper, in which the Zurich Reformer insisted that the Bible should be read, not literally, but figuratively, a view that is very much in the heritage of Greek philosophy's predisposition for allegory (*Account of the Faith*). Zwingli's commitments surfaced in another way in the differences he had with Luther regarding the Eucharist.

Luther's Catholic commitments entailed a break with Greek philosophy insofar as his belief that Christ was present in the elements implied the contention that the spiritual works through, is received in, the material. Luther's belief that finite things can contain the infinite (Christ) is also reflected in his biblical literalism and belief that finite words adequately communicate the Word of God. By contrast, Zwingli, heavily influenced by Neoplatonism through humanism, contrasted matter with spiritual reality. As a result, the Swiss Reformer regarded the material realm (the bread and the wine) as a barrier to spiritual life (*Account of the Faith*). His views led to an allegorical hermeneutic, for if the finite realm (the words) must be contrasted with, seen as a barrier to, the spiritual realm (the Word of God), then we must bypass the literal sense of the words (interpret them allegorically/spiritually) to get to their spiritual meaning. In regard to biblical interpretation, Zwingli insisted that the Bible is only properly understood with divine guidance, and as such is the Spirit's work. Is this not akin to Luther's employment of the letter-spirit dialectic?

Another methodological commitment of Zwingli's theology, also compatible with his admiration of the insights of Renaissance humanism, surfaces in his claim that God has given all human beings (including philosophers) the knowledge of God. Note that this knowledge is not a "natural knowledge" of God in the strict sense, which maintains that human beings know God "naturally" by virtue of their humanity. Zwingli insisted that the knowledge of God given to all is revealed by God. But it is not a full knowledge of God. Yet Zwingli did see much agreement between classical Greek insights and God (*Of the Clarity and Certainty or Power of the Word of God; On True and False Religion*).

### God/Providence/Predestination

The impact of classical Greek philosophy through the Renaissance is evident even more clearly in Zwingli's view of God. Some (including Zwingli's contemporaries) might argue that these suppositions informed his thinking on this doctrine more than the biblical picture. Just as the Greek universal forms were eternal and unchanging (in the sense of not being affected by what happens to finite things), so Zwingli's God is omnipotent, omniscient, and unchanging. The portrait of the omnipotent God that results from these reflections must be a God who determines all things in eternity, lest his counsel be said to be dependent on the contingency of his creatures. And if God determines *all* things (a strong doctrine of providence), then God must have determined who is saved and who is damned in eternity. The affirmation of double predestination necessarily follows from these suppositions (*Account of the Faith*).

This mode of affirming predestination is very different from Luther's treatment of the doctrine (even in those instances when, like Zwingli, he endorsed double predestination). For Luther, the doctrine was rooted in the human condition (in knowing the self as impotent before sin). Though Zwingli may have had a sense of his own moral laxity, he does not seem to have been tortured by it as Luther's own sense of sin tortured him. For the Zurich Reformer, the affirmation of predestination was much more a function of his philosophically conditioned view of God.

To be sure, Zwingli taught that faith alone gives the assurance of forgiveness (*Exposition of the Faith*), which is a necessary consequence of his affirmation of predestination. Tied to this commitment is his claim that we are all trapped in sin (*Account of the Faith*). If we were not so trapped, then we might be able to contribute to our salvation, but this prospect would negate Zwingli's prior commitment to the absolute providence of God (for it would mean that God does not totally determine salvation). In any case, the doctrine of justification by grace is not the pressing issue for Zwingli that it was for Luther but is rather only a consequence of Zwingli's prior commitments. Insofar as justification is a function of God's eternal decree, it seems that Zwingli's construal of justification is more forensic in character than a model like justification as conformity to Christ, which would entail that sanctification (and a desire to do good works) is necessarily linked to justification. This may have been a factor in Zwingli's concern self-consciously to exhort good works (to assert a third use of the law), not to assume that works follow faith, as Luther often did.

### Eschatology

Zwingli expressly rejected the Anabaptist idea (which Luther also held) that the dead sleep in death, insisting instead that the faithful enter heaven in death. The soul is always active, he insisted; it never sleeps (*Exposition of the Faith*).

### Law-Gospel Relationship

Given his view of God's unchanging nature, Zwingli logically posited more continuity between the law and gospel than Luther did. Only if the law and gospel are in continuity can God be said to be unchanging, for then the claim can be made that the gospel is essentially what God has been doing all along. Thus, the Swiss Reformer insisted that the gospel does not abolish the moral law. On the contrary, he asserted, the commandment to love summarizes the moral law. In essence, in these remarks Zwingli presupposed a kind of third use of the law. The law is not a terrifying enemy; rather, it and the gospel are practically the same (*On True and False Religion; Sermon, Aug. 20, 1530*). Despite this concern with the ongoing positive significance of the law, Zwingli's commitment to the primacy of grace still led him to insist that there can be no good works without faith. Yet, he insisted, works necessarily result from faith (*Exposition of the Faith*).

Zwingli's concern to relate the law to the gospel also logically intertwined with his concern about the moral fiber of the Swiss people, which he perceived to have been compromised by their exploitation as mercenaries. In view of this agenda, it was important for him that the gospel not be license for more moral laxity. Given such pastoral concerns, Zwingli called upon the Christian faith to teach a wholesome morality, which is precisely where his affirmation of a third use of the law (the law's intimate connection with the gospel) fits.

### Church-State Relations

Given the close continuity Zwingli posited between the law and the gospel, it is hardly surprising that he spoke as if church and state were coextensive. If the state is the realm of the law and the church the community of the gospel, it follows that as law and gospel are correlated, so church and state must be correlated. However, as the gospel has the final word over the law, so the Christian law must be higher than the civil law. It (the gospel) should be legislated; Zwingli posited a kind of theocracy (*Exposition of the Faith*). Another way of making the point is to claim, as did Luther, that the political use of the law must function as a criterion for determining just laws in the state.[11] However, insofar as Zwingli correlated the gospel with the law, the gospel as well as the law must function as the criterion for determining justice.

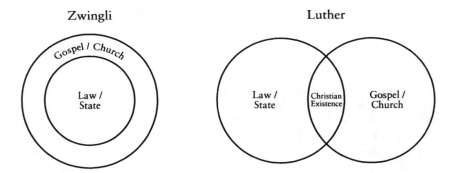

Zwingli's views on church and state can be illustrated by two concentric circles: the gospel-governed church (the larger circle) enveloping the law-governed state (the smaller circle). This model represents Zwingli's view that the laws of the state must conform to the principles of

---

11. All the Ten Commandments functioned in this authoritative role for the Zurich Reformer, in contrast to Luther, for whom only the second table of the Ten Commandments was relevant in the political sphere.

the gospel. By contrast, recall that the German Reformer's position can be diagramed with two overlapping, but not concentric, circles, one representing the church and the other representing the state (see chap. 2).

Zwingli's views on the relation of church and state also seem to have grown out of his concern for the welfare of his beloved Swiss people. In rejecting the foreign domination that had characterized medieval Swiss life (and was still occurring due to the exploitation of mercenaries), Zwingli saw the need for the establishment of a new society with new norms. What better criterion for these new social norms than the gospel? Given this agenda, Zwingli conferred on Christians a role in guiding society in the midst of its present chaos. The emphasis Zwingli placed on good works followed logically, which may also have been a function of the broader social responsibility the church had for society in Zurich's more democratic form of government (as opposed to the German monarchy in which Luther lived).

Zwingli's equation of God's elect with the population of Zurich meant that sloth was a problem to be addressed by theology. In this context, everyone was a "Christian," but certainly not everyone was a sincere Christian. Here is yet another reason why Zwingli's theology was preoccupied with the practice of the Christian life.

## Church and Sacraments

Zwingli defined the Church as the company of the elect, which is hardly surprising given his affirmation of predestination. The visible church is a sign of the invisible church, he asserted, an affirmation made necessary by Zwingli's role in the creation of a state church in Zurich, in which every citizen of the town was a member of the church. Consequently the visible church (the state church of Zurich) must be an ensign (more or less inclusive) of those who have been elect. However, since not every member of the visible church is a sincere Christian, the Swiss Reformer quite logically insisted on the obligation to discipline members. Excommunication is the responsibility of the Church, he argued, though the lapsed might be readmitted upon giving signs of their election through visible expressions of faith manifest through regular church attendance (*Exposition of the Faith; Reply to Emser*).[12]

Zwingli's views on the sacraments follow logically from his preoccupation with disciplined Christian living and the use of Renaissance

---

12. Church attendance was mandated in Zwingli's Zurich, another example of the intimate connection between church and state that he posited. This policy helped further ensure that every citizen of Zurich was a member of the church.

(Greek philosophical) suppositions in biblical interpretation. He defines *sacraments*, of which there are only two (baptism and the Lord's Supper), as acts of initiation or pledges. As such, they have no power to free consciences; they are mere symbols (*On True and False Religion*). For Zwingli, then, believers have a necessary role in the reception of the sacrament, whereas for Luther the sacrament is God's objective act. To portray the sacrament as a pledge means that it is of no value if the recipient is not pledging his or her faith wholeheartedly. Such a portrayal is certainly compatible with Zwingli's overall preoccupation with teaching morality and ordering society. When the Church observes the sacraments, these occasions are ceremonials by which those in the community of believers prove to or inform the Church that they are or aim to be soldiers of Christ.

With regard to the doctrine of baptism, Zwingli broke with Luther and the Roman Catholic tradition in rejecting the idea of baptismal regeneration. This rejection in addition to his view of the sacraments as testimonies of faith made it harder for him to justify infant baptism. Consistent with his insistence on the continuity between law and gospel (between the Old Covenant and the New Covenant), Zwingli posited an analogy between circumcision and baptism. As infants are circumcised, so infants may have access to baptism. Besides, infants are already elect, he argued. Baptism is merely the sign of their election (*Account of the Faith*).

In this connection, Zwingli claimed that the gift of tongues (the baptism of the Holy Spirit) was ordained by Christ for the benefit of providing a witness to unbelievers, just as water baptism provides a testimony of faith to others. *Glossolalia* (the experience of speaking in tongues), he insisted, is not necessary for salvation, as it is only given to a few. It is, though, a miracle (*On Baptism*). The Zwinglian tradition is obviously friendly to the subsequent development of Pentecostalism.

Like Luther, Zwingli rejected transubstantiation and the idea of the Mass as a sacrifice. Recall, the Zurich Reformer even abolished the Mass in favor of the idea of the sacrament as "Communion," a celebration of community (*Exposition of the Faith*). As with baptism, Zwingli construed the Lord's Supper as a symbol. Thus he denied that Christ was really present in the sacrament (*Account of the Faith*).

Zwingli's views on the Eucharist clearly relate to his Renaissance/Greek philosophically oriented approach to interpreting Scripture. He insisted on reading Jesus' words, "This is my body" (Matt. 26:26; Mark 14:22), figuratively (as one would read the "I am" passages in John 6:41; 10:11; 14:6). "Is," Zwingli insisted, means "signifies" (*Account of the Faith*). Also related to the denial of Christ's presence in the sacrament is Zwingli's endorsement of a Christology more typical of the ancient Antiochene school of thought, rather than Luther's "Alexandrian" viewpoint. Like the ancient Antiochenes, the Reformer of Zurich expressly rejected the Alexandrian *communicatio idiomatum*. The humanity of Christ is not omnipresent as is his divinity (*Exposition of the Faith; Of True and False Religion*). The omnipresence of Christ's humanity must be affirmed in order to posit that Christ is really present in every celebration of the Eucharist in every locale. In this connection, Zwingli offered little insight about the Trinity and, significantly, did not seek to articulate the nature of its unity as emphatically as Luther had (*Account of the Faith*).

Zwingli's beliefs pertaining to both Christology and sacramentology reflect the Neoplatonic spiritual-material dichotomy that followed logically from his devotion to the Renaissance agenda of recovering the riches of classical Greek thought. His philosophical assumptions render it logically impossible to conceive of *finitum capax infiniti*, that is, the material (Christ's body) as bearing the marks of the spiritual (Christ's divinity). Likewise this assumption conflicts with any affirmation of the physical affecting the spiritual being, as the Alexandrian *communicatio idiomatum* affirms. Similarly, it is also not possible on grounds of Zwingli's Renaissance humanism to affirm that salvation can be gained through the power of any elements of the world like bread and wine.[13]

Zwingli's attempt to take seriously the avant-garde intellectual assumptions of his day and to propose a more rationally intelligible view than Luther and Catholicism seems defensible. Also, his view of the sacraments appears better able to explain how they might stimulate a more committed practice of the Christian life. However, what may be compromised by the Reformer's sacramentology is the primacy of God's grace, a commitment that is more unambiguously affirmed in the real-presence view, for the sacraments in Zwingli's view seem contingent on the faith of the recipient. One receives no spiritual meaning from them apart from faith. In addition, Zwingli's view breaks with virtually all precedents in the Christian tradition. It is tempting to ask, as Luther suggested, if he has not made reason (in this case, Greek philosophy) more authoritative than the biblical witness (*Marburg Colloquy*, in *LW* 38:76). Luther clearly repudiated Greek philosophical assumptions in affirming Christ's real presence in the sacraments, in implicitly conceding the contribution that physical realities (the consecrated bread and wine) make to spiritual well-being.

---

13. It is at least implied in Luther's version of the sacraments that the elements are a vehicle for receiving grace. After all, Zwingli insisted, "body and spirit are such essentially different things that which one you take it cannot be the other" (*On True and False Religion*).

Both Luther's and Zwingli's views of the sacraments have strengths and weaknesses, and readers should seek to sort out which arguments seem most persuasive. Be aware, however, that both Reformers may also have had nontheological reasons to cling to their respective positions with such tenacity. It is likely that Zwingli and his Swiss colleagues held nationalistic suspicions about Luther's continuing fidelity to the papacy and Roman Catholic worship styles. As such, they could not fully trust him as an ally in the struggle against false teaching of the gospel. In fact, Luther's continuing loyalties to such a foreign institution as the papacy might have rendered him an enemy of the Swiss agenda to purge all foreign influence. Luther and his followers may have seen similarities between Zwingli's free-worship style (as well as his discrediting of traditional modes of worship) and the spiritualism that characterized the already-rejected Peasants' Revolt and the Zwickau Prophets.[14]

Is it possible to definitively assess the controversy between Luther and Zwingli? Was there any common ground? The Marburg Colloquy led to one apparent point of convergence. When pressed by apologetic concerns, such as Zwingli was addressing (for his view, after all, is eminently more compatible with reason), Luther conceded an openness to calling the sacrament a "sacred symbol" (*LW* 38:34). Luther also deemphasized the real presence early in his career when, like Zwingli, he focused on issues related to sanctification. When theologians address similar pastoral concerns, do they characteristically agree? Are theological differences ultimately a function of differences in context? Certainly the differences between Luther and Zwingli seem related to the distinct overall pastoral concerns they were addressing.

## Assessment: Why Zwingli and Luther Disagree

Both Luther and Zwingli clearly affirmed the primacy of God's grace. However, since Zwingli clearly did not share Luther's existential despair, his theology does not address and is not organized around existential anxiety about salvation. The Swiss Reformer's theology is more preoccupied with relating the faith to the intellectual trends of his day. Which of these two agendas is more important for faith to address?

A factor in Zwingli's failure to concentrate as much on the assurance of salvation was his preoccupation with nurturing higher standards of morality among his beloved Swiss. Consequently, he placed more emphasis on the role of the law in the Christian life than did Luther, who was more concerned with freedom from the law (distinguishing it from

---

14. See chap. 4 for a discussion on the credibility of these intuitions. The early Anabaptists looked to the leaders of these discredited movements as allies.

the gospel) in order to avoid the slightest appearance that salvation (the gospel) might be related to our performance of works of the law.

Differences likewise surface in the Reformers' views on the sacraments. Luther's preoccupation with justification by grace led him to insist that Christ is present in the sacraments regardless of our response. Zwingli's view of the sacraments as symbols, by contrast, means that the sacraments function primarily as occasions for exercising faith, since they are worthless unless one has faith and uses them as occasions to remember Christ.

The Reformers' two agendas — both Luther's more single-minded emphasis on the assurance of salvation and Zwingli's preoccupation with nurturing Christian morality — have had an effect on a number of doctrinal formulations. As such, their comparison serves to remind us of the richly diverse character of the Reformation. Which of these agendas needs to predominate in a contemporary theology embodying the Reformation?

# CHAPTER 4

# THE ANABAPTIST MOVEMENT
## A RETURN TO NEW TESTAMENT CHRISTIANITY?

The Anabaptist movement, also known as the Radical Reformation, refers to a loosely related group of Reformers distinct from Luther, Calvin, and the Anglicans. The movement is distinguished by the radical nature of its reform, for it broke most radically with the Roman Catholic Church. Most of its adherents became convinced that Luther and Zwingli had not gone far enough in their reforms, that the Church of their day needed to cut through and renounce Roman Catholic accretions in order to return to a truly New Testament version of the faith.

Though representing very distinct viewpoints, these Radical Reformers shared commitments to (1) the voluntary character of church membership; (2) the separation of these churches from the national or territorial state, with the accompanying belief that the Church needs no support from the state in any way; and, perhaps most importantly, (3) the rejection of infant baptism and insistence that only believers should be baptized, commitments that follow from the movement's emphasis on personal decision and New Testament practice. As a result of this practice, the Radical Reformers were pejoratively dubbed "Anabaptists" (rebaptizers), since most of those that the movement baptized had been previously baptized as infants.

The emphasis on personal decision and a believers' church had uniform implications for the church life. As a community of the converted, members enforced discipline, including the practice of the *ban* (the practice of excommunication of the lapsed), which was regularly employed. So radical was the break with the Catholic tradition that, in the tradition of Zwingli, typical worship in Anabaptist communities involved simple religious ceremonies, without excessive ritual. Another interesting characteristic of the movement was its radically egalitarian character. Women had the same rights as men in most groups. The poor and ignorant were regarded as being as important as the rich. The organizing principle in all of these commitments was a fervent concern to restore the New Testament church. The key word in much of their rhetoric was "restitution."[1]

As a whole, the Anabaptist movement endured much persecution. Large segments of it were exterminated. Only the Mennonites, Amish, Hutterian Brethren, and the Schwenkfelder Church are its true descendants. It is not the direct forebear of modern Baptist churches, which have their institutional roots in Puritanism, albeit inspired by certain earlier Anabaptist reforms.

The Anabaptist movement was richly diverse. There was no one Anabaptist movement. At least four quite distinct groups (each of which may be divided into subgroups) have been lumped together as Anabaptists, largely by their critics. The four groups may be identified as (1) spiritualists, (2) early Anabaptists, (3) revolutionary Anabaptists, and (4) later Anabaptists.

## Spiritualists

Spritualists, at least the early spiritualists, are not properly speaking Anabaptists; however, they shared enough commonalties with later spiritualists, who are identified with the Anabaptist movement, to warrant identification as forerunners of the movement. Basically what unites these various Reformation and post-Reformation figures grouped under this rubric was their strong mystical tendencies. These Reformers tended to be more concerned with the spiritual life of the individual than with reformation of the Church at large. Many felt that the inspiration of the Spirit is more authoritative than Scripture and so believed that the written Word may be set aside. Corresponding to these commitments was a low view of the sacraments, to the point of even dismissing their utility.

### Early Spiritualists

The Zwickau Prophets, who descended on Wittenberg while Luther was in exile at Wartburg, are perhaps the paradigmatic example of the early spiritualists. They claimed that God had spoken directly to them and also taught that the Bible was not necessary, since they were possessed by the Spirit. They were premodern Pentecostals. But is this not a Pentecostalism detached from biblical faith?

Also counted among the early spiritualists are Thomas Müntzer (also Münzer; ca. 1490–1525) and his followers. Because they advocated

---

1. Observe the close links between this commitment and Zwingli's similar agenda.

revolution, this group may more properly belong to the revolutionary Anabaptists. Yet like the Zwickau Prophets, Müntzer also claimed
special inspiration; however, he was convinced, unlike them, that God
would soon bring the present age to an end, punishing those who oppressed the people (*Sermon before the Princes*). Müntzer also apparently
wrote against the practice of infant baptism (Conrad Grebel *Letter to
Thomas Müntzer*), but there is no evidence that he actually practiced
the baptism of believers only. In that sense, he and his movement are
not fully Anabaptist.

With the peasants, Müntzer sought a new political order that would
be conformed to the gospel. The peasants in the region of Memmingen
(a town in southern Germany) articulated these commitments in early
1525 in what has come to be known as the Twelve Articles. The articles
also included specific economic demands, such as the end of inheritance
taxes, indentured servanthood, and restrictions on hunting by the poor.
One interesting religious proposal was that the entire community alike
(rich and poor) would have the authority to appoint a pastor. It was
advocated that, if necessary, these aims should be achieved by force. The
peasants and their revolution failed.

### Later Spiritualists

The later spiritualists held many of the preceding theological commitments (as distinct from the peasants' sociopolitical agendas) but
joined the movement after Anabaptism was formally initiated in Zurich.
Several of them gave rise to modern Unitarianism in the seventeenth century. Such spiritualistic propensities also may have influenced George
Fox (1624–91), founder of the Quaker movement in the seventeenth
century.

*Caspar Schwenkfeld.* Silesian by birth, Caspar Schwenkfeld (also
Schwenckfeld; 1490–1561) was originally a follower of Luther's. His
reform agenda aimed to find the "middle way" between Protestants and
Catholics. He insisted that neither the Church nor the Bible binds the
Holy Spirit. Schwenkfeld held other controversial views, a number of
which drew the attention of Luther as he sought to refute them.

Schwenkfeld affirmed what might be called the "deification of
Christ's humanity." While claiming to support the Chalcedonian formula, he sounded very Monophysite (the belief that Christ has one
nature) in orientation. According to Schwenkfeld, Christ is of celestial
flesh, and his body is of the Spirit (*Answer to Luther's Malediction* III).[2]

---

2. Such language seemed to connote that even Christ's body was fundamentally divine
in nature, not truly human.

Schwenkfeld's Christology set the stage for his spiritualism. Having implicitly denied the creaturely (not created) character of Christ's body, Schwenkfeld could assert that the flesh of Christ is potentially available to every spiritually perceptive believer.

With regard to the Eucharist, Schwenkfeld believed that Christ is really present but also that neither the elements nor his body are corporal, corruptible food. The presence of Christ, then, is a mystical communion but not in the elements. The eminent Silesian referred to a "spiritual eating," insisting over against Luther that Christ is not received through the mouth (*Answer to Luther's Malediction* II.2,6). He seems to have had a similarly low, almost critical, view of the value of baptism.

Schwenkfeld had no aims to start his own church, for in his view the ideal of the New Testament church that he sketched could no longer be implemented. Nevertheless, a few followers in his native Silesia kept his views alive after his death. They immigrated to Pennsylvania in the eighteenth century and eventually founded the Schwenkfelder Church.

*Sebastian Franck.* A German humanist, heavily influenced by Erasmus, Sebastian Franck (ca. 1499–ca. 1542) became a Lutheran in 1525. He developed much empathy with the Anabaptist agenda, especially the claim that the Apostolic Church had been distorted by its accommodation to the state (*Letter to John Campanus* 3ff.). He also endorsed *pacifism* (the sword must not be drawn to protect the faith). Like Schwenkfeld, though, he did not apparently believe it desirable or possible to implement the New Testament model in his own time.

Eventually Franck advocated complete freedom of thought and defended an undogmatic freedom in Christianity. His view of the Bible as an unclear manifestation of the Eternal Word led him to assert that one could not understand its true meaning apart from revelation of that Word (*Letter to John Campanus* 17–18, 24), which happens through a confirmation of the heart (23). This Word he called "Christ," but he did not identify it with Jesus.

Franck's spiritualism is evidenced not just in the preceding claims but also in his assertion that there is a spark of the divine in each of us. All externals are unnecessary, he asserted. Sacraments are necessary only because of spiritual immaturity, which is why the early Church required them. In his view, because the Spirit is among all peoples, all Turks and heathen who fear God and work righteousness have been drawn by him (*Letter to John Campanus* 13–14).

*Michael Servetus.* An Italian scholar, Michael Servetus (1511–53) became a physician in Viene (in southeast France). In his principal work, *Christianismi Restitutio*, he denied the Trinity and the divinity of Christ. Servetus's rejection of the Trinity was likely related to his Spanish background. Growing up in a region with a still significant Jewish and Moslem population, he found that the doctrine had been the stumbling block for relating to these faiths. He also rejected Luther's views on predestination, insisting instead on free will (*On Faith and the Righteousness of the Kingdom of Christ* 1.2). Condemned by the Catholic Church, he escaped to Geneva but was captured and martyred under the auspices of its Reformation leader, John Calvin.

*Faustus Socinus.* An Italian ethnic residing in Poland, Faustus Socinus (Fausto Paolo Sozzini; 1539–1604) denied the divinity of Christ and the immortality of human beings. He did much to spread a kind of Unitarianism among the elite. The movement he initiated was more or less institutionalized in the seventeenth century but suffered severe repression. As a result, the center of Unitarian thought came to be focused elsewhere, though Socinus continued to be a major inspiration for its more modern appearances as his writings greatly influenced the first British Unitarians.

## Early Anabaptists

Among the early Anabaptists were the radical followers of Zwingli in Zurich in the 1520s. Their most prominent figures include Conrad Grebel (ca. 1498–ca. 1526), George Blaurock (1491–1529), and Felix Manz (ca. 1498–1527). Since the origins of this movement (known as the Swiss Brethren) and the fate of its leaders have already been noted (see chap. 3), it is sufficient at this point to outline its core theological commitments.

Essentially the Swiss Brethren, in seeking to return to New Testament Christianity, were preoccupied with the doctrine of sanctification. This commitment is evident in the strong emphasis they placed on the purity of the Church and the purity of the lives of Christians. They also insisted that the Church should not seek support from the state because Christianity is a matter of personal conviction.[3] The Brethren's insistence on believers' baptism (as an exercise of the believer's personal conviction) logically followed from these commitments. Other Brethren beliefs included pacifism and a concern to keep the community pure, which resulted in the excommunication and shunning of hypocrites, that is, those not living out their conversion.

Similar movements developed elsewhere in western Europe. One in Augsburg, Germany, was led by Hans Denck (ca. 1495–1527), a

---

3. This belief was clearly aimed at the state-church arrangement that Zwingli had established in Zurich.

Bavarian humanist scholar who had become increasingly critical of the Lutheran reform. Probably the most scholarly of all the German Anabaptists, he was forced to resign his academic position on the faculty at a leading humanist institution in Nuremberg due to the radicalism of these critiques. Eventually he became engaged in controversies in Strasbourg with Martin Bucer, one of Luther's admirers. On most issues, such as the introduction of believers' baptism, his reform closely paralleled that of the Swiss Brethren. His idea of the voluntary character of the Church (*Retraction* 7) is another commitment Denck shared with the Brethren.

The connections that Denck and the Swiss Brethren shared pertaining to the Church as well as their insistence on a believers' baptism seem to presuppose an affirmation of free will. Denck largely made the case for this view, as over against Zwingli and perhaps Luther, in his work *Whether God Is the Cause of Evil.* Offering a negative conclusion to the thesis, Denck insisted that our will, in rebellion against God, creates evil. We must "yield" (*gelassenheit*) to the Will of God the way God yields to the human will and does not violate it. Christians are to imitate Christ, offering themselves as he offered himself for all. A key issue in assessing the validity of these remarks in relation to possible Pelagian tendencies is Denck's claim that before God "our activity is passivity." Have he and the Anabaptist emphasis on free will and the decision of faith freed themselves from the Pelagian abuse?

Similar express affirmations of free will were made by Balthasar Hübmaier (ca. 1485–1528), perhaps the most theologically creative of the early German Anabaptists (*On Free Will*). A student both of Luther's debating partner John (Johann) Eck and subsequently of Zwingli, this former Catholic priest also qualified his affirmation of free will. He warned that we dare not rely on human strength (*Eighteen Dissertations* 16). Hübmaier himself precipitated some controversy in the Anabaptist community, as he never took a totally negative view of the social order in the manner of some of his compatriots. By contrast, he insisted on the legitimacy of the state.

Hübmaier was a man dearly beloved by the Catholic parish he had served in Germany. Indeed, the town was willing to defy the episcopal hierarchy in order to protect him. But Hübmaier renounced their support and went into exile in order to spare the citizens armed intervention by Catholic authorities.

## An Early Anabaptist Confessional Statement

The movement begun in Zurich was obviously not confined to the Swiss territories. We have already observed how it spread elsewhere in western Europe, such as to Germany. Michael Sattler (ca. 1490–1527) was an important leader in this development. He also played a major role in a full statement of beliefs drawn up by a number of the Swiss Brethren (including Brethren in Germany), the Schleitheim Confession.

The confession is, not a full statement of Brethren belief, but a confession of certain distinctions they held over against some Anabaptists whom the Brethren perceived as teaching falsely. The confession has become the paradigm for virtually all subsequent Anabaptist statements of faith. The core beliefs noted are (1) believers' baptism, (2) excommunication and separation from all that is evil (entailing an insistence on the establishment of a pure church, not one marred by sinners), (3) a Zwinglian-like view of the Lord's Supper, (4) the affirmation of pacifism, and (5) the separation of Christians from involvement in government.

The Brethren's commitments regarding the absolute separation of church and state represented a dissolution of the whole structure of medieval society in a way that Luther and Zwingli had not previously challenged it. This challenge to the structural conventions of the day may help further explain why the institutions of society retaliated so strongly against the Anabaptists as they did. Not just in Zurich were many martyred, for numerous accounts of mass executions of Anabaptists were recorded. There seems to be little doubt that the fierceness of the persecution and the stories of heroism of the movement's martyrs helped stimulate growth.

## Revolutionary Anabaptists

Though the first leaders of the Anabaptist movement were scholars and pacifists, the movement began to assume an expression of popular resentment to society, which had earlier resulted in the Peasants' Revolt.[4] No doubt the persecution and martyrdom that many of the early Anabaptist leaders endured heightened an eschatological sense among adherents of the movement and a sense that something climactic was to happen or be made to happen. At any rate, pacifism gave way to the hope of violent revolution (in the tradition of Müntzer's revolt, which may more properly be categorized here).

### Melchior Hofmann

In Strasbourg, Melchior Hofmann (ca. 1500–ca. 1543), a German convert to Lutheranism turned lay preacher, inflamed crowds in hopes that

---

4. This dynamic suggests how we have come to regard Anabaptism as a movement of peasants, when in fact it had its origins in the upper class.

the New Jerusalem would come there. He ran afoul of authorities for his eschatological speculations. In 1530, he found a home in the Strasbourg Anabaptist fellowship. In this later period of his life, he began to teach a believers' baptism and spoke of the soul's betrothal to the Lord and a light that enlightens all human beings (*Ordinance of God* 149, 155–59). Hofmann also enjoyed significant missionary success in the Netherlands.

In 1533, Hofmann predicted that he would be imprisoned and then the Lord would come. He attracted a significant number of fanatical followers who followed him to Strasbourg. He also claimed that it might be necessary to take up arms. A usually tolerant government arrested him, and the end never came. Hofmann languished in prison a forgotten man.

### The Kingdom of God in Münster

The next development occurred in Münster, Germany, where the more or less even distribution of Protestants and Catholics forced a measure of tolerance towards Anabaptists. When the word got out that it was a relatively safe city, numerous Anabaptists began flooding the environs. Their numbers were so great that, led by the Dutch baker John Matthys (Mattys) and his disciple John of Leiden (Leyden), Anabaptists actually took over the city by force, expelling Catholics. John of Leiden named himself king.

The Anabaptists in Münster engaged in complete *iconoclasm* (destruction of all religious icons or statues). Believers regularly reported visions, said to be divinely inspired, concerning the imminence of the end, which would transpire in Münster. Aiming to restore not just New Testament practice but also Old Testament practice, the Anabaptists practiced polygamy.

Food supplies began to dwindle in Münster, which was isolated from its "sinful" neighbors. Eventually the citizens of the town put an end to it all. New Jerusalem was no more.

# Later Anabaptists

The fall of Münster effectively put an end to the revolutionary Anabaptist movement. New leaders worked to restore pacifism and put aside the other vagaries of the revolutionaries, such as polygamy. The most prominent, the Dutchman Menno Simons (1496–1561), became founder of the Mennonites (from which the Amish come). Another leader was the pacifist Jacob Hutter.

## Jacob Hutter and the Hutterian Brethren

Seeking to restore the fortunes of the Anabaptist movement, Jacob Hutter (d. 1536) organized the Hutterian Brethren, a group which continues to practice pacifism and a kind of spiritual communism (Ulrich Stadler *Cherished Instructions on Sin, Excommunication, and the Community of Goods;* Acts 4:32–5:11). Not the founder of the first community, Hutter effectively organized one that was already sharing goods. His efforts stimulated much interest, many converts, but also much persecution. He died a martyr for the cause, burned as a heretic.

The core commitment of the Hutterian Brethren was their view of private property as the greatest enemy of love. At an early stage, the group practiced strict discipline and the shunning of the persistent sinner. Hutterian Brethren also spoke of the faithful having a free will, though prepared by God's grace (Ulrich Stadler *Cherished Instructions on Sin, Excommunication, and the Community of Goods*).

By the seventeenth century, the Hutterian Brethren were flourishing in Moravia, often sponsored by local nobility. Later persecution of the community led to their migration to eastern Europe in the eighteenth century. The handful of survivors immigrated in the nineteenth century to North America, where several small communities still exist. They function as separatists, continue the use of the German language, and run their own schools in their communities.

## Menno Simons and the Mennonite Heritage

From a peasant background, Menno Simons had been ordained as a Catholic priest in his late twenties, without the benefit of a distinguished education. He had been appointed to a comfortable position as a parish priest and had embarked on a lifestyle far more economically secure than his earlier situation in life could have afforded. These creature comforts and subsequent study led him more in the orbit of Renaissance humanism. Though never renouncing these new intellectual commitments, Simons's lifestyle changed dramatically in 1536.

After some years of careful study of the New Testament, which had already caused him doubts about Roman Catholic teaching on baptism, Simons was exposed to a community of Anabaptists in his homeland in an encounter that changed his life. So impressed was he with their devotion to God and so shamed by their life of devotion, he finally submitted in 1536, renouncing his life of comfort and joining the Brethren (*Reply to Gellius Faber*). The combination of his publications and his opposition to what the Münster experience had done to the Anabaptist movement propelled him into leadership of the movement, which explains why most of its adherents came to be known as Mennonites.

The peaceful posture Simons took with regard to the state (he never advocated disobedience to the state, save refusal to serve in the military or to swear governmental oaths) was still perceived as subversive to many regional governments. This pressure led to the scattering of Mennonite communities to eastern Europe and their eventual immigration to North and South America.

Simons's primary agenda was to follow the doctrine and practice of the apostles, that is, to return to the New Testament, cutting through the Catholic inheritance as an unnecessary accretion (*New Birth* 4:315). The Word of God, he insisted, is infallible (*Foundation of Christian Doctrine* III.D; *Christian Baptism*). Yet he did endorse the Trinity doctrine, and this tradition has continued in historic Mennonite confessional statements, such as the seventeenth-century Dordrecht Confession. Early Swiss Anabaptists even confessed the creed (*On the Trinity*).

Of course, there does seem to be some suggestions of a Monophysite Christology like Hofmann taught in Simons's thought. Seeming to deny that Christ received his body from Mary, Simons held that Christ's body was a new creation of the Holy Spirit (*Confession against Jan Laski* 1; *Incarnation of Our Lord* II). This contention logically followed from the Mennonite founder's patriarchal belief that the generation of human life rests solely with the father, that the woman is passive in the birth process (*Reply to Gellius Faber* VIII).

Simons's agenda to restore the Church meant that its sole authority must be Scripture, since those attempting to get back to the New Testament church viewed church practice in the intervening centuries, the heritage of the Roman Catholic tradition, as having no binding authority (*Reply to Gellius Faber*). The Catholic inheritance, in Simons's view, needed to be rejected because it included the Constantinian inheritance of the state church, to which one belonged by the mere fact of having been born into it. Anabaptists, and especially in this case Simons, stressed a believers' church; that is, one becomes a Christian by deciding for it. The Church is the community of the converted (*Why I Do Not Cease Teaching and Writing*).

The Anabaptist-Mennonite concept of a believers' church necessitates that the Church can receive no support from the world. Christians are to obey the laws of the land, suffering persecution if need be, not wielding the sword, which entails a commitment to pacifism (Dordrecht Confession 14). Simons advocated a kind of separation from the world, at least from the worldly church (*Foundation of Christian Doctrine* II.G). In order to maintain its purity, the Church as the community of the converted must enforce discipline, by practicing the ban or ex-communication (Dordrecht Confession 16–17; *Why I Do Not Cease Teaching and Writing; A Kind Admonition on Church Discipline*). At these points, the Anabaptists strongly advocated something akin to a third use of the law.

In the tradition of Zwingli, and for much the same reason as the Zurich Reformer, Simons construed baptism and the Lord's Supper as mere symbols of inner realities. According to the former Catholic priest, Christ is not present in them; consequently, baptism does not save (*Foundation of Christian Doctrine* I.F; Dordrecht Confession 6). Because infants do not have sanctifying faith (cannot decide for Christ), Simons taught they should not be baptized (*Foundation of Christian Doctrine* I.F).[5]

Simons's emphasis on the Church as a church of converts and discipline, as the community that lives by the Law, requires critical analysis. His ecclesiology could raise the specter of legalism. The Mennonite founder claimed, however, that such obedience and conversion are the work of the Spirit (*Why I Do Not Cease Teaching and Writing*) and that faith is a gift (*Foundation of Christian Doctrine* I.F). Though such commitments would seem to lead to an affirmation of predestination, the Dutch Anabaptist reneged on such speculation, sometimes only claiming that God elects Christ (*Incarnation of Our Lord* III). In another instance, Simons did assert that God's election is about the celebration of God's free grace that grants salvation and moves believers to godly lives (*Meditation on the Twenty-Fifth Psalm* 14). Compatibility with the Lutheran notion of single predestination is obvious at this point.

Simons endorsed the concept of original sin and spoke of salvation by Christ (*Meditation on the Twenty-Fifth Psalm* 14; Dordrecht Confession 2–3). Anabaptists affirm justification by faith (*Confession of the Distressed Christian* I; Dordrecht Confession 6). To be sure, though, this doctrine is not as central to the Mennonite-Anabaptist heritage as it was for Luther. Of course, that is understandable given the overriding Mennonite concern with conversion and sanctified community life.

A schism late in the seventeenth century in the Mennonite community in Switzerland, led by Jacob Ammann (ca. 1644–ca. 1730), resulted in the creation of Amish communities. This movement emerged as a result of a debate over shunning, in particular whether excommunication entailed that the faithful should shun the one who had lapsed. The Amish

---

5. One suspects that a Neoplatonic ontology similar to Zwingli's, which precludes the possibility of the finite bearing the infinite, may be in operation at this point. Despite the great Anabaptist's affinities with a Monophysite Christology, Simons concurred with Zwingli's rejection of the Alexandrian idea of a communication of idioms between Christ's two natures (*Incarnation of Our Lord* II).

practice this stricter discipline. There is much debate over where Simons stood on this matter. The 1555 Mennonite Conference in Strasbourg asked Simons to relax his severity in discipline. He held firm (*On the Ban: Questions and Answers*), and as a result, various branches of the Mennonite movement split over the question of the proper degree of discipline to administer. Perhaps the most influential of all Mennonite statements of faith, the 1632 Dordrecht Confession (17), affirmed shunning of the expelled. It did so, however, in a moderate way, akin to Simons's mature position, such that the shunning be undertaken with discretion and so as not so to deprive the excommunicated of earthly needs. In any case, on American soil, the Amish have practiced a ghetto-like existence (living in small, socially homogenous, segregated, and exclusive communities) not unlike the Hutterites.

## Assessment: Did the Anabaptists Offer a Version of the Reformation Superior to That of Luther and Zwingli?

In rediscovering the original principles of Anabaptism, readers should be reminded that these sects have separated from the world and endured persecution. Their continuing persecution (taking form today usually in critiques of their lifestyle but also in acts of violence against members of Amish communities in the United States) may be related to the tendency of their sixteenth-century critics to lump all Anabaptists into one, including heretical spiritualists and revolutionaries. Today modern Evangelicals are included in the critique. In order to evaluate the contribution of the Anabaptists — to decide whether their version of the Reformation is superior to that of the other Reformers — it is first necessary to make judgments concerning the various versions of the Anabaptist movement. Except for a few of the most radical spiritualists, Anabaptists understood their project as an endeavor to reestablish New Testament Christianity. Did each of the versions succeed?

Certainly given the Anabaptist preoccupation with becoming Christian through deciding for Christ, their characteristic position on the various doctrinal themes follows logically. Their symbolic view of the sacraments follows, since only with such an understanding can the role of the sacraments as primarily occasions to exercise faith and give testimony to faith be ensured. If Christ is present in the sacraments, the focus is more on God's action than on the response/decision of the faithful. The Anabaptist view of the Church as the community of the converted serves to highlight the importance of conversion, as without it one is not a church member. The strict standards of discipline (something like a third use of the law) serve further to emphasize one's decision for Jesus and sanctification. The separation of the Church from the things of the world is a further witness to this emphasis.

Are these overall theological emphases what New Testament Christianity is all about? Or with Zwingli should we be concerned that they are not in sufficient dialogue with the thought currents of the day and are guilty of abdicating responsibility for society as a whole? With Luther should we worry instead about a creeping Pelagianism and the compromise of the primacy of grace?

# CHAPTER 5

# JOHN CALVIN AND THE SPREAD OF THE REFORMED TRADITION

Many scholars agree that John Calvin (1509–64) was Protestantism's most important systematizer. In one sense, his theological proposals diversified the Protestant tradition. The more diversity we find in the Church, the more likely it is that the Church will be inclusive. In another sense, though, Calvin's work as an influential systematizer of Protestantism has contributed, not to diversity, but to unity within the Church — especially to Protestant unity. Calvin's profound impact on the theology of various segments of Protestantism will become increasingly apparent.

It is appropriate to draw distinctions between Calvin and Luther. In some ways, Renaissance humanist scholar that he was, Calvin was more like Zwingli and the early Anabaptists than the peasant Luther. Yet he also differed from these men in that he was French, and all of the other Reformers, except Simons, were German.[1] Calvin holds a middle position between the extremes of Luther and Zwingli. He was a man of the middle in another way. Not impetuous like Luther, Calvin was more inclined to hang back and keep his options open as long as possible. Another significant difference is that Calvin was the first of the great second-generation Reformers. Born in 1509, he was not in the first wave of reform, as were Luther and Zwingli, which afforded Calvin a different perspective on it.

## Life of Calvin

Calvin was born into a somewhat higher social standing than was Luther. However, like Luther, this French Reformer had a father who had great plans for his son. Calvin's father was a pious Catholic layman, a widower, who served as secretary to the bishop and as procurator of

---

1. Such cultural differences are not insignificant. More so than German culture, French culture values individualism and individual creativity, with somewhat less emphasis on systemic detail.

97

the Cathedral Chapel in Noyon. He aspired for a career in the ministry for his son. To that end, Calvin's father obtained early clerical appointments for him, which meant that the income from the parish to which young John had been appointed could defray his educational expenses.[2]

Despite these well-laid plans and the comfortable lifestyle they seemed to afford, for some reason Calvin's father dictated that his son, then in his teen years, should switch to the study of law. There is a possibility that the father had been discredited among his ecclesiastical superiors, causing him to suspect that he would be of little use in advancing his son's career in the Church or that in fact the son might suffer from his father's reputation. Yet another possibility is that reform-minded friends of Calvin's father had convinced him of the bankruptcy of the Catholic theology of his day, leading him to fear that his son would gain nothing from its study. In any case, ever obedient, Calvin agreed to the father's directive regarding a curriculum change.[3] Calvin's obedience would lead one to assume the presence of great affection between father and son. However, it is striking how little affection he expresses in his writing for his father, especially in comparison to Luther's remarks about his father. In a sense, Calvin seems to have been a man spending his life searching for and carrying out the wishes of father figures.

## Humanist and Reformer

Much like Zwingli and the early Anabaptists, Calvin was a man thoroughly schooled in the Renaissance humanist tradition. Having studied in Paris, he received the best education possible in his day, in contrast to Luther, whose doctorate was not obtained at a leading school. How thoroughly Calvin accepted the tradition's agenda is evident in his greatest work — the *Institutes of the Christian Religion* (1.5.2) — as he claimed that those with a liberal arts background were more readily able to penetrate the divine mysteries. Such commitments forced him throughout his career to endure criticisms of his thought as too much influenced by the agenda of Renaissance rationalism (*Institutes of the Christian Religion* 4.17.24–25; hereafter cited as *Institutes*).

It is not clear why Calvin adopted the reform agenda. Certainly humanism's impact on him was a factor, as humanists of the day were

---

2. Of course, the boy could not serve in such a capacity until reaching adulthood and completing his education, but that did not matter. In late medieval Catholic church life, plagued by simony as it was, leaving ecclesiastical positions vacant while still collecting their tithes was nonetheless standard operating procedure.

3. Calvin's background in law seems relevant to his own theological preoccupation with law, which will become evident as we analyze his theology.

characteristically critical of the Catholic Church. In fact, in France since the fourteenth century prominent voices for reform had sounded, ever since conciliarism had been heartily defended. Various Parisian intellectuals were reading Luther while Calvin studied in the city. A crackdown on Reformers in Paris in 1533 led to Calvin's banishment, which was largely due to negative reactions to a controversial sermon preached by one of his friends, Nicolas Cop, the new rector of the Sorbonne. Calvin may have helped write the sermon. A year and a half later, Calvin resigned his clerical benefices. His break with the Catholic Church was complete.

Following these episodes, Calvin decided to devote his life to a career as a Christian scholar. The *Institutes*, the Reformation's first and perhaps greatest summary of the Christian faith, was initially published in 1536 and frequently revised during his life. Its initial publication created much interest and rendered Calvin a much admired young scholar. It is this classical voluminous summary of the faith that has established Calvin as the chief systematizer of the Reformation, while the other Reformers' writings, including many of Calvin's other writings, are merely occasional pieces addressing specific problems.

## The Reformer of Strasbourg

In the year the *Institutes* was published, Calvin resolved to settle in Strasbourg, where Protestantism had been established. The leader of the Reformation in Strasbourg was the eminent Martin Bucer, who had created a stimulating intellectual climate in the city. Military operations closed the direct route to Strasbourg, and Calvin took a detour, which led him to Geneva. While in Geneva, he met the leader of its Reformation, William (Guillaume) Farel (1489–1565), a French humanist and already a successful Reformer elsewhere in Switzerland.

Farel quickly realized, given Calvin's budding reputation, what the young scholar might mean to his reform efforts. He was soon urging Calvin to join him in the project. Farel needed all the help that he could get. The only reason there was a reform in Geneva was because the city's rising bourgeoisie had advocated it on account of economic reasons.[4] An older man, Farel turned the pressure on Calvin, who only desired a career as a scholar, in order to cajole him to stay and work for reform. Calvin's affirmative response after many attempts to say no indicates again his need to please "father figures."

---

4. Recall that in this period of the transition to capitalism, people generally perceived the Catholic Church as the defender of feudalism. Consequently, to the capitalists Protestantism appeared to be better for business.

The reform efforts in Geneva were rocky. Calvin's insistence on enforcing regulations for admission to the Lord's Supper (in some cases, these regulations pertained to picayune behaviors, like strictures against having one's fortune told by a gypsy or laughing during a sermon) and his use of excommunication to enforce such behavioral standards (*Institutes* 4.12.1ff.) led to his own and Farel's voluntary expulsions in 1538. Calvin was eager to return to life as a scholar. He was again drawn to Strasbourg (at this time still a German city) to the company of the great humanist Reformer Martin Bucer. The older Bucer was yet another father figure who prevailed on Calvin to undertake an unwanted task — in this case to minister to the French congregation in town.

Calvin's three years in Strasbourg were fruitful. Besides a successful and happy ministry in this period, with Bucer's encouragement he also married a French widow, Idelette de Bure, with whom he lived very happily until her death in 1549. During this period, Bucer's polity and ideas on the Eucharist began to exert influence on Calvin (Martin Bucer *Confession of Faith concerning the Eucharist*). The theological influence that Bucer had on him was most significant because though the Reformer of Strasbourg was a Lutheran, he functioned as a go-between for his heritage and other Reformation traditions. In addition, Bucer had significant influence on the reform in the British Isles.

Finally in 1541, urged again against his will by Bucer and Farel and coupled with popular support from the Geneva Council after Catholic efforts to regain influence during Calvin's and Farel's exile, Calvin returned to Geneva. There Calvin was truly able to implement reform. He took control of revamping the town government to ensure the input of clergy. Though he never established a pure *theocracy* (a form of government in which the Church in the name of God rules the state), Calvin's prestige was such that he usually got his way. The town government was clearly in the business of promoting religion (*Institutes* 4.20.2–3, 9). The law was used to enforce Christian standards. Sometimes those standards were so rigorous, so nit-picking, so severe, as to warrant the reputation that Calvin has among many as a stern, almost fanatical, man. The persecution of dissenters was a regular affair in sixteenth-century Geneva.

## The Spread of Calvinism and the Reformed Tradition

Calvin's influence spread widely to sections of Germany, the Netherlands, France, Hungary, and Scotland (through his famous student John Knox; ca. 1513–72). His thought also came to influence the Waldensians, a community of dissident Roman Catholics that had practiced a lifestyle of extreme poverty since their formation under the leadership of the French merchant Peter of Waldo (Peter Valdes; d. ca. 1205) in the Middle Ages. After their excommunication in 1184, they fled to the Alps. Calvin's views were adopted by the sect, and they renounced recognition of the Roman Catholic Church in 1532. To this day the Waldensian Church, though small, retains its Reformation orientation.

Calvin's opening of an academy in Geneva placed him in contact with an international group of students, who carried his theological views into their homelands when they returned. Gradually contemporaries perceived Calvin's views as a distinct theological alternative to the Lutheran and Anabaptist models. The key dividing issue was Calvin's view of the Lord's Supper, which resembled his mentor Bucer's view (see the discussion below). In 1526, Luther and Bucer were reconciled on this matter in an agreement called the "Wittenberg Concord." However, Calvin's similar views were still perceived as distinct.

Another dynamic related to the perception that Calvin offered a distinct theological alternative was the eventual reconciliation of the views of Calvin and Zwingli. Calvin's views spread widely, first in Switzerland and even to Zwingli's Zurich. Zwingli's successor, Johann Heinrich Bullinger (1504–75), became especially appreciative of the Genevan Reformer, and in 1549 he, Calvin, other Swiss Protestants, and some southern German Reformers signed the Zurich Consensus. From then on, observers of the Calvinist and Zwinglian heritages regarded them as a unity, just as the two traditions would see themselves as essentially one.[5]

Since the title "Lutheran" was an inappropriate identification of the followers of Calvin and Zwingli and since they were not Anabaptist, in time the title "Reformed" came to be attributed to their tradition. Of course, this epithet is appropriate insofar as the views of Calvin and Zwingli have their origin in the Reformation. The term implies that the Reformation must continue, that the Church must always be in reform, as also suggested by Calvin's more critical perspective on the Catholic tradition. Luther's view, by contrast, was that the Reformation is complete once the Catholic tradition is preaching and teaching the gospel of unconditional grace.

---

5. In 1566, Bullinger prepared the Second Helvetic Confession, which became and has remained a most influential statement of this tradition's beliefs. The confession clearly embodies beliefs consistent with Calvin's, the one possible exception being its treatment of the Lord's Supper (XXI), which some have speculated might be more Zwinglian in orientation.

## Calvin's Pastoral Context

To understand Calvin's theology, we need to understand him as a man torn by anxiety and special circumstances in Geneva (*Institutes* 3.14.6; *Letter to Somerset*). Calvin, unlike Luther, was not so concerned about personal salvation; he was more anxious about the world's being out of joint, in chaos. Like many sensitive and culturally sophisticated people in the late Middle Ages, he sensed startling changes on the horizon. Medieval society as they had known it was withering away.

In Geneva, things were certainly in chaos when Calvin first arrived. The old feudal economy was changing, replaced by capitalism. Influenced by the Reformation in Bern, the town leaders had sought to oust the duke of Savoy and the Catholic bishops, who had previously ruled the town. They succeeded in establishing a government ruled by a council, but everything was in flux. There was no order. In the midst of chaos, discipline was necessary. Many of the revolutionaries, now free of ecclesiastical oppression, had no desire to submit again to Christian discipline. Some among the Genevan elite had even raised questions about the existence of God; the Church's credibility was that badly damaged. In this sort of personal and social context, Calvin's theology developed.

## Calvin's Theology

Not surprisingly, the overriding concern of Calvin's theology was with discipline in the Christian life and, to a lesser extent, apologetics (*Institutes*, pref. 7–8; 1.3.2; 3.10.1; 4.11.1). The situation in sixteenth-century Geneva dictated this agenda.

Clearly Calvin was not as preoccupied with justification as Luther was. Yet Calvin did claim that justification was the main hinge on which religion turns (*Institutes* 3.11.1). His primary concern, though, was to promote God's glory (*Necessity of Reforming the Church*). Indeed, the knowledge of God, particularly knowledge of the sovereignty of God, is at the heart of Calvin's system. This knowledge of a sovereign God who does and works all things logically entails a belief in God's justifying us by grace, for all that happens, including our salvation, is construed as God's work.

For Calvin, the knowledge of God is existential, not merely theoretical (*Commentaries on II Timothy 3:16–17; Geneva Catechism;* cf. *Institutes* 1.1.1ff.). It is "heart knowledge," not mere "head knowledge." So important is the knowledge of God for Calvin that in one context he insisted that we cannot know ourselves apart from the knowledge of God (*Institutes* 1.1.2). In another context (1.1.1), he reversed the order of the two spheres of knowledge, claiming that the knowledge of ourselves arouses us to seek the knowledge of God. Generally speaking, with atheism in view as his polemical target, the Reformer's response was to emphasize the knowledge of God and divine providence or divine sovereignty (1.4.5; 1.16.1ff.). The attainment of such knowledge, he asserted, leads to a lifestyle of constant praise, a life lived in awe that looks for every good from God (1.2.2). All of these commitments point us again to the heart of Calvin's theology — an affirmation of God who is in control of all that happens.

## Sin

So thoroughly are we enmeshed in sin in Calvin's view that he referred to human nature's total depravity, which of course denies human free will (*Institutes* 2.2.1ff.), much as Luther had (2.1.5). The Genevan Reformer refers to our corrupt nature (2.1.11), a belief also based on his emphasis on a sovereign God. If human beings were free, God would not be entirely in control.

## Law-Gospel Relationship and the Shape of the Christian Life

Calvin's reflections on the relationship between law and gospel are best understood in light of his views on the nature of the Christian life. In his treatment of the doctrine of justification by grace through faith, which he claims is only a sign of election (*Institutes* 3.21.7), Calvin tends primarily to assume a forensic view (3.11.2), though with some references, like Luther, to the idea of justification as conformity to Christ (3.1.1; cf. 3.11.9ff.). Recall that forensic justification is the idea that God declares the believer righteous, much as a judge in a court of law may declare a guilty defendant innocent. Therefore, the declaration does not make the guilty party good, that is, does not sanctify the believer. Such a view of justification, then, mandates that the theologian needs to devote express attention to exhorting the faithful to good works. When that happens, it is usually by way of teaching a third use of the law (see pp. 53–54, 56–57 for a discussion of these concepts). Consequently, advocacy of the forensic view of justification characteristically mandates a third use of the law; we can observe this to be the case in Calvin.

The Genevan Reformer did not distinguish the law and gospel as Luther did. Gospel confirms law (*Institutes* 2.9.4). The law is not a curse for believers; it merely awakens them (22.7.14). These suppositions reflect his openness to affirming a third use of the law. Unlike for Luther, it is the most important use (*Institutes* 2.7.12; 2.8.51). Also unlike the German Reformer and again more in the spirit of Zwingli and the Anabaptists, Calvin believed in the possibility of progress in the Christian life (3.7.5). If the law is to guide Christian life, obedience is mandated. And so Calvin refers to the faithful's obedience to God (4.20.32). This emphasis on sanctification and obedience tended to nurture a work-oriented vision of the Christian life, such that the Genevan Reformer is often credited as the originator of the so-called Protestant work ethic.

The correlation of the law and gospel led Calvin to correlate Old and New Testaments, which he regarded in turn as distinct, though related, covenants (*Institutes* 2.11.23). Though not at the heart of his theology as some later interpreters allege, the theme of covenant (or agreed-upon federations) was an important one for Calvin, as he regarded it as "the first union of us with God" (3.14.6).

## Church-State Relationship

In view of the correlation Calvin posited between the law and gospel, and inasmuch as the gospel has the final word over the law, it logically follows that he would hold that the gospel rightly exercises influence on the state. It aids magistrates in their responsibility to curtail sin, he asserted. As such, it joins with the functions of the state (*Institutes* 4.11.3). Thus, the ideal for the state is to seek to legislate gospel norms, at least insofar as magistrates must be subject to the Church (*Institutes* 4.11.4). In fact, government should promote religion (4.20.2, 39). It is in this qualified sense that we may understand Calvin to advocate a theocracy. In the strict sense, sixteenth-century Geneva did not embody such a system, since as the council, not the Church, continued to exercise supreme political authority. The Church's political authority was more indirect, through influence on the magistrates and popular opinion.

Essentially Calvin and Zwingli agreed in their views of church-state relations (Christian social ethics). Both disagreed with Luther's two-kingdom ethic. Thus, the diagrams used to compare Luther and Zwingli (see p. 78) are appropriate for comparing the German Reformer and Calvin.

Other differences emerge between the German and Genevan Reformers. While Luther was critical of capitalism, Calvin was more open to it, which is not surprising insofar as the new bourgeoisie led the Reformation in Geneva. Private property was a fundamental right in Calvin's view. He even exhibited a certain appreciation of wealth, which he believed was not inherently evil (*Commentary on Exodus 16:17; Commentary on Exodus 11:2*). However, Calvin may not have been a wholehearted supporter of capitalism (*Commentary on Exodus 22:25*). In the style of contemporary liberation theology, he did claim that the poor are often more pious than the upper class (*Commentary on Isa-*

*iah* 28:14). He also asserted that Christians are called to share with the poor (*Institutes* 2.8.46).

The Genevan Reformer mandated obedience to those in power (*Institutes* 4.20.23–32). Yet while hardly a proponent of revolutionary change, he did not advocate unquestioned obedience to political authority. Rather he advocated change "inside" the system, claiming that constitutionally authorized magistrates (though not private citizens) may act against an evil king (4.20.31).

### Double Predestination

Insofar as Calvin did not feature predestination prominently in his writings (contrary to the assumptions of many), it is not at the heart of Calvin's thought. In fact, predestination is merely a logical consequence of Calvin's view of sin and his stress on God's sovereignty or divine providence (*Institutes* 1.16.1; 1.17.1ff.; 2.4.7). If God is sovereign, totally in control, then all aspects of salvation, even our faith or lack of it, must be God's work.

Calvin affirmed, as Zwingli did, *double predestination* (the belief that in eternity God determines both who will be saved as well as those who are to be damned; *Institutes* 3.21.1, 7; 3.23.1). God's decree is not based on foreknowledge, he insisted (3.21.5). In fact, the divine decree is eternal. Thus Calvin teaches a *supralapsarian election* (the belief that God decreed who would be elect before the Fall into sin; see 2.12.5). Historically some students of Calvin have been put off by his views on this subject and the idea that God would elect to damn some in eternity even before they existed.[6] The Reformer responded by asking who are we to judge God and by reminding us that it is good to be humbled by double predestination (*Institutes* 3.21.1–2; 3.24.17). As such, it is a salubrious antidote to our sinful pride, which would try to seize governance of the world from God by questioning his sovereign ways.

Calvin also has a word of comfort for those existentially struggling with double predestination, that is, for those concerned about whether they are among the elect or might be damned. His word of assurance is the idea that *perseverance* (constancy in the faith) is a sign of election (*Institutes* 3.22.7; 3.23.10). If you have walked the walk of faith consistently for some length of time, you can be assured of your election. Another word of hope is that grace is irresistible and the elect cannot fall from grace (3.24.5ff.).

---

6. Calvin's fidelity to the Augustinian heritage is certainly apparent in these commitments.

## View of Scripture

Historically many in the heritage of Calvin have embraced in his name a Fundamentalistic view of Scripture. Certainly there is some evidence in the great Frenchman's writings to warrant this conclusion. He did seem on at least one occasion to affirm something like the divine dictation of Scripture (*Commentary on II Timothy 3:16;* cf. *Institutes* 4.8.6). Elsewhere he claimed that the gospel is an infallible truth (*First Sermon on Pentecost*).

A more potentially critical approach to the Bible is evident in other writings of Calvin. One can identify Christocentric hermeneutical suppositions in his thinking (*Commentary on John 5:39*). Apart from Christ, there is no saving knowledge, he claimed (*Institutes* 2.6.4). Yet paradoxically he also asserted that the whole Christ is never fully revealed — a concept that has come to be known pejoratively among non-Reformed theologians as the "extra Calvinisticum" (4.17.30). Such a view is implicit in Calvin's affirmation of double predestination. Christ cannot be said to have wholly revealed God if there is something in God that is not unconditional love but would damn human beings in eternity. Calvin's "Bucerian" view of the Lord's Supper also presupposes that the whole of Christ is not revealed, at least not in the sacrament.

At any rate, the Bible is never a dead book of doctrine for Calvin. His notion of the knowledge of God (which Scripture reveals) as a life-transforming, existential knowledge precludes that possibility. Thus he speaks of Scripture as illuminating experience (*Institutes* 1.6.1). Experience is also critical for Calvin in understanding Scripture as the Word of God. If God is sovereign, then even our understanding of the Word must be God's work. Thus, we only know the Word if the Holy Spirit testifies to it, a concept called the "internal testimony of the Spirit." The Spirit seals the testimony of the Word (*Institutes* 1.7.4). Similarities to Luther's and Augustine's letter-spirit dialectic certainly seem suggested at this point.

The correlation of experience and the Word of God emerges in some of Calvin's sermons and expositions that reflect a kind of narrative approach. Not unlike Luther, Calvin aimed in these instances to have the interpreter identify with the biblical characters in the pericope studied (*First Sermon on Pentecost*). When one considers again its many proponents, such a venerable narrative, storytelling approach has obviously had an enormous impact on the history of the Church.

## Trinity and Christology

With regard to his views on the continuing authority of the Catholic tradition, Calvin stood between Luther and the Anabaptists. His reflections on the nature of God resemble Luther's. Time is in God, he claimed, and so in principle God is affected by time (*Institutes* 3.21.5). Yet elsewhere in the *Institutes* (1.13.8; 1.17.13), he asserted that God has not changed.

With regard to the Trinity, Calvin broke with Luther's Christocentric focus, which emphasized the unity of the persons. Rather Calvin spoke of the Father as the fountain from which the Son and Spirit were begotten and proceeded (*Institutes* 1.13.8, 26) in a way that not only emphasizes the distinctions among them but also prioritizes the Father as the source of the other persons.

Calvin was more Antiochene than Alexandrian in his Christology. He denied the *communicatio idiomatum* (communion of attributes; *Institutes* 1.13.6; 2.14.1; 4.17.29). As previously noted, he did indeed espouse an "extra Calvinisticum" in the sense that God is not totally revealed in Christ, for Christ is not wholly present in Communion (4.17.30). In the final analysis, we do not know God as he is in himself, but only know him as he is towards us (1.10.2). This assertion relates to Calvin's contention that God "accommodates" himself to our finite capacities (1.13.1). These commitments also further emphasize the distinctions between the persons of the Trinity (the Son is not fully able to reveal the Father) in contrast to Luther's stress on the unity of the persons (the Son fully revealing the Godhead).

### Church and Ministry

Calvin rejected the Anabaptist idea of the Church as a believers' church, a church of the converted. For him, the Church is a community that includes sinners (*Institutes* 4.1.13). Given his emphasis on divine sovereignty, it follows that the Church must be created by God's act (4.1.10–12; Genevan Confession 18). In this regard, he shares a like mind with Luther. However, unlike the older Reformer, Calvin at least at one point in his career defined the Church in relation to discipline (*Reply to Sadolet*). His insistence that the Church be marked by such discipline is certainly consistent with his overriding concern with discipline in the Christian life.

To be sure, worship for Calvin is at the heart of the life of the Church. Much like Zwingli, though by no means as militant, Calvin had low-church propensities and did not retain the Catholic liturgy, as Luther did. Such commitments, much like the other great Swiss Reformer, were related to Calvin's preoccupation with avoiding idolatry (*Institutes* 1.11.3; *Necessity of Reforming the Church*).

Like Luther, Calvin was open to the threefold ministry (ministers as bishops, presbyters, and deacons). Of course, he preferred to refer to presbyters but identified three different roles or orders (*Institutes* 4.3.4–9; 4.4.1–5). Also like Luther, Calvin was open to regarding ordination as a sacrament (4.19.31). However, the Genevan Reformer also affirmed the priesthood of all believers (2.15.6; 4.19.28; *Commentary on I Thessalonians 4:3*), yet this was not his dominant way of talking about the ministry.

Ministers, he insisted, must exercise authority over the laity (an affirmation no doubt related to his own need to exercise such authority over some of the slothful laity in Geneva; *Institutes* 4.8.2ff.). Indeed, ministers rule over the Church (*Reply to Sadolet*), representing Christ's person (*Institutes* 4.3.1; *Reply to Sadolet*). Furthermore, clergy must have a special role in presiding over the elections of ministers (*Institutes* 4.3.15). This sort of attention to church polity, though not an unambiguously presbyterian system of church organization, certainly bears sufficient affinities to such a polity as to authorize the subsequent impact that Calvin has had on the Presbyterian tradition.

### Sacraments

Calvin typically only refers to two sacraments (*Catechism of the Church of Geneva*). There is little of the ambiguity in Calvin that we observed in Luther on that matter.

**Baptism.** Much like Zwingli, Calvin claimed that the sacraments provide occasion for giving testimony to one's faith (*Institutes* 4.1.8). Also like Zwingli, he opted for infant baptism because of its analogy to circumcision (4.16.3). In addition, he argued that children are as entitled to receive the promises as any other elect members of the Church (4.15.20, 22; *Catechism of the Church of Geneva*).

Calvin rejected the concept of baptismal regeneration. The sacrament provides knowledge of one's cleansing, he argued, but is not the cause of such cleansing (*Catechism of the Church of Geneva; Institutes* 4.15.1–2). It is something like a seal, a government seal that confirms the authority (the official character) of what is proclaimed in a document (*Institutes* 4.14.5). For example, Americans cannot be sure that the tax refund is really in the mail unless the notification includes the governmental (Internal Revenue Service) seal.

**Lord's Supper.** Essentially, as he had on other issues, Calvin staked out a middle ground on this sacrament between Zwingli and Luther. Like them, he rejected the concept of the Mass as a sacrifice and insisted that the laity receive the wine as well as the bread (*Institutes* 4.17.47–50; 4.18.1ff.) With regard to Christ's real presence in the sacrament, Calvin affirmed this with Luther, but with Zwingli he argued that Christ is not in the elements (4.17.16–17). The elements function as holy symbols, means by which the believer is elevated to Christ's heavenly presence (*Confession of Faith concerning the Eucharist; Best*

*Method of Obtaining Concord; Institutes* 4.17.18, 31). Christ remains in heaven (*Institutes* 4.17.26; *Two Discourses on the Articles* 1; *Catechism of the Church of Geneva; Confession of Faith concerning the Eucharist; Summary of Doctrine concerning the Ministry of the Word and the Sacraments* VIII).

The similarities at this point between Calvin and his Lutheran mentor Bucer are obvious. Insofar as Bucer subscribed to Lutheranism's historically authoritative doctrinal summary, the Augsburg Confession, can the case be made that Calvin's view (which was Bucer's) is essentially "Lutheran"? Are the differences between the Lutheran and the Reformed tradition on this point essentially insignificant? Of course, some would argue that there are important differences. For example, Calvin rejected the concept of a *manducatio oralis* (receiving Christ through the mouth when one partakes of the consecrated bread and wine) as well as the *manducatio impiorum* (eating or drinking to one's judgment; *Institutes* 4.17.6). After all, unbelievers in Calvin's view do not have Christ present (4.17.33, 40). Recall that for Luther, Christ is present even for unbelievers, albeit to their detriment.

In view of the fact that Calvin's treatment of the Lord's Supper was perceived as the issue that divided his tradition from Lutheranism, we must raise anew questions about the compatibility between Luther and Calvin on the Lord's Supper. Are their differences enough to justify the continuing division between the Lutheran and the Reformed traditions? In connection with possible ecumenical links to Lutheran and Catholic Communion practices, it is interesting to note (and often overlooked) that Calvin advocated weekly Communion (*Institutes* 4.17.43, 46; *Articles concerning the Organization of the Church*). Of course, in actual practice in Geneva it was only celebrated monthly (*Articles concerning the Organization of the Church*), a practice that has more characteristically typified the Reformed tradition.

### Social Concern

Calvin's views on social issues, as with his economics, represent an interesting mix. He was perhaps not as open to women's leadership as Luther was, though clear similarities exist. Those bearing the title "father," he said, were lit with the spark of God's splendor (*Institutes* 2.8.35). The Reformer opposed women baptizing (*Institutes* 4.15.20–22), in contrast to Luther's openness to the practice in emergencies (Luther *Concerning the Ministry*, in *LW* 40:23). On the other hand, though, Calvin did claim that it is merely a practical matter that women were not given ecclesiastical leadership positions or were directed by Scripture to dress in certain ways (*Institutes* 4.10.30–31; *Commentary on Mark*

*16:1*). Calvin accepted many of his era's sexist attitudes, such as advocating that a woman's place is in the home (*Commentary on Isaiah 3:17; Sermon 16 on II Sam.* 138). We have already noted Calvin's happy marriage. In addition, the Geneva Reformer praised sex (*Commentary on I Corinthians 7:6*) and claimed that women have equal rights in sexual matters (*Commentary on Matthew 19:9*).

Regarding African peoples, Calvin cited, as did Luther, the Coptic and Ethiopian Orthodox churches with favor in arguing that churches long before his own time had thrived without exhibiting obedience to the papacy (*Acts of the Council of Trent*). However, unlike Luther, he did not praise ancient Egyptian culture but criticized it for its alleged pride and cruelty (*Commentary on Genesis 12:20*). It is also interesting that Calvin did not deal with the vicious rumors circulating among the late medieval masses regarding Africans that Luther noted and tried to refute. Could Calvin's silence on the matter be a function of the fact that this cultured man was not in touch with peasant lore?

In any case, there are indications that Calvin loathed the exploitation of African people through the institution of slavery. He rejoiced at the disappearance of slavery from Europe (save Spain) during his lifetime, claiming that the survival of the institution was the result of the heathen Turks and the Africans themselves. Recognizing that the Old Testament patriarchs had practiced slavery (Gen. 24:2ff.; Exod. 21:1–11), Calvin felt that he could not absolutely condemn the abhorrent practice (*Commentary on Jeremiah 34:8–17; Commentary on Genesis 12:5*).

## Assessment: Were the Adjustments Made by Calvin to the Thought of the Other Reformers Precisely What the Church Needed?

In the final analysis, Calvin's theology boils down to a commitment to affirming the sovereignty of God in face of a turbulent secular culture and the perceived breakdown in moral standards. Is this proposal a viable model for ministry in our present setting, marked as it is by cultural turbulence and the decline of moral standards? Certainly Calvin's emphasis on the sovereignty of God (an affirmation that everything that happens is God's work) and an attempt to uphold Christian morality are reflected in virtually every doctrine. In response to atheism or skepticism, Calvin contended that we need a God big enough, powerful enough, to command respect. In response to moral laxity, Calvin would have the Church emphasize the "Protestant work ethic," the third use of the law, and a view of the sacraments in which nothing happens for the faithful unless they have exercised their faith.

The grace reflected in Calvin's thought seems to be a rather joyless one, which is accounted for by Calvin's view that all grace is by divine condescension. It is an exception; as such, it is not totally free. Such a picture of grace seems in line with Zwingli and even with the Anabaptists. Only Luther appears to contradict this portrait, proposing instead a joyful, unconditional love of God. Or does Luther's portrayal effectively diminish the awesome and transcendent character of grace, rendering it little more than a deified version of human love? Which of these portraits is more faithful to the biblical witness?

# CHAPTER 6

# THE REFORMATION IN GREAT BRITAIN

## TOWARDS AN INCLUSIVE CHURCH?

A consideration of the Reformation in the British Isles follows logically after a study of John Calvin's theology. Much of the Anglican, as well as the Scottish, reform bears the imprint of Calvin's influence. During this time period, England and Scotland were still separate countries, each with a different history. The focus of this chapter will be the Reformation in England and the early stages of reform in Scotland. Not until a century later, during the Puritan era, did the Reformation in Scotland come to full fruition.[1]

Despite the clear influence of Calvin, in a most fundamental, rudimentary sense, the founding of the Church of England comes down to Henry VIII's (1491–1547) desire for a male offspring and a new wife who would be able to provide him with one. To the mind of a sixteenth-century man, if an heir is lacking (and only a male heir counted), it was the woman's fault.

### Non-Theological Factors in the Anglican Reform

England had a special relationship with Spain early in the sixteenth century.[2] The British-Spanish ties had been further strengthened in 1509 when Henry VIII married Catherine of Aragon (1485–1536), daughter of the Spanish king.

The original plan had been for Catherine to marry Henry's older brother Arthur, who was heir apparent to the British throne. Four months after their marriage, the British prince died, leaving Catherine a widow. Almost immediately the Spanish throne, with an eye towards

---

1. A fuller exposition of the reform in Scotland will be considered in chapter 9.
2. Scotland was an ally of France, and this in part accounts for the tensions between these two kingdoms on the British Isles.

Catherine's welfare, suggested that ties between the nations could be preserved were she to be remarried to the new heir apparent, Henry. Catherine's father, King Ferdinand V (1452–1516), was also motivated by the concern that he not forfeit the dowry he had bestowed on the British royal house for the first marriage. Granted, there would be complications. Leviticus 18:16 forbade sexual relations between a man and the wife of his brother. A papal dispensation would be necessary to allow the marriage of Henry and Catherine. Of course, obtaining such favors was no problem for the elite. Pope Julius II (1443–1513), himself a wheeler-dealer in politics, was only too pleased to grant the favor, although his decision created much controversy.

### Ecclesiastical Consequences of Henry's Divorce

The failure of Henry and Catherine to produce a male heir — their only surviving offspring was Princess Mary Tudor (1516–58) — was a source of much consternation and controversy. The nation had only recently suffered through wars of succession. It could not afford another episode of chaos. Only a male heir could ensure peaceful succession. It seems that Henry did have an illegitimate son, but declaring him legitimate was apparently not a viable option given the standards of morality and litigation of the day. In addition, the failure of Henry's union with Catherine to produce a male heir was increasingly seen as a sign of God's displeasure with the union. Given the medical suppositions of the day, the one viable option was obvious: Henry needed a new mate who could provide him with the male heir that he and the British people needed so desperately!

Good Catholic that he was, Henry could not merely put his wife aside through divorce (Matt. 5:31–32; 19:9; 1 Cor. 7:10–11).[3] The only option available was to request an annulment of the marriage from the pope on grounds that the marriage to Catherine had never been valid. Pope Clement VII's (1478–1534) failure to grant the annulment was mostly a function of politics. He did not dare to offend Spain, whose king (Charles V [1500–1558]; also the Holy Roman emperor during Luther's reform career) was Catherine's nephew.

That Henry was no supporter of Protestantism was obvious. However, many in England who were attracted to Luther welcomed the growing distance between Henry and the pope. They regarded the Reformation as in the spirit of John Wycliffe, whom many still admired. The king's main religious advisor, Thomas Cranmer (1489–1556), envi-

---

3. Early in Henry's reign, he had been commended by the pope as a "Defender of the Faith" for writing a critique of Protestantism.

sioned the Reformation of the Church under royal authority. Cranmer sought and received the opinions of various theological faculties regarding the validity of Henry's marriage to Catherine. Both he and Henry got the answer they wanted to hear.

The king proceeded to place more pressure on the pope. He had ancient laws forbidding appeals to Rome reenacted (Restraint of Appeals). He threatened to retain funds normally sent to Rome and in so doing was able to secure Cranmer's appointment as archbishop of Canterbury (the highest office in the Catholic Church based in England). The final break came in 1534 when Parliament forbade payment of funds to Rome, declared the king to be head of the Church of England (Dispensations Act; Supremacy Act), and even ruled that Henry's marriage to Catherine was not a true marriage. This decree was not a Reformation, but it clearly represented a schism.[4]

As soon as he was declared head of the Church, Henry had the archbishop of Canterbury declare his marriage to Catherine void and regularized his secret marriage to Anne Boleyn (1507–36), who had been a maid of honor to Catherine. The union with Anne was short-lived, producing only one child, a daughter, Elizabeth (1533–1603), who was obviously born before their marriage was made official. Finding Anne tiresome by 1536 and inasmuch as she had not "provided" him with a male heir, Henry had her put to death (on some apparently trumped-up charge) and proceeded to spend the rest of his life in a series of one temporary marriage after another. Staunch Catholics in England were by no means prepared to put up with these developments. In addition to protests by Catherine of Aragon, one of the most prominent protests was stated by the chancellor of the kingdom, Sir Thomas More (1478–1535). His opposition to the new policies eventually led to his execution; as much as the persecuted Anabaptists, he was a sixteenth-century martyr for the faith.

Henry seemed to feel that his break with the papacy would go down easier with his subjects if nothing else changed in daily church life. This commitment to minimizing change was officially stated by Parliament in the 1534 Dispensations Act. Nevertheless, Cranmer and other advocates of reform saw in these developments the opportunity to bring about a real Reformation in the English church. Various humanists and those with a feel for Wycliffe's agenda joined the cause. Cranmer even ordered the Bible to be translated into English, and Henry actually decreed that the Great (English) Bible be placed in every church in a place where all could read it. The suppression of the monasteries was also instituted, as

---

4. The idea of a national church under the direction of civil authorities resonated well with the British, as it had been an aspect of Wycliffe's reform program.

it was politically beneficial for Henry. In so doing, he effectively silenced some of the harshest critics (the monks and nuns) of his policies.

One of the monarch's marriages finally produced a male heir in 1537, Edward VI, whose mother was Jane Seymour (ca. 1509–37), whom Henry had married after disposing of Anne Boleyn. Subsequent marriages following Jane's death meant different religious policies for Henry's regime. When he married the relative of a German prince (Anne of Cleves), the Anglican reform proceeded along Lutheran lines (as evidenced by the Ten Articles). When she was shunted and replaced by a queen more conservative about the reform, Henry reached an accord with the Holy Roman emperor and began to direct church life more towards Rome. The shift to Catholic practices and beliefs is evident in the Six Articles of 1539, which reaffirmed transubstantiation and clerical celibacy as well as the continuance of private Masses and confession. Nevertheless, even during these years, Henry never advocated obedience to the pope and refused to restore the monastic properties that he had confiscated. Henry's last wife was a supporter of the Reformation, so when he died in 1547, the Reformation was firmly established in England.

## The Reign of Edward VI

Upon Henry's death, his single male heir, Edward VI (1537–53), succeeded him. Edward was but a child when he came to the throne, and he reigned only six years. During his reign under the regency of staunch supporters of the Reformation like Cranmer, the Protestant side made great advances. The Communion cup was restored to the laity, and Cranmer issued the *Book of Common Prayer* (the authoritative book of worship of the Anglican reform). The first version of the book had a Lutheran or Catholic theological profile. It appeared in the period in which the great Reformer of Strasbourg Martin Bucer was living in exile and teaching in England. His influence is definitely reflected in the tone of this earlier edition, notably but not exclusively insofar as the prescribed order of service was based on a liturgy Bucer had composed for Cologne. Even though the second edition of the *Book of Common Prayer* had a more Zwinglian profile, the influence of Bucer was never totally silenced, as the authoritative view of the Eucharist for the Anglican tradition clearly demonstrates. On the other hand, the reform had moved in a definitively Reformed (esp. Calvinist) direction.

## Mary Tudor: A Restoration of Catholicism

Edward's death at a young age created marked turmoil. His half sister Mary Tudor, the daughter of Catherine, succeeded him. Raised a

Catholic, Mary had good reason to deplore Protestantism, as it had been the Reformation that had brought her and her mother into disgrace. She was a politically astute leader and did not immediately show all her cards. First she undertook the task of consolidating her position in England by solidifying her ties with the most influential Catholic royal family in continental Europe — the Hapsburg family, which ruled Spain. She did so by marrying the Spanish king, Philip II (1527–98), who also happened to be her cousin.[5]

With this alliance in place, the new British monarch sought to restore Catholicism. She restored the feast days of the saints. Married clergy were ordered to put their spouses away. Protestant leaders were persecuted, and almost three hundred were martyred. The queen came to be known as Bloody Mary as a result. Even Cranmer was martyred. At one point he recanted, but he eventually withdrew the recantation and faced his execution as an unrepentant Protestant. Heartened by his witness, true believers in the reform in England persevered in the face of Mary's continuing persecution.

## The Elizabethan Settlement

Mary died in 1558 and was succeeded by her half sister, Elizabeth. A committed moderate Protestant, Elizabeth aimed to restore many of her father's policies, such as demanding clerics to renounce allegiance to papal authority (Supremacy Act), but she also resisted Zwinglian and Calvinist proponents who rejected all Catholic liturgical elements (Act against Puritans). Elizabeth sought uniform worship practices, as had her father, in order to unite the kingdom (Act of Uniformity). This policy was well expressed in a new edition of the *Book of Common Prayer* published during her reign and in the Thirty-nine Articles (the 1562 authoritative doctrinal summary of the Church of England). Both embody a kind of via media between Protestantism and Catholicism. This sort of theological "inclusivism" was especially evident in the theological commitments finally articulated by the reform.

In establishing her ecclesiological policies, Elizabeth was putting off resistance to policies on two fronts. Efforts were being made to bring Mary Queen of Scots (1542–87), a Catholic who was next in line, to succeed her. At the same time, people with Calvinist ideas (who came to be called "Puritans") were calling for a full Reformation, the restoration of New Testament practices. The political task, then, in this context was to find a middle ground between these two agendas and their sup-

---

5. Recall that Mary's mother, Catherine, was a member of this Spanish royal family.

porters — in other words, (1) to develop an ecclesiastical ethos that was so Protestant as to preclude forever any attempt by loyal Catholics to bring the Church of England back to Roman jurisdiction but also (2) to preserve enough Catholicism to help Elizabeth's Catholic subjects feel at home in the newly reformed church. This "Elizabethan Settlement," an endeavor to keep both sides happy, still characterizes the Church of England and the Anglican community (all churches with origins in the Church of England, such as America's Episcopal Church) as a whole. Elizabeth's legacy to the Church has not waned in the centuries since her death. One still continues to find in the Anglican tradition some with more Protestant sentiments (usually referred to in modern times as Anglican Evangelicals) and those with more Catholic sentiments (referred to in modern times as Anglo-Catholics).

## The Early Stages of the Reformation in Scotland

Elizabeth feared that the successor to her throne would be the Catholic monarch of Scotland. What shape was the reform taking in this neighboring nation (which has today become yoked with England in the United Kingdom)? Essentially the Reformation in Scotland involved a controversy between an emerging Protestantism (drawing upon the heritage of the Lollards and the Hussites, indigenized by older traditions of Scottish sympathy felt towards these movements) led by John Knox (c. 1513–72) and the Catholic king James V (1512–42) and after 1543 his daughter, Mary Stuart (later Mary Queen of Scots, who was the great-granddaughter of Henry VIII's father). The controversy was further exacerbated by certain subplots pertaining to the question of whether Scotland should continue its historic alliance with France or become allied with neighboring England. Part of the dynamic during the regime of Henry VIII was that England favored the Protestant party in Scotland while those more loyal to the French and relying on these allies to fend off British designs were Catholic in religious orientation.

When the infant Mary succeeded to the throne, loyal Catholics were able to fend off proposals that she be betrothed to Henry VIII's son and heir. Rather, she was educated in France and reared a Catholic. In the interim, John Knox was gathering the support of Scottish nobles to the Protestant side, and there was a period of armed rebellion against the throne, which the French in the region finally quashed. Knox and other Protestant leaders were arrested and tortured. He was able to escape, first to England. When Edward VI died and was succeeded by his Catholic half sister, Mary Stuart, Knox fled to Geneva to study with John Calvin. It was there that he fully absorbed Calvin's Reformed version of the Reformation, a most profound development for the history of Christianity in Scotland and for the eventual development of the Presbyterian Church.

While Knox was in exile, Mary of Guise, the young queen's mother, had acted as her regent and harshly persecuted the Protestants. Her action effectively united the Scottish Protestant leaders, and in 1557 they pledged a solemn covenant, promising faithful service to the Word and to God's congregation.[6] The next year they organized themselves into a church and wrote to Geneva asking Knox to return as their leader.

In Geneva, Knox had been busy in ways other than absorbing the teachings of Calvin. He wrote a controversial work, *The First Blast of the Trumpet against the Monstrous Regiment of Women*, aimed at women Catholic rulers at the time in Scotland, England, and France. The book may have been directed solely against these sovereigns, but it contained so much antifeminine prejudice that when Elizabeth came to the throne in England, she took it offensively. That effectively closed for a time channels of possible cooperation between the Scottish Protestants to be led by Knox and Elizabeth's own Reformation cause.

After Knox's return to his homeland and through a number of political maneuverings, the Reformed Church of Scotland (later to become the Presbyterian Church) formed. Mary abdicated under pressure, and Protestants ultimately took control. The transition was by no means a smooth one, even within the Protestant camp, as Knox came to clash with the Protestant nobles while Mary still reigned. Many of the nobles, it seems, may have joined the Protestant cause for the sort of insincere reasons that attracted the early capitalists of Geneva to Protestantism. Thus they sought possession of the riches of the Catholic Church, while Knox and his supporters had more socially benevolent plans for use of this wealth. In the spirit of Calvin and much of the later Reformed tradition, Knox employed these resources for establishing a system of universal education, to lighten the load of the poor, and to support the newly formed church.

The basic theological profile of Knox's reform was essentially that of his mentor, as discussed in the preceding chapter devoted to Calvin's theology. The reform in England, though itself heavily influenced by Calvinism, is sufficiently unique to warrant special attention.

---

6. The theme of *covenant* would from that time on play an important role in theology inspired by the Scottish Reformation.

## Did the Anglican Reform Truly Mediate between Rome and the Other Reformers? Was It a Truly Catholic Expression of the Faith?

In order to assess the Anglican reform, it is first necessary to determine whether the Anglican Reformation was indeed a true reform or rather the accidental outcome of the political dynamics involved in Henry's concern about having a male heir. Such a determination can only be made after considering the theological profile that emerged from the reform.

### Catholic Orientation

In the spirit of the Roman Catholic Church, the Thirty-nine Articles (XXXIV) maintained fidelity to traditions that do not conflict with the Word.[7] Another influential voice striking a similar chord was that of the great apologist for the Elizabethan Settlement Richard Hooker (ca. 1554–1600). He claimed that though Scripture is not insufficient, wisdom may be discerned in other realms. Hooker also insisted that we should not lightly esteem the ancient practice of the Church (*Laws of Ecclesiastical Polity* 2.8.7; 5.7.1). An appreciation of the Roman Catholic heritage, as in Lutheranism, is again apparent in these sentiments.

### Legalistic Orientation?

Thomas Cranmer claimed that in Scripture one finds what is needed to be learned — the threat of damnation and exhortation diligently to labor (*Preface to the Bible*). Elsewhere he urged readers to conform their lives to the Commandments. Something like a third use of the law is clearly suggested in these and other remarks in his *Short Declaration of the True, Lively, and Christian Faith*. This preoccupation with the Christian's obedience to the law of God is also reflected in the subsequent writings of Hooker, who was particularly concerned about obedience to church law (*Laws of Ecclesiastical Polity*).

Such preoccupations with "the keeping of God's Commandments" surface in the royal injunctions of 1536 and those of 1538. This emphasis did not merely advocate a ritualistic obedience, however, but called for a true education of laity in a manner similar to Luther's concept of the priesthood of all believers. The Thirty-nine Articles reflect the same concern. At one point (XXXIV), the document claims that all traditions should serve to guard discipline. To be sure, the doctrine of justification

---

7. The influence of Lutheranism, particularly in its late sixteenth-century forms, is evident at this point.

by faith is affirmed (XI), but it does not play the central role it does in the Lutheran tradition. The document merely identifies justification as "a most wholesome doctrine." Found in the Thirty-nine Articles is a clear departure from Reformed theological propensities, as in the claim that one can fall away from grace (XVI). The document also seems to affirm something like a third use of the law in endorsing the volume *The Book of Homilies*, which advocates specific behavior directives (XXXV).

## Church and Ministry

Both church and ministry are defined by the Thirty-nine Articles (XIX, XXIII) in a way compatible with the Lutheran and Reformed heritages (and also with the Roman Catholic tradition) as works of God (in terms of the preaching of the Word and the administration of the sacraments). In accord with Elizabeth's commitment to maintain as much of the Catholic tradition as possible, the document maintains the historic episcopacy. Insofar as some of the first Anglican bishops, such as Cranmer, were previously consecrated as Catholic bishops in the apostolic line, the Anglican Church has contended that apostolic succession has been preserved.

## A Reformed View of the Lord's Supper?

The Thirty-nine Articles (XXVIII) allude, as did Calvin, to a "heavenly ascent" of the believer to Christ's presence. Yet the Anglican liturgy, which is more authoritative, says nothing about encountering a heavenly presence of Christ (*Book of Common Prayer*, Order for Celebrating the Holy Eucharist).

## Baptism

The Thirty-nine Articles identify baptism as an "instrument" by which one is grafted into the Church and affirm infant baptism (XXVII). There is a suggestion that this article is more in line with the Lutheran tradition, which maintains along with the Catholic heritage that the baptized is regenerated (born again) in baptism. However, reference in the article to the sacrament as a "sign" and "seal" is most suggestive of Calvin and the Reformed heritage.

## Predestination

The Thirty-nine Articles (XVII) seem to endorse supralapsarian election, as the Reformed tradition did. However, unlike Calvin and his heirs, the document makes no reference to an election to reprobation. The Lutheran view of single predestination is suggested by the claim that all begin in damnation and God passes over some.

### Assessment: Was This a Real and Catholic Reformation?

The Anglican reform was unique in several ways. A first mark of uniqueness surfaces in its relative lack of concern about theological distinction. In contrast to the other Reformation traditions, it was more precise about matters of liturgical form and episcopal polity. A second mark of uniqueness is that this reform was inspired, not by Augustine's theology, as were other earlier sixteenth-century reforms, but by pre-Augustinian strands in the history of the early Church. In view of these characteristics, could we say that the Anglican reform is really a movement preoccupied with reform of liturgy and polity based on ancient Catholic principles?

The lack of theological precision in the Anglican movement could also be taken by some as an indication that the Anglican Church's creation was largely a sociopolitical, not a theological, matter. Does it all ultimately boil down to Henry's desire for a male heir and his determination to get one? However, it could also be argued that the theological profile embodies an openness not characteristic of the other Reformation traditions, whose concern about doctrinal or behavioral precision bordered on sectarianism. Could it be that the genius of the theological profile of the Anglican Reformation is that it patently avoided theological precision for the sake of inclusion of a broad range of theological profiles, which then in turn may be considered validly Anglican? In that sense, is the theological imprecision indicative of the Anglican reform's truly catholic character?

The inclusiveness seems obvious, as one can identify Catholic, Lutheran, and Reformed strands in the documents we have been considering. Certainly such inclusivism has been most congenial to British culture, as it is characterized by a propensity to take all sides into account (at least if they emanate from a sufficiently "respectable" social class). Such theological inclusiveness poses anew the questions of whether a true reform transpired in the Anglican Reformation and whether the Anglican heritage is a model for a truly catholic, mediating version of the Christian faith?

# CHAPTER 7

# THE CATHOLIC REFORMATION

The desire for reform was not just an agenda of the sixteenth-century Protestant Reformers; the movement was too inclusive and catholic to be limited only to emerging Protestantism. Indeed, this desire had its roots in the Roman Catholic Church in the late Middle Ages and was especially prevalent among Renaissance humanists and pre-Reformers, such as John Wycliffe and John Huss. A general popular call for reform was in the air. The task of this chapter is to evaluate how the Catholic Church disposed of these yearnings and what its reaction was to the Protestant schism. Did the Catholic Church succeed in addressing Protestant concerns? Could it be that the issues that so disturbed the Reformers are no longer issues with regard to the Catholic Church?

The key theological issue that occasioned the Reformation, at least from the perspective of the first Reformer (Luther), was the doctrine of justification by grace through faith. Consequently, it is necessary to focus on what position the Roman Catholic Church took on the issue. Does the Catholic Church teach a kind of Pelagianism, as some of its theologians (the nominalists) of the late Middle Ages did? If not, and insofar as the Reformation was occasioned by this dispute, does the Counter-Reformation negate the need for the divisions caused by the Reformation? Suppose the Catholic Church since the Counter-Reformation has spoken about salvation and Christian life in a way compatible with Protestant denominations. In that case, there would not seem to be any justification for the continuing existence of such denominations estranged from Rome.

Scholarship has for the most part offered a negative assessment of the Counter-Reformation with regard to its ecumenical consequences. It is thought to have erected barriers that block Protestant-Catholic relationships to this day. Is this assessment accurate?

## Pre-Reformation Reforms: The Reformation of Spanish Catholicism

An impulse for reform existed in the Catholic Church well before Luther's lifetime. Such efforts took concrete, institutional form in Spain during Luther's childhood, as Queen Isabella (1451–1504) with Cardinal Francisco Ximénez de Cisneros (1436–1517) pushed educational efforts aimed at untrained clergy. Both the cardinal and the queen were themselves of notable scholarly repute. Their educational emphases were combined with their on-site visits of monastic houses and the punishment of recalcitrant monks and nuns.

The Spanish reform was biblically oriented. A multilingual edition of the Bible was published. Scripture was even prioritized over the authority of tradition. Studies that contributed to the reformation of customs and morals were also encouraged.

Isabella's reign with her less devout husband, Ferdinand V (1452–1516), was a great period of humanistic learning, as the reform inspired in the following generations the work of Miguel de Cervantes (1547–1616) and Ignatius Loyola (ca. 1491–1556). It was, though, by no means an era of intellectual freedom. Doctrinal deviation was not tolerated. The *inquisition* (a judicial persecution of heresy by ecclesiastical courts that may lead to temporal punishment) had been formerly only used under papal authority. However, during this period, it was placed under the authority of Isabella and her husband by the pope. This decision proved to be a forerunner of papal policy throughout the period of the Counter-Reformation, as increasingly the papacy conferred authority on local sovereigns to persecute heresy through juridical proceedings.

Isabella and her colleagues certainly carried on this mandate with insidious excellence. Jews and Moslems were harshly persecuted. Jews were either to accept baptism or be exiled. Most accepted the latter option, which resulted in the decimation of the Jewish community in Spain. Many of the exiles died in transit. The historically tense situation with Moslems in Spain, who dominated much of the territory for centuries since the Islamic Invasion, may have contributed to the zealousness with which their persecution sanctioned by the inquisition was carried out. It was only during Ferdinand's and Isabella's reign that the last stronghold of the Moors (Spanish Moslems) was captured and a united Spain as we know it today was established. Forced conversion was practiced on this community, which also experienced a violent backlash from those Moors who continued to practice under cover the religion of their ancestors.

During Ferdinand's and Isabella's reign, Spain undertook the colonization of the Americas. Consequently when Spanish missionaries exhibited a general intolerance towards indigenous religious traditions in these regions, it is hardly surprising. However, the actual official administration of the inquisition in the New World was executed in a less harsh manner against converted Native Americans than was the persecution of Jews and Moslems in the Spanish motherland. In any case, the intolerance to doctrinal deviation that characterized the Spanish reform became typical of the Catholic Reformation in general.

## Catholic Polemics

The advent of the Protestant Reformation altered the style of Catholic theology. It began to assume a more polemical tone in order to extol Catholic truth over against Protestant "errors." We consider some of the most prominent theologians of this genre.

John (Johann) Eck was Luther's Catholic debating partner in the Leipzig Disputation. During the course of Eck's career, he prepared a German translation of the Bible. Yet he always insisted that Scripture was not authentic without the authority of the Church (*Enchiridion* 1). As a polemicist, Eck first lumped Luther with all Protestants, charging them all with iconoclasm (*Defense of the Images of Christ and the Saints*, Pr.; 14).[1] Later, he commended the German Reformer for his defense of images against the Radical Reformers (*Enchiridion* 16). He sided, of course, with Erasmus regarding the necessity of affirming free will (*Defense against the Ritian Attacks*).

James Latomus (Jacobus Masson; ca. 1475–1544) was another of Luther's theological debating partners. This Belgium Catholic attacked both Protestants and humanists for their undue confidence in the authority of the Bible's original languages. Latomus argued that in order to understand Scripture, it was necessary to read it in Latin in light of the tradition of the Church. With regard to the Reformers' efforts to restore pure doctrine, he insisted that this was not justification for overthrowing the authority of the ages (*Defense against Martin Bucer* 2).

Robert Bellarmine (1542–1621), the greatest Catholic theologian of the era, became the main systematizer of Catholic polemics against Protestantism. He vigorously contended against Pelagianism, insisting in the spirit of Thomas Aquinas that all human efforts were in vain unless God added his grace (*Disputations on the Controversies over the Christian Faith* 14.6.4).[2]

Bellarmine was engaged in polemics not just with Protestants. Involved in the trial of Galileo (1564–1642), the Catholic polemicist eventually condemned the scientist with the declaration that the notion

---

1. At some point in his career, Eck criticized each of the first generation of Reformers.
2. Some scholars suggest, however, that Bellarmine may have made the gift of grace contingent on God's foreknowledge of the human's free decision to accept or reject grace.

that the earth revolves around the sun is heretical. Later in his career, Bellarmine did run into some trouble as a result of his contention that the pope had only an indirect, not a direct, power in temporal affairs. On the other hand, he still attributed to the papacy something like infallibility in the realm of faith and morals insofar as Bellarmine insisted that the office could not ever teach contrary to the faith (*Disputations on the Controversies over the Christian Faith* 3.4.3).

## Monastic Reform

Although monastic life had fallen on hard times in the late Middle Ages and was characterized by much corruption, there were still many practitioners who took their vows most seriously and yearned for reform. During the sixteenth century, several new monastic orders were created in order to facilitate reform. Two different strategies in the formation of these reform orders developed. Some created orders with the express intention of merely renewing strict observance of ancient vows. Other orders were created self-consciously in order to respond to the new conditions of the sixteenth century.

### Orders Aimed at Restoring the Ancient Monastic Ideals

The Discalced Carmelites clearly embodied the attempt to renew a strict observance of the ancient monastic vows. The Carmelite Order had itself been founded in Palestine early in the thirteenth century for the practice of an ascetic lifestyle in order to enhance contemplation. By the sixteenth century, adherence to the discipline and its associated spirituality was very lax. The Spanish mystic Saint Teresa of Avila (1515–82) sought to revive the rigorous discipline. One who experienced many ecstatic visions, Teresa was apparently a woman of great charm, a cause célèbre among the Spanish nobility. These qualities, as well as her administrative talents, may account for the success of the movement that she initiated. Her reform movement, in which she was joined by the Spanish mystic Saint John of the Cross (1542–91), received its name from the fact that the nuns (and later monks) wore sandals instead of shoes. They appeared to be barefoot (*discalced* in Latin).

Founded by the Italian Franciscan Matteo da Bascio (di Bassi; d. 1552), the Capuchins are another example of an order that aimed at stricter observance of Franciscan ideals, in this case extreme poverty. It is so named for the brown pointed hoods worn by its first monks.

## The Society of Jesus: A New Monastic Paradigm

The Society of Jesus (Jesuits) was founded by Ignatius Loyola (ca. 1491–1556), the son of Spanish aristocrats. His commitments to monastic life really began with a serious wound, which ended his military career. He resolved to become a saint, first by undertaking a pilgrimage to Jerusalem. On the way, a plague prevented him from entering Barcelona. During the delay he devoted himself to a life of austerity and spiritual discipline.

Like Martin Luther, Loyola found that such discipline failed to bring peace of mind; in fact, he was tormented by a profound sense of sin. Unlike Luther, however, he became convinced that the way to respond was not by seeking his own salvation but by dedicating his life to serve the Church and its mission, especially through obedience to the Church's representatives, to the pope in particular (*Constitution* vi.I). One suspects that this emphasis on unquestioned obedience to ecclesiastical authorities may reflect Loyola's military background.

Originally Loyola had intended the order that he formed to be a missionary order to evangelize Turks in the Holy Land and indigenous peoples in the Far East and the New World. However, the order's commitment to unquestioning obedience to the papacy made it a most attractive ally for sixteenth-century popes in their struggles with emerging Protestantism. As a result, the Jesuits came to be pressed into service by the papacy in its polemical endeavors against Protestantism.

But the Jesuits' original purpose — the evangelism and education of indigenous peoples and the impoverished — was not forgotten. Indeed, the Jesuits have fulfilled that role successfully. Among their most impressive early accomplishments was the culturally sensitive work of Roberto de Nobili (1577–1656) on behalf of the order in India. He so identified with India's cultural traditions that he took up the upper castes' vegetarian diet, permitted converts to continue celebrating Hindu feasts, indigenized worship, and in the traditions of Indian/Hindu culture did not allow Christians born in lower castes to worship with converts from the higher castes. An earlier Spanish-Basque Jesuit, Francis Xavier (1506–52), had previously conducted an effective ministry among the lower castes as well as undertaken successful missionary work in Japan.

Despite the Jesuits' impressive history of work in the foreign mission fields, the additional papal mandate during the Counter-Reformation to function as theological "hit men" against Protestantism effectively transformed the Society of Jesus into a leadership role in Roman Catholic education outreach in the universities. As a result, the order has been at the forefront of theological endeavors of the post-sixteenth-century Roman Catholic Church.

## Other Reforms

With regard to missionary work, the efforts of the Catholic Church in endeavoring to indigenize Christianity for indigenous peoples in various parts of the world during the Counter-Reformation period were admirable. Beginning in 1537, when Paul III (Alessandro Farnese; 1468–1549) condemned the enslavement of Native Americans, the popes of the era steadily condemned the doctrine of slavery for New World Indians. Of course, the Spanish clergy in America and Portuguese clergy in Brazil and Africa were unperturbed by slavery. Other pioneer missionaries, in addition to Roberto de Nobili and Francis Xavier, were Archbishop Toribio Alfonso de Mogrovejo, Pedro Claver (ca. 1580–1654), and Matteo Ricci (1522–1610).

Ricci's ministry was in China, where he took the lead in Jesuit efforts to relate Christian faith to the indigenous culture. An accomplished student of geography, mathematics, and astronomy, he gained the attention of the Chinese elite. He committed himself to the disciplined study of Chinese and Confucian classics and became an expert in them. As a result, the Chinese intellectual elite grew increasingly intrigued with his erudition, opening the door to informal proselytizing with a gospel that affirmed Chinese cultural traditions like the veneration of ancestors. Ricci's approach to missions came to be known as "accommodation." After his death, a protracted debate about its legitimacy emerged in Catholicism.

Claver and Mogrovejo both worked in the Americas, in the regions of Colombia and Peru, respectively. Claver was a Jesuit missionary from a family of nobility who devoted his life's work to the improvement of the welfare of African slaves in the region. He cared for them when they first landed on American shores, visited them later once they were settled, baptized them, and insisted they have access to worship services. Although largely a lonely voice in his lifetime, in his later years he began receiving the attention he deserved, leading to his canonization as a Catholic saint in the nineteenth century.

Mogrovejo, as archbishop and a committed advocate of the reforms of the Council of Trent, convened a regional synod in 1583, the Third Lima Council, which passed laws to defend the liberties of Indians and the relatively few number of African slaves in the diocese. Mogrovejo also advocated the education of the slaves and oversaw the preparation of textbooks in original Native American languages.

These dedicated and culturally sensitive ministries invite a reassessment of the adequacy of the Catholic Church's missionary work in this period. Can we speak of a reform in missions during the period of the Catholic Reformation?

Papal reform in the period after Luther was inconsistent. At the time of the Reformation in 1517, the papacy was in the hands of Leo X (Giovanni de' Medici; 1475–1521), whose major interest was in the Renaissance humanist embellishment of Rome through building projects. Some of his successors, though not all, had reforming instincts. Paul III, though very concerned with making Rome a wealthy center of the Renaissance, had reforming instincts and did convoke the reforming Council of Trent in 1545. Ten years later, Paul IV (Giovanni Caraffa; 1476–1559) was instrumental in cleansing the Roman curia of corruption.

# Council of Trent

The Council of Trent was the official expression of the Counter-Reformation. Though called for by Luther and other Reformers, there was great hesitancy by the papacy to convene such a council for fear of giving rebirth to the conciliar movement. The council was convened in 1545 under difficult negotiations with the Holy Roman emperor regarding the site. The pope and the emperor each wanted the council held on his own territory, presumably in order to be in a position to influence the bishops with threats of force. The council's first session was poorly attended; Emperor Charles V refused to recognize it as a true and authoritative council, and the turf fight caused a recess of several sessions. Consequently, the council continued meeting on and off through 1563. The council basically had a twofold agenda: (1) moral reform and (2) expunction of (Protestant) heresy (*Decree concerning the Opening of the Council*). In order to evaluate the success of the Counter-Reformation, it is necessary to cut through the stereotypes about it and carefully study its core theological commitments. The theology of the Council of Trent needs to receive particular special attention.

## Biblical Authority and Tradition

In order to appreciate the council's reflections on biblical authority and its relation to the Reformers' appeals to *sola scriptura* (the belief that Scripture, not tradition, is the ultimate authority for the Church), it is important to consider the council's context in earlier reforms within the Roman Catholic Church. There is growing scholarly consensus that the Spanish reform placed emphasis on the authority of Scripture over tradition, even before Luther did.

The Council of Trent echoes modern Protestant Fundamentalism in its claim that Scripture is divinely dictated (*Decree concerning the*

*Canonical Scriptures*), but it also declared that the Vulgate is author-itative in matters of dogma (*Decree concerning Edition and Use of the Sacred Books*). To be sure, the council did concede that the sav-ing truth is contained both in Scripture and in "unwritten traditions," which might lead one to conclude that tradition has an authority on par with Scripture. In other decrees (*Decree concerning the Edition and Use of the Sacred Books;* Pius IV *Injunctum nobis*), it more clearly affirmed that tradition is merely a guide for ruling out improper interpretations of Scripture.

Another methodologically relevant commitment of the council's de-crees is its establishment of Thomas Aquinas as the dominant theologi-cal spokesman for the Catholic Church. In view of Luther's tendency to equate Roman Catholic views of how we are saved with the nominalists' Semi-Pelagianism, Reformation traditions now need to reconsider their assessment of Roman Catholicism in light of a fresh look at Aquinas's theology and the teachings of Trent.

### Ecclesiastical Reform

In dealing with the ecclesiastical abuses of the day, the council ordered bishops to reside in their sees and included lists of general clergy obliga-tions (*Decree concerning Reform* 6th Session; 7th Session). The bishops also established the founding of seminaries for the training of clergy (5th Session, chap. I). Although Trent by no means invalidated relics and in-dulgences, it did regulate their use in order to prevent their further abuse (*Decree concerning Indulgences*). The Jesuits held similar commitments (Ignatius Loyola *Spiritual Exercises* ii.6).

### Sacraments

The council endorsed all seven of the Roman Catholic sacraments (Pius IV *Injunctum nobis; Decree concerning the Sacraments*, Canons of the Sacraments, can. 1). The Mass's status as a sacrifice was affirmed (*Doctrine concerning the Sacrifice of the Mass*, chap. II). Likewise, the council endorsed transubstantiation (*Decree concerning the Most Holy Sacrament of the Eucharist*, chap. IV; Pius IV *Injunctum nobis*).

### Ecclesiastical Authority

The council unequivocally endorsed obedience to the pope (Pius IV *Injunctum nobis*), much as the Jesuits did. Though inquisition had al-ready become the practice of the Church, broader use of it and policies even less tolerant of doctrinal diversity than in the Middle Ages were officially sanctioned (Pius IV *Bull of Confirmation*). More theological diversity had been permitted in the Church in the Middle Ages, it could be argued, than was permitted following Trent.

### Justification

Essentially the council affirmed the views of Thomas Aquinas and the larger medieval Scholastic tradition. Justification is a process initiated by grace, with the cooperation of the will. The will cooperates with God in preparing for grace, but even this movement of the will is derived from God (*Decree concerning Justification*, esp. chap. VII; Canons). Consequently, in the view of the bishops and influential Catholic reformers, sin does not entirely extinguish free will (chap. I; Ignatius Loyola *Spiritual Exercises* ii.14). Contrary to the view of Luther and Calvin, the council did not deem every deed a sin (*Decree concerning Justification*, can. 7), which is a point crucial to any attempt to determine whether official Roman Catholic theology is compatible with Protestant traditions. It appears that, at least in this period, the Catholic Church had broken with the anti-Pelagian strands of Augustine's thought.

The council did not deny predestination, which is no surprise. The Jesuits had expressly affirmed the doctrine, albeit related to free will (Ignatius Loyola *Spiritual Exercises* iii.14). Insofar as the bishops insisted that no one can state with absolute certainty that he or she is among the predestined, the council affirmed predestination by implication (*Decree concerning Justification*, chap. XII). The council's affirmation of the authority of the theology of Thomas Aquinas likewise implies an endorsement of double predestination, inasmuch as this was his view (*Summa Theologica* I.23). To be sure, the bishops and reformers differed significantly, the former unable to affirm the certainty and confidence about election that Luther and Calvin did. Unlike Calvin, the bishops claimed that grace can be lost (*Decree concerning Justification*, can. 15).

## Was the Counter-Reformation an Unmitigated Success, a Great Resource for Future Ecumenical Work?

At one level it seems indisputable that the Council of Trent and the Counter-Reformation were successful. After all, they had a pronounced impact on the Roman Catholic Church. Most of the major abuses in church life during the late Middle Ages, like rampant simony, were curtailed. In that sense was not the reform a resounding success?

Many scholars implicitly concur with the assessment of the reform's success with regard to its impact on the Roman Catholic Church. They concede this point insofar as they assert that the Council of Trent marked the birth of the modern Catholic Church. However, it is argued this is a church that bears the marks of the sixteenth-century Counter-Reformation's reaction against Protestantism to such an extent that only since the mid-twentieth century could the Catholic Church truly set its own agenda as something more than mere (negative) reaction to Protestantism. Since the Catholic Church reacted by recognizing no evangelical legitimacy in Protestant churches, it does not seem possible to assess the Counter-Reformation as an ecumenical success. Indeed, was it actually counterproductive ecumenically?

On the other hand, are the core theological commitments of the reform, especially of the Council of Trent, really so unpalatable to Protestants, or might they have potential for building ecumenical bridges? To be sure, there are some characteristically Roman Catholic affirmations, such as the authority of the papacy, transubstantiation, and the continuing validity of indulgences, which will not sit well with Protestants. However, when we recall that these were not the real issues that occasioned the Reformation, that the split between Luther and Catholicism was over the Reformer's sense that the Catholic Church had compromised the Pauline-Augustinian emphasis on justification by grace, perhaps one can discern more ecumenical promise in the teachings of the Counter-Reformation.

Trent affirmed *sola gratia*, insofar as the entire process of justification is initiated and worked by grace.[3] Given this apparent Roman Catholic affirmation of such Pauline-Augustinian themes, are the remaining differences between the Catholic Church and Protestantism really sufficient to warrant their continuing separation? Of course, unlike the Reformers, Trent seems to have construed justification as a process that is ongoing, rather than as a once-and-done event; in other words, we may increase in justification. Aquinas himself qualified this conclusion, claiming at least in a "supratemporal" sense that justification is an event (*Summa Theologica* I/II.113.7). Something like a third use of the law is implied insofar as it is by doing good works in accord with the Commandments that the believer has signs of justification, presumably meriting more grace by these grace-initiated works (*Decree concerning Justification*, chaps. X–XI; can. 24). Also, grace is not external as it was for the Reformers; it is an internal substance.

Are these differences between the Protestant and Catholic views of

---

3. The way in which this Thomistic conception weaves together grace and human works in a compatible whole is most reminiscent of the Eastern Orthodox notion of salvation as deification. In that sense, can we talk about the Counter-Reformation as contributing to a more positive ecumenical climate between the churches of the West and the Eastern Orthodox tradition?

justification sufficient to keep the churches separated? After all, while rejecting the unequivocal identification of good works with the fruit of justification, the council did not condemn them, asserting in a way compatible with Luther and Calvin the belief that good works are fruits of justification. Are the differences still enough to justify the ongoing separation between Protestantism and Catholicism, and if so, why? If they are not, is not the Counter-Reformation a great resource for future ecumenical work?

# CHAPTER 8

# SEVENTEENTH-CENTURY RELIGIO-POLITICAL CONFLICTS AND THE AGE OF ORTHODOXY

Martin Luther, John Calvin, the Anabaptist movement, and the Counter-Reformation, as trendsetting people and events, had international significance. However, the Reformation, as the inclusive movement that it was, had an immediate, albeit less widely known, impact on other geographical locations in western Europe. Apart from an understanding of the spread of the Reformation to these other European regions, we cannot understand these nations' cultures and cannot comprehend much of what is happening in the contemporary political dynamics involving these nations. In addition, certain women behind the scenes also made significant contributions to the Reformation. A survey of these lesser-known figures sets the stage for identifying developments in Europe in the seventeenth century that were significant for the history of the Church.

## Women of the Reformation

A number of the internationally prominent women of the Reformation have already been noted: Katherine von Bora (b. 1499), Teresa of Avila (1515–82), Mary Tudor (1516–58), Mary Stuart of Scotland (1542–87), and Elizabeth I (1533–1603). To this distinguished list should perhaps be added Catherine of Aragon, whose faithfulness to the validity of Catholic orders manifested in her unwillingness to have Henry VIII declare their marriage illicit, which was an important factor in the Reformation. It is important to note how many of these prominent women were political leaders.

### Women Martyrs

British Protestant author John Foxe (1516–87) relates accounts of several women martyrs of the Anglican Reformation, among them Anne

Askew, who suffered in 1546 in the later stages of Henry VIII's reign, as Mary Tudor (Henry's daughter by his first marriage and a devoted Catholic) was gaining influence. Askew died confessing it to be idolatry to trust the Mass more than Christ. Elsewhere other women paid the ultimate price for their faith; many Anabaptist martyrs were women.

## Anne Locke

A confidant of John Knox during the Scottish Reformation, Anne Locke is thought to have been the woman he loved most. A devoted Protestant, she went into exile with him (without her husband, a Scottish Protestant merchant) to Geneva. After the death of her husband, she married a committed Puritan. After his death, she married another. Locke bears testimony to the intellectual contribution of women to the Reformation. She translated some of the work of John Calvin and work written in French by a Dutch Reformer.

## Maria of Hungary and Bohemia

Maria (1505–58) was born to royalty, a sister of Emperor Charles V. Early on she was sympathetic to the Lutheran cause. In 1526, Luther himself comforted her on the loss of her husband, Prince Louis II of Hungary (*Four Psalms of Comfort*, in *LW* 14:209ff.). She attended the 1530 Diet of Augsburg, where Philip (Philipp) Melanchthon perceived her as someone trying to mollify the harshness of her brother. It is likely her final position on the reform was in line with the irenic perspective of Erasmus — that is, seeking to reconcile Protestants and Catholics. Her final years were spent as the emperor's regent in the Netherlands, where she issued edicts against Lutherans, as per her brother's policies. However, she also repeatedly showed Lutherans leniency in the execution of the sentences, much to the chagrin of even liberal Catholic bishops in the region. The survival of Protestantism in the Netherlands owes much to Maria.

## Anna Pedersdotter Absalon

Burned as a witch in Norway in 1590, Anna Pedersdotter Absalon died a martyr for the faith of the Reformation. In the patriarchal climate of the late Middle Ages, any woman who violated social convention in some way was a likely target. Accusations against women for witchcraft continued in the West until well into the eighteenth century. It is estimated that some three hundred thousand women were condemned in the West as witches between the years 1484 and 1782.

Anna was the spouse of one of Norway's most illustrious humanist scholars and theologians, Absalon Pederson Beyer (d. 1574), a student of Melanchthon's. Absalon Beyer was a radical Protestant who supported the destruction of images in the Catholic churches of his region. He and the bishop of Bergen removed several images from the high altar of the cathedral. The town council was incensed. Both Absalon and the bishop were too powerful, though, to remove from office. The best way to get at them seemed to be to accuse their wives of witchcraft. The court exonerated Anna in 1575, but the allegation would not go away. She was eventually brought to trial on such a charge fifteen years later, long after the death of her eminent husband. Women of the Reformation suffered much for their support of spouses committed to reform.

## The Further Spread of the Reformation in Western Europe

Two political realities in particular influenced the shape of the establishment of Protestant churches throughout western Europe. The first is the political influence of the papacy in the late Middle Ages. Equally significant is the fact that the prevailing political forces in continental Europe, notably the Holy Roman Empire and its emperor in the post-1517 era, Charles V (also king of Spain), were staunch Catholics.

In 1532, Charles and Protestant princes (known as the Smalcald, or Schmalkaldic, League) negotiated the Peace of Nuremberg, a treaty that allowed German Protestant princes and their territories to remain Protestant as long as they did not try to propagate their faith in regions other than their own. Protestants had to promise not to seek reforms other than those described in the Augsburg Confession.[1] In return, Charles got the German princes' support in any conflict between him and King Francis I (1494–1547) of France, as was threatening to transpire. Most historians think that Charles was just trying to buy time with this agreement, that he hoped to contain the advance of the Lutheran "heresy" until he was able to marshall the military strength he needed to stamp it out. But in fact Lutheranism continued to spread. The complex military situation never permitted Charles to marshall the military coalition of Catholic leaders he needed.

The Catholic cause then began to suffer other setbacks. In the German territory of Württemberg, the prince who had been exiled was returned and, with the support of his people, converted to Protestant-

---

1. In a way, then, the treaty was a kind of Lutheran-Catholic agreement.

ism. On top of that, one of the territories ruled by Catholic princes, a section of Saxony, turned Lutheran when the old monarch died and the successor identified with Protestants. In addition, several bishops who were also feudal lords made themselves hereditary lords and declared themselves Protestant so that they could keep the properties.

## Protestant Setbacks

When everything seemed to be going Protestantism's way, when it looked like it might overrun all of Germany, it experienced several setbacks, which undercut its credibility. One was the polygamy practiced by the leader of the Smalcald League, Prince Philip of Hesse. Philip claimed to have been in a marriage totally devoid of sexual expression and did not feel that he had the gift of celibacy. Faced with a situation with which he could no longer cope, and filled with guilt over it, the prince sought the advice of Martin Luther, Philip Melanchthon, and Martin Bucer. Divorce and remarriage were certainly one option. The Reformers suggested another — that Philip take a second wife secretly, one able to afford him the sexual satisfaction he needed. When the secret became public, Philip and his theological advisors lost enormous credibility with the German public.

Other events transpired that weakened the Protestant coalition, but Luther's death in 1546 was probably as severe a blow as any. The Protestant disarray happened at an auspicious time for Charles, just when foreign affairs gave him an opening to concentrate on Germany. He launched an invasion and captured two German Protestant princes.

## The Interim of Augsburg

Despite the military victory, Charles realized that it was too late to reimpose Catholicism on all the German territories. He settled in 1548 for promulgating the Interim of Augsburg. Written by a joint commission of Protestant and Catholic theologians, this document was expressly intended as an interim agreement (until a general council could be convened, which would decide on the issues being disputed). Of course, the Council of Trent was already underway, but that was but a mere detail for Charles. The pope might say that Trent was a general council, but Charles, as emperor, did not recognize it as such.

Charles's motives were good ones. He hoped to reform the church in Germany, as his grandmother Queen Isabella had in Spain during the Counter-Reformation. In another lesson learned from his grandmother, he hoped to buy time with the agreement in order to prosecute abuse and corruption in the church, encourage piety and learning, and disallow any doctrinal divergence. However, the Interim of Augsburg, which became the law of the land in Germany, satisfied no one, but Protestants probably had the most grounds for complaint. Essentially the agreement conceded the cup to the laity in Communion and marriage to clergy, but every doctrinal point made in the document was purely Roman Catholic. As a result, several prominent Protestant theologians refused to obey the decree. Theologians in Luther's old university, Wittenberg, led by his principal colleague, Philip Melanchthon, offered a compromise, called the "Leipzig Interim." Largely perceived as a sellout, it was generally discounted by Protestants.

### The Peace of Augsburg and the End of Charles's Reign

The unrest among German Protestant princes paid off. Princess Maria of Saxony established an alliance with King Henry II of France, an alliance that effectively put enough pressure on Charles that it forced him to agree in 1555 to a new settlement — the Peace of Augsburg. Essentially the treaty provided any territory espousing the Augsburg Confession with the guarantee of religious freedom; in return, those same territories would not persecute or attack territories that were Catholic. Only pertaining to Lutheran and Roman Catholic territories and rulers, the treaty was of no benefit to adherents of the Reformed or Anabaptist Reformations.

Charles's failure to restore Catholicism in Germany may have led him to relinquish his power. Not long after the 1555 legislation, he resigned the emperorship and entered a monastery. His successors were so tolerant of Protestants that at least one of them was rumored to have converted to Protestantism. In any case, the permissiveness of these rulers created an ethos in which Protestantism could prosper and expand into new areas, notably into Austria. This dynamic itself created more tensions between Protestant and Catholic rulers, culminating finally in the next century in the Thirty Years' War.

### Lutheranism in Scandinavia

Luther's impact was felt in Scandinavia. In Germany, the Reformer's impact and ensuing struggles divided the region and as a result helped the high nobility assert its power in relation to the monarchy; in Scandinavia, the Reformation had just the opposite result. Monarchs embraced the Reformation, which had the effect of enhancing their power.

Officially, Denmark, Norway, and Sweden were a united kingdom in the sixteenth century (and Iceland was a Danish possession). The truth is that the king ruled only in Denmark, while elsewhere powerful regents held sway. When the Reformation broke out, King Christian II (1481–1559) was frustrated by his failure to be able to rule in Sweden. He tried to remedy this situation by engineering (with foreign help, as he was the brother-in-law of the emperor) a massacre in Stockholm in order to seize more power. His efforts to use the Reformation as a tool to enhance his power ultimately backfired. It seems that the entry of Protestant preachers into the region resulted in exacerbating the clergy's enmity towards Christian. Eventually he had to flee, landing in Norway and setting himself up as the champion of Catholicism. His successor was Frederick I, a committed Protestant, though he promised at the time of his coronation not to use the crown to further the interests of Protestantism over Catholicism. Nevertheless, by this time many of the new king's Swedish subjects were of a similar persuasion.

Frederick recognized the pointlessness of trying to exercise any rule in Sweden, and so in 1523 he relinquished all other claims to power, save in his native Denmark. Norway proceeded to elect him as its king. Given Frederick's religious policies — at the very least he assumed neutral positions on Reformation disputes — Protestantism spread rapidly without impediment. Frederick's successor, Christian III (1503–59), was a sincere and firm believer in the Lutheran cause; he had even attended the Diet of Worms. With help from Lutheran teachers, a national church in Denmark, and therefore nominally in Norway (which at that time was merely its appendage), was established in 1537. It would take decades of Christian education in Norway before its church became Lutheran, as is evident from the resistance that the reforming husband of Anna Pedersdotter Absalon encountered. In fact, Icelandic Catholics resisted these developments until the island's church became Lutheran in the 1550s. Nearly two centuries later a combination of Danish colonialism and missionary outreach would bring Lutheranism to Greenland.

The situation was more complex in Sweden after Frederick abdicated authority to rule. Gustavus Vasa (Gustavus Erikson; 1496–1560), who had been the leader of an earlier resistance movement to King Christian, was declared king. Through political maneuverings, he succeeded in undercutting the political influence of the episcopacy. From that point on, Lutheran influence was on the increase, usually joined with royalist convictions. Olaf (1493–1552) and Lorenz Petri (1499–1573) were two very influential Reformers among the clergy, the former being not only one of Luther's first students but also a staunch advocate of criminal reform. The transition to a national Lutheran church was not complete until 1593. As a dependency of Sweden, Finland became Lutheran at the same time, just as it originally had become Christian in the same way.

## The Reformation in the Low Countries

The Low Countries — present-day Belgium, the Netherlands, and Luxembourg — offered a wide range of sixteenth-century responses to the Reformation. Adherents of the reform were present from early times. All the major Reformation groups made inroads, but circumstances made success of the movement problematic.

A yearning for reform predated the Reformation in the region. The late medieval mystic Gerhard Groote founded the Brethren of Common Life in the Low Countries. The ideal of the movement was a monastic-like call to devotion and holiness, but without necessarily practicing the monastic vocation. Groote's vision was that those not called to that vocation would remain in their present vocations, practice the "common life," but do it by following principles of modern devotion. Though many of Groote's followers did feel called to monastic life, the concern about the common life was never diminished in these communities, a concern that came to expression particularly in strong educational outreach: the founding of many schools that stressed both scholarship and devotion. These schools became centers of renewal for the Church, as most of their alumni were possessed of a critical and reforming spirit. The renowned humanist Erasmus was trained in such a school. One of the characteristic commitments of the Brethren of the Common Life education program was the necessity of reading Scripture in the language of the people. To the degree that this attitude had permeated to the people of the Low Countries, it is obvious that the Reformation would receive a favorable hearing in these societies.

The emperor Charles tried to quash the reform, especially its Anabaptist manifestations. These efforts produced many martyrs but largely failed. Charles, though, was a popular ruler in the region, so his efforts had the effect of swaying most people to regard Protestants as heretics deserving punishment. Charles's successor as king of Spain and ruler of the region, his son Philip II, was by no means as popular. It was widely known that he had used the inquisition in Spain. Many feared that he would try to do the same in the Low Countries. In fact, he did try to enact the decrees of the Council of Trent against Protestants.

Catholics began to refer to the Protestants in the region as "Beggars," and they in turn adopted this epithet with pride. The Protestants became a kind of fierce "countercultural movement" that resisted every royal effort to suppress them, even by military means. The Beggars had been able to organize an especially effective navy. For a while there were indications that the rebels might get English and French support.[2]

---

2. The French support waned after the French monarchy turned on the Protestants following a period of flirtation with their movement (see pp. 140ff.).

Philip could and did rely on Spanish troops to accomplish his aims. The Spaniards made a smart move: they exploited religious differences among the people of the region.[3] They proceeded to negotiate a separate peace agreement with Catholics in the southern provinces (present-day Belgium and Luxembourg). These nations remain largely Catholic to this day. However, Spain spent decades trying to suppress the northern regions (present-day Netherlands), which were heavily Reformed. Finally in 1607, the Spanish king (Philip III) threw in the towel and ceded the land to the nationalists. In this way, the Protestant Reformed Netherlands was born, while in the predominantly Roman Catholic southern regions, Belgium and Luxembourg were born.

## The Reformation in France

In the early sixteenth century, France had the greatest degree of national unity and centralization of any western European nation. Its king, Francis I (1494–1547), was Catholic but was inclined to make things difficult for his enemy Charles V, who was the Holy Roman emperor and king of Spain. Francis did this by encouraging German Protestantism. Consequently, he allowed Protestants (mostly of Reformed persuasion, like the native son Calvin) a measure of freedom in his land. However, the strategy backfired. Protestants gained adherents, especially among the intellectuals.

After the death of Francis's successor, Henry II (1519–59), Protestants (called "Huguenots" in France) married into the royal family. At one point, a plot led by Protestants aimed at turning the monarchy away from Catholic influence was thwarted by an influential Catholic family, the house of Guise of Lorraine. This Catholic family's influence became so great during the early part of the reign of Charles IX (1550–74) that the new king's mother, Catherine de' Medici (1519–89), who functioned as his surrogate since he was but a child, began cultivating Protestants in retaliation. This created more Protestant-Catholic tensions.

Especially significant was a 1572 massacre of thousands of Huguenots in Paris, the Massacre of St. Bartholomew's Day, because King Charles had been convinced that there was a Huguenot plot against him. Protestants were persecuted elsewhere. News of the massacre spread widely; it became an international event, a cause of celebration for Catholics and dispiriting news for Protestants.

When Henry III (1551–89) ascended the throne in 1574, he tried to make peace with the Protestants. Catholic leaders objected, and a new

---

3. Some of the support for the Beggars' rebellion was nationalistic, as even Catholics in the region resented the occupation of their lands by foreign troops from Spain.

war of religion began. When Henry died with no direct heir, legal succession to the throne belonged to Henry Bourbon (1553–1610), royalty from a Protestant family. France had a Protestant king (though not a very good Protestant)! The Catholic party could not tolerate this. Earlier there had been much turmoil regarding succession to the throne. Pretenders to the throne, both named Henry, emerged. Bourbon took the name Henry IV. Realizing that the Catholic party would never accept him as a Protestant, he turned Catholic. It is claimed that he said, "Paris is worth a Mass." Henry did not forget his former allies, which led some Catholics to claim that he was still a (Protestant) heretic. At any rate, in 1598 he issued the Edict of Nantes, granting Huguenots freedom of religion as long as they renounced foreign alliances.

Henry's manipulation of religion to serve political aims in many respects was the passageway to the modern world. It is, after all, common today for politicians to function in this way. To be sure, other rulers had used religion to serve political aims in the past. However, Henry seems to have been one of the first in the West to manipulate religion publicly to these ends. In this sense, his actions prefigure the style of modern Western politics.

After Henry IV was assassinated in 1610, Protestants had grave misgivings about the future and with good reason. Henry's wife, Marie de' Medici (1573–1642), who became regent because the new king (Louis XIII; 1601–43) was still a boy, tried to allay mistrust. Her principal advisor, Cardinal Armand Jean du Plessis Richelieu (1585–1642), was a real wheeler-dealer. At the time, the Thirty Years' War was underway (see below). Richelieu was convinced that the main enemy was the Hapsburgs, the Catholic monarchy in Switzerland and Germany. Consequently, to further the interests of the French monarchy help was given to the Protestants in Germany so that the Catholic Hapsburgs would have trouble on their hands. Having done that, Richelieu took just the opposite tactic in France, thus cracking down on the Protestants in the homeland. They were deemed a threat to start a rebellion because under the Edict of Nantes they held several fortified French cities that could readily become bases of operation for a revolution. Once he succeeded in weakening their military position, French Protestants were left in peace. However, all that ended in the 1660s when the next king, Louis XIV, came to manhood.

Louis was determined to be in complete charge. Though a Catholic, the king demanded that the Catholic Church be run his way. He refused to submit to the claims of papal authority that had been officially articulated by the Council of Trent. Instead he proclaimed and defended the liberties of the Gallican Church. *Gallicanism* was a largely nationalist movement that insisted on the "ancient freedoms" of the Gallican (French) Church that Trent had rejected. It and related movements in other European nations insisted that the locus of ecclesiastical authority rested with the bishops, not just with the pope. Such a view meant that there would be more local, national control of the Church. Those who backed the authority of the pope were in the majority among the French clergy and came to be called the "Ultramontanes." However, they were forced to achieve their aims by means consistent with Gallicanism, insofar as the papal decrees were not promulgated in France until the local clergy themselves backed these decrees. So entrenched did Gallicanism become that ultimately it was quashed only by the French Revolution.

Louis XIV's support of Gallicanism was matched by his measures to stamp out Protestantism. To that end, he abolished the Edict of Nantes in 1685. Many Protestants fled to North America and other nations of western Europe where Reformed Christian communities had already been established. Though the bureaucratic fiction was that no more Protestants were left in France, and the official French policy was one of public violence towards Protestantism, including the forcible conversion of thousands back to Catholicism, French Protestants (some of whom "officially" converted back to Catholicism) continued to meet. Under this sort of persecution, a Protestant resistance movement began to organize. Motivated by an apocalyptic, mystical orientation, the movement developed and continued until 1709, even though it had predicted that Christ's second coming would transpire twenty years earlier. During this period, it engaged in armed rebellion.

Meanwhile a different group of French Protestant leaders came forward. They did not trust the apocalyptic visions of the new leaders and called for a return to strict Reformed theology. Led by Antoine Court, the group formed the French Reformed Church in 1715. It taught obedience to civil authorities in all things except where they demand what is contrary to the Word of God. The French kings responded with the same policies of persecution. The Reformed Church needed to operate underground, with headquarters and educational resources in Switzerland. Nevertheless, the Reformed Church became firmly rooted in France. Finally in 1787 King Louis XVI (1754–93) declared religious tolerance.

The Catholic-Reformed struggle led to a general distrust of dogmatism in France, a sense of horror that theological doctrine could divide people. This distrust of things religious and of dogmatism became an important factor in giving rise to the secular attitudes that shaped the French Revolution.

## The Thirty Years' War

So named for its length during the first three decades of the seventeenth century, the Thirty Years' War was apparently another religious conflict, primarily fought in Germany but with international participation. Many scholars believe, however, that it and other wars of the seventeenth century, though fought with a religious veneer, were not truly religiously oriented, as the controversies of the sixteenth century had been. Certainly the prosperity generated by the capitalist economy of the recently liberated, predominantly Protestant Netherlands encouraged and/or motivated the Spanish Catholic emperors to invade other Protestant allies of the Dutch.

The Peace of Augsburg of 1555, which put an end to religious wars in Germany in the sixteenth century, was only a temporary armistice. It merely allowed rulers to determine the religion of their region; the Reformed tradition and Anabaptists were not included in the agreement. A gathering storm was precipitated by Protestant distrust of the staunch Catholic emperor Rudolf II, who took office in 1576. The city of Donauworth, near staunchly Catholic Bavaria, opted for Protestantism. The Catholic duke of Bavaria invaded. Though Protestant princes organized in the Evangelical Union, it was not as strong as the union of Catholic princes, the Catholic League.

The confrontation came in Bohemia, the land of the ancient Hussites. This group had aligned with the Reformed tradition. German Calvinists were also settling the region. As a result, Reformed Christians made up the majority of the population. The successor to Rudolf, Matthias, appointed his cousin Ferdinand, a Catholic, king of Bohemia. Protestants revolted, calling Frederick the elector of Palatinate in Germany to be their king. This was a logical choice since Frederick was a Reformed Protestant.

Catholics responded, especially when the Protestant rebellion spread to other regions. The new emperor, Ferdinand II (1578–1637), called on the Catholic League to invade Bohemia. Catholics not only conquered Bohemia, thus reestablishing the Catholic king there, but also overthrew Frederick in Palatinate, which in turn brought it under Catholic rule. Protestants in both regions were persecuted.

The Protestant League formed by England, the Netherlands, and Denmark aimed to support the German Protestant princes.[4] Denmark withdrew from the coalition, but help came from Sweden and its king (Gustavus Adolphus; 1594–1632), who had succeeded in eliminating Danish rule of Sweden. Swedish support turned the tide so that by 1648

---

4. Frederick of Palatinate was the son-in-law of the English king James I (1566–1625).

after thirty years of war (Protestants were by now receiving moral support from France), all sides were ready to make peace. The Peace of Westphalia was the treaty that all parties of the peace signed. Its terms were most significant in shaping modern Western society.

The terms of the treaty may be summarized in three points. (1) Independence was granted to the German states, the Swiss cantons, and the Netherlands. (2) Subjects professing a religion different from that of their prince were given equal rights. (3) Under the agreement, Reformed Christianity was recognized alongside Lutheranism and Catholicism as protected. The last two points represent new developments, not typical of the earlier treaties. The idea that subjects should be granted religious tolerance, even if they are not in agreement with the views of their sovereign, is strikingly modern.

Is it possible that the religious tolerance of the treaty was in fact born of a deeper understanding of Christian love? Or could it have been a manifestation of the growing indifference to religious matters by the state? There are indications here that the modern secular state was beginning to develop. With the Peace of Westphalia, history is well on the road to modernity.

## Are the Subsequent Developments in the Reformation on the European Continent As Well As Early-Seventeenth-Century Developments of Historical Interest Only?

Subsequent developments in the Reformation had long-lasting effects. The state church system in Europe was further and more widely established by the territorial settlements of the various treaties, as the ruler was given authority in each case to establish a religious preference in the region over which he or she ruled. In a sense, these dynamics effectively preserved the Constantinian era into early modernity. Has that been good for the Church?

Another consequence of the events late in the Reformation period is that (apparent) religious wars had the effect of hardening Protestant-Catholic disputes along national lines. Ethnic disputes worsened because these rivalries now had a religious sanction. Many of the ethnic rivalries among Western nations, such as the mutual suspicions between the French and the Germans, have taken on a more complex character as a result of the religious tensions between the majority of the citizenry.

With these intensified rivalries, the official theologies of both sides hardened into dogmatic orthodoxies. In a climate in which the masses perceived themselves to be fighting religious wars, it is hardly surprising that the older, more pastoral and storytelling models of Reformation theology would give way to a new model. When loved ones and friends were engaged in war against a power that nationalized a different religious persuasion, it is little wonder that the theologies focused more on the distinct teachings of the contending traditions, that is, became more doctrinally oriented and polemical. Protestants and Catholics had reason to seek clarity and precision about their own beliefs (what their adherents were fighting and dying for) and to demonize the other side.

These dynamics led not just to the development of orthodox theology but also of Pietism, spiritualism, natural religion, and Enlightenment secularism. The last four were responses to the orthodox preoccupation with doctrine (without saying much about spirituality), polemics, and its insistence on the parochial character of truth (effectively denying that those outside a particular church can have access to truth). The widespread contemporary attitude that denominations really do not matter is a modern phenomenon rooted in early Enlightenment reaction against orthodoxy and the Enlightenment quest for natural religion.

## Development of Orthodox Theology

Orthodox theology's character as dogmatically focused and polemical led naturally to a preoccupation with authority. Luther and the other Reformers had challenged the historic Roman Catholic claim that the Church teaches with authoritative reliability through the episcopacy and the papacy. The Reformers' theological heirs found it necessary to assert that Scripture alone had such authority. Consequently in the orthodox period we observe the development of modern views of biblical inerrancy and/or divine dictation (John Gerhard *Loci Theologici* II.286; Westminster Confession I.8–9; IX.2). At the Council of Trent, largely in response to these Protestant claims on behalf of the authority of Scripture, the Catholic Church likewise asserted orthodox theories of biblical inspiration.

The new, more doctrinally focused form of theology effectively marginalized the sort of "popular theology" espoused by a number of the Reformers, such as Luther. Of course, the process of locating theology in the universities began in the Middle Ages. However, the conceptual, quasi-scientific character of orthodox theology expedited the "academization" of Western theology. As such, theology became the domain of the educated elite, and preaching, which focused increasingly on such doctrinal conceptual concerns, likewise became increasingly estranged from the undereducated masses.

Virtually all of the major pre-seventeenth-century Western traditions had a number of theologians who adopted the orthodox model of theology. Predictably, the dogmatic, polemical orientation that typifies the model led to the emergence of a number of controversies. Readers should take sides in each of these controversies, identifying which positions they think are correct and giving reasons for their preferences.

### Catholic Orthodoxy

Growing nationalism in Europe led to discontent with Tridentine (Council of Trent) claims that further emphasized papal authority. Out of this milieu emerged Gallicanism; several related national movements arose in other regions.

*Gallicanism.* According to the Gallicans, ecclesiastical authority resides with the bishops, not with the pope (Four Gallican Articles). Since the Jesuits functioned as the pope's army in carrying out papal aims, Gallicans called for their suppression. In fact, not just in France but elsewhere due to their unquestioned loyalty to the papacy, Jesuits were banned. As already noted, Gallicanism and its related movements were not ultimately thwarted by papal pronouncements (as the papacy was losing temporal power in the seventeenth and early eighteenth centuries). Only the French Revolution succeeded in putting the movement to rest.

*Febronianism.* The anonymous work of a bishop appearing in Germany in the 1760s under the pseudonym Justinus Febronius led to the emergence of Febronianism. In the spirit of Gallicanism, the movement went so far as to argue that bishops, as representatives of the community of the faithful, ought to rule the Church (Justinus Febronius *State of the Church and the Legitimate Power of the Roman Pontiff*). Needless to say, Pope Clement XIII condemned the movement.

*Jansenism.* Cornelius Jansenius (1585–1638), a theological educator in France who became one of the nation's bishops, was the namesake for this movement. It emerged out of a concern that the Catholic condemnation of the Reformers might effectively entail a denial of Augustine's thought. Jansenius was condemned in 1643 because his version of Augustine sounded too much like Calvin's to the Catholic hierarchy.[5]

There had been earlier efforts to reassert Augustine's heritage in the Catholic Church, but that heritage had to some extent been compromised since the time of Pope Gregory I's (ca. 540–604) reinterpretation

---

5. Recall that all of the Reformers, save the Anglicans and to a lesser extent the Anabaptists, had self-consciously invoked Augustine on behalf of their views.

of it. Gregory had transformed Augustine's emphasis on salvation by grace into a theology about how we can offer satisfaction to God, which opened the way to Scholastic notions of the faithful cooperating with grace in order to be saved. The Augustinian agenda had become especially problematic after the Council of Trent condemned Protestantism and its Augustinian propensities.

The Augustinian themes of Jansenism had resonated earlier in the sixteenth century with a number of prominent Catholic theologians, such as Domingo Báñez (1528–1604) and Michael Baius (1513–89). Tensions developed between the Dominicans (backing such an Augustinianism with a denial of free will and an insistence on unconditional election) and Jesuits, like Luis de Molina (1535–1600), who defended Trent and who maintained (perhaps incorrectly) that the council taught predestination based on foreknowledge (Molina *On Predestination* 23.4–5.1.9). Jansenism spread in France, where it evolved into more of a reform movement than a theological movement concerned about predestination and grace. Its French adherents became vigorous critics of all ecclesiastical corruption. Among its most prominent French proponents were Blaise Pascal (1623–62) and Antoine Arnauld (1612–94). Pascal himself was born into a prominent family and had an impressive background with notable accomplishments in mathematics (esp. thermodynamics). After a mystical experience, he became a Jansenist. His work is an especially notable resource for Protestants seeking resources in the Catholic tradition, as his classical work *Pensées* (192, 273, 418, 468) is a model for the affirmation of grace alone and a thoughtful apology for the truth of the Christian faith. In the great traditions of Augustine's synthesis of reason and faith, Pascal also insisted that religion could not totally submit to reason, but that reason must be used to explore faith.

The debate in France raised by Jansenism gave rise to several counter-proposals offered by the Jesuits. One of these, which came to be called "probabilism," taught that a probability that an action might be correct, no matter how slight, made it morally acceptable. The aim of this proposal was to undercut the confidence and insistence on rigor in the Christian life that characterized the Jansenists' reform proposal. To French Jansenists, it had the ring of moral indifferentism, leading them to advocate more discipline and rigor.

The Jansenist movement gained much popular support, even among the aristocracy. Papal condemnation in 1713 did not do it in. What led to its withering away was its popularity because, like Gallicanism, it gradually became more like a political movement opposing the undue influence of Rome and France than a theological reform. As it became increasingly amorphous, it gradually disappeared. Christian movements without a strong confessional base tend to wither away.

*Quietism.* A controversial mystical movement, quietism had its origins in some of the same dynamics that gave rise to Jansenism. It originated in the work of the Spanish scholar Miguel de Molinos (ca. 1640–97) and was carried forward in France by Madame Jeanne Guyon (1648–1717), who gained numerous influential adherents for her views. She won to her side the influential young bishop François Fénelon (1651–1715), who further propagated the movement. Molinos and his cohorts, following an extreme Augustinian course, taught total passivity before God. The believer is simply to disappear, to die and be lost in God.[6] Contemplation must be on purely spiritual matters, having nothing to do with visible or physical means, including the humanity of Christ (Molinos *Spiritual Guide*).

As a radical form of mysticism, quietism rendered the Church and its mediatorial function less essential. Also the ascetic discipline that the Church advocated was rejected. Quietist commitments were said to promote moral laxity. The inquisition condemned Molinos in 1685. Pope Innocent XI (1611–89) also partially condemned the French version of his views two years later.

The opposition to papal power reflected in all of these movements had the effect of weakening the authority of the Catholic Church in France, paving the way for the French Revolution. Readers should reflect on which of these movements seems most helpful for the present context. Does the Church ever require the Jansenist recovery of Augustine, or are one of the other Catholic options of the sixteenth and seventeenth centuries more in touch with the gospel?

## Lutheran Orthodoxy

After Luther's death, Philip Melanchthon became the main spokesperson for Lutheranism. The feeling began to emerge that he and his supporters (who came to be known as Philippists) had broken with Luther by endorsing humanism and the need for good works. Melanchthon's diplomatic work with Catholics and his irenic disposition had always made him suspect in the eyes of some Lutherans. Other issues in dispute related to his alleged compromises to Catholicism in preparing the Leipzig Interim by appeal to the concept of *adiaphora* (the idea that some practices of the Church are indifferent to the gospel and so may be compromised or adopted in the interests of unity, good will, and practicality). One critical point was Melanchthon's openness to positing a role for free will in cooperating with the Holy Spirit when one is being converted (*Elementa Rhetorices* IV; *Loci Theologici* C). The similarities

---

6. Note that a mystical union with Christ is also presupposed.

to the Council of Trent's treatment of justification seem obvious. On top of that, there was some perception that Melanchthon might be Calvinist, at least open to Calvin's view of the Lord's Supper. He had, after all, arranged the 1536 Wittenberg Concord with Martin Bucer endorsing the legitimacy of the Strasbourg Reformer's view of the Eucharist.[7] In 1540, he had produced a revised version of the Augsburg Confession, which had made room for Reformed views, though the revision was never considered authoritative in Lutheran circles like the original version.

Melanchthon's accommodations were intolerable to many Lutherans, especially to those in Germany who thought that one must be faithful to Luther's heritage at all costs. However, in this regard they were not quite faithful to Luther, since the Reformer himself, recall, did not insist on doctrinal uniformity but quite commonly embraced apparently conflicting doctrinal positions. These "Luther-fundamentalists" came to be called "Gnesio-Lutherans." Their prime leader was Matthias Flacius (also known as Illyricus; 1520–75).

Eventually the controversy between the Gnesio-Lutherans and the Philippists was resolved. At the very least, a truce was called in 1577 with the signing of the Formula of Concord, a consensus document that a leading Lutheran theologian of the era, Martin Chemnitz (1522–86), influenced significantly. To this day, the controversy continues in a fraternal way within Lutheranism. The document, which has official status in the Lutheran Church to this day, represented a compromise. It endorsed the concept of *adiaphora*, though not in such a way as to concede the validity of all of Melanchthon's compromises to Catholic practice, on grounds that in contrast to his approach, concessions on *adiaphora* matters should not be made under political pressure (Ep X). In a highly qualified sense, the Formula of Concord also endorsed, though also in the same article rejected, the validity of Melanchthon's concept of concurring causes of good action, one of which is the will (SD II). The controversy over free will between the Philippists and the Gnesio-Lutherans was called the "Synergist Controversy." Regarding Calvin's views, the Formula of Concord affirmed a third use of the law, but condemned his view of the Eucharist (Ep VI, VI), which fractured the hope of Lutheran-Reformed collaboration and unity until our own time, rendering Lutherans especially inhospitable to the Reformed overtures about unity.

*The character and legacy of Lutheran orthodoxy.* The next generations of Lutherans developed a Scholasticism not unlike medieval Catholic Scholasticism. Efforts were made to reconcile Melanchthon's views to Luther's thought in a systematic way. These endeavors charac-

---

7. Recall Bucer's impact on Calvin's conception of the sacrament (see pp. 100, 108–9).

teristically employed Aristotelian schemes, which were of course foreign to Luther's way of thinking. Indeed, the unsystematic, contextual character of Luther's thought was foreign to the spirit of the Scholastics. In addition, Luther was a theologian highly critical of the value of Aristotle for theology (Luther *Disputation against Scholastic Theology* 41).

Orthodoxy did leave lasting legacies on Lutheranism. In addition to its theories of biblical inspiration, a strict *confessionalism* (fidelity to confessional documents like the Augsburg Confession, the Formula of Concord, and Luther's catechisms) also developed. Such confessionalism became a permanent feature of virtually every subsequent strand of Lutheranism. Even though the emphasis on biblical inspiration was a sort of innovation, never universally accepted among Lutherans, certain seeds for the development of a theory of biblical inspiration and biblical inerrancy, as well as confessionalism, are rooted in Luther himself (see chap. 2).

*Syncretism.* The controversy that developed in the period of Lutheran orthodoxy and further contributed to its doctrinal rigidity grew out of the work of Georg Calixtus (1586–1656), a Lutheran professor of theology in Helmstedt, Germany. In many ways, his proposal foreshadows the suppositions of the modern ecumenical movement. Reacting against the doctrinal rigidity and polemics he experienced in the orthodox theology of his day, Calixtus proposed that rapprochement with believers of other traditions was possible by distinguishing what is essential from what is secondary. What is essential, in his view, are the doctrinal commitments about which there was consensus in the first five centuries (Calixtus *Desire and Zeal for Concord in the Church* 8ff.). On this basis, he argued that the insistence that justification be the central doctrine cannot be a church-dividing issue, for justification was not clearly taught that way, or Luther's way, in the first five centuries.

Generally speaking, the reactions from orthodox Lutherans to Calixtus's proposals were that such a view compromises the authority of Scripture. Abraham Calovius (1612–86), a prime spokesman for the critics, claimed that everything God revealed in Scripture is absolutely necessary. He was also critical of Calixtus for making tradition, the consensus of the first five centuries, authoritative (Calovius *Systema Locorum Theologicorum* I.304). He and fellow critics began to term Calixtus's proposals "syncretistic," on grounds that the Helmstedt theologian had "mixed" elements of various confessional traditions.

### Reformed Orthodoxy

Similar patterns observed in Lutheranism are also identifiable in the orthodox theology that developed in the Reformed tradition. In a controversy initiated by Jacob (Jacobus) Arminius (Jakob Harmens; 1560–1609) of Holland, a major debate transpired over the issue of predestination. Arminius had all the proper Reformed credentials; he was a student of Calvin's successor in Geneva, Theodore Beza (1519–1605). After much struggle with his conscience, the Dutch Reformed Arminius concluded that the Calvinist view of double predestination was not biblical and seemed to make God responsible for sin. It was only on this view that he departed from the great Genevan; on every other doctrine, he was a committed and orthodox Calvinist.

By 1610, Arminius and his followers, called the "Remonstrants," went on record in stating their alternative to Calvin's view of predestination. In a manner similar to that of Anselm (ca. 1033–1109) and the Jesuits of the Counter-Reformation period, the Remonstrants affirmed predestination but said it was based on God's foreknowledge of who would later have faith; for Calvin, predestination was not contingent on foreknowledge. Arminius and his followers also affirmed that Christ's death was for all (a commitment logically precluded by double predestination) and claimed that grace is not irresistible and can be lost. On the question of whether the saints will inevitably persevere and cannot fall from grace, the Remonstrants designated this an open question requiring further study (*Five Articles of the Remonstrants*).

Early in the controversy, the Remonstrants had the support of the merchant class. Intent on preserving the purity of the Reformed church, the clergy and the lower classes were the Remonstrants' primary opponents. Economics and politics also divided these parties. Simultaneous with the theological debate was a political one: whether the relatively newly independent Netherlands should renew links with Spain. Merchants, of course, supported such policies, as it would be good for business. Clergy and those of the lower classes did not support the renewed links with Spain for fear that it would attenuate Reformed, as well as Dutch, identity.

The political fortunes changed when Prince Maurice of Nassau came out against those who wished no contact with Spain. With his position came the support of the staunch defenders of Calvin, who were called "Gomarists" after the leading spokesman for predestination, Francis Gomarus (also Gomar; 1563–1641). These developments entailed that the Gomarists' political policies were no longer in conflict with the interests of the Dutch government, making government support of the Gomarist theological position more likely. Furthermore, merchants who might have been attracted to the Arminian view, because most Gomarists had previously held a political position so detrimental to these merchants' economic interests, were now inclined to withdraw their original support of Arminianism. For such (formerly Arminian) merchants could now find economic allies among the Gomarists as well.

Gomarists feared that Reformed identity would be compromised by the Arminian position. They were also explicitly troubled by the apparently Pelagian agenda of the Remonstrants, who seemed to imply that our decision for Christ is what ultimately saves us, since it is the foreknowledge of such a human decision that determines God's election. The Remonstrants did insist, however, that the decision for Christ is itself a work of grace (*Five Articles of the Remonstrants* IV). However, in response to these Gomarist concerns, and perhaps in response to the support of Gomarists for its foreign policy, the government convened an ecclesiastical assembly at Dort in 1618 to put an end to the debate.

This Synod of Dort condemned the Remonstrants. It was mostly composed of Dutch theologians, but Reformed theologians from France, Germany, Switzerland, and Great Britain were also invited to participate. In essence, the participants affirmed unconditional election (that is, double predestination, not based on foreknowledge), limited atonement by implication (the idea that Christ only died for the elect), and they denied that there exits in fallen human beings a natural light that can be properly used. In addition, the synod affirmed the irresistible character of grace and the perseverance of the saints.

Persecution of the Remonstrants followed Dort. However, after Prince Maurice died, measures against the Remonstrants were less rigorous, until by 1631 they were given full religious tolerance. Their greatest ongoing impact has been on Methodism, though their heritage is by no means dead in the Reformed-Presbyterian tradition.

The Westminster Confession is the other great manifestation of Reformed orthodoxy. Its genesis and theological commitments will be analyzed in the next chapter. Suffice it to say that its basic theological affirmations are in harmony with Dort, notably with regard to the way in which it features the doctrine of predestination (Westminster Confession III).

The emphasis on predestination by the Westminster Confession and the Synod of Dort illustrates the degree to which the strict orthodoxy of Reformed Scholasticism departed from Calvin, who did not feature the doctrine. Recall that predestination for the Genevan Reformer was nothing more than a logical consequence of his core commitment, the sovereignty of God. Focusing on predestination also effectively squeezed Calvin's humanistic bent out of his tradition for centuries, at least until our own time.

## Assessments of Orthodox Theology:
## Can We Use These Theologians Today?

Were the controversies of the seventeenth century good for the Church or detrimental to it? They are clearly related to the development of orthodox theology in the Western churches. This raises the broader question of whether the rise of this style of theology was good for the Church, indeed whether it is still good for the Church. In a way, this question relates closely to the matter of how one evaluates Fundamentalism or the Evangelical movement, which are both clearly indebted to Protestant orthodox theology (see chaps. 11 and 15). In a context (like today's) that is characterized by relativism and uncertainty about truth, the orthodox preoccupation with doctrinal truth may be a valid way of calling the Church to the riches of the gospel and the Church's tradition. On the other hand, is the focus on doctrine likely to reduce the faith to a cerebral exercise to the detriment of a lively and egalitarian spirituality?

# CHAPTER 9

# THE PURITAN REVOLUTION

Despite a number of affinities to the orthodox theology of the seventeenth century, Puritanism was a distinct English movement. It has had a great impact on American religiosity.

## The Fracturing of the Elizabethan Settlement

The Elizabethan Settlement forms the backdrop for Puritanism. Recall that Elizabeth, herself a Protestant, was committed to following the "middle way" between conservatives, who tried to retain ancient Catholic practices pertaining to worship and governance, and Calvinists, who had influenced most Protestant sentiments in the Anglican Reformation. The tensions between these two parties were always not far from the surface.[1]

Tensions became more visible after Elizabeth's death in 1603 with the ascension to the throne of James I (1566–1625), who was already king of Scotland (the son of Elizabeth's cousin Mary Stuart (Mary Queen of Scots; 1542–87). James was not fully accepted. His efforts to unite England and Scotland caused resentment, and conflicts with the merchant class emerged. Elizabeth's trade policies had enhanced the power of the merchant class, which definitely resented James's agenda to establish an absolute monarchy, in which the nobility would be given more favor.[2] However, the biggest problem for James came from another quarter.

The Protestants in England felt that the Reformation had not gone far enough in their land, a logical conclusion given their Calvinist propen-

---

1. It is interesting to consider what might have transpired if the original Lutheran influence of Martin Bucer, who worked for a while in England, had a more lasting impact on the Anglican reform. The reform might have been easier because Luther's version was less radical than Calvin's version of the Reformation. The radical nature is clearly evident in the Calvinist-Reformed insistence on the need to continue "reforming" tradition, not just to passively accept whatever in the Catholic inheritance that does not conflict with the gospel. Consequently, a follower of Calvin's reform could not as readily accept the old traditions as Elizabeth had tried to retain.

2. The emergence of capitalism typically pitted the rising capitalists against the nobility, which had prospered under feudalism.

sities. And they saw, with the influence of John Knox, how more of the old Catholic traditions had been stripped away in Scotland. It is likely that the English Protestants were hoping that that would happen in their land. Besides, inasmuch as James was the son of the infamous Catholic queen of Scotland, Mary Stuart, they never felt that they could trust him.

## The Character of Puritanism and Its Distinct Parties

The more radical Protestants in England were not organized in a single group, so generalizations about them are difficult. Others gave them the name "Puritans" because they insisted on the need to "purify" the Church by a return to biblical religion. These ultra-Reformed commitments led Puritans to oppose many of the traditional elements of worship which the Church of England had preserved (including priestly garments and celebration of Communion at an altar). Many rejected an episcopacy. They also insisted on the need for a sober life, guided by the Commandments of Scripture (and so endorsing a third use of the law) and strictures against drunkenness and participation in theatrics, along with mandated strict observance of the Sabbath, a day on which no frivolous activity would be condoned (Millenary Petition; Book of Sports).

Puritanism's diversity essentially manifested itself in four distinct, only loosely organized, parties: Episcopal loyalists, Presbyterians, and Independents (a party itself subdivided in two distinct groups). The Episcopal loyalists (Prelatical party) were Puritans committed to working for reform while remaining in the Church of England and maintaining its episcopal polity. The Presbyterians were Puritans who, while remaining loyal to the Church of England, believed that reform (the purification of the Church) could best be accomplished by the adoption of a presbyterian polity, that is, a representative form of church government in which presbyteries (pastors and selected elders) exercise authority on behalf of the whole body. The most prominent early spokesman for this party was the well-respected Cambridge University professor Thomas Cartwright (1535–1603). The Independents, the most radical of the Puritans, had given up on the possibility of reforming the Church of England and so resolved to establish a new independent church that could truly embody biblical principles. Believing that each congregation should be independent from others in governance, the Independents called for a congregational polity.

Two distinct groups made up the larger party of Independents: Congregationalists and Baptists. The Congregationalists were those Puritans who called for a new church with a congregational polity while re-

maining loyal to a largely Calvinist theological profile. The first of the
Pilgrims in America, those who sailed on the Mayflower, belonged to
this party of Puritans. The Baptists, the most radical of the Independents, believed that baptism ought only be administered to believing
adults. As such, they drew inspiration not just from Calvin and Zwingli
but also from the Anabaptists. In fact, a number of these early English
Baptists, led by John Smyth (ca. 1554–1612), an Anglican clergyman,
fled to Holland at the turn of the seventeenth century in order to avoid
persecution. Direct contact with Mennonites there highlighted for the
Baptists both similarities and dissimilarities between them and the Anabaptists. Smyth associated with the Mennonites, while others among
his followers, led by Thomas Helwys (ca. 1550–ca. 1616), found the
dissimilarities between their own commitments and the Mennonite positions too great. This segment of Smyth's congregation returned to
England, where Helwys organized the first Baptist congregation in 1612.
Like the Anabaptists, both of these early Baptist leaders were more
Arminian than Calvinist in theological orientation. A Calvinist Baptist
strand would form later in the 1610s in England.

## The Reign of James I

In view of the overall Puritan agenda as well as the position of the most
radical Independents, the Elizabethan Settlement and subsequent efforts
by leaders of the Church of England to maintain the best traditions of
Catholic worship, without much of an explicit theological agenda, understandably led Puritans to fear a "Romanism" in their church. King
James's efforts to hold together the Elizabethan Settlement did not stand
much of a chance. In general, he sought to follow Elizabeth's agenda,
but with several religiously significant differences. For one, he persecuted Anabaptists. As a result, it was in this period that some Puritans
(the ones who eventually sailed on the Mayflower for America) began
settling in Holland. For another, James's desire for absolute authority
led him to seek to strengthen the episcopacy as a means of increasing
his own power. The connection he perceived between the two is evident
in this statement attributed to him: "Without bishops, there is no king."
Among the Presbyterians in Scotland was an unwillingness to grant him
absolute authority, and so he became suspicious of presbyterian, non-episcopal polity. Another factor in his growing unpopularity was his
solicitousness towards Puritan Arminians, rather than arch-Calvinists.

James's popularity level was also not helped by his personal characteristics. Besides his autocratic propensities, he was erratic in his
administrative, legislative style, wavering between rigidity and weakness. He was also extravagant in spending public money on seemingly

superfluous projects. Perhaps most controversial, he was a known homosexual.

The antipresbyterian, proepiscopal ethos that James inspired reached its high-water mark in 1604 when, no doubt with the king's blessing, Richard Bancroft (1544–1610), the archbishop of Canterbury, affirmed the divine origin of episcopal hierarchy. Discussions in support of apostolic succession, the use of indulgences, confession, and prayers for the dead, as well as an openness to a reformed papacy by prominent Anglican Church leaders, gave the appearance of an increased endorsement of Roman Catholic traditions by the Church of England in this period (Jeremy Taylor *Letter to a Gentleman Seduced to the Church of Rome;* John Cosin *Letter to the Countess of Peterborough;* Herbert Thorndike *Just Weights and Measures* 1–3). Some directives by the archbishop of Canterbury were against Puritans.

Tensions brewed between James and Parliament, especially with the largely Puritan House of Commons. The king did make some efforts to mend fences. He sanctioned a new English translation of the Bible, a move that was calculated to please the biblically oriented Calvinist Puritans. This document, which has come to be known as the King James Version of the Bible, was thus the result of efforts in political fence-mending under the auspices of a ruler known to be practicing sodomy. In view of the circumstances of its composition, can we still conclude that it was truly a divinely inspired translation as some contemporary English-speaking Christians still believe?

James had other political problems that the translation project would not solve. He lost further credibility for failing to support a deposed Protestant elector in the Thirty Years' War. Twice the tensions with Parliament became so pronounced that he dissolved it. In addition, tensions with English Catholics also developed.

## The Puritan Revolution

Similar dynamics immersed the next king of Scotland and England, Charles I (1600–1649); his openness to Catholics (possibly a function of his marrying a French princess) exacerbated tensions with Protestants even more. In 1633, the archbishop of Canterbury strengthened the pro-Catholic commitments by instituting harsher measures against the Puritans. In this period, Puritans in England, who were not separatists, organized the Massachusetts Bay Company for colonizing the New World.

Committed as he was to the beauty of the Anglican liturgy and the need for uniformity for the good of the state, Charles tried to impose that liturgy on the Reformed Church of Scotland through the decrees and policies of the archbishop of Canterbury, William Laud (1573–1645), who was no friend of Puritanism. Rebellion followed. The General Assembly of the Church of Scotland abolished the episcopacy, and the church reorganized itself as a presbyterian church. This was the formal beginning of the Presbyterian Church as we know it.[3] Crucial in these dynamics was the development of and subscription to a covenant of Scottish rebellion by the Scottish Reformed community. Like the earlier covenant of 1557, this 1639 national covenant further established the importance of the covenant theme in the Presbyterian-Reformed theological heritage.

Charles could get no support from the British Parliament to quash the rebellion. The episode had the effect of drawing Scottish Presbyterians and English Puritans closer together, further estranging the crown and Parliament. Matters in England came to a head in 1641 when Parliament passed a law forbidding the monarch to dissolve it. Civil war seemed inevitable. The Puritan factions drew together. Partly as a means of attracting Scottish support and also in order to obtain funds from property held by bishops that might then be confiscated, Parliament also abolished the episcopacy in the Church of England.

In the midst of this turmoil with both king and Parliament (the House of Commons) marshaling troops for conflict, Parliament convoked in 1643 in a borough of London a group of theologians for the purpose of charting a course for the "purified" Church of England, which now seemed in reach. The group was to function in an advisory capacity, though the course had already been charted. As a condition for the military support that the British Puritans had received from Scotland, the mandate of this conclave was essentially set: it was to develop a presbyterian church, akin to the Presbyterian Church that had been formed in Scotland (Solemn League and Covenant), as the British had already pledged to the Scots in a 1643 covenant patterned on the earlier 1639 Scottish covenant.

Called the "Westminster Assembly," the conclave met from 1643 through 1647. The assembly included Scots as well, no doubt in another effort by the British Puritans to build more bridges with them. Among the several documents produced by the assembly, the Westminster Confession of Faith is the most notable. In the spirit of the Synod of Dort, the document is Reformed orthodox in theology and Presbyterian in polity. It soon became the measuring gauge of Puritanism in the British Isles and subsequently in the United States. Given Scottish

---

3. The polity of the older Reformed Church of Scotland since its inception had affinities to a presbyterian form of government.

Presbyterian participation in the assembly, it is not surprising that the document has also become the defining document for Presbyterianism.

With armies on both sides assembled for civil war, conflict was inevitable. Oliver Cromwell (1599–1658), a prominent Puritan, came to the fore as the leader. When the king was captured, Puritan measures were installed as laws of the land. While the majority of Parliament consisted of Puritans wanting a national presbyterian church, the majority of the army was aligned with the Independents, who opposed such a polity. The tensions between these two segments of Puritanism contributed to tensions between Parliament and the army. The army purged Parliament, set up its own Rump Parliament, and beheaded Charles.

The Scots, fearing the loss of independence from England, acknowledged the dead king's son, Charles II (1630–85), as their ruler. The Irish took the opportunity to rebel against Scottish domination. In England, the split among the Puritans led to chaos. Presbyterians and Independents continued to compete. In addition, a new radical group emerged — the so-called Diggers, who advocated a social order in which the right to property would be universal. Such preaching was of course threatening to the merchant class, even though the majority of them were Puritan sympathizers.

In the midst of the chaos, Oliver Cromwell took power, setting up a "Protectorate" — really a Puritan dictatorship. He also stamped out the Irish rebellion and forced Charles II to flee Scotland. Basically Cromwell opted for legislating Puritan beliefs. Given the climate of the times, he was fairly tolerant. Though himself an Independent, he made room for Presbyterians and Baptists. Of course, he did install legislation regarding strict observance of the Sabbath and a ban on frivolous entertainment (Agreement of the People; Instrument of Government; Humble Petition and Advice). His economic policies were more favorable to the middle class than to the rich or the poor. These two economic extremes launched a campaign against the Protectorate, eventually bringing it to an end with Cromwell's death.

Parliament moved to restore the crown to Charles II in 1660, which brought about a reaction against the Puritans. The episcopacy and the *Book of Common Prayer* were restored. Attempts to eradicate dissidents who were outside the Church of England were also enacted (Corporation Act; Conventicle Act; Five-Mile Act). When it became evident these measures could not totally stamp out the Puritan movement, and that it continued to exist outside the law, toleration was eventually decreed late in the seventeenth century. In Scotland the turmoil was even greater. Charles's decree to restore the episcopacy did not have a chance in such staunch Presbyterian country. When the royals deposed clergy who refused to see Charles's way, riots ensued.

On his deathbed, Charles declared himself a Catholic, and his successor, James II (1633–1701), resolved to restore Roman Catholicism in both kingdoms. He decreed the death penalty for all who attended unauthorized worship in Scotland. Perhaps in hopes of winning friends in view of the coming invasion of William of Orange, in 1688 he did declare rights to the Nonconformists in England (Declaration of Indulgence).

William Prince of Orange (1650–1702) and the king's daughter, Mary (1662–94), were brought to the British throne after just three years of James's intolerable rule. They also gained possession of the Scottish throne. The new monarchs instituted tolerant religious policies towards any who would subscribe to the Thirty-nine Articles or, at least, did not conspire against sovereigns. In Scotland, Presbyterianism was instituted as the official state religion. The influence of Puritanism remained ongoing not only among the Scots but also in England for some years after the restoration of the Church of England to a more Catholic orientation.

## Are the Baptist Tradition and to Some Extent the Presbyterian Heritage Fundamentally Puritan Movements?

On historical grounds, the Presbyterian and the Baptist heritages have Puritan roots. Might these roots in Puritanism also be of a theological nature? In order to answer this question, we need to examine historic Puritan statements of faith, notably the Westminster Confession of Faith, which functioned as *the* authoritative summary of Puritan beliefs, as well as two early Baptist confessions (the 1644 and 1677 London Confessions), which were inspired by Westminster.

### Discipline in the Christian Life

The overall Puritan agenda to "purify" the Church of all vestiges of Catholicism and sloth (along the lines of an even stricter, no-nonsense Calvinist Reformation) manifested itself in an emphasis on discipline in various Puritan statements. This included rubrics on the strict observance of the Sabbath and a commitment to excommunication of the lapsed, which is most reminiscent of the strictness of Anabaptist practice (Millenary Petition; Cromwell, Humble Petition). The concern with discipline is also strongly affirmed in the Westminster Confession (XIX.5; VII), as it asserts that the justified are forever bound by the law and gospel, which are virtually identical in substance, not radically distinguished.

These themes relate to other Reformed commitments reflected in the same Westminster document. It affirms a forensic view of justification (XI). If justification is a mere pardoning of sin distinct from sanctification, then justification does not render the faithful holy and spontaneously predisposed to practice the regenerate lifestyle. It is necessary then to be prodded to live such a life of holiness as through a third use of the law. Though this forensic view is clearly reflected in the confession (XVI), at some points, the document attests to justification as conformity to Christ, whereby sanctification is given in justification so that good works happen spontaneously (XII.1). However, this view of justification as conformity and what that means for the Christian life is, as it was in Calvin, clearly a subordinate theme.

### God, Covenant, Predestination

Covenant is a major theme in the history of Puritanism. Covenantal agreements such as the Solemn League and Covenant served to facilitate the organization of various Puritans for the sake of advancing the movement's impact on society (see Westminster Confession VII).

The austerity of the Puritan lifestyle seems to presuppose an angry God who compels us to obey in fear and trembling. Such a conception of God is consistent with Westminster's affirmation of double predestination (III), which is featured more prominently in the confession than it was in Calvin's thought. In the tradition of the Synod of Dort, the confession likewise claims that the elect cannot be lost; grace is irresistible (XI). Also related to these claims is an apparent affirmation that Christ dies for only the elect (VIII.5).

### Other Doctrines

In several other ways, the Westminster Confession reflects the characteristics of Reformed orthodox theology. These features of the confession anticipate the emergence of Fundamentalism in the twentieth century. Such theological predispositions are reflected in the confession's notion of Scripture as the infallible rule of interpretation (I.1). Although there is much debate among scholars about whether this statement is in fact an unequivocal endorsement of the infallibility of Scripture, it is no accident that Puritanism gave rise in American Christianity to Fundamentalism. Another feature suggestive of latter-day Fundamentalism is the confession's endorsement of dispensationalism (the belief that in different historical periods, or dispensations, God has interacted differently with his creatures and has had different expectations of them in each era), as expressed in the claim that the Old and New Covenants are really the same "under various dispensations" (VII.6).

Just as was the case in Reformed orthodoxy, there are indications that Puritanism, as embodied in the Westminster Confession, departed from Calvin in making predestination so central and in squeezing Calvin's humanistic bent out of his tradition. Was that for the good of the Church or to its detriment?

The Westminster Confession and Reformed orthodox theology share several other doctrinal convergencies. These are points they share with the positions of the Reformed heritage as a whole. Westminster's views of the sacraments and church-state relations are identical to the positions of Calvin on these issues (XXV, XXIX–XXXI). Are these convergencies indicative of the Westminster Confession's success in truly maintaining the heritage of Calvin?

## Early Baptist Theology

The key to understanding the theology of the early Baptists is to consider the London Confessions of 1646 and 1677, two statements of faith that appear Puritan in character. Both confessions endorse double predestination, as expressed in terms of those with faith being unable to fall away (London Confession III, XXIII; Second London Confession III, X.4). Of course, in the spirit of Luther and Calvin, the documents insist that God does not force his will on humanity in such a way that what humans do is by necessity (Second London Confession IX). As in Westminster (XVII), the Baptist statements view perseverance as a sign of election (London Confession XXXI; Second London Confession XVII). In fact, the Second London Confession was deliberately modeled after the Westminster Confession in an effort to help unite Puritans in face of the harassment they were experiencing after Charles II was restored to the British throne.

## Particular Baptists versus General Baptists

Deriving from Reformed orthodoxy, the London Confessions represent the Particular Baptist strand. The epithet "Particular" refers to the notion, based on the group's affirmation of double predestination, that only certain people will be saved. Another group of Baptists, whose theological commitments emerged even earlier in the work of Helwys and Smyth, rejected predestination in favor of Arminianism and its idea that grace is available to all, that is, "generally" available (Helwys *Declaration of Faith of English People at Amsterdam* 5). Consequently this group, which came to be known as the General Baptists, exhibited more openness to free will (Short Confession of Faith 5) than Westminster's assertion of our passivity and bondaged will (Westminster Confession IX; cf. Second London Confession V).

These two strands of Baptist thinking have continued and are still present in the Baptist Church to this very day, though they are known by different labels. Of the two, which seems more in touch with the biblical witness? In America, the Particular Baptists (known as Regular Baptists) had pronounced success in the pre-Revolutionary War South. Their heritage seems discernible in the African American Baptist churches (National Baptist Convention, Articles of Faith 9) and, to a lesser extent, in the Southern Baptist Convention (Statements of Faith V).

### Other Distinct Early Baptist Theological Commitments

The Puritan concern with discipline is also evident in the early Baptist confessions. Christ is identified as a "Law-giver," thus implying an appeal to a third use of the law (London Confession LI); the Church is identified, not in terms of God's act, but as the community of visible saints (XXXIII). Christ thus functions as the enforcer of discipline, which is so necessary if discipline is to be maintained and if the Church is to be visible in its saintliness.

The early Baptist view of the sacraments, which were typically called "ordinances" as a way of distinguishing them from Catholic teaching (London Confession XXXIX), was in line with earlier Anabaptist views. Of course, only believers' baptism by immersion was deemed valid (XXXIX, XL). Elect infants dying in infancy were still assured of eternal life (Second London Confession X.3). The Lord's Supper was deemed merely as a symbol (XXX).

Like Westminster, the Second London Confession (I) posits a kind of biblical inerrancy. Also in line with the Puritan understanding of church-state relations, clearly breaking with the later Anabaptists, the early English Baptists held that the state is duly ordained by God and that Christians rightly serve in governmental offices and affairs (XXXIV, XXXIII).

## Assessment: How Puritan Are These Traditions?

Are Baptists and Presbyterians the theological heirs of Puritans? If so, it is important to sort out the nature of the differences among these traditions. After all, Baptists are not Presbyterians. Do these institutional differences have a theological basis?

Presbyterians and Baptists have theological disagreements over the sacraments. The initial response to this last question seems to be that Baptists do not practice *pedobaptism* (infant baptism), and Presbyterians do. The former is Zwinglian on the Lord's Supper, and the latter is Calvinist. The differences between these traditions seem, though, to be deeper and more fundamental than these differences in regards to the sacraments.

Baptists, in the tradition of the Anabaptist heritage, are more critical of the Roman Catholic tradition than is Presbyterianism. Insofar as the Baptists emphasize individual conversion (Second London Confession IX.4; London Confession XXV), they seem more preoccupied with individualizing the Puritan preoccupation with discipline and a purified church. The rigorous congregational polity of the Baptist tradition may also be a manifestation of its stronger anti-Catholic stance. Yet Puritanism, as embodied in the Westminster Confession (IX, XXVIII), also concerns itself with the conversion and regeneration of the individual, not unlike the Baptist focus on conversion. In that sense, the uniquely Baptist agenda may be said to accord with Puritan emphases.

Also on the side of arguing for the Puritan character of the Baptist and Presbyterian traditions, it could be noted that both were embodied in the Puritan movement, and in that sense Puritanism as a whole endorsed both characteristic Presbyterian and Baptist themes. In addition, on numerous topics Baptist and Presbyterian theological commitments accord with each other and with the teachings of the Westminster Confession. Of course, it could be argued that insofar as the Presbyterian tradition more fully represents the theological commitments of the Westminster Confession, it is more Puritan than the Baptist heritage. After all, the Presbyterian Church throughout the world has adopted this confession (in some denominations, a revised version) as authoritatively representing its beliefs. Or could it be that both the Presbyterian and the Baptist heritages are adaptations of the Puritan movement that have so significantly departed from their spiritual mother as to no longer be properly deemed Puritan?

The Puritan characteristics of the Baptist and Presbyterian traditions raise an interesting question. Could their Puritanism explain why these denominations seem so "American," why they have thrived so well on American soil? Is this related to the fact that American society, because its earliest cultural influences were Puritan, is still a Puritan culture resonating best to Puritan religious movements?

CHAPTER 10

# THE EMERGENCE OF RATIONALISM, SPIRITUALISM, AND PIETISM

With the close of the seventeenth century, church history crosses the threshold to the modern world and its distinctive worldview. The modern world is marked by confidence in reason. By contrast, premodern peoples considered spiritual insights, matters of faith, to be more in touch with truth and of greater certainty. That is not the way modern people operate. Even believers who live in the world after Darwin and the industrial revolution are more likely to defer to and trust the fruits of rational explanation and scientific research than the articles of faith. Are not modern Christians more inclined to trust the biblical witness when its claims can be squared with science, history, and reason? In general, modern people intuitively think that way.

The first real expression of the modern worldview was rationalism. Spiritualism and Pietism are to some extent reactions to the emergence of modernism and its rationalistic impulses as well as reactions against the predominance of orthodoxy in the Church of the day.

## Rationalism and the Development of the Modern Worldview

*Rationalism* is a worldview characterized by interest in exploring the world with humanity's unlimited powers of reason. Modern people still generally display this kind of confidence in reason and science. When rationalism truly became the philosophy of the European intellectual elite in the eighteenth century, the period historians call the Enlightenment began. In the era of the eighteenth and early nineteenth centuries, European intellectuals were prone to discard all false authorities in order to permit enlightened reason, no longer chained by tradition, to dictate social and intellectual agendas. Contemporary readers still live in an Enlightenment, or a post-Enlightenment, period.

In a sense, the Renaissance began the process of restoring the sort

165

of confidence in reason that characterizes the modern period. A no-less-important pre-Reformation historical precedent was the Middle Ages' replacement of Plato by Aristotle as primary philosopher in western European society, which primed the West for a more empirical orientation, that is, an interest in investigating the physical. Aristotle held that the universal form is located in the individual thing (*Metaphysics* I.9), whereas Plato deemed the universal form to exist in another realm, one having no contact with the dimensions of space and time (*Timaeus* 1.51–52). Aristotle's view provides, then, a framework that stimulated an interest in the empirical investigation of individual things. On his grounds, the universal form — truth — is *in* the individual entity. Such empirical investigation makes no sense on Plato's grounds. For him, truth is not in the empirically observable individual thing.

## René Descartes

Scholars are generally agreed that the best starting point for understanding rationalism is the work of the great French mathematician and philosopher René Descartes (1596–1650). His admiration for mathematics and the absolute certainty it provided led to a longing for a kind of certain knowledge in all spheres of human knowledge. Descartes proceeded to develop a method of inquiry modeled on mathematical inquiry. Though the starting point for the Cartesian method was scientific, his purpose was not indifferent to religion. He wanted to place faith in God, he claimed, on firm intellectual footing (*Meditations on First Philosophy* I).

Like all good scientists, Descartes was convinced that we should assume nothing. In order to know, we must begin with doubt, which in turn led him to consider what might be certain. Reflecting on these questions, thinking about them, presupposed that he was thinking. Of that he could be certain. But if he was thinking, and certain of it, he must exist. Moreover, the certainty of his existence must be as sure as the fact that he thinks. There is no thought, then, without an existing "I." In the words of Descartes, "I think therefore I am" (*Discourse on Method* V).

With these certainties established, Descartes could move on to prove God — the idea of a more perfect being. Insofar as he could think of this more perfect being, the idea must come from somewhere, for he himself could not be the source of such an idea. Thus God must be the source of the idea; God must certainly exist. With this established, the certainty of the existence of physical things, of our body, was proven, he maintained. God's existence is necessary in order to certify that our clear and distinct ideas of these physical existences are true, for truth could not be derived from nothingness, which would be the case if God did not exist (*Discourse on Method* V).

In his cultural context, where orthodox theology and its dogmatism still reigned, Descartes's views became the brunt of criticism to the point that he became dismayed. Already established as a mathematician, his fame was international. Consequently, Swedish royalty invited him to live in Sweden during the period of controversy, which he did in his final days. His international renown is obvious in the widespread impact his ideas have had.

It is readily apparent how thoroughly the modern view of reality is reflected in and indebted to Descartes — how significant a break he made from the premodern worldview. Premodern religious people seeking truth begin with the Bible or the oral stories of their tradition, for that is where reality is to be found. By contrast, "modern" people like Descartes seek truth first by rational investigation and, if at all, only then turn to God. Premodern, pre-Enlightenment folk find truth in communities, wherein deliberation and thought take place. Modern people, however, seek truth through individual reasoning, as Descartes did. They get to truth from the perspective of the individual, not of the community.

Descartes set the agenda for the development of rationalism in another way — with respect to what he failed to accomplish. By beginning with individual thought, he was never really able to relate on convincing scientific grounds rational reality to the body, to physical things. He could not answer the question on grounds that would convince scientists what the mind had to do with the body, how the mind could know bodily things, for he needed to have recourse to the reality of God to do that. This set an agenda for the Enlightenment: how to relate reason and the physical. Subsequent philosophers tried to solve this dilemma. Thus, Descartes's philosophy effectively immersed the modern Western intellectual tradition even more deeply in the struggle with the dualistic tendencies it inherited from Greek philosophy.

## Options for Solving the Cartesian Dilemma

At least three major streams of thought developed for dealing with the dualistic dilemma introduced by Descartes. One of these efforts is rooted in the work of a French priest, Nicolas Malebranche (1638–1715). Home-schooled and physically debilitated, Malebranche joined a religious group oriented to Augustine, which was also studying Descartes. Persuaded by the rationalism he encountered, he developed a view that has come to be known as "occasionalism." His solution to Descartes's problem was to concede that body and soul (rationality) do not communicate directly with each other. Of course, there are times when the body acts on the mind's direction and when the mind's decisions are occasioned by the body's feelings and the requirements of religious traditions. However, Malebranche insisted, these are only "occasions," acts of God, miracles, if you will (*Dialogues on Metaphysics* I.III; VII.XV). Were these insights related to the fact that Malebranche was crippled?

A second, related alternative was proposed by the eminent German philosopher and mathematician (a man who invented calculus just as Isaac Newton was arriving at similar conclusions) Gottfried Leibniz (1646–1716). Truly cosmopolitan in outlook and scholarship, a true embodiment of Renaissance ideals, Leibniz spent much of his career as a German diplomat. Intellectually he sought to deal with the relationship between the physical and the spiritual by suggesting that there is a "pre-established harmony" of the various substances. These monads (physical monads and spiritual monads) have no windows, that is, cannot really communicate with each other. At this point, he and the occasionalists agreed. He diverged from them, though, by claiming that the monads work together in accord with an *order* (a preestablished harmony) established by God, not merely on occasion (*Monadology* 7, 14, 80ff.).

Benedict de Spinoza (1632–77), a Spanish/Portuguese Jew born and bred in the Netherlands, offered a third alternative for addressing the Cartesian problematic. Spinoza is the father of modern *pantheism* (the idea that God and world are the same). This identification entails that the spiritual and the physical are necessarily related (*Theologico-Political Treatise* XV). Is this a satisfactory way out of the dualism that Descartes bequeathed to the modern Western intellectual tradition?

### Empiricism

The development of *empiricism* on the British Isles (a philosophy that maintains truth can be obtained, not through rational speculation, but only by sense experience) was a way out of the unsatisfactory impasse created by Descartes's agenda. The most prominent figures in this philosophical movement were John Locke (1632–1704), David Hume (1711–76), and Thomas Reid (1710–96).

*John Locke.* The eminent Oxford University professor Locke was the most optimistic of the empiricists regarding his confidence in the powers of observation. He insisted that in the quest for knowledge, we must begin, not with innate ideas, but with experience, from which, in his view, all knowledge is derived. In this sense, the order of the mind corresponds to the order of the world (*Essay concerning Human Understanding* II.I; II.VII.15). For anyone who is confident about the ability of empirical, scientific investigation to yield truth, Locke is one of the philosophical guiding lights undergirding such a belief.

Locke's theory of how we know what we know (epistemology) has had important implications for Christian faith. On his grounds, religion is only true if it conforms to reason and empirical investigation (*Essay concerning Human Understanding* IV.XVIII.5). Since faith, and thus religion, is merely a matter of probability, it never results in certain truth. Religious toleration is then a logical consequence (*Letters concerning Toleration*). Given Locke's influence on America's founders, it is no accident that religious freedom was a central commitment in the origins of the American republic. Has the price religion needed to pay for this freedom, its (at least implicit) relegation to the status of mere opinion, been in its best interest?

Locke himself did not reject Christianity. He argued that it was the most reasonable of all religions, teaching nothing not available to reason. As such, he placed little emphasis on Christ, except in a role of his making clearer what reason reveals or rendering reason's insights accessible to the masses (*Reasonableness of Christianity* 234ff., esp. 252).

Though not unambiguously affirming such a view, Locke opened intellectual doors for thought currents that would lead to the development of *Deism* (the belief that God is like a clockmaker who created the world but no longer intervenes in creation, allowing it to run as a clock that once wound runs according to its own natural course). A contemporary of Locke's who expressly advocated such a view in the work *Christianity Not Mysterious* was John Toland (1670–1722). A more radical version was developed in the next half century in Germany by Hermann Samuel Reimarus (1694–1768). He concluded that the only miracle with any rational credibility was creation, for Christianity as a whole must be rejected as a barrier to natural religion (*Apology or Defense for the Rational Worshippers of God*). The quest for natural religion ("natural" in the sense of being rationally intelligible) was an understandable response to the quibbling over narrowly dogmatic issues that characterized the orthodox theology still prevailing in this period. The concept also provided a way in which the value of Christianity could continue to be affirmed in face of the emerging critical approach to Scripture that came increasingly to characterize the Enlightenment.[1]

---

1. A younger contemporary of Reimarus's, the German scholar Johann Salomo Semler (1725–91) is in some respects a forerunner of modern biblical criticism. He began to examine each individual text with a view towards evaluating its rationality and adequacy in depicting the original historical event it purports to represent (*Vorbereitung zur theologischen Hermeneutik*).

**David Hume and reactions to the Humean critique.** The Scottish philosopher David Hume challenged Locke's optimism about reason and the rationality of Christian faith. Starting with Locke's empiricism, he concluded that the scope of true knowledge is in fact more limited than imagined. All empirical evidence gives us is a series of phenomena, he claimed. Cause and effect is a mere construct of the mind, not really given by sense experience or reality; likewise substance is not rational knowledge but a mere construct of the mind (*Enquiry concerning Human Understanding* IV.I; XII.I). On Hume's grounds, all knowledge is to some extent arbitrary — a conclusion certainly familiar in the midst of the cynical tenor of the Western cultural ethos at the beginning of the twenty-first century. Hume's challenges effectively undercut the Deist solution and other efforts to posit a natural religion/theology, for their arguments for God's existence are based on cause and effect. If that is nothing more than a human construct, then the existence of God is not a rational certainty (XI).

Several attempts to recover from the Humean critique developed. In France, the famed poet, novelist, and philosopher Voltaire (François-Marie Arouet; 1694–1778) was critical of both Descartes's and Locke's optimism. Yet he did have a certain confidence in the use of reason as common sense. It was common sense, he argued, that man has made progress in human rights. The seeds of the French Revolution were thereby planted. One of his contemporaries, Baron de Montesquieu (Charles-Louis de Secondat; 1689–1755), applied the principles of reason to his theory of government and concluded that because power corrupts, three branches of government can provide a good balance (*Spirit of the Laws*). The internationally renown political philosopher Jean-Jacques Rousseau (1712–78) advocated a return to the original order, from which present governments had departed (*Discourse on the Arts and Sciences*). This original order was established on the principle that the general will of the people, not the ruler, was sovereign (*Social Contract*). In Rousseau's view, the only good state is one that observes this principle in its social contract and allows human beings to rule themselves.

**Thomas Reid.** In Scotland, another important reaction to Hume emerged in the philosophy of Thomas Reid and his school of Scottish Common-Sense Realism. This philosophical school was very influential on America's Founding Fathers, the American political system they created, and much of pre-1960s grassroots society in America. In response to the skeptics' claim that all knowledge is arbitrarily constructed, Reid taught that constructs like cause and effect and a sense of right and wrong are common sense; that is, they are accessible to all rational people (*Essays on the Intellectual Powers of Man* I.ii, p. 422; *Essays* *on the Active Powers of Man* pp. 580, 582, 589). This Scottish philosophy's view of common sense probably inspired the "self-evident truths" to which the Declaration of Independence refers. Proponents of this philosophy believe that people truly can reason together.

### Immanuel Kant

Another reaction to Humean skepticism was framed by the great modern German philosopher Immanuel Kant (1724–1804). Kant's alternative has exerted more influence than any other philosophy on the European university and high culture, on American colleges and society since World War II, as well as on modern Protestant theology. In fact, it is generally said that he is *the* philosopher of all modern Protestants. Readers should consider whether they do in fact share his basic suppositions.[2]

Kant's dialogue with Hume's skepticism is evident in the German philosopher's rejection of innate ideas. He did claim, though, that there are fundamental structures of the mind (what he calls "synthetic a priori judgments," such as space and time) in which we must place the data provided by senses. We cannot get to the "thing in itself" (the *noumenon*) when we study an object. We only perceive the object as *phenomenon* (not the noumenon), which the mind orders under the appropriate synthetic a priori categories (*Critique of Pure Reason* Int.; I.I; II.III).

The Kantian view of how we know entails that all our knowledge is subjective and thus is not knowledge of the thing-in-itself. The interpreter always makes a creative contribution to what is known. Are not our late-twentieth-century attitudes concerning knowledge as a matter of one's perspective or the existential baggage one carries thoroughly Kantian? Most of the theology done since Kant has been carried out in light of these suppositions. There is ample evidence that the Kantian assumptions define modernity.

## Modern Spiritualism

Orthodox theology dominated the intellectual and ecclesiastical worlds of the seventeenth and eighteenth centuries. In some respects, the quest for intellectual freedom and scientific precision were reactions to the authoritarianism (the subordination of reason to faith) mandated by the orthodox theology of the day. In the same sense, spiritualism, as well

---

2. Inasmuch as Kant's career extended into the nineteenth century, many aspects of his thought will be covered in chap. 13.

as Pietism, should be deemed reactions to the endless debates on dogma and to the intolerance of orthodox polemics. In that sense, Protestant orthodoxy had a role in enriching the diversity of Western theology.

Another apparent factor in the emergence of spiritualism was its adherents' wish to find refuge from all the fast-paced changes. The focus of the movement was, not on doctrine and church practice, but on spiritual life. During the orthodox period in Western Christianity in the seventeenth and eighteenth centuries, the Western church was not truly a "people's church," for leadership in the church presupposed an educated mind that had been trained in and could grasp the theological subtleties of orthodox theology. Though spiritualism appealed to members of the upper class critical of religious intolerance, it also appealed to the less educated who were not readily able to grasp the subtleties of the orthodox theological agenda.

Spiritualism is a movement whose adherents believe themselves to be directly in touch with the divine/spiritual realm. Moreover, they believe, such fellowship can be obtained without the mediation of visible means like church structures or rites. In its modern form, spiritualism is distinct from the sixteenth-century versions associated with the Anabaptist movement but is to some extent indebted to the latter (see chap. 4). Among its important leaders include the German Lutheran layman Jakob Boehme (1575–1624) and the eminent Swedish scientist-turned-mystic Emanuel Swedenborg (1688–1772). But the leader who founded a vast long-standing movement was George Fox (1624–91), the seventeenth-century English spiritualist who founded the Society of Friends (Quakers).

### Jakob Boehme

Originally a wandering cobbler, raised in a devout German Lutheran family, Jakob Boehme is reported to have experienced in his mid-twenties a series of divine visions that confirmed his earlier insights about nature and human life. Consequently he claimed in his writings to describe only what he had learned by divine illumination. His spiritualist propensities are obvious in his assertion that believers should be guided, not by the Bible, but by the Spirit.

Boehme contended that God the Father is the *Urgrund*, that is, the indefinable matter of the universe, containing the germ of both good and evil. As such, God has two wills — one good, one evil. The *Urgrund*, the abyss of being, tends to know itself in the Son, who is light and wisdom. The fate of human beings is worked out in the midst of this God who is both good and evil. According to Boehme, human character depends on the constellation of the stars under which the body is formed. However, people can avoid hell by uniting with Christ through faith, which renders them conquerors on earth, making it possible for them to replace the devil in the heavenly city.

Although Boehme's posthumous literature never launched a formal movement, it has enjoyed wide readership. During his lifetime, he was interrogated by the prince in his home region of Saxony about his views but was not condemned, allegedly because of their ethereal character. It is also likely that his critics recognized much that was solidly Christian in them.

## Emanuel Swedenborg

Perhaps most famous as a scientist, Emanuel Swedenborg notably founded the discipline of the classification of crystals, which is known as "crystallography." After many years in this field, he experienced a vision that, he claimed, had carried him into the spiritual world, where he had been able to observe eternal truths and so felt commissioned to make his doctrines known. All that exists is a reflection of the divine attributes, his vision taught him; consequently, the visible world corresponds to the invisible one. So authoritative was his revelation, he claimed, that what he had received was what the Bible meant when it spoke of Christ's second coming. Swedenborg also associated these insights with health and healing.

Given the eschatological character of his "revelation," the Swedish scholar sought to establish an agency for these ideas that would be a spiritual fraternity, not separated from the existing churches; he called it the "New Church." Wesleyan preachers in London, among the many disseminators of his view, formed a distinct congregation of Swedenborgians late in the eighteenth century after his death. Originally known as the Church of the New Jerusalem, it is now known simply as the Swedenborgian Church and persists today as a small body of less than several thousand members.

## George Fox and the Quakers

Unlike Swedenborg, more like Boehme, Fox was a man of humble origins. He was merely a devout ordinary English layman who came to the conclusion, after leaving his job as a cobbler in order to become a religious wanderer, that the various religious sects in England were an abomination. He soon became critical of their ostentation and structured worship forms. After a time of struggling with these new insights, which in the fashion of other spiritualists he felt had been revealed to him directly by the Spirit, Fox began to declare his views at various church meetings. Of course, he was ostracized for such verbalizations but soon began to attract a group of followers.

Seeking divine illumination, Fox and his followers became convinced that the "inner light" was the basis for true knowledge of God because the inner light is a seed existing in all humans providing immediate access to God (Robert Barclay *Chief Principles of the Christian Religion* II). The inner light does not contradict Scripture, yet it is not to be subjected to Scripture, for it is prior to any communication by external means (III). The religious enthusiasm associated with Fox and his followers, manifested in trembling, led critics of the movement to refer to the group pejoratively as "Quakers." Fox himself preferred the name "Society of Friends."

The priority of internal spirituality to its external forms manifested in the group's criticism of structures in worship and avoidance of the sacramental rites (Barclay *Chief Principles of the Christian Religion* XI–XIII). Worship was held in silence until someone felt moved by the Spirit. It would have seemed logical to reject the Calvinist idea of total depravity, for such a concept could be understood to mean the rejection of the presence of the inner light in all human beings. However, one of Fox's primary disciples, Robert Barclay (1648–90), prepared a still influential statement of fifteen propositions of Quaker faith, *The Chief Principles of the Christian Religion* (IV), in which he asserted that all human beings are fallen and degenerated, deprived of the feeling of the inner light until they actually join themselves with it. To be sure, he and Fox did posit the possibility of perfection as a goal for which to strive (VIII). However, in a fashion most consistent with British Calvinism, they expressly rejected Pelagianism and affirmed that justification was merely nonresistance to God's aims (IV, VII).

The Quaker emphasis on the freedom of the Spirit could lead to excessive individualism, but Fox and his followers avoided this danger by a strong stress on community. Consequently to this day, decisions in the Society of Friends are made, not by majority vote, but by consensus, as the meeting continues in silence until consensus is achieved. Regarding another matter of polity, there was no paid ministry when the movement began (Barclay *Chief Principles of the Christian Religion* X), though today clergy are paid.

The early growth of the Society of Friends led to a backlash in England. Fox was imprisoned for blasphemy. A contributing factor in the resentment his movement stirred was the Quaker lifestyle, which characteristically violated accepted norms of social convention. The Quakers treated all people as equal, even those higher up on the social scale. They ignored such practices as men tipping their hats or women curtsying (Barclay *Chief Principles of the Christian Religion* XV). In addition, the Friends always dressed in very simple attire and violated the linguistic conventions of seventeenth-century English by addressing everyone, even those of a higher social standing, with the familiar form of the second person singular, "thou," rather than with the polite form, "you."

Perhaps the most famous of Fox's followers was William Penn (1644–1718). The well-educated son of a British admiral, Penn spent years as a Quaker arguing for religious tolerance. He received land from the crown in the New World (what eventually became the colony of Pennsylvania) to establish a "holy experiment," a colony in which there would be full religious freedom.[3] Another feature of the colony was its generous treatment of Native Americans. Unlike in other American colonies, all land that was obtained was through purchase. Penn spent most of his life after the settlement cultivating relations with the Indians.

The Quakers had a largely positive and progressive social ethical agenda. Penn and his movement were pacifists (Declaration to Charles II), which manifests today in condemnations of capital punishment (Friends United Meeting *Faith and Practice* III). Already by the late seventeenth century, Quakers expressed dissatisfaction with slavery and officially condemned the institution by 1776, if not before.[4] An earlier eloquent and influential spokesman for this cause was the American Quaker John Woolman (1720–72; *Journal* 29–30, 41–44, 128–29). The unambiguous rejection of slavery of Woolman and the Quakers in general grows out of the commitment that everyone has some sense of the divine presence and an inward awareness of Holy Spirit. No social policy demeaning any individual can therefore be tolerated. Correspondingly, the Quaker tradition also affirmed women's leadership from the time of its inception. Women were given the same right to speak as men in all meetings of the Society of Friends.

With Fox and his tradition we can identify a pattern previously observed: free-church movements (like the Anabaptists and the early Church before it gained respectability in the Roman Empire) seem to have done the best job in preserving and nurturing women's leadership. A similar pattern of more positive Christian social outreach seems notably exhibited in Pietism.

## Pietism

A movement begun in the late seventeenth century in reaction to orthodoxy, Pietism differs from spiritualism in that Pietism maintained

---

3. Note the harmony between these commitments and Enlightenment ideals. The spiritualist movement is clearly a post-Enlightenment religious phenomenon very much presupposing many Enlightenment conceptions.

4. Sources are not clear regarding the precise date of the Philadelphia Yearly Meeting's condemnation.

the doctrinal commitments of orthodoxy, while spiritualism was more heterodox. Pietism is so named by reference to its emphasis on small-group Bible study in the large parishes of European Protestantism. These groups were called "colleges of piety." The basic commitment of all parties of this diverse movement was that the heart of Christianity is the nurturing of a living faith, rather than doctrine or rationalism. It prioritized the *fides qua creditur* (faith by which one believes — one's piety) over the *fides quae creditur* (faith that one believes — doctrine). In essence, the movement involved calling the faithful to a different, higher life than merely that of respectable citizen.[5]

## Origins of Pietism: Philipp Jakob Spener

The father of Pietism is usually identified to be a Lutheran from Alsace, Philipp Jakob Spener (1635–1705). He was a talented pastor from the region that had become Lutheran during the Reformation through the work of Martin Bucer (1491–1551). Born into an aristocratic family, he received the very best education one could obtain in his region in this era. However, like almost every subsequent Pietist and his intellectual/ spiritual forebears, he had become disappointed with the practice and piety of the Church of his day (*Pia Desideria*, Sal.; I). Spener's perception of laxity in the Church was no doubt related to his almost "puritan" lifestyle standards, which may have been the outcome of his early nurture by a devout mother and the influence of a competent pastor, Joachim Stoll (1615–78), who eventually became his brother-in-law.

At least three other influences on Spener's development of the Pietist option are noteworthy. One was the writings of Johann Arndt (1555– 1621), a Lutheran mystic whose interests included a concern to renew the practice of the Christian life among his contemporaries (*True Christianity*). Earlier he had studied the writings of the late medieval German mystics who had also influenced Luther, such as John Tauler (ca. 1300–1361) and the anonymously penned work *German Theology*. An additional influence was the French Reformed preacher Jean de Labadie (1610–74), whose mystical, almost pietistic, views eventually led to fanaticism in the organization of communities practicing a communist ideal. Another, perhaps more significant, influence was the young Spener's reading of various Puritan works, a first indication that the Pietist movement is intimately connected to the Reformed tradition, that is, is more in the heritage of Calvin than of Luther. When one considers that the Anabaptist heritage was rooted in Reformed (Zwinglian)

---

5. By the eighteenth century, with the combination of a state-church system and the dominance of orthodox theology in Western Christianity, respectable citizenship was about all that being a Christian had come to mean for the average layperson.

sources and that the Anglican Reformation was aligned with Calvin, it seems justifiable to conclude that the Reformed tradition is in fact the dominant theological strand in Protestantism, which means that to some extent Lutheranism may not genuinely belong to the Protestant coalition.

Spener became especially preoccupied with the concept of the priesthood of all believers and with nurturing this awareness as a tool for stressing the common responsibility of all Christians. For laity to exercise the priesthood necessitates that they undertake a more intense life of devotion and study (*Pia Desideria* 3.2). Indeed, an emphasis on the laity, the movement teaches, entails a corresponding emphasis on the laity's responsibility to undertake disciplined Bible study as part of what God expects of lay ministers. Such a strong emphasis on Scripture became typical of Pietism and led Spener to advocate the small-group Bible studies (colleges of piety) in the large parishes of the European Reformation (*Pia Desideria* 3.1), from which Pietism received its name.

The small groups were of significant sociological consequence, for they effectively broke down the social barriers that had begun to divide the Church in Europe. Under the state-church system and the dominance of orthodox theology, European Christianity had come to be dominated by the educated elite. However, in the colleges of piety, Christians from a diversity of social classes could and often did meet to study Scripture on an equal footing. These egalitarian tendencies made Pietism especially attractive to lower classes, and it meshed well with the rise of urbanization and democratization. A related consequence of the colleges of piety and Pietism as a whole was that they served to encourage the development of public education. All Christians, even those of the lower classes, needed to learn how to read the Bible.

The Pietists' emphatic belief in the priesthood of all believers coupled with the expectation of lay Bible study prefigures an important modern development in the concept of the office of the ordained ministry in contemporary Protestantism. An emphasis on the universal priesthood to some extent deemphasizes the authority of the ordained ministry. In addition, Spener contended that pastors would be provided more opportunities to know their members, nurture their growth, and support their weaknesses (*Pia Desideria* 3.1). Exercising less authority, the pastor is then engaged, not so much in pedagogy, as was the principal role of the pastor in the orthodox theological model, but rather in a ministry of pastoral care. Modern models of ministry in almost all denominations are far more indebted to Pietist suppositions, with all Pietism's strengths and weaknesses, than most church leaders realize.

Though committed to Luther's theology, Spener tended to emphasize, not justification, but (more like Calvin) sanctification (*Pia Desideria* 1).

Here is yet another affinity between Spener's Pietism and the Reformed heritage. Such links are hardly surprising. Hailing from Alsace, Spener experienced a Lutheranism that was already in the mode of the Strasbourg Reformer Martin Bucer, who consciously built bridges between Luther and Zwingli and directly influenced Calvin. With its focus on sanctification, Pietism in general seems more Reformed than Lutheran. Furthermore, the Great Awakenings in America (see chap. 11), which were Puritan/Reformed-based, illustrate Pietism's Reformed character.

Spener's emphasis on sanctification and piety is particularly interesting in light of his friendship with Gottfried Leibniz. Like his Pietist friend, the great Enlightenment scholar had a religious interest that was primarily inspired by a concern with piety and moral behavior. This motive led Leibniz to seek a reconciliation between traditional religion and Enlightenment science (*Theodicy*, pref.). This link between the Enlightenment and Pietism is most important for understanding Pietism's character and is a reminder that Pietism is a truly modern theological movement (in contrast to the other Protestant strands of thought, save perhaps modern spiritualism) in its close dialogue with the assumptions of the Enlightenment. Both Spener and Leibniz became committed to the possibility of uniting the various Protestant churches (a Lutheran-Reformed merger). Of course, this was a logical step for Spener given the "Reformed" orientation of his Lutheranism. Pietism would henceforth be a largely interchurch, ecumenically oriented movement.

Lutheran that he was, Spener continued to affirm justification by faith and a somewhat Lutheran view of the sacraments (*Pia Desideria* 1). The mystical influence of Tauler and *German Theology* led Spener to use language that implies the believer's "mystical union" with Christ (3.6). Of course, there were precedents for this image in Lutheranism, as it likely inspired Luther's concept of justification as conformity to Christ. However, when this conception was combined with Spener's claim, like Fox's, that perfection is a goal for which to strive (2), some Lutheran orthodox theologians (typically committed to an exclusively forensic view of the doctrine of the justification) began to accuse Spener of speaking of the new being in Christ as if the believer were divine. Affinities between Spener's view and the Eastern Orthodox notion of salvation as deification are certainly suggested at this point. The overlap between Pietism and the Eastern Orthodox tradition will become even more apparent with other figures, notably Wesley.

Directives for Christian living often accompany a strong belief in sanctification. Spener offered many such directives, especially for pastors, in a manner similar to the Reformation's third use of the law. He considered such questions as whether a Christian may wear gold ornaments or dance, and he of course condemned drunkenness. In a quite "un-Lutheran" appeal to Christ as an example for Christian life, Spener urged the faithful to imitate him (*Pia Desideria* I; Sal.; III; *Theologische Bedencken*).

Spener's approach to Scripture (his suppositions about how one knows God) is both characteristically Lutheran and also suggestive of modern theological trends. Like Luther, Pietism's founder used the stories of the Bible to interpret the readers' present reality. Also like the German Reformer, in a break with the Lutheran orthodoxy of the great Pietist's own day, Spener makes no reference to doctrines of verbal inspiration or biblical inerrancy. Instead he preferred to claim that Scripture is not properly understood apart from faith and the work of the Holy Spirit (*Pia Desideria* 1; 3.5), which is perhaps similar to Calvin's "internal testimony of the Spirit" (*Institutes* 1.7.4). Taken to its most radical extreme, the belief that the Word cannot be understood apart from faith means that the reader assumes a critical perspective on Scripture, that is, judges whether a given pericope does in fact function effectively. The idea that one assumes such a critical perspective on the text was not new; Luther in fact held it. Such an approach had even more ancient precedents, as it was employed by the Apologists of the early centuries, such as Justin Martyr (ca. 100–ca. 165) and Clement of Alexandria (ca. 150–ca. 215), when they interpreted Scripture allegorically in order to render it relevant to the issues of concern in the Roman Empire of their day. The Enlightenment's characteristic approach to Scripture was also critical and laid the foundation for the emergence of the historical-critical method. In yet another sense — approach to Scripture — Spener's Pietism has a link to modern intellectual trends, indicating again how closely associated Pietism and the Enlightenment are.

A final feature of Spener's thought should be noted. He had a very strong eschatological, almost apocalyptic, orientation. He was convinced that the end was near.

### The Movement Spreads

Thousands came to embrace the Pietist movement, though proponents of orthodox theology regarded it as emotional and overly subjective. Lutheran orthodox theologians were especially and perhaps justifiably critical of the Pietist movement's apparent Reformed, rather than Lutheran, orientation in light of its emphasis on sanctification rather than justification. In any case, by the late seventeenth and eighteenth centuries, there were proponents of the movement in all parts of Protestant Europe.

In Norway, with notable success in the city of Bergen and in the nation's south, the lay Pietist Hans Nielsen Hauge (1771–1824) staged revivals that both led him to be counted as the Viking homeland's greatest evangelist and changed Norwegian religious and cultural life forever. Hauge undertook his preaching partly because a childhood accident had convinced him of a call to preach. Raised in a deeply religious family, influenced like Spener by Johann Arndt, Hauge was highly critical of the spirituality of the leaders of the state church of his day. Like most of the early Pietists, he left the orthodox doctrines untouched. Despite remaining a loyal son of the state church, Hauge was imprisoned for his various activities.

Hauge's revivalist preaching, which appealed to the will more than to emotions, did have a legalistic tone, as he insisted that apart from the law one could not believe. He tended to deemphasize the sacraments. In typical Pietist fashion, he stressed sanctification and the priesthood of all believers (including lay preaching and the value of work in one's vocation). His revival had economic dimensions, as he encouraged his followers (mostly farmers) to build mills and factories in order to enhance their economic status.

Hauge's reaching out to the common people in his revivals had staggering social implications (perhaps because of Norway's small size). The confidence of rural people, their sense of worth, was strikingly enhanced. The Norwegians' adoption of a liberal constitution early in the nineteenth century and the egalitarian ethos of its culture, many believe, were immeasurably forwarded by the revival.

Similar dynamics can be observed in Sweden and Denmark, although the most important manifestations of the Pietist revival in these regions occurred decades into the nineteenth century. In Sweden, some critics of rationalism and orthodoxy who developed themes suggestive of Pietism emerged. Of these, Henrik Schartau (1757–1826) was perhaps the most influential. He himself had been influenced by the Moravians; however, he attached great importance to theological doctrine and a piety rooted in the Church, which included a strong liturgical sensibility. In this way, he marked subsequent Swedish Lutheran Pietism with a theological and liturgical sensibility that has perdured. Hauge's later Swedish equivalent, Carl Olof Rosenius (1816–68), also a layman, had even more influence.[6]

### August Hermann Francke

Perhaps the most renowned of all Lutheran Pietists were earlier German figures — August Hermann Francke (1663–1727) and his well-to-do family. Francke, who was self-consciously indebted to the insights of

---

6. See the discussion of Rosenius's thought in chap. 12 on p. 240.

Spener (save the latter's apocalyptic bent), was quite concerned about the level of spirituality among the Church's leaders and so insisted that a clergy's blamelessness become the presupposition for all other attributes of the preacher (*Sunday Sermons*, Mis.). This emphasis on the pastor's spirituality, as a leader embodying higher levels of spirituality, would continue to characterize Pietism.

Besides his duties as a professor at the University of Halle (in southern Germany), Francke became heavily engaged in organizing activities on behalf of the poor, orphaned, and aged, as well as administering Lutheran work in foreign missions. His role in these ministries forever linked Pietism to ministries of social outreach, social justice, and evangelism. Of course, this social concern was a logical development given the character of Pietism as an egalitarian movement that leveled class distinctions in its colleges of piety and insisted on the responsibility of all Christians, regardless of social standing, to read and study the Bible. Generally speaking, Lutheranism's best moments on social-justice issues have occurred when the Lutheran Church was represented or led by Pietists.

The links between social justice and foreign missions have also characterized Pietism since Francke. Among those missionaries whom Francke's institutional legacy commissioned was the greatest Lutheran missionary to colonial America, Henry Melchior Muhlenberg (1711–87), as well as Bartholomaeus Ziegenbalg and Heinrich Plutschau, who founded a mission in India, awakening great interest in foreign missions work on the European continent. The modern missionary movement (considered in chap. 12) is unthinkable apart from Pietist leadership.

Though originating in Lutheranism, Pietism was clearly interdenominational. The first prominent Reformed Pietist leader was F. A. Lampe (1683–1729), who was also an advocate of dispensationalist thinking. His hymns, sermons, and books did much to spread the spirit of Pietism in the Reformed tradition. In fact, his popularity among the masses was so marked that he wound up enduring much sustained criticism from orthodox theologians in the German universities. Tensions between proponents of orthodoxy and Pietism characterize Protestant church life from the late seventeenth century to the present.

### Radical Forms of Pietism

Not all of those caught up in the Pietist revival remained in the established churches of Europe. Particularly in Germany a number of Reformed Christians revived ideas of the early Anabaptists, including insistence on believers' baptism and immersion. They came to be known as the Dunkers. Virtually all the members of these communities emigrated to America after several decades of persecution and founded the predecessor bodies of the Church of the Brethren. The Brethren in Christ Church emerged from an expressly American version of this sort of revival. The theological profile of these bodies still closely resembles Mennonite theological commitments.

## The Emergence of the Moravian Church

Intimately related to the Pietist movement is the work of Count Niko-laus Ludwig von Zinzendorf (1700–1760), founder of the Moravian Church. Reared in a devout Lutheran Pietist home (Spener had been a sponsor at his baptism), he grew up and studied with Francke. The turning point in his role as a religious leader came when he offered asylum to a group of Hussites (more likely their forebears had been Taborites) who had survived as a community (a kind of brotherhood) leaving their native Moravia under the persecutions initiated during the Counter-Reformation. His affiliation with them, which was related to his efforts to convert them to his own brand of Evangelical Pietism, gave rise to a strong missionary impetus, eventually leading the Moravian community to undertake the sponsoring of independent mission work. After Zinzendorf's death, tensions with the Lutheran Church over such matters led to a rupture with Lutheranism and to the creation of the Moravian Church as it is known today. This development was clearly not in line with Zinzendorf's own vision, as he originally directed the Hussite Brethren community that settled on his land to join the local Lutheran church, and he believed that his community could cooperate with any church that shared his Evangelical faith. In fact, the Mora-vians continued to accept the Augsburg Confession of Lutheranism as a statement of their faith.

Theologically, the count and his followers claimed that outward con-fession without inner conviction was a tragedy (Zinzendorf *Nine Public Addresses on Important Matters Pertaining to Religion* 2). Of course, Zinzendorf was not without doctrinal concern and did develop some unique theological insights. For example, he taught that the Holy Spirit is Mother, alongside Father and Son (*Public Addresses to the Congrega-tion* 3, 27). Yet even when dealing with this doctrine, he hastened to add that the decisive issue in considering the Trinity is, not what the persons are to each other, but what they are to us (*London Sermons* 5.12).

Consistent with these commitments was Zinzendorf's claim that the entire content of Christian doctrine could be summarized as "that we belong to the Savior and become one heart and one soul with him" (*Twenty-one Discourses on the Augsburg Confession* 9). As with Spener, the Eastern Orthodox concept of salvation as deification certainly seems suggested in such Pietist descriptions of the new life in Christ (*Remarkable Conversations between a Traveler and Various Other Persons* 3). Also consistent with these commitments was the count's insistence that it is the Holy Spirit who works faith and brings us to Christ (*Twenty-one Discourses on the Augsburg Confession* 4). The Moravian founder's insistence on the primacy of God's work may suggest the continuing indebtedness of his thought and his tradition to Lutheranism. Such a theological orientation subsequently led John Wesley and others to criticize the Moravians for espousing a kind of quietism. Zinzendorf did concern himself with sanctification, especially insofar as he followed Spener's lead in speaking of the possibility of moral perfection (*Remarkable Conversations between a Traveler and Various Other Persons* 1). However, his writings and the character of his tradition are less inclined than the first Lutheran Pietists to spell out precisely how a Christian should live (*London Sermons* 4.7).

The Moravian missions in America were notably successful in their early stages with African Americans in the West Indies and with Native Americans on the mainland. Among the significant contacts that the Moravian missionary ventures had was with the young Anglican missionary John Wesley on his way to America. Through this contact Pietism would perhaps have its greatest, certainly largest, institutional impact on the Christian Church.

## John Wesley

Born the child of an Anglican priest in a Reforming family, shaped by a remarkable mother, Susanna Wesley (1669–1742), who was herself the daughter of a Nonconformist (Puritan) pastor, John Wesley (1703–91) was reared in a family climate that was all about loyalty to the Church mixed with discontent about its present state and a commitment to reforming it. His mother's piety and spiritual roots bear witness that a Puritan influence was still very much in the air in late seventeenth-century England. Albeit not formally trained, Susanna Wesley was quite a learned theologian in her own right. Her children, including John, readily sought out her theological and spiritual advice even in adulthood. In correspondence (7/18/1725) with her son John, she seems to articulate a kind of Arminian Calvinism. Her Puritan inclinations appear even more clearly within the family, especially in her emphasis on discipline in the spiritual life.

The influence of Wesley's father should not be discounted. Samuel Wesley, also the son of a Puritan clergyman, was a converted High Church Anglican but clearly a reformer with strategies of renewal much like that of the Pietists: he instituted small-group Bible studies in his parish during John's childhood. The father's influence on his fifteenth child seems evident not just in John's mature orientation towards small-group Christian nurture but also in his stubborn loyalty to the Church of England as well as its liturgy and polity.

John Wesley's career was in many respects launched when he along with his brother Charles (1707–88) and others, outstanding young university students, who were concerned to help each other progress in the Christian life, plunged into spiritual discipline. University life has never been very conducive to such pursuits. Consequently the group was an object of derision for other students, who mocked Wesley's circle, calling its members the "Holy Club" or "Methodists," for they were so disciplined in spirituality that they were perceived as having a "method" for nurturing Christian life (J. Wesley *Character of a Methodist* 4). The latter moniker, pejoratively intended, stuck and would forever be associated with those who were spiritually fed by such discipline.[7]

Following graduation and ordination, Wesley undertook a missionary venture in America that was spectacularly unsuccessful. Young and perhaps too idealistic, he had come hoping that the colonists in Georgia could be nurtured in a vibrant piety that would reflect the discipline of his beloved Holy Club at Oxford. Needless to say, things did not work out that way (J. Wesley *Journal* 4/17/1736; 4/22/1736; 8/11–12/2/1737). His brother Charles, who had undertaken a similar mission in the New World, fared no better. Another complication for John Wesley was that he had become attracted to a woman who eventually married another man. Exercising ecclesiastical discipline as her priest, Wesley began to sense frivolity in her and felt compelled to deny her Communion. She and her family sued for defamation. Wesley's ministry in America could not be continued (7/3–7/16/1737).

A highlight of the entire venture was the budding Pietist's voyage to the Americas. On board he met a group of Moravian missionaries going to the Americas to undertake a mission among the Indians. Wesley became a great admirer of the Moravians' piety. So confident were they in their faith that Wesley came to doubt his own piety and certainty of salvation (*Journal* 2/7/1736; 2/29/1738).

Returning to England, Wesley was not quite sure of his next step. Increasingly uncertain about whether he truly had a saving faith, he resolved not to preach but received comforting counsel from the Moravian preacher Peter Bohler (J. Wesley *Journal* 3/4/1738). The turning point in his spiritual crisis came in 1738 when he experienced a new assurance of

---

7. The early Methodist emphasis on discipline is most suggestive of the movement's links to Puritanism.

salvation, the so-called Aldersgate experience, while reading the preface to Luther's *Epistle to the Romans*. He tells the story this way:

> In the evening I went very unwillingly to a society in Aldersgate-Street, where one was reading Luther's preface to the Epistle to the Romans [*LW* 35:365–80]. About a quarter before nine, while he was describing the change that God works in the heart through faith in Christ, I felt my heart strangely warmed. I felt I did trust in Christ, Christ alone for salvation. And an assurance was given me that he had taken away *my* sins, even *mine*, and saved *me* from the law of sins and death. (J. Wesley *Journal* 5/24/1738)

Though he appreciated Luther's treatment of justification, Wesley believed that the Reformer had not adequately treated the matters of sanctification and the practice of the Christian life (*Sermon* 107.5). Is that a fair characterization of the whole corpus of Luther's works? Certainly Luther's preface to the *Epistle to the Romans* includes a discussion of Paul's view of sanctification. Could Wesley's assessment of Luther have been based on a selective reading of the Reformer?

Following the experience, Wesley visited the Moravian community in Germany and, while deeply admiring their spirituality, became convinced that he ought not join them. He became critical of a sort of quietism and mysticism that he thought he observed in their theology. Their piety was too passive (awaiting the grace of God, as Luther had taught), not sufficiently active (J. Wesley *Journal* 12/31/1739; Extract 11/1/1739–9/3/1741). Another influence on the great Pietist, though he critically amended their strict Calvinism, was the Puritan-inspired Great Awakening in America (J. Wesley *Preface to a Treatise on Religious Affections*). This dialogue with the American Puritan heritage is another indication of how Pietism is really a Reformed-inspired movement.

From then on Wesley entered a career as an itinerant and independent preacher. His friend from the Holy Club during student days George Whitefield (1714–70) brought him into this ministry in earnest. Whitefield himself had become a preacher of great renown in both England and in the Georgia colony. Wesley had some initial difficulties with Whitefield's fiery preaching style and his use of outdoor sites, even in England, for his worship services. However, the final break between the two came over theological differences. Whitefield was an orthodox Calvinist, and while Wesley's emerging theology was Calvinist on almost every point, he opted for something more like the Arminian position on predestination (J. Wesley *Journal* 3/28/1741).

During his years of working with Whitefield in the leadership of the Methodist movement, Wesley gradually became the main leader. After their break, Whitefield organized the Calvinist Methodist Church, which had its strength in Wales. Though Wesley wanted his movement to re-main in the Church of England, circumstances, especially in America, hastened the dynamic of independent organization. Against Wesley's will, tensions over the itinerancy of Methodist preachers (their assum-ing various preaching posts without regular appointment by Anglican bishops) and the need to regularize the ministry, especially in the United States, finally brought matters to a head.[8] These tensions, to some ex-tent class motivated insofar as the Methodist movement was effectively granting ecclesiastical authority to some from lower-class backgrounds, which caused resentment among some upper-class clergy of the Church of England, manifested in interruptions of some Methodist religious gatherings by ruffians. Wesley was himself often threatened.

After American independence, about which Wesley himself was criti-cal (*Some Account of the Late Work of God in North-America*), when the Church of England, which was said still to have jurisdiction over the parishes, refused to ordain personnel in the United States, Wesley pro-ceeded in 1784 with his own ordination of preachers and appointment of acting bishops (which he designated as "superintendents"). Through it all, the Methodist founder refused to believe that he had not sepa-rated from the Church of England, for he was too much a man of the Church to want this to happen (*Letter to Dr. Coke, Mr. Asbury, and Our Brethren in North America; On Separation from the Church*). The die for ecclesiastical independence had been cast. In 1784–85, American Methodists became the Methodist Episcopal Church. In England, there was no clear break even at the time of Wesley's death in 1791, but by 1795 it had occurred.

When it came to Methodism as a distinct church, American Method-ism set the agenda. In some respects, it is tempting to say of the Methodist Church what we did of Lutheranism. There is a sense in which both are "accidents."

### Factors in Methodist Growth

Concerning the Methodist movement's growth, its success in the New World was related to the westward movement of settlers with no eccle-siastical links and to whom the established churches were not reaching out. In England, the reasons for the movement's success seem no less related to sociological and economic factors, specifically to the new circumstances brought about by the industrial revolution. In fact, Wes-ley's movement cannot be understood apart from the social upheaval

---

8. The mission in America was particularly growing under the leadership of Francis Asbury (1745–1816), whom Wesley commissioned in 1771.

wrought by the new economic dynamics. The industrial revolution created a mass movement of the British population that had lost connection with the Church as a result of their dislocation in the urban setting. Among those masses, Methodism had its greatest success, for many of the same reasons that the egalitarian emphases of Pietism itself appealed to the disadvantaged.

## Did John Wesley and His Pietist/Methodist Heritage Bring the Insights of the Reformation to Perfection?

What was the relation between John Wesley and the Reformation? To answer the question requires examining Wesley's theology in relation to the views of the Reformers. In a sense, however, it is unfair to evaluate Wesley and his movement by this standard, for in his view Methodists are not distinct by actions, customs, or usages. They are marked by having the love of God in their hearts — just plain old Christianity. They are distinguished by fruits of a living faith but are not distinguished at all from other real Christians (*Character of a Methodist* 1–4, 17–18). The nature of true religion consists, not in orthodoxy or right opinions, but in "the hidden man of the heart" (J. Wesley *Sermons* 7.1.5–6). These are typical Pietist commitments. At the same time, as the loyal member of the Church of England that he was, Wesley also claimed that there are no Methodist practices that do not agree with the laws of the Church of England (*Journal* 8/16/1742). This loyalty to the Anglican tradition means that one can identify some of the same inclusive diversity in Wesley that characterizes the Anglican heritage.

### The Doctrine of God

A practical theologian, Wesley did not engage in speculation about the Trinity. He avoided all attempts to explain how the three can be one. By his own account, he was concerned only with the actions of God (*Letter to a Member of the Society* CCLXII).

### Perfection and Sanctification: The Heart of Wesley's Methodism

On only one doctrine did Wesley function as a kind of innovator. He believed that he had recovered the doctrine of Christian perfection, a theme that we have seen featured in the emergence of Pietism in general and in modern spiritualism (Matt. 5:48; 19:21). Though several theologians of the early Church, notably those influenced by monasticism, did stress this theme, it was not evident in the Church in subsequent centuries. Wesley, however, made much of this recovered theme.

Wesley claimed that perfection is the "peculiar doctrine committed to our trust" (*Journal* 8/14/1776). In that sense, it is the central doctrine for Methodists, not unlike how the sovereignty of God functions for Presbyterians, justification by grace through faith for Lutherans, and the restoration of the New Testament church for the Anabaptists. Wesley made this point even clearer when he claimed that "all our Preachers should make a point of preaching perfection to believers constantly ...and all believers should mind this one thing" (*Plain Account of Christian Perfection* 26). In this respect, he self-consciously broke with Luther's emphasis on justification as the article on which the Church stands or falls, though conceding earlier sympathy with this commitment (*Some Remarks on Mr. Hill's "Farrago Double-Distilled"* VII; cf. *Thoughts on Salvation by Faith* 1).

What Wesley meant and did not mean by the concept of Christian "perfection" is easily misunderstood. In his view, perfection is not exemption from ignorance, mistakes, or temptations (*Plain Account of Christian Perfection* 26; *Sermons* 40.I.7–8). It is simply another term for holiness; it is nothing more than entire sanctification (*Sermons* 40.I.9; *Late Conversations* V.1–2). Perfection is the ability not to commit sin (*Sermons* 40.II.20), a desire not to sin (*Plain Account of Christian Perfection* 10). Perfection is manifest when all thoughts, words, and deeds are governed by love (19). It is loving God with all that we have (25 Q.6). Christian perfection is a process, not a state. It is an instant but also "a gradual work, both preceding and following that instant" (*Brief Thoughts on Christian Perfection* 2). The instant occurs generally, though not necessarily, at death. In any case, it usually transpires many years after justification (3).[9]

Many scholars believe that in recovering the idea of Christian perfection, Wesley borrowed from the *Macarian Homilies*, which are either the work of the Egyptian desert monk Macarius the Great (ca. 300–ca. 390; *Apophthegmata Patrum* 33) or of a Syrian monk indebted to a group of fourth-century Turkish church leaders known as the Cappadocian Fathers, especially Gregory of Nyssa (ca. 330–ca. 395). In other ways also Wesley was a student of the monastic piety of the Desert Fathers. In this sense, one may legitimately refer to the impact of early African Christianity on the Methodist heritage.

Generally speaking, Wesley spoke of justification as forensic. His

---

9. Wesley's ambiguity about the sense in which perfection is a state or a process closely parallels the way in which most theologians have characterized sanctification (and deification).

inclination was to regard entire sanctification as transpiring after justification; thus, later American Methodists did not totally distort Wesley in deeming entire sanctification a "second work of grace" (Articles of Religion 9; *Sermons* 5.II.1–5). As a result of his endorsement of a forensic view of justification, which entails that nothing happens to the believer when justified save the proclamation of forgiveness, an emphasis on discipline and the striving for perfection were logical affirmations. This (Puritan-like) concern with discipline manifests itself in Wesley's formulation of strict lifestyle standards, which effectively function as a kind of third use of the law within the Methodist tradition. Among these standards are strictures against drinking alcohol, conducting business on the Sabbath, participating in theater, and donning ostentatious attire (*Directions Given to the Band-Societies* I.1–2, 6). In 1789, American Methodism even added strictures against slavery (*General Rules* Negative Rules 4). Such a commitment to the positive use of the law in guiding the Christian life positions Wesley against Luther and on the side of the Reformers. As did the majority of sixteenth-century leaders, Wesley argued for a close relationship between the law and gospel (*Sermons* 25.2–3).

Wesley's discussions of the doctrine of justification illustrate how the practical, unsystematic character of his thought meant that he, like Luther and in accord with his own Anglican heritage, endorsed a rich diversity of theological options. Thus, at times he seems to bracket the forensic model of justification and instead employs the language of Christ in us, who purifies us, implying that justification actually cleanses from sin (*Sermons* 49.II.25–26, 28) and that sanctification begins in justification (43.I.4). At these points, the Methodist founder's language suggests the concept of justification as conformity to Christ or even the concept of deification (becoming like God), as was typical of Gregory of Nyssa and the other Cappadocians. In one sermon, Wesley even refers to our thirsting after a deified state, "to partake as truly of God as we do of flesh and blood, to be glorified in His nature" (141.II) As with the Eastern Orthodox monastic tradition, in Wesley's thought there are links between affirming the possibility of Christian perfection and construing salvation as deification.

### Arminianism and the Freedom of the Will

Wesley opted for a consistent, if not self-conscious, Arminianism (*Question, "What Is an Arminian?" Answered*). Some scholars claim that this label was foisted on him by critics. Others maintain that he was self-consciously influenced by the Dutch Reformed revisionist Jacob

Arminius.[10] In line with the best in Arminius's thought, Wesley affirmed justification by faith and prevenient grace as well as original sin. Like Arminius, he also asserted that the atonement is for all, that election is conditional, and that grace can be resisted. In fact in at least one of his sermons (58.5ff.), Wesley went so far as to speak explicitly of election based on divine foreknowledge. Does it follow, then, that in Wesley, as in Arminius, there is a connection with Aquinas's treatment of justification insofar as the three of them posit cooperation between grace and the human will? In harmony with the logic of the Roman Catholic heritage, he on occasion spoke of salvation as a process, not given in justification but completed only in sanctification (*Sermons* 43.I.1ff.). He even defended Pelagius as a holy man who, in fact, taught nothing more than that Christians may go on to perfection by the grace of God (68.9).

Clearly Wesley affirmed that human beings have a free will (*Sermons* 120.19). However, in the spirit of Aquinas and the Eastern Orthodox tradition, he insisted that whatever measure of free will we have must be first supernaturally restored by grace (*Predestination Calmly Considered* 45). Elsewhere, on the other hand, the British Pietist aligns himself even more closely with the Puritan/Calvinist/Reformed orthodox heritage as he affirms that in sin every man "is of his own nature inclined to evil" and that after the Fall we cannot turn to God by our own natural strength (*Farther Appeal to Men of Reason and Religion* II.5.IX–X) Wesley even referred to God's "sovereign pleasure" with regard to when he grants perfection to the believer (*Plain Account of Christian Perfection* 21).

## The Sacraments

Given Wesley's self-understanding of preserving the practices of the Church of England, it is hardly surprising to discern apparently Anglican conceptions of the sacraments in Methodism. Wesley identified only two sacraments: baptism and the Lord's Supper (*Articles of Religion* 16). As in the Anglican tradition, he affirmed infant baptism. Not construed as a mere symbol by Wesley, baptism is a "sign of regeneration" (17). In fact, at one point he asserted this position so firmly as to claim that the Church often ascribes regeneration to baptism (*Treatise on Baptism* II.4).

As in the Church of England's Thirty-nine Articles, Calvin-like language appears in the Methodist founder's reflections on the Lord's Supper. His *Articles of Religion* (18) claim that the bread we break is

---

10. In either case, the Reformed influence (through Arminius) on Pietism is once again evident.

a partaking of Christ, who is eaten "only after a heavenly . . . manner."
There has been controversy about this understanding within Methodism
since many Methodists have been inclined to interpret their heritage in
terms of a Zwinglian symbolic view of the sacrament. However, it seems
highly unlikely that Wesley, a committed son of the Church of England,
would have rejected Anglicanism's higher view of the sacrament, the
heritage of his father. The Calvinist view of Christ's real presence was
clearly the piety John Wesley learned at home from his mother; one of
her letters to him (2/21/1731/2) during his days as a university student
and leader of the Holy Club affirms such a Reformed understanding of
the Lord's Supper. Another of Wesley's commitments, largely rejected in
the Methodist Church, is his almost Catholic or Anglo-Catholic piety
that is reflected in the calls for and practice of frequent reception of the
sacraments by Wesley and his colleagues (*Sermons* CI).

## Church and Ministry

The combination of Roman Catholic and Reformed Protestant elements
is evident in Methodist Church structure, which is another illustration
of the inclusiveness of the Wesleyan heritage and how its practical orientation opens the way to embrace diverse views. Methodism retained
the office of bishops, even though Wesley believed in thought as well as
in practice that ordination is not dependent on its being performed by
bishops in the apostolic line. Wesley gets no credit for this Reformed
Episcopal structure, which was the creation of the American Methodist
Church, not of Wesley, who preferred the title "superintendent" to designate the movement's leaders (*Letter to Dr. Coke, Mr. Asbury, and Our
Brethren in North America* 2, 4).

Outreach was built into Methodist structures by Wesley. "Woe is me,
if I preach not the Gospel wherever I am in the habitable world," he
proclaimed (*Conversation with the Bishop of Bristol*). Such beliefs had
evangelistic and financial implications for Methodism, as it also opened
the way to the use of lay preachers, some of whom were women. Built
into the character of the Methodist heritage is a fluid, not too carefully
determined, relation between pastor and laity.

## The Quadrilateral

What is the degree to which Pietism is a post-Enlightenment movement
and is expressly in dialogue with the suppositions of the Enlightenment?
Most scholars of John Wesley have concluded that such suppositions appear in the Methodist founder's thought with regard to his openness to
gaining insights from secular sources like reason and experience, which

were the primary sources of truth for Enlightenment scholars. In support of their conclusion, these scholars refer to the Wesleyan Quadrilateral — the idea that in Wesley's thought are four guidelines for interpreting Christian belief: (1) Scripture, (2) tradition, (3) experience, and (4) reason (*Articles of Religion* 5; *Address to the Clergy* 2; *Sermons* 11.7; 70.6; *Earnest Appeal to Men of Reason and Religion* 22ff.). The endorsement of all of these sources for theology, with a priority on Scripture, is quite suggestive of the Roman Catholic heritage, which seems embedded in this Protestant movement. Insofar as the reform, not eradication, of this Catholic heritage was the original goal of the Reformation, could the case be made that Wesley's endorsement of the Catholic heritage at this point witnesses to the fact that Methodism truly perfects the Reformers' thought, represents what the Reformation at its best is all about?

Much in line with the view of biblical authority observed in Spener and other Pietists, Wesley seems to break with the characteristic models of Protestant orthodox theology and their insistence on verbal inerrancy. He does not acknowledge these conceptions, save some denials that the Bible contains error. Though he did refer to the Bible's divine inspiration and lists the canonical books in a way most reminiscent of the Westminster Confession, the great Pietist only remarks that the Scriptures "contain all things necessary to salvation" (*Articles of Religion* 5; *Popery Calmly Considered* 3). In fact, Wesley so qualified the Protestant orthodox commitment to portraying the truth of Scripture as the basis for faith that he claimed that even if the external evidences of faith were challenged (the Bible's historicity), the internal evidence of Christianity's truth that believers have in their own lives would be sufficient evidences for Christianity's truth (*Plain Account of Genuine Christianity* II.10–III.4). Is this still a useful perspective for addressing challenges to Christianity issued by historical criticism and science?

### Social Justice

Pietism's colleges of piety effectively broke through class barriers, thus elevating the underclasses to new status. Pietism in general and Wesley in particular were out in front on issues of sexism and racism. The quest for holiness/perfection permeated all aspects of his thought and so had social implications (*Sermons* 107.V.4–5; *Thoughts upon Slavery* IV.4–5). His belief that the Christian faith (the gospel) must structure social ethics is in harmony with a Calvinist-Puritan concept of social ethics. However, Wesley combined this commitment with an openness to the separation of church and state (*Of Former Times* 20), which is akin to the Augustinian belief that the law, not the gospel, is the primary determining factor in Christian social intervention.

Wesley's use of lay preachers tore down lay-clergy barriers, and as noted, some of these preachers were women. He himself endorsed this practice in a surreptitious way (*Letters to Mrs. Crosby* [1761, 1769]). There is a precedent for female ministers in Methodism, then, from its origins.

Apparently Wesley was genuinely concerned about the impoverished and was himself actively engaged in a ministry to the poor (*Journal* 1/4/1785; 6/11/1747). In the style of modern liberation theology (see chap. 15) with its call for an identification with the poor, Wesley urged making contact with the impoverished and praised their taste (*Letters* CCLXX; CCLXXI). But his emphasis on striving for perfection and obedience to the law in turn nurtured a work ethic that tended to enhance the wealth of Methodist adherents and could render them intolerant of the poor (*Sermons* 116.17–18).

The position of the Methodist tradition on slavery is indeed a most commendable witness. Wesley himself condemned slavery (*Thoughts upon Slavery*), and American Methodists included a prohibition against it in its discipline (4) as early as 1789, the only major denomination to make abolition an article of faith. On the other hand, Wesley was somewhat demeaning in his assessments of African and Native American culture (*Imperfection of Human Knowledge* 5–6; *Of Former Times* 7).

## Assessment: Has the Reformation Been Perfected?

The case can certainly be made that Wesley brought the insights of the gospel to perfection. In addition to its emphasis on living the Christian life (sanctification) and striving for perfection (the latter commitment embodying the best elements of the early Church), Methodism has demonstrated impressive flexibility in its polity for enabling mission. Not to be discounted either is the strong witness of Wesley's tradition in the realm of social justice, especially in its stance against slavery at an early date.

As an interdenominational movement, Pietism overall has had a stellar history in fighting slavery and other forms of social injustice. For example, in Pietism's embodiment in the Lutheran heritage was the sterling social witness of August Hermann Francke. In addition, in America the early-nineteenth-century Norwegian American and German American Lutherans who rejected slavery or practiced integration were Pietists, most notably the Franckean Synod and the most controversial American Lutheran theologian of the century, Samuel Simon Schmucker (1799–1873; see chap. 11).

What is it about Pietism that makes it so effective in addressing social-justice issues? Could it relate to the Pietist quest for perfection, since such commitments in turn mandate a quest for perfection even in the social order? Such questions pose a problem for those not whole-heartedly committed to Pietism. Has the Pietist perspective alone dealt effectively with social justice? Does a higher view of ministry or an emphasis on God's transcendence lead to conservatism on social issues? Without doubt, Pietism has been notably effective in the area of social justice, but courageous social-justice stands have also been taken by non-Pietists in the Lutheran and Reformed traditions (orthodox theologians of a sort).

Another characteristic of Methodist (albeit not unequivocally Wesley's own) thought that could be deemed a strength is the way in which he wove together Roman Catholic and Reformed Protestant elements in his ecclesiology and view of ministry. Should one praise his inclusive ecumenicity at this point or critique him for failing to expunge Catholic vestiges from his thought?

On the negative side, critical questions must be posed to Wesley and Pietism about whether the doctrine of justification by grace through faith has been effectively compromised by their emphasis on sanctification, the practice of the Christian life, a third use of the law, and a role for the will. Is the emphasis on experience in Pietism (the belief of Spener that the Word is not fully understood apart from a proper piety or the belief of Wesley that the believer's experience is sufficient to prove Christian truth) a compromise of the transcendence of the Word of God, an objectivity that orthodox theology properly sought to protect?

# CHAPTER 11

# CHRISTIANITY IN AMERICA

Both the colonization and the Christianization of America occurred in the modern period. Neither can be understood without looking at the precolonial and colonial sociocultural and religious dynamics of the region. Students of church history may need to unlearn some of the stereotypes schools and popular culture have taught them about American colonization.

## Early Colonial Ventures in the New World

While the sixteenth century was a period of building the great, but infamous, Spanish and Portuguese empires, the new century was a time for other powers to emerge. Of these, Great Britain was the most prominent. It had a different colonial agenda. Spain established its colonies while seeking gold. Portugal also became involved in colonial ventures for the sake of commerce. Though with some exceptions, many of the British colonizers came to the Americas for religious motives.

The economic dynamics of the first British efforts in colonization mandated a preference for settlers who came to the New World, not as free landowners, but as indentured servants who would work land already owned by the colonial companies. In fact, in some of the earliest colonies it was not even possible for colonizers to own their own land.

The first permanent settlement in what would become the United States was by the Spanish at St. Augustine in 1565. The (Roman Catholic) church life in this and every subsequent colony of New Spain reflected the ethos of earlier Spanish reforms during Isabella's reign. The savagery associated with this reform in its systematic use of the inquisition to blot out all infidels was apparent in the Spanish colonizers' massacre of an earlier colony of French Huguenots who had settled just north of the new Spanish colony. Though not unambiguously successful in Florida, strong missionary efforts directed towards Native Americans characterized the life of the Catholic Church in New Spain in general.

The first permanent British settlements were, not with the Pilgrims in New England, but in Virginia more than a decade before the Pilgrims landed. In fact, the successful settlement in 1607 was the third attempt to settle the region. Two earlier ventures in 1585 and 1587 led by Sir Walter Raleigh (who named the territory "Virginia" in honor of Queen Elizabeth) had failed. The purpose of Raleigh's settlements was economic and political, not religious, but there was some Puritan influence early in the successful venture. Many of the stockholders and settlers believed that Puritan principles should govern the colony, the settlement of which took place at the high point of Puritan influence in the Church of England. Consequently, early legislation in Virginia mandated twice-daily attendance at worship, strict observance of the Sabbath, and stern punishment for profanity and immodest attire.

By 1622, Puritan influence in the Church of England was on the wane. A series of economic and ecclesiastical-political maneuverings contributed to the rapid dissipation of Puritan sentiments in favor of the evolution of a rather aristocratic version of the Church of England. In the British colony of Virginia, increasing economic prosperity effectively contributed to a decline of religious fervor. It also soon led to the importation of slaves. The church climate of the colony fit the bill perfectly for this new development. Virginia's comfortable aristocratic Christianity was just right for plantation owners but was not much concerned with the plight of the poor and certainly not with the slaves.

Generally speaking, the Church of England did little to convert slaves, the majority of whom, it is usually assumed, were not from Christian regions. Some contend that the majority of these African people were Moslem. Other scholars suggest that most of the first slaves hailed from regions in the present-day locale of Nigeria and were practitioners of indigenous African religions. The question of the slaves' origin is not moot and warrants further research, especially by those concerned with the origins and future direction of the African American church.

One reason for the inattention to slaves was an ancient principle, rooted in the decrees of the Third Lateran Council, prohibiting Christians from holding fellow believers in slavery (see 1 Cor. 7:22). Consequently, in order for slaveholders to avoid difficulties on this score, the best move was to not baptize any slaves. In 1667, the colony's legislature passed a law declaring that baptism does not change a slave's status. Can the Church's position be viewed as anything but a "cop-out" at this point?

Despite a reluctance to convert slaves, an informal pattern of evangelizing them evolved. When slaves were in fact baptized and joined the Church, it was typically the church of their masters. Some African Americans, especially Baptists, did organize their own churches in the South as early as the 1770s, the first being at Silver Bluff, across the Savannah River from Augusta, Georgia.

The Church of England's aristocratic airs were alien to slaves but also to white settlers in Virginia not included in the elite. In the eighteenth century, these alienated British colonists began turning to dissident movements, like the Quakers and the Methodists, to the latter through the efforts of Francis Asbury, early American Methodism's most prominent evangelist. Others fled to colonies, like Pennsylvania and Maryland, that had established principles of religious toleration. Rhode Island was also formed for the sake of guaranteeing religious tolerance and became a stronghold for Baptists. The colonies to the south of Virginia were established in the seventeenth and early eighteenth centuries. The society that developed in the Carolinas, especially in South Carolina, closely resembled the aristocratic flavor that characterized Virginia itself. Again, the higher classes belonged to the Church of England, while the lower classes tended to affiliate with either Quakers or Methodists. On the whole, though, the populations in these colonies lacked regular contact with the Church.

Georgia was founded in the 1730s for two distinct purposes. Politically the British established the colony to halt a Spanish advance from their base of operations in St. Augustine, Florida. As this was also a period in England when many religiously minded people were concerned, much as was Wesley, to better the lot of the poor, British Christians founded Georgia to provide the impoverished with an alternative to incarceration for debts: the poor could go to Georgia and work.

Once Georgia was founded, the missions of the Church of England had little influence on the colony. Wesley failed in his work in the region, but the Moravians did establish some missions in the territory. The most significant religious movement in the colony's early years was the popular response to the preaching of George Whitefield, an early Pietist who eventually became the Wesleys' Methodist colleague. The stamp he placed on Georgia's religious life helps account for the predominance of Methodist and Baptist piety in the region to this day.

## Puritan Colonies in New England and America's Puritan Paradigm

The earliest New England colonies were formed as religious communities. They were intentionally Puritan in orientation and aimed to create an ethos in which a truly living gospel with all its Puritan emphasis on discipline permeated the whole society. But not every Puritan colonizing effort was the work of Independents like the Pilgrims of the Mayflower, who settled at Plymouth in 1620. Many settlers associated with the efforts of the Massachusetts Bay Company and with the colony in Connecticut were Puritans who had remained loyal to the Church of England. During the Puritan Revolution in England, the migratory wave to the New World trickled away to nothing, as the hope of establishing a holy commonwealth in the motherland was reborn. The Restoration of the Stuarts to the British throne did not notably affect the Puritan colonizers as it did those in England.

American historians vigorously debate the impact of Puritanism on American history. The prevailing thesis is that Puritanism provided the primary paradigm for understanding American religiosity; that is, whenever people in American society have thought about what religion was like, inevitably the images upon which they drew were conceptions typical of Puritanism. In that sense, we may speak of a "Puritan paradigm" for understanding religion in America and for understanding American society throughout its history.[1] For example, it is no accident that in the popular mind-set, American history (except for perhaps Columbus's "discovery" of America) begins with the 1620 landing of the Pilgrims/Puritans. After the same fashion, one of the major American holidays, Thanksgiving, is at least mythologically rooted in expressions of Puritan piety.

The Puritan paradigm is reflected in American attitudes towards religion in other, more subtle ways. For much of the prevailing European American culture, to be religious means to be serious and disciplined, not unduly joyful, and the leadership of religion is largely the province of white men. This is the way the media and educational textbooks that dare mention religion tend to portray Christianity. For example, in the successful TV comedy *The Simpsons*, the family patriarch, Homer, is regularly lulled to sleep by the topic and mode of the "serious" sermons he hears. These portrayals reflect the Puritan agenda. The media also often portrays Christians either as "goody two-shoes" whose faith is always obedient to laws or else as Bible-thumpers who believe the Bible to be inerrant. Again, these characterizations link with Puritan teachings; they are not characteristic of Lutheran, Quaker, Roman Catholic, and Jewish doctrinal emphases.

Despite the American public's (and its media's) increasing awareness of religious pluralism and of the wealth of religious life in America, it can be argued that the Puritan paradigm is still controlling, as it always has, prevailing American cultural attitudes towards religion. In assessing the validity of this claim, readers should note that the concept of the Puritan paradigm does not negate the presence of very distinct

---

1. Given Puritanism's roots in the theology of John Calvin, this paradigm is also one more indication of the profound impact of the Genevan Reformer on Protestantism as a whole.

attitudes towards religion in certain subcultures of American society. African Americans do not characteristically construe religion in this Puritan manner as "serious" business in which joy and celebration are not appropriate. The Italian American subculture, shaped as it has been by the Roman Catholic heritage, is also likely to find this prevailing Puritan image of religion in America as an oddly incomplete version of the faith, unduly stripped of appropriate ritual. Even the Norwegian American subculture (at least those truly Lutheran segments of it, not unduly affected by Pietism) would not characteristically think of religion in terms of Puritan discipline and seriousness. Perhaps these subcultures do not regard religion in America in terms of the Puritan paradigm, but the prevailing culture does.

When one lives in a culture that adheres to the Puritan paradigm, it is bound to have an effect on the adherents of other religious traditions. Against their will, even, members of these minority traditions begin to conform their religious communities ever so gradually to the prevailing attitudes until even non-Puritan traditions begin to work and act like Puritans.[2] This is what is meant by the Puritan paradigm and its profound impact on the American social psyche.

Working in other subtle ways, the Puritan paradigm helps the American public define which religious traditions are most American, most socially acceptable. Puritan conceptions are sometimes identified with what the cultural gurus of American society deem to be "genuinely American," that is, those values of the upper middle class. Certainly the concept of "family values" in the latest version of fashionable American political rhetoric reflects Puritan commitments (Westminster Confession of Faith XXIV; Larger Catechism, qq. 138–39).

What are the truly American churches? Congregationalism (especially in New England, where it functions as the true heir of Puritanism), Presbyterianism, Methodism, and Baptists appear to be likely candidates. It seems that the closer one's tradition is theologically to Puritanism and its Reformed heritage, the more socially advantageous it is to belong to it — for because like tends to seek out like, the greater the percentage of higher social classes reflects in its membership. Perhaps this is why it is more prestigious, at least more in line with the image of having made it in America, to be Presbyterian than to be Methodist.[3]

---

2. For example, one may see this in American Lutheran congregations where the preaching and teaching of a Christian ethic of freedom from the law has instead become a matter of legal obligation. It is no less reflected in African American congregations whose worship is totally bereft of gospel music and spontaneous response.

3. Generally speaking, this pattern of higher social classes being attracted to Presbyterianism rather than to Baptist or Methodist churches, which are in turn themselves solidly middle class, is evident in the African American community as well.

The Presbyterian tradition is a more direct heir of the Puritan heritage. It is true that in the American context, very few of the first Puritan settlers had Presbyterian inclinations; however, in the colonial era one detects the increasing influence of Presbyterian polity on the structure of New England Congregationalism in a way that resembled the emerging Presbyterian interest in the middle colonies. The significant influx of Scotch-Irish (staunchly Presbyterian) immigrants after 1714, swelling to a tide in the following century, firmly established American Presbyterianism. The higher social standing accorded Episcopalians is simply a function of the higher social status reflected by the Church of England in the original colonial scheme.

Presbyterian, Episcopal, Congregational, Methodist, and Baptist churches, then, appear to be the truly "American" religious traditions, which is hardly surprising when one considers their origins in Puritanism and/or in the Reformed heritage.[4] As part of the Puritan tradition (or in virtue of being theologically related to it), Presbyterian, Episcopal, Congregational, Methodist, and Baptist churches more naturally fit American religious expectations, for those expectations have been defined by Puritanism. Of course, the case can be made that there is a price for all the benefits accruing to these denominations in virtue of their association with the Puritan paradigm. The price that they and American religion in general pay (no less than in the case of "minority" churches previously noted) is that Puritanism and American society have transformed them. Some analysts have argued that this close association has transformed the Puritanism of the Puritan paradigm into a kind of *civil religion* (a syncretistic set of beliefs shared by all members of a society that serves to provide religious justification for that society), which is no longer distinctively Christian. Such a development, the analysts argue, has had an inevitably "secularizing impact" on the denominations associated with the Puritan paradigm and the general American religious society, rendering them in some ways to be communities shaped as much by American aspirations as by the gospel.

The case for such a Puritan paradigm embedded in the American social psyche is all the more persuasively made when it is recognized that the paradigm has affected the lives and religious communities of Lutherans and Catholics as well as Jews and African American Christians.

---

4. Though the Episcopal/Anglican tradition and Methodism were not established as Puritan movements, the theological profile of these traditions, particularly as further developed in the American context, are most compatible with core commitments of Puritanism. The Puritan influence on Methodism is evident through Susanna Wesley's piety, with its emphasis on discipline in the spiritual life, and its impact on her sons. Nor can it be denied that Calvin was the primary influence of the Continental Reformation on the Anglican reform.

As a result, these Americans have been historically marginalized in the American religious psyche. This dynamic is not just a function of these traditions being mostly composed of members ethnically related to the last wave of European immigrants prior to present Asian influx (though the ethnic composition of Lutheran and Catholic memberships could be a factor in their marginalization). No, the relative disestablishment of Lutheran and Catholic traditions in the American context is also a consequence of their theological and liturgical distinctness over against the Puritan establishment.

In scholarly circles today, there is some talk about the inappropriateness of the Puritan paradigm for understanding American religious experience. Some are suggesting, instead, a Methodist or revivalist paradigm. Subsequent stages in the history of American religion following settlement bear witness to the intimate relationship between Puritanism and the Pietist heritage, which is not unlike the intimate relationship between Calvinism and Pietism on the European continent. The links between these two traditions suggest that perhaps we cannot meaningfully refer to one of these paradigms without the other. In that case, the concept of a Puritan paradigm for interpreting American religious life seems sufficiently rich to explain characteristic American thinking about religion.

# The Middle Atlantic Colonies

A picture of the religious profile of early America is not complete without an examination of New York, New Jersey, Pennsylvania, Delaware, and Maryland. It is hardly surprising to find early Reformed, if not Puritan, influence on these colonies. The Dutch were the first settlers in New York (originally New Netherland), and so the Reformed dominance was well established in the territory. When conquered by the British in 1664, the earlier Dutch inhabitants of the colony became British subjects. The Church of England was established in the colony, and with a wave of British immigration, it soon became the region's majority church.

The eastern part of New Jersey followed the same pattern as in New England with strict Puritans in control. In the western part of the state, though, the influence of Pennsylvania's Quaker settlement was strong. In that region, Quaker principles of religious tolerance were put in place, though as the Quaker community in the colony prospered and began to hold slaves, relations with the Society of Friends in Pennsylvania became very strained.

Pennsylvania was settled under the leadership of William Penn. Although the basic inspiration for Penn's "experiment" was to found a colony for Quakers, from the very beginning it was a colony comprising people of varied confessional traditions. Among the early settlers were Scotch-Irish Presbyterians, German Lutherans and Reformed Christians, and even a Swedish Lutheran parish left over from the establishment of the colony of New Sweden in what would become Delaware.

The situation in Delaware was similar to what transpired in Pennsylvania, to some extent because Delaware was part of Pennsylvania until 1701, while earlier having been a territory of New Sweden. In Delaware and in all the other locales where early Swedish Lutheran congregations were established, the American melting pot, if not the Puritan paradigm, was in operation at a very early date. When the colonies in which they were located became British possessions, virtually all of these congregations left Lutheranism to become part of the Church of England. Lutherans in America have never been very confident of their "American" character, in part because the Lutheran Church has always been on the fringes of the American religious establishment.

A consideration of significant traditions outside the establishment leads to Maryland, the main center of Roman Catholicism in the North American British colonies. Established in 1632, it was part of King Charles I's policy of seeking Catholic support. However, given the religious attitudes in England at the time, it would have been unwise to allow for the establishment of a Catholic colony. Consequently, it was decided that the colony would permit religious freedom. As a result, though Catholics governed during the colony's early stages, Protestants were always in the majority and after the fall of King James II in 1688 even succeeded in establishing churches in conformity to the Church of England. The early history of all the colonies in the Middle Atlantic region serves to remind us that no religious influence is long-standing in the American context if it does not link itself in some form to the Puritan paradigm and its related traditions.

## Periods in American Church History

One way to approach summarizing the history of American Christianity prior to the 1950s is to identify important developments/periods. This typology also serves to highlight the rich diversity that exists in the midst of a core commonality that has characterized American Christianity. There are ten such distinct historical periods: (1) breakdown of the Puritan communities and the fix: the Half-Way Covenant; (2) Jonathan Edwards, the Great Awakening, and early African American Christianity; (3) reaction of the churches to independence; (4) immigration; (5) the Second Great Awakening; (6) denominational division over slavery; (7) Reconstruction, response to urbanization, later immigration, and revivalism; (8) emergence of new African American denominations; (9) the liberal-Fundamentalist controversy: end of the American Evangelical era; and (10) new religions.

## Breakdown of the Puritan Communities and the Fix: The Half-Way Covenant

A number of theological controversies developed in colonial New England. One of the most pressing was what to do about the tradition of infant baptism supported by the Reformed heritage and the Puritan insistence that one must have a regeneration or conversion experience in order to be Christian (Westminster Confession XXVIII, IX). A crucial issue in this debate was the meaning of baptism. Some Puritans advocated the Baptist approach of baptizing only those who had professed their faith as adults. The adoption of this strategy, though, would conflict with the avowed Puritan agenda of founding a society guided by biblical principals. A Christian commonwealth was only conceivable if, as in ancient Israel (the Reformed/Puritan paradigm for a Christian society), one becomes a member by birth. Civil and religious communities must be coextensive, or the society is not "Christian." The presence of an increasing number of adults among colonists who had not experienced conversion made the problem even more complex for Puritans.[5] What was to be done with their children?

One of Massachusetts's most prominent Puritan leaders championed the way out of the impasse. Solomon Stoddard (1643–1729), the grandfather of Jonathan Edwards, advocated the Half-Way Covenant. The proposal, which was formally adopted by ministerial councils in the New England colonies, was that children of those never converted might be baptized because both the children and their parents were still members of the covenant. Baptism, after all, was sufficiently constitutive of church membership to allow its recipients to bring their children into the baptismal covenant. But only those who had had the conversion experience were full communicant members of the Church with power to participate and make decisions. In fact, Stoddard took more radical steps, downplaying the emphasis on covenant and opening the Lord's Supper to all morally responsible "professors" of the faith.

Although there was some dissent from these new ecclesiastical developments, the general consensus among New England Puritans about them is an indication that the original Puritan optimism concerning

---

5. Most of these unconverted colonists were professing Christians leading morally respectable lives.

the possibility of establishing Christian commonwealths was becoming increasingly clouded with cynicism. New England Puritans generally settled on congregational polity with a confession that was based on the Westminster Confession of Faith. As a result, and given its impact on Presbyterian immigrants to America, the confession has served as the *most* authoritative expression of Reformed faith in the New World.[6]

## Jonathan Edwards, the Great Awakening, and Early African American Christianity

The eighteenth century brought to America the same Pietistic currents that we have observed in England and continental Europe. A controversy developed, particularly among Presbyterians, between the orthodox adherents of the Westminster Confession, called the "Old Side," and those more concerned with the experience of redeeming grace, called the "New Side." A coalition of both sides was made possible by a great Pietistic, revivalistic wave, which spread throughout all of the American colonies called the "Great Awakening." To some extent, the awakening was a reaction against the spiritual indifference nurtured by the Half-Way Covenant.

**Jonathan Edwards and the Great Awakening.** The revival, though it clearly had earlier precedents in New England, first broke out sometime in 1734 in the Massachusetts parish of the most profound American theologian of the colonial era — Jonathan Edwards (1703–58). It is common to think of Edwards as a crotchety old Puritan who preached a fearsome Word: his best-known sermon is "Sinners in the Hands of an Angry God." But that is by no means a full picture of Edwards's theological orientation. What most of us know about this sermon and its author from our earliest exposure to American history is an unfair characterization of its message.

Edwards was, not a "hellfire-and-brimstone" preacher, but a sophisticated and faithful Reformed theologian who was also well schooled in Enlightenment philosophy. He needed all of these skills to confront the spiritual listlessness of his and his eminent grandfather's day. No less did he require these skills in the struggle against the rising tide of Arminianism in Puritan circles that challenged the Reformed emphasis on the sovereignty of God.

Edwards's major point in his well-known sermon is that life is precarious (here today, gone tomorrow). That is a sobering appraisal of

---

6. Those New England Puritans more inclined to prefer a presbyterian polity eventually participated with other Presbyterian ministers in the Middle Atlantic colonies in the organization of America's first presbytery in 1706.

human life, but a realistic one. To be sure, we would like to ignore such reminders of the transience of life. Perhaps that is why so many think of the sermon as a quaint statement of the piety of the era. On the contrary, though, its message calls for an authenticity about the human condition. We dismiss it at great cost.

Elsewhere one can discern a softer, more Pietistic side of Edwards, as is evident in publications like his *Treatise concerning Religious Affections*. People are not really changed by what they learn, he argued, unless their affections are moved. Edwards was a theologian of great depth and creativity, regularly offering insights that may still be relevant in our era. Espousing a view reminiscent of the ontology of several modern philosophers, he claimed that every intelligent being is related to Being in general. One who loves Being in general, the equivalent of loving God, will be more disposed in turn to benevolent action towards individual beings, who also belong to Being in general (*Nature of True Virtue*). He also spoke of the Trinity in a very Augustinian way as the mutual love of Father and Son united (made one) by the Holy Spirit, who is the love that unites them.

Edwards had an impressive way of combining Pietist and revivalist concerns without compromising his orthodox Calvinism. This perspective helped him refute critics of the awakening who were concerned about its alleged undermining of the solemnity of worship and study in favor of a mere feast of emotion. On the other hand, the Great Awakening did have an important impact not just on Congregationalists and Presbyterians but also on the nascent Baptist and Methodist churches. The awakening's emphasis on conversion led many Congregationalists and Presbyterians to align with Baptists. It also proved to be the impetus to Methodist and Baptist outreach to the frontier West as well as the impetus for a new, more inclusive outreach in the South. The preaching of George Whitefield had its greatest impact during the Great Awakening, and he must be considered one of its main propagators.

The awakening is the period of the first serious outreach to African American slaves in the South. It is likewise significant in that, as a movement extending throughout all the American colonies, it had the effect of providing the first bonds of unity among colonists — a common religious experience. Prior to the Great Awakening, each of the colonies was an island unto itself, with little appreciation of what they had in common, but with the awakening, the perception grew among Americans that they had something in common. This soon led to the circulation of common American views regarding human rights and the nature of government. As such, the Great Awakening, with its combination of strict Puritan orthodoxy blended with revivalism, indelibly shaped American religious sensibilities. It is largely through the awakening that the Puritan paradigm was established in American culture (inasmuch as the awakening had its origins in the Puritan ethos and was related to Edwards's Puritan theology).

Another unique aspect of American religiosity warrants consideration in relation to our examination of the Great Awakening. In America, it is noteworthy that distinct ecclesiastical bodies are called "denominations" (different names for Christians in a pluralistic society) and not distinct "churches," mutually exclusive of each other. This way of construing Christian diversity in America conveys the idea that common religious experience holds all Christians together despite religious preference. This ecumenical propensity is no doubt a reflection of the Great Awakening's ecumenical orientation and its profound impact on the American social psyche.

***Early African American Christianity.*** Another exciting consequence of the revival was the challenge it issued to the southern legal and cultural order regarding slavery. Prior to the 1720s, it had been common to justify reluctance about evangelizing African Americans by arguing that slaves were not included in God's plan of redemption. In the revival setting, though, the preacher proclaimed the Word to all who could hear. Very few of the revival preachers actually challenged slavery, but the awakening clearly introduced the idea of equality before God into the American psyche. The typical pattern of evangelism was for slaves to be incorporated into the churches of their masters. Because the Great Awakening brought about so many Baptist and Methodist converts in the South, most of the slaves converted in this period became Methodist or Baptist.

Semi-independent religious life for slaves began developing in the South in the eighteenth century, if not before. Black preachers became a fact of life early in the movement in regions with many slaves. Largely an invisible institution in its early stages, because the converted slaves often worshiped in their own way clandestinely on the plantations, African American Baptist congregations were established late in the eighteenth century. In regions with few African Americans, slaves officially worshiped with white masters in segregated settings.

Given the apparent interconnections between African American Christianity and European American Christianity (specifically Puritanism in its revivalistic forms), questions of pressing contemporary significance arise concerning the character of the African American church, that is, whether it is unique and how it has served the African American community. True enough, much of African American Christianity reflects aspects of the Puritan paradigm, just as the rest of American Christianity does. It is hardly surprising that there would be certain theological continuities with Puritanism in the case of those

African American congregations affiliated with Reformed-Presbyterian and Baptist denominations. Of course, Methodists also share, with significant modifications, certain theological commitments of the typical Puritan/Reformed theological profile. These three denominational families include the vast majority of African American Christians; consequently, it seems justified to speak of African American Christianity's compatibility with Puritan theological commitments.

Worship was another way in which Puritan, or at least European American, styles influenced the African American church. One can walk into the sanctuary of some predominantly African American congregations and experience a sedate, controlled, serious worship marked by European music and style of singing. However, this profile is by no means the predominant style of worship in African American congregations. Indeed, African American Christianity by no means fits the Puritan paradigm in all its aspects. This branch of Christianity is truly unique. The African American church's uniqueness is symptomatic of the uniqueness of other churches in America (esp. Roman Catholic and Lutheran churches, not to mention Judaism and Islam) that do not fit the Puritan paradigm.

One of the most unique characteristics of African American Christianity is worship. These churches view worship as celebration — a different mood from that of the typical European American church. This unique character may in fact reflect general African cultural attitudes towards worship, an ethos that even the bondage of slavery could not crush. Certainly the African American church has never been totally bereft of its unique music, hand clapping, use of drums, and sacred dancing; these elements are very much in evidence in congregations today that are self-consciously Afro-centric.[7] The African American Christian emphasis on celebration in worship is an ecumenically relevant contribution to Western Christianity, for it puts the black church in touch with the way in which the earliest Christians worshiped. By contrast, Western Christianity has been much more preoccupied with forgiveness of sin and the Cross, and so has placed more emphasis on repentance than celebration.

Characteristic worship in the African American church offers at least one other significant ecumenical contribution. It is increasingly common in ecumenical circles to identify two poles in a catholic view of ministry, both of which are evident throughout the history of the Church. On one side, the ordained minister is part of the priesthood of all believers. On the other, the ordained minister exercises authority, standing over

---

7. Such practices are also common in the ancient indigenous African churches, specifically in Ethiopian Orthodox worship.

against the universal priesthood. In many traditions, one of these aspects of the ordained ministry is emphasized more than the other. The Roman Catholic and Eastern Orthodox traditions, for example, tend to emphasize the more authoritarian pole. In the African American tradition, perhaps reflecting the hierarchicalism of indigenous African culture, is a tendency to emphasize the authority of the minister (even in Baptist traditions, which characteristically emphasize the priesthood of all believers). In worship, though, with its characteristic openness to spoken responses from the laity even to the sermon, we see in the African American church a living witness to the priesthood of all believers. In this tradition, then, the catholic view of ministry in the unadulterated richness of both its strands is on full display.

Another aspect of the African American church's unique contribution is in the realm of social ethics. To be sure, there have been points in history when these churches have been apolitical and unduly concerned with the individual's salvation. On the whole, though, beginning with these churches' contribution to the abolitionist movement, the African American churches have played an important role as agents of social justice, most visibly in the civil rights movement. Compared to the most socially active of predominantly European and European American churches, the African American church has been a consistent agent for sociopolitical reform, though its theological orientation for dealing with these issues has been identical with that of the denominational traditions with which particular African American churches are affiliated.

Scholars have offered various characterizations to capture the uniqueness of the African American church. Until recently, the classic study of the African American church was *The Negro's Church*, a 1930 publication by Benjamin Mays and Joseph Nicholson. They identified pride of ownership, democratic fellowship, and the spirit of freedom afforded for African Americans in their own churches as the genius (uniqueness) or soul of the black church. A more recent study by C. Eric Lincoln and Lawrence Mamiya entitled *The Black Church in the African American Experience* referred to the black church as "the cultural womb of the Black community" (8). Gayraud Wilmore has offered an even more detailed discussion of the African American church's uniqueness in *Black & Presbyterian* (79–85). He notes that the special contribution of the African American church lies in its historic ability to relate the secular to the sacred. Everything exists in a divinized world: "There ain't no difference between 'praying and plowing.'" That is, the same beat that lets the good times roll on Saturdays stirs the soul on Sundays. A related factor noted by Wilmore is the persistent tolerance of black religion for the mysterious and occult. In that sense, can we say that the African American church is premodern, pre-Enlightenment, in character?

Wilmore also noted four additional resources characterizing the black Christian tradition: (1) concern with personal and group freedom (linking salvation to political liberation), (2) reliance on the image of Africa as the land of origin, (3) emphasis on the Will of God for social justice, and (4) creative style and artistry in worship (worship as exciting and to be enjoyed). Wilmore's provocative reflections pose a challenge to all readers, regardless of their ethnic or denominational background, to offer similar reflections on the uniqueness of their own traditions, how their traditions converge with and differ from the Puritan paradigm of American religion. Such reflections can be a most relevant exercise in theological/ecclesiastical "roots."

Scholars of American religion do well to devote more attention to the African American church (and other "minority" churches in the American context). Such study provides insights about the nature of the Puritan paradigm's impact on American religion as a whole. It reminds scholars of the pluralism of American religion, and in view of the thriving character of the African American church today, a study of its heritage and ethos may teach all Christians valuable lessons concerning how churches may thrive in our present context.

### Reaction of the Churches to Independence

The dynamics that led to the American Revolution were not exclusive to the North American continent. The new democratic political ideals, rediscovered in Greek culture by the Enlightenment, were fused with eighteenth-century economic dynamics in the Western Hemisphere that pitted those who had profited from the emerging capitalism and trade (the new aristocracy) against the older aristocracy of blood/royalty. The American Revolution is clearly a product of these international dynamics.

The Revolution and its success certainly had an impact on religion on the North American continent. The first reaction of the American elite, educated in Enlightenment thinking, was to see it as proof that religion is truly rational, living proof of the inevitability of human progress when set free from traditions of the past, including traditional religion. These dynamics account for the emergence of the Unitarian and Universalist religious traditions. The ethos of both of these exhibits their rejection of orthodox theology and beliefs in favor of a rational religion that stresses human freedom and the intellectual capacities of humanity. Unitarianism is so named for its explicit rejection of the Trinity doctrine. Although the movement had earlier precedents and had begun to organize in England in the previous century, the origins of Unitarianism in America, particularly in Congregationalist (old Puritan) and Anglican circles, were contemporaneous with independence. Universalists, so named for their belief that in the end all will be saved, were organized in 1793 in America, primarily by Methodists. The similarity between Universalism and Unitarianism eventually resulted in their merger in 1961 into the Unitarian Universalist Association.

The American Revolution forced difficult adjustments on several churches. The Church of England in the colonies included many Tory members. In 1783, in order to respond to their image as unpatriotic Tories and to protect church property, Anglicans who remained in the former colonies renounced membership in the Church of England and renamed their organization the Protestant Episcopal Church. The majority of its members were from the old aristocracy. Not much has changed in the twentieth century.

Methodism at first had the same problem as Anglicanism. Wesley had been a loyalist, as had most Methodist preachers, except their prime leader Francis Asbury. Under pressure from English legislation aimed at making him declare himself a separatist, Wesley had ordained ministers for America without official authorization from the Church of England. Finally in 1784, no longer feeling the need to receive Wesley's permission for all their ecclesiastical actions and policies, American Methodists organized themselves, long before the founder had, as an independent Methodist church, separate from the Church of England.

In the same period, a spirit of unity of all American Christians nurtured by the Great Awakening began to emerge. Put off by barriers to ministry erected by their traditions, these American Protestants began to organize themselves as a nondenominational body dedicated to proclaiming the purity of the gospel. In essence, the agenda of this so-called restorationist movement was to bring about a return to primitive Christianity (although this was tinged by healthy doses of the rationalism typical of the age). Finally, against the original designs of one of the founders, Thomas Campbell (1763–1854), the Christian Church (Disciples of Christ) organized itself as a new denomination in 1832, uniting most of the followers of founders Alexander Campbell (Thomas's son; 1788–1866) and Barton Stone (1772–1844). All three of the founders had been Presbyterian pastors of a New Side persuasion, critical of the Westminster Confession. To this day, the nondenominational, ecumenical character of the movement continues to be preserved. The church is somewhat unique in that while it practices believers' baptism, its congregations characteristically celebrate the Lord's Supper weekly.

Other revolutions in American Christianity began taking place in response to independence. Baptists grew rapidly, particularly in the southern states. This planting of congregations and their loose congregational polity, which did not mandate an educated ministry, placed Baptists in a particularly strategic position to penetrate the new territories of Tennessee and Kentucky. Congregationalism had gained much prestige in the newly formed nation as a result of its unambiguous support for independence. However, this translated into growth in membership only in regions colonized from New England. The next period in American history brought about even more radical changes in the religious scene.

## Immigration

An unprecedented wave of immigration to the United States began late in the eighteenth century. The Napoleonic Wars and other unsavory political dynamics plagued Europe. In addition, the rise of industrialization on the European continent was causing great social turmoil and famine, increasing the gap between rich and poor so that land available in the American Western frontier was a most alluring prospect. The growing need for cheap farm labor in the Americas increased the slave trade as well.

The wave of European immigration markedly increased the Roman Catholic population in the United States. By the middle of the nineteenth century, the Roman Catholic Church, due first to French and then to Irish immigration, had become the largest religious organization in the United States. Many in the older American establishment perceived this immigration as a threat to Protestant (and English) hegemony, eventually culminating in a backlash. Indeed, Catholicism's growth and the maintenance of its various constituencies' ethnic heritage became the object of the Ku Klux Klan's wrath in the next century, as the Klan broadened its fanaticism not just against African Americans and Jews but also against Catholics.

Increased immigration likewise led to the growth of Reformed and Lutheran communities. These traditions were already planted on the continent in the colonial period through German and Dutch immigration. Lutherans were well established in Pennsylvania. However, many of an early wave of Swedish Lutherans in the colony of New Sweden (Delaware) were lost as Lutherans after Anglicizing and joining the Episcopal Church.

It is typical of immigrant Catholics, Lutherans, Reformed, Mennonites, Moravians, Greek Orthodox, Russian Orthodox, and Jews that their religious bodies retained a distinctively ethnic character through much of the nineteenth century and even into the twentieth, which helped immigrants maintain ties to their roots. The ethnic character of these religious communities was a source of strength (guaranteeing communal fidelity and insulating them from the dynamics of secularization) but also a liability in evangelism and in maintaining members who had become Anglicized/Americanized. For instance, many Lutherans and Presbyterians became Baptists and Methodists in the next period, during the Second Great Awakening. The ethnic character of these traditions is by no means dead. Until well into the twentieth century, as much as any other factor, differences in national background of the denominations occasioned the differences between distinct Reformed denominations and between Lutheran denominations.

The immigrant influx of this period also championed a religious ideal that had characterized the earlier Puritan immigration — creating a community totally governed by Christian ideals. Earlier eighteenth-century Amish and Mennonite immigrants from continental Europe had established such communities in Pennsylvania. Among such communities established in the period include various other Mennonite settlements in the Western territories, a German radical Pietist (Dunker) settlement observing a seventh-day Sabbath led by Conrad Beissel (1691–1768) in Ephrata, Pennsylvania, and in the late nineteenth century the Oneida Community (New York), which practiced an extreme form of community property to the point of sharing spouses. America has been a great showcase for experimentation in religion.

## The Second Great Awakening

Towards the end of the eighteenth century, a second great revival began in New England. It was marked, not by great emotional outbursts, but by earnestness in Christian devotion and living. Worship attendance markedly increased. These developments also had significant consequences for inspiring greater concern for outreach and social justice.

Among organizations founded in this period to facilitate the revival were the American Bible Society (in 1816) and various foreign missions societies. The first American Baptist Convention was formed in 1814 to promote missionary work. Movements for temperance and abolition of slavery also developed in this period.

Women played prominent leadership roles in the awakening, particularly in the formation of various women's missionary societies and in the Women's Christian Temperance movement. In fact, this organization, under the leadership of Frances Willard, became a foremost voice for women's rights. Modern American feminism is clearly rooted in the awakening. Likewise, the American Colonization Society, founded for the purpose of purchasing slaves so that they might return to their native homeland, also had its origins in this period.[8]

In the West or on the frontier, the revival was more emotional, less intellectual. Camp meetings characterized the revivalist style. These developments split Presbyterianism in 1810 when a great revival in Kentucky and Tennessee raised questions about how such revivals could be reconciled with core Presbyterian convictions articulated in the Westminster Confession regarding predestination. In some respects, this dispute was a continuation of an earlier eighteenth-century debate in American Presbyterianism concerning the Great Awakening — the so-called New Side versus Old Side debate. A continuation of this debate leading to the 1810 schism resulted in an even more significant schism in Presbyterianism in 1837. The church split into an Old School Presbyterian denomination (the new designation of those with Old Side sympathies) and a New School denomination (the theological heirs of the New Side tradition). They divided not just over questions concerning the value of revivals and the importance of subscription to the Reformed confessions but also with regard to whether traditional Presbyterian polity should be deemed unequivocally binding on church practice.

The revivals of the Second Great Awakening also stimulated the greater growth of Methodists and Baptists. Their efforts in evangelism through the use of camp-meeting revivals cut across ethnic lines. A number of the recent immigrants of this period converted to Baptist or Methodist churches. For example, Germans in Pennsylvania influenced by Wesleyan piety formed the Church of United Brethren in Christ (a predecessor to the United Methodist Church). During this Great Awakening, these churches in the leadership of the revivals gained the reputation of presenting a simple, easy-to-understand gospel, which was in part related to their openness to employing theologically untrained preachers. This feature of their polity gave them a kind of flexibility in reaching out to the frontier regions of the new republic, accounting for why by the middle of the nineteenth century Methodists and Baptists were the two largest Protestant denominations in the country. The ability of these churches to attract settlers in the West by cutting across ethnic lines tilted American Christianity away from an unequivocal correspondence between ethnic origin and denominational affiliation. On the frontier, Germans, Scots, and Irish might become Baptists.

What was the awakening's impact on the West? Its Arminianism promoted a spirit of optimism (for on its grounds anyone has the capacity to be elect by doing the right thing) and further undergirded the Puritan paradigm's sense of America as an elect community, as the Promised

---

8. The founding of the Republic of Liberia was largely the result of the society's work.

Land. Such commitments were already becoming "politicized" in colonial days and were more or less formally articulated in the concept of *manifest destiny* (the idea that expansion into Western territories was America's divinely mandated destiny). The impact of such American expansion on American religious life was most readily apparent in the marked growth of the Roman Catholic Church in the United States.

The War of Independence of Texas and the ceding of the Southwestern Territories to the United States by Mexico as a result of the Mexican War placed a larger number of Mexican, Spanish Catholics on American soil. With their membership came new challenges for the American Catholic establishment, as it was now called upon to incorporate into its fellowship a large flock belonging to an entirely different culture than the rest of the membership. American Catholicism committed itself to the "Americanization" of this new segment of its church, a policy that effectively marginalized Hispanic Catholics for almost a century.

Any discussion of the Second Great Awakening is incomplete without noting the first of the modern revivalists (America's first "Billy Graham"), Charles Grandison Finney (1792–1875). He launched numerous successful crusades in the period of the Second Great Awakening. Reared on the western frontiers of New York State, trained as a lawyer, Finney was a born leader — handsome, musical, excitingly energetic, with a tough and forceful rhetoric. Finney's renown as a preacher spread. Originally a Presbyterian, he adopted methods (including an emphasis on the human role in producing conversions) that exacerbated tensions in the church. Given the impact of his revivals, Finney's abolitionist position brought much national attention to the antislavery cause.

In this period, Lutherans in the South gained African American members. Southern Lutherans, not unlike other denominations, regrettably imposed on the slaves special requirements for baptism, requirements pertaining to obedience and a period of additional instruction. Worship was also directed to be held on a segregated basis.

A combination of camp meetings and a renewal of Wesley's perfectionist ideal applied to slavery or care for the poor originated another new movement in this period. The Methodist Episcopal Church, it seemed, had become increasingly lax about these commitments and was developing into a middle-class church with newfound respectability. In response, several Methodists seeking to recover these emphases were reprimanded for their theological and abolitionist commitments. Institutional breaks with Methodism transpired, resulting in the initial formation of the Holiness movement (so called for its special emphasis on perfection). Holiness denominations that formed in this period for these reasons include the Wesleyan Methodist Church of America (today part of the Wesleyan Church) and the Free Methodist Church of North America.

In this context of growing antislavery and human-rights sentiments, it is not surprising that certain African American Methodists in Philadelphia and in New York began objecting to segregation in church life and the second-class status that was imposed on them as a result. In Philadelphia, Richard Allen (1760–1831) led a 1787 secession in reaction to such segregation. He was an ex-slave who had been a traveling preacher since his manumission in 1786 and had settled in Philadelphia working among African Americans. After Allen's and his colleagues' secession, American Methodism's unchallenged leader at the time, Francis Asbury, consecrated Allen as a bishop. The secession eventually led to the formation in 1816 of the African Methodist Episcopal Church (A.M.E.).

Allen's loyalty to Methodism manifested itself in several ways throughout his career. After the secession, a majority of the African American activists in the city preferred affiliation with the Church of England, urging Allen to function as their pastor. He reneged, asserting his loyalty to Methodism, insisting that its simple gospel, popular teaching style, and discipline were just right for his people. Certainly the Methodist preoccupation with sanctification and advocacy of something like a third use of the law clearly reflect in his thought, as they do in the Articles of Religion of the church (*Life Experience and Gospel Labors of the Rt. Rev. Richard Allen*). The activist heritage of those who originally seceded from the Philadelphia congregation, their commitments to abolitionism and black solidarity, including support of the Back-to-Africa movements, have endured in the denomination's ethos.

In New York, a later 1793 African American separation from Methodist ecclesiastical segregation led to the formation of the African Methodist Episcopal Zion Church (A.M.E. Zion) in 1824. Largely as a reaction to undesired interference from Bishop Allen in seeking to plant his own church among the faithful in New York, the leaders of the secession proceeded to develop structures for their own church, one that reflected a more democratic, less hierarchical polity. After modest beginnings, both A.M.E. and A.M.E. Zion began to enjoy great success among freed slaves in the South after the Civil War. Both have maintained classical Wesleyan theological and lifestyle commitments.

African American Methodist churches protested not just against ecclesiastical segregation but also heroically witnessed against slavery, actively protesting the unjust laws articulated during this period and supporting the Underground Railroad. Among the leaders of the abolitionist movement were such A.M.E. Zion members as Sojourner Truth, Harriet Tubman, Jermain Loguen, and Frederick Douglass. Such active social concern was not merely a function of the experience of slavery. Social concern is, after all, part of the legacy of both the Methodism of these denominations and of the Christianity of the Second Great Awakening. This is all the more evident when it is noted that Truth's, Loguen's, and Douglass's objections to slavery were authorized in a manner characteristic of both Methodism and the Puritan roots of the awakening, by appeal to the essence of the gospel of Jesus Christ, not just to common human decency (*Narrative of Sojourner Truth* 146–48; *Frederick Douglass Papers* I[1]16–17, [2]181–83; Rev. J. W. Loguen *As a Slave and as a Freeman* 391–94).

## Denominational Division over Slavery

Quakers in America, in the tradition of earlier British Quaker opposition to slavery, had refused membership to any person holding slaves since 1776, though the first declaration may have been in the previous decade. Recent scholarship suggests that this policy statement may have also been originally endorsed by Mennonites in Pennsylvania. Methodists banned slavery in 1784. In subsequent years, though, not only American Methodism but also many Baptists compromised such commitments in order to gain members in the South. In fact, by 1843, numerous Methodist ministers were slave owners. Presbyterians went on record in 1818 as opposing abolition, even while conceding that slavery is against the law of God. These dynamics were also perhaps related to the development of the idea of manifest destiny, which justified westward expansion by suggesting the superiority of white Protestant America.

Many Lutheran Pietists, notably a German group organized in 1837 called the "Franckean Synod," took a strong abolitionist stand.[9] Gettysburg Seminary, also a Lutheran Pietist stronghold, educated African Americans for the synod under the seminary's founder, Samuel Simon Schmucker (1799–1873). In addition to being a strong critic of slavery and providing a haven for escaped slaves in his home, Schmucker was also a proponent of trying to "Americanize" Lutheranism, that is, to minimize the impact of Luther's unique themes on the church. One particularly eminent graduate of his seminary was Daniel Alexander Payne (1811–93). Ordained by the Franckean Synod, he eventually returned to his Methodist background, becoming a great African Methodist Episcopal Church historian and its foremost educator in addition to being perhaps its most renown nineteenth-century bishop.

---

9. It was named for August Hermann Francke, Germany's great Lutheran Pietist who is especially notable for his social concern and role in focusing the Pietist movement on such an agenda.

Two aspects of Payne's thought and career warrant consideration. His passion for education led him to seek the seminary training he received among Lutherans. He regarded education as the key to the advancement of his people and also to a deeper faith through the study of Scripture (*Welcome to the Ransomed; or Duties of the Colored Inhabitants of the District of Columbia*). The influence of these commitments remains very much alive in the A.M.E. denominational ethos to this day. One segment of its leadership emphasizes social action (claiming the heritage of the founder, Richard Allen), and another segment places more emphasis on advancement of African American people through education clustered around Wilberforce University, which was founded by Payne. Are these strands of thought ultimately compatible, or should one be prioritized over the other?

The other aspect of Payne's thought is the way in which he tends to reflect Puritan emphases on discipline, industry, thrift, and duties of religion (*Welcome to the Ransomed; or Duties of the Colored Inhabitants of the District of Columbia*). Making these points with a kind of third use of the law (using the Ten Commandments and/or the values they imply as a guide and prod to Christian living) is most compatible with Payne's Methodist commitments and is also characteristic of the Lutheran Pietism of Schmucker, his instructor. Insofar as these commitments are rooted in Calvin, the compatibility between Payne and the Puritan heritage must be conceded. As such, Payne is one more example of the degree to which American Christianity truly reflects something like the Puritan paradigm.

The Franckean Synod was not the only example of a strong Lutheran testimony against slavery. The Norwegian Lutheran Synod severed its cooperative alliance with the German-dominated Lutheran Church-Missouri Synod over the latter's unwillingness to have slavery declared to be sin.[10] Consequently, the record of American Lutheranism is a mixed one, but Lutheranism was by no means the only confessional tradition in America to be splintered institutionally by the slavery issue.

The Methodist Church split in 1844 over slavery, leading to the formation of the Methodist Episcopal Church, South.[11] Similar developments are evident in the Baptist Church in 1845 when the convention refused to commission for missionary service a candidate who owned slaves, and in response the Southern Baptist Convention was born. This rift has never been healed. Southern presbyteries of the Old School denomination withdrew in 1861 and founded their own denomination

---

10. Norwegian laity took the leadership in this episode, while the clergy never officially registered such a condemnation of the institution.

11. Reconciliation of North and South did not occur until 1939.

after the General Assembly had expressed its loyalty to the Union. Four years earlier the New School had split after its General Assembly had repudiated the view that slavery is divinely sanctioned. African American Presbyterian clergy largely provided leadership for their tradition's opposition to slavery.

Lutherans in the East (German Lutherans of the General Synod) split when the southern synods seceded after their home states seceded from the Union. In response, the General Synod officially backed the federal government.

### Reconstruction, Response to Urbanization, Later Immigration, and Revivalism

The period following the Civil War through the end of the nineteenth century involved significant increases in immigration and urbanization. The immigration brought larger numbers of Christians to America who, because of ethnic background, were not inclined to join churches associated with the Puritan paradigm. For example, Lutheran, Eastern Orthodox, Roman Catholic, and Jewish ranks swelled during these years. Christians associated with free churches (largely Scandinavian bodies originating in nineteenth-century European Pietist revivals; see chap. 12) also arrived in America in this immigration wave. Many of these new immigrants encountered prejudice and hostility from longtime American citizens, which continued into the twentieth century.

The period was also one of virulent racism, both in society (with the institution of legalized segregation, the infamous Jim Crow laws) and in church life. To some extent, this was the result of a backlash by southern whites against their exploitation during Reconstruction. However, in this period there was general Anglo-Saxon racism in the air. Even at high levels of influence in the Church it was manifest. No less than Josiah Strong, the general secretary of the Evangelical Alliance (a late-nineteenth-century coalition of theologically conservative Christians dedicated to defending faith from modernist movements), declared in 1893 that God was preparing the Anglo-Saxon race for a great moment — to dispossess weaker races deficient in the purity of their Christianity and level of their civilization. His aim was to "Anglo-Saxonize" mankind (Strong *New Era; or, the Coming Kingdom* 79–80).

Despite these trends, Reconstruction and the decades immediately following witness signs of hope. The African American Methodist Church had good success in the South; A.M.E., A.M.E. Zion, and northern Methodist churches experienced marked increases in membership among African Americans. A number of other American denominations based in the North launched efforts at educating liberated slaves in the region.

The postbellum decades were also a time, however, when the expanding urban centers, stimulated by the increasing impact of the industrial revolution on American soil, started trapping many of the newest immigrants in poverty. Secularization likewise began making significant inroads among the uprooted masses. The Protestant response to these disturbing dynamics took the form of establishing various organizations aimed at reaching the urban masses. Two of these originating in England, the Young Men's Christian Association (YMCA) and the Young Women's Christian Association (YWCA), have been successful for over a century. The Sunday school movement also had its origins in this period, as a response to declining Christian-education discipline within families among the urban masses. If it were not for the secularizing consequences of the Enlightenment and the industrial revolution, there might be no Sunday schools today. Instead, the home or the Pietist "colleges of piety" would likely be the primary means of Christian education. Are these now more (or less) viable structures in our postindustrial context?

*The Salvation Army.* Several new denominations had their origins in this period. The Salvation Army (the Army) was founded in 1865 in England (coming to America in 1880) by Methodists who were distressed about their church's apparent abandonment of Wesleyan ideals in favor of middle-class respectability. William Booth (1829–1912) and his wife, Catherine Mumford, were the movement's true patriarch and matriarch. Organized and operated on a paramilitary pattern, the Army originally aimed, and has continued, to provide for the spiritual and physical well-being of the urban masses. Early in the movement's history, it became apparent to the Booths that they would not attract the working poor with only revivals. As a result, the Army shifted gears and has become well known for its relief work among the poor. No less noteworthy has been its commitment to radical equality of the sexes, as evidenced in the role women have played in the Army's leadership since its inception.

*Seventh-Day Adventists.* William Miller (1782–1849), a farmer-preacher from upstate New York who had concluded early in the nineteenth century that the Christ would come again in 1843, instituted a prophetic movement that led to the forming of the Seventh-Day Adventists. When Miller's prophecy was not fulfilled, and his remaining followers experienced great disappointment, they organized under the leadership of Ellen Harmon White (1827–1915). After marrying an Adventist elder, she came to function as a new prophet for the movement. Under her leadership, belief in the seventh-day Sabbath became an article of faith, along with the earlier apocalyptic orientation. White's special views on health, diet, and the legalistic way in that she believed we are saved have also become part of the denomination's teachings. In this century, it has truly become an international movement.

*Holiness denominations.* Several other denominations associated with the Holiness movement also had their origins in this era. These churches (such as the Church of the Nazarene, founded in 1907, and an 1897 predecessor body of today's Wesleyan Church, the Pilgrim Holiness Church) represent a modification of some of the concerns of the first Holiness churches, which were formed before the Civil War. Modern revivalism influenced this new segment of the movement, especially in its postbellum form. These new Holiness bodies are also distinct from the earlier Holiness churches because of the later bodies' tendency to equate the Wesleyan emphasis on entire sanctification with the "baptism of the Holy Spirit," which identifies entire sanctification as an event, rather than as a process. Seeming to represent a break with Wesley, this conception is a theological commitment rooted in the ministry of Finney (*Lectures on Revivals of Religion* II). Subsequently Phoebe Palmer (1807–74), one of the great leaders of this branch of the Holiness movement, advocated and widely promulgated this conception (*Present to My Christian Friend on Entire Devotion to God*). As one would suspect, these emphases became very influential in the eventual development of the modern Pentecostal movement. The precise nature of these emphases, especially their more individualistic tenor, becomes clearer after we consider the way in which American revivalism was transformed in this period.

*Dwight L. Moody.* In response to the new sociocultural situation, the new "Finney," Dwight L. Moody (1837–99), reworked and urbanized revivals. A lay preacher who had been actively involved in the Sunday school, YMCA, and related new ecclesiastical movements, Moody had been a shoe salesman. He gave up this successful career in his twenties to take up a task as a missionary to the city and its poor. His sales talents were put to a new, successful use when his career as a revivalist was launched somewhat accidentally. He had been invited to fill a pulpit in England during a business trip. The result of his sermon was spectacular. From then on, he would be a full-time revivalist.

Moody's was a revivalism without as much social conscience as Finney's and those of the Great Awakening. His prime, almost exclusive, concern was to save souls by calling people to repentance, not to transform society. He assumed that conversion of the masses was the only way to transform society. American revivalism has largely adopted Moody's model for revivals, which is why revival movements since Moody have usually failed to address social issues.[12] The lack of social concern in the revivalism of the era had its impact on all the religious

---

12. One thinks of Billy Graham's generally apolitical tendencies as a prime exemplification (see chap. 15).

movements influenced by the revivals. Consequently, it is hardly surprising that those strands of the Holiness movement that began in this period (most African American Holiness churches have spiritual roots in this era) were less socially conscious than Holiness groups that began prior to the Civil War.

*Retreat of the African American church from social concern.* The beginnings of a similar demise of social concern and lack of formal education of the clergy typical of the new revivalism surface in the predominantly African American churches of the era. The great nineteenth-century African American author William Wells Brown lamented this development (*My Southern Home: or, the South and Its People*). Such an explicit advocacy of political noninvolvement rises from the voice of a prominent early leader of the Christian Methodist Episcopal Church, Lucius Holsey (1842–1920; *Autobiography, Sermons, Addresses and Essays*). Noninvolvement seems implied in the speeches of Elias Morris (*Sermons, Addresses and Reminiscences and Important Correspondence*), the longtime president of the largest African American Baptist denomination — the National Baptist Convention.

The black church mounted little organized resistance to Booker T. Washington's accommodationist policies, which were articulated in this period. In essence, Washington was willing to concede that African Americans should continue to endure political inequality as long as they received an education and had opportunity to contribute economically to society. Granted, his agenda may have had some salubrious long-term effect on the black clergy, as he awakened in them the concern to address the everyday problems of the economic well-being of those they served. Yet Washington was disdainful of the clergy's outlook. On the whole, the turn of the century was not a period of great leadership on behalf of social justice by the churches influenced by American revivalism.

### Emergence of New African American Denominations

The development of a yet more virulent racism, even in the Church, marked the first part of the twentieth century. The new dynamics gave rise to the creation of several additional predominantly African American denominations. During Reconstruction, independent African American Baptist churches in the North and South had begun to collaborate. It was a period of great revival among the liberated slaves, which was facilitated by Northern Baptist work in the South. The number of black Baptists swelled.

However, a combination of heightened race consciousness, of the desire for segregation among white Southern Baptists, and of the paternalism of the Northern Convention working in the South facilitated the desire for an independent black Baptist denomination.[13] Another fascinating factor in this dynamic was Reconstruction political dynamics. Black congregations could be used to strengthen the Republican Party (helping to organize the African American vote) to the benefit of the freedmen and the detriment of southern whites, who would surely not support the use of these churches for such purposes.

To be sure, there were strong sentiments among nineteenth-century black Baptists for continuing cooperation with the Northern Baptist Convention. The reticence about secession manifests itself to this day insofar as many African American Baptists are found in the membership of both the Northern and Southern Baptist Conventions. Nevertheless, in 1895, the majority of African American Baptists already grouped into three distinct predominantly black Baptist associations merged to form the National Baptist Convention, U.S.A.

Twenty years after the formation of the united convention, a controversy on how to control the convention's property and publishing house divided the new body. At the time, R. H. Boyd administered the publishing house. Relying on his personal credit, he was its main developer. When the convention claimed ownership, and Boyd won the legal skirmishes, a division was inevitable. The publishing house and Boyd's supporters became the nucleus of a new convention, which remained unincorporated, that took the name National Baptist Convention of America. To this day, it is the second largest predominantly African American Baptist body. The National Baptist Convention, U.S.A., lost the court case for ownership of the publishing house because it had hitherto been unincorporated. It responded by becoming incorporated and is often identified as the "Incorporated Body."[14]

*Christian Methodist Episcopal Church.* Related efforts by southern white Protestants to segregate from African American members during and immediately after the era of Reconstruction are evident in the Methodist Episcopal Church, South. It "released" its African American members in 1866 so that they could form the Colored Methodist Episcopal Church, which is today called the "Christian Methodist Episcopal Church" (C.M.E.). In the same year, the Northern Methodist Church, whose ranks of African American members markedly increased imme-

---

13. The outreach to the freed slaves by denominations based in the North was quite typical in the Reconstruction and post-Reconstruction decades, explaining why many African Americans in the South joined the Northern Presbyterian churches and the (Northern) Methodist Episcopal Church. The same dynamic with regard to Lutheranism occurred.

14. In 1988, however, the newer convention lost members as a result of another controversy over ownership of the publishing house. In this controversy, the Boyd family and its supporters seceded, creating the National Missionary Baptist Convention.

diately after the Civil War, made provision to create a separate Negro conference.

Although black initiative for independence played a crucial role, there is great ambiguity about the degree to which the creation of this and other independent African American denominations in this era was merely a matter of African American choice. White segregationist desires to rid their churches of African American membership may also have contributed to the formation of these new church bodies. Lucius Holsey, born a slave of mixed parentage, was a major force in the new Methodist denomination. A former school teacher and forceful personality, Holsey was one of its founders. He wrote most of the denomination's founding documents and became a bishop. Holsey himself noted opposition to a separation from the larger Southern Methodist body, some even voiced by African American church leaders (*Autobiography, Sermons, Addresses and Essays*). Although they were not the majority of white members of the Southern Methodist Church, a number of vocal whites wanted to dispense with black membership since the breakup of slavery no longer made the "inconvenience" of black membership necessary. In that sense it seems fair to speak of the "push-pull" dynamic (the push by white racists and the pull by African American leaders) in the creation of the new denomination.

The Southern Methodist Church did place some restrictions on the new denomination, giving the C.M.E. ownership of certain properties on the condition that it not become engaged in political activity of any sort. This was aimed at keeping the new denomination somewhat in the orbit of the parent church and free of the African movement. Holsey's remarks unwittingly reflected this agenda as he spoke of the "fatherly directorship" of the Methodist Episcopal Church, South, over his own denomination.

The strategy of discretion adopted by the C.M.E. became even more solidified as Ku Klux Klan terrorism intensified in the South in subsequent years. Given the circumstances of its origin and because it lacked the tradition of abolitionist involvement of the older African American Methodist churches, the C.M.E. from the time of its early development bore the stigma of ultraconservatism and political inconsequence. More recently the church has demonstrated an increasing sense of social concern. From its inception, it has always been concerned about the education of African American people. Another appealing aspect of its heritage, in light of the current interest in interpreting African American Christianity as a movement that permitted its members essentially to maintain their African spirituality, is its endorsement of certain themes characteristic of African spirituality. Holsey, at least, insisted that all people, particularly "the colored man," have a religious sensibility that their culture presumably nurtures (*Autobiography, Sermons, Addresses and Essays*).

The heritage of the Christian Methodist Episcopal Church provides a distinct alternative to the approaches of the other major African American Methodist churches for the upbuilding of the African American peoples. In its origins, it has been a church of black Christians concerned not to cut all ties with white Christians. Is that strategy in the best interests of African American liberation? The Christian Methodist Episcopal Church at the end of the twentieth century remains the smallest of the three African American Methodist churches. Of late, it has been in some dialogue with the African Methodist Episcopal Zion Church about the possibility of merger.

*Alpha Synod.* Lutherans in North Carolina had been ministering to African American members since 1814 and in 1868 licensed a number of African Americans to serve congregations in the region.[15] Difficulties in funding the ministry were the North Carolina Lutheran Synod's official reason for the establishment of a separate African American synod, the Alpha Synod, in 1889. When it obtained no money, the new synod appealed to the theologically conservative Lutheran Church-Missouri Synod, which absorbed these African American Lutheran congregations, though with some stated, but never substantiated, reservations about the orthodoxy of their theology.

At the same time, the Missouri Synod was doing excellent work in providing education for the children of the freed slaves. Its leader in this missions work was Nils Bakke, a Norwegian American Lutheran. Booker T. Washington claimed that these Lutherans were doing more for African Americans than any other denomination, which accounts, with its absorption of the Alpha Synod, for why the Missouri Synod had the largest African American membership of Lutheran bodies prior to a schism in the 1970s. This had the long-term effect of bringing most African American Lutherans into the membership of the newly formed Evangelical Lutheran Church in America.

The period also saw the beginnings of African American migration to the cities. On the whole, the historic African American churches were not adequately prepared to deal with the new realities. One response to the new conditions was the development of storefront churches, which were sometimes little more than sects. This was also the period that marked the beginnings of the secularization of the African American community, a process that had begun much earlier in the white establishment.

---

15. A sister body, the Tennessee Synod, had been doing so since 1866.

*Pentecostal revival: Church of God in Christ [C.O.G.I.C].* In the same era, at the turn of the century, Pentecostalism emerged nationwide and in the African American community. This great modern outbreak of tongues had links to the Holiness movement. In a sense, the revivalist's version of the Holiness movement and its identification of entire sanctification with the baptism of the Holy Spirit established both the problematic for Pentecostalism and offered it the conceptual tools for addressing that problematic.

Consider the spiritual quandary of those who became the first leaders of the Pentecostal movement. These devout Holiness believers were yearning for the second work of grace, for entire sanctification. For them, it was to be a distinct event necessary to assure salvation. Yet they had not experienced it; they yearned for it.[16] The study of one such Holiness leader, the former Midwestern Methodist preacher Charles Parham (b. 1873), was crucial. He established Bethel Bible College in Topeka, Kansas, and in 1901 along with his students began to discern that the Bible offered tangible evidence for the comfort sought. They concluded that God gave concrete evidence of the baptism of the Holy Spirit (which their Holiness commitments taught them was associated with entire sanctification) through speaking in tongues. Several of them in turn received this experience. The first was reportedly a woman, Agnes Ozman. The Pentecostal revival had begun.

To be sure, Parham and his students had not been the first to speak in tongues. Outbreaks of glossolalia had been reported in the nineteenth century (and earlier, in the sixteenth century). A number of scholars believe that such outbursts were particularly prominent in the African American Christian community. However, it was only with Parham and his followers that such outbursts were interpreted as evidences of the baptism of the Holy Spirit.

These manifestations and the distinct new interpretation that they were given in turn offered these Holiness Christians the assurance that they were redeemed and sanctified. Having spoken in tongues, and so having evidence of receiving the third work of grace (the baptism of the Holy Spirit), the Christian in turn received assurance of being sanctified (of having received the second work of grace, following the first work, conversion), since God would clearly not have given the third apart from the second.

News of the revival in Topeka spread to one Holiness Christian, an African American, William J. Seymour. There are reports that he received some instruction from Parham at a school that had been opened

---

16. For a good example of such yearnings by early Pentecostal leaders, see Elsie Mason, *The Man, Charles Harrison Mason [1866–1961].*

in Houston (though there are certain indications suggesting that Parham practiced a kind of segregation that did not allow Seymour to sit in his classes.) In any case, Seymour did adopt Parham's views regarding speaking in tongues as a manifestation of the baptism of the Holy Spirit. Seymour was the principal leader of the famed Azusa Street revival (a great interracial, though African American led, outbreak of tongues) that began in Los Angeles in 1906. Parham had been invited to play an advisory role. At first he declined, and when he finally did participate, his role was largely marginalized, perhaps because he criticized what he perceived as extremes in the revival. Parham and Holiness theology may have provided Pentecostalism with an initial theological orientation, and the first visible stirring of the movement may have originated with him and his followers. However, it was the black-led Azusa Street revival that truly gave the new movement international exposure.[17]

One of the eventual leaders of the movement, Charles H. Mason, along with other African American colleagues. had founded a predecessor of the present-day Church of God in Christ (C.O.G.I.C.) in 1895/1906 as a Holiness body. Mason, yearning for assurance of his holiness, subsequently came to have the Pentecostal experience, even participating in the Azusa Mission. In 1907, he and those in agreement with him founded the C.O.G.I.C. denomination as a Pentecostal church body, while the non-Pentecostal faction seceded.[18]

The early Pentecostal movement was interracial in character and had significant black leadership. Pentecostalism, not just the American Holiness movement, appears to have roots in African American, if not African, spirituality. Indeed, African Americans, such as Seymour and Mason, mentored many of the first European American leaders of the early Pentecostal movement. In fact, Mason ordained several who eventually formed the Assemblies of God (the largest Pentecostal denomination in the world). The tragedy of the Pentecostal movement has been that it divided into racially segregated denominations, for it was truly an egalitarian movement in its origins. Not only was it interracial, largely black led, but it included women among its prominent leaders and was a movement largely of the uneducated and lower classes. With regard to women's leadership, note that one of the major Pentecostal denominations, the International Church of the Foursquare Gospel, was founded by a prominent and controversial woman evangelist, Aimee Semple McPherson (1890–1944). This egalitarian profile has largely di-

---

17. The first great European Pentecostal and founder of much European Pentecostalism, a Norwegian named T. B. Barratt (1862–1940), participated in the revival at Azusa Street.

18. C.O.G.I.C. is presently the largest predominantly African American Pentecostal body and has been the fastest-growing denomination in America.

minished in the ensuing years, as the Pentecostal movement became increasingly mainstreamed and institutionalized.

As the movement grew, segments of it began to distance itself from the original Holiness theological orientation. This was primarily a function of the increasing numbers of new Pentecostals early in the century who did not come from a Holiness background. Many of these did not regard sanctification, as the Holiness movement did, as a crisis experience (a distinct work of grace temporally distinguished from regeneration/justification). Rather, these new Pentecostals held a Reformed/Baptist view of sanctification understood as a process, initiated in justification. Consequently for them, the baptism of the Holy Spirit was a "second work of grace," not a "third work," as it was for the old-line Holiness Pentecostals.

To this day, the theological distinction between the relatively newer two-step Pentecostalism and the Holiness-oriented three-step Pentecostalism is still in place. Certain denominations, like the Church of God in Christ and the Church of God (Cleveland, Tennessee) maintain the three-step orientation, while the Assemblies of God churches are two-step in orientation. The two approaches distinguish themselves not just denominationally but also in terms of their piety. Three-step Pentecostalism continues to covet the baptism of the Holy Spirit and the experience of tongues as a necessary sign of the assurance of one's salvation.[19] Two-step Pentecostals do not need the baptism of the Holy Spirit to claim the assurance of salvation since that is guaranteed, as is sanctification, in justification. For them, baptism of the Holy Spirit is only an enrichment of what has already been given.

In the decades immediately following the Azusa Street revival, Pentecostalism lapsed into popular oblivion, except for its reputation among many as a movement of fanatics. After the decline of Fundamentalism at the end of the liberal-Fundamentalist controversy, Pentecostal churches, like the Fundamentalists, gradually flourished (behind the scenes) until publicly reappearing in new forms after the Second World War (notably at first with the emergence of the charismatic movement).

## The Liberal-Fundamentalist Controversy: End of the American Evangelical Era

Until the end of the nineteenth century, the inroads of modernism had not really hit America as they had earlier in Europe. When they did, it

---

19. In the practical piety of these churches, if one has not spoken in tongues, it may be that he or she has not been sanctified (experienced the second work of grace) and so is not saved.

became increasingly evident to the intellectual elite of American culture that the old assumptions of orthodox Protestantism that had governed so much of America's cultural suppositions since the colonial era were no longer unquestionably valid. And if these theological suppositions could be undermined, presumably America itself could no longer be so unambiguously regarded as a (Protestant) Christian nation. The cultural dynamics that led to the posing of these questions were most painfully appropriated. Their eventual permeation of American society truly put an end to the "Evangelical era" in America. No longer could Americans be so confident of and assume that their society was based on Protestant (Puritan) Christian principles.

Protestant liberal theology (see chap. 13 for details on it and the social-gospel movement, with which it is often associated) tried to deal with these new dynamics by translating the gospel into the categories of the modern worldview. A conservative reaction to these social dynamics and to liberalism's efforts to accommodate them as well as to the social-gospel movement's liberal social agenda developed in a loose amorphous movement called "Fundamentalism," which tried to retain the fundamentals of faith.

Fundamentalists gradually evolved five fundamentals of faith: (1) the inspiration and infallibility of the Bible, (2) the deity of Christ and his virgin birth, (3) the substitutionary atonement by Christ's death, (4) the Resurrection of Jesus as a literal truth, and (5) the second coming. There are at least some indications that these fundamentals were originally articulated at an 1895 Bible conference in Niagara Falls. Such theologically conservative Bible and prophetic conferences like the Niagara Conference, rooted in the revivalist movement, were theologically conservative, apocalyptic/millennialistic oriented, and dispensationalist. They were typically premillennialist in orientation, that is, believing that Christ must come again prior to the establishment of his thousand-year reign, which will be preceded by distressing times (Rev. 20; 2 Tim. 3:1). Many of the participants in these conferences had been strongly influenced by the Plymouth Brethren (a mid-nineteenth-century apocalyptic, separatist movement) and its prime theoretician John Nelson Darby (1800–1882), who taught dispensational premillennialism. Inasmuch as the Bible and prophetic conferences represented one of the two main constitutive streams of the emerging Fundamentalist movement, it is hardly surprising that much of the movement has exhibited a pronounced dispensational, premillennialist orientation.

The scenario of the movement's course is perhaps familiar. Originally it enjoyed great success. Besides its roots in the Bible and prophetic conferences, Fundamentalism also owes its existence to the coalition the participants in these conferences forged with prominent members of

American society, most notably the theological elite of the Presbyterian Church based at Princeton Theological Seminary. At Princeton, a sophisticated orthodox theological conservatism had been maintained. In the previous generation, Charles Hodge (1797–1878) had been the premier spokesperson for this theological school that eventually provided Fundamentalism's intellectual underpinnings.

*The Fundamentals*, a series of booklets written by eminent theologically conservative authors, distributed free to every rostered American clergyman by well-to-do supporters of the Fundamentalist cause between 1910 and 1915, created much attention for the movement. Another publishing event of great magnitude for the movement was the 1909 publication of the Scofield Reference Bible. Fundamentalists continue to endorse wholeheartedly and widely employ this dispensationalist-oriented commentary.

The media became increasingly impressed and favorable to the movement. Fundamentalist factions of several major denominations, notably the Northern Presbyterians, Northern Baptists, and the Christian Church (Disciples of Christ), briefly, or at least nearly, assumed complete control of these church bodies. When their efforts failed, the Fundamentalists left these churches to establish what became small denominations still in existence today, such as the Orthodox Presbyterian Church and the General Association of Regular Baptists.

These outcomes forever marked Fundamentalism in several ways. Henceforth, the movement was committed to a separatist orientation. No longer would bona fide Fundamentalists associate in a formal way with other Christians in "liberal" denominations. In addition, bereft of all viable hope of taking over the major denominations, Fundamentalists devoted attention to making their mark on American society through exerting influence on important social issues. In its general opposition to alcohol consumption, the movement had allies throughout American Christianity, and so by 1919 and during the 1920s, Prohibition became one of the ways that Fundamentalists and their allies sought to affect American society. However, the question of what to make of new scientific theories that seemed to call the authority of the Bible into question, specifically whether the theory of evolution should be taught in public schools, became the ultimate battleground for the Fundamentalist cause.

Efforts by Fundamentalists to legislate against the teaching of evolution succeeded in several states. Tennessee had passed such a law in 1925. The stage was set for the famed Scopes trial. Essentially John T. Scopes, a young biology teacher, challenged the law, receiving top-notch legal support. The state's expert witnesses included none other than the former presidential candidate William Jennings Bryan. A "media event," the trial received intense coverage. The very reputation and credibility of the Fundamentalist cause were on the line. Though the state won the case, Fundamentalists lost the media's image contest. They and their cause were portrayed by the press as uneducated, unsophisticated, and as southern "hicks." Many of the pejorative stereotypes commonly held by Americans of Fundamentalists have their origins in the Scopes trial.

The brutal press coverage of the trial spelled the end of Fundamentalism's popular support, at least in centers of American power and influence. With this negative image firmly fixed in the press and in the minds of most Americans, academia and the press soon lost interest in Fundamentalism — especially by the 1930s after the burnout of the antievolution crusade. After 1930, the media image began to become self-fulfilling. Fundamentalist support increasingly became restricted to those regions and persons farthest removed from the centers of power, like the rural South. The Fundamentalist retreat in the next decades into this new status as a "cognitive minority" had a salubrious outcome, for in these enclaves it significantly, though in a most unobtrusive way, began to thrive. Though Fundamentalism and its theological heir, the Evangelical movement, have a heavy concentration in the South, Fundamentalism was not originally an illiterate redneck movement. As already noted, the movement had some of its origins in Princeton Seminary and the intellectual leaders of Presbyterianism.

There was little African American, Pentecostal, Lutheran, and ethnic Reformed and free-church involvement in Fundamentalism and the ensuing controversy. The question is why. Besides sociological factors (members of these church traditions were not part of the intellectual and cultural elite that comprised large segments of early Fundamentalism), theological issues were also perhaps involved. Pentecostals were excluded simply on grounds of their allegedly "demonic" behavior and beliefs with regard to speaking in tongues. Interesting dynamics are identifiable in the other traditions that remained uninvolved with the movement. Enlightenment challenges to biblical authority were not a problem for churches in these "Bible-believing" traditions. They were so theologically conservative as not to be tempted, as were like liberals, to accede to modernist impulses. Consequently, the Fundamentalist theory of an infallible Scripture was simply not necessary in these Christian subcultures. Modernist challenges to biblical authority were not part of the agenda.

Of course, Fundamentalism did have a subtle impact on these traditions: many of their members (especially Pentecostal and free-church Christians) have subsequently identified with the concept of an inerrant Bible. This has typically led them to identify themselves as allies of the Fundamentalist heritage and its spiritual successor — the Evangelical movement — and even to adopt the conservative social agenda associated with much theologically conservative Christianity. Of course, these dynamics bring us to the threshold of the twentieth century's final decade. One can no longer cavalierly dismiss Fundamentalism and its theological/spiritual heirs as a misguided escape from the realities of modernity.

## New Religions

In the decades between the end of the Fundamentalist controversy and World War II, new religions emerged at the same time as one dynamic became typical of almost all of the religious traditions of American Protestantism. Various related, though distinct, denominations began to consolidate.

After the Civil War, Presbyterian Old School and New School factions in both the North and South began merging. The northern and southern branches of Methodism finally reunited in 1939. The Civil War had divided eastern Lutheranism on regional lines. Another division took place in the North right after the war; it was between German American Lutherans of the North who supported Samuel Schmucker's agenda to "Americanize" Lutheranism (by appropriation of more Pietistic/revivalist emphases) and a group of Lutherans especially committed to the heritage of the Lutheran confessions as interpreted through seventeenth-century Lutheran orthodox theology. This latter group formed the General Council. This General Council, the General Synod from which it seceded, and the General Synod, South (the southern synod that had seceded during the Civil War), united in 1918 as the United Lutheran Church. Of course, American Lutheranism was still a long way from fully uniting after these developments. It remained divided along ethnic, regional, and theological lines. However, after World War II, it and virtually all of American Protestantism were caught up in a spirit of unity, which brought about many additional and larger corporate denominational mergers.

Prior to these institutional developments and consolidations, several new religious movements developed. Unique to the American scene, these movements have exerted significant national, even international, influence.

**The Church of Jesus Christ of Latter-Day Saints (Mormons).** Joseph Smith (1805–44) was a poor, biblically literate, rural New York farmer and itinerant treasure hunter who was very troubled by the pluralism of American denominationalism. Believing that God had told him that none of the denominations' teachings were true, he claimed to have received a new revelation — ancient plates relating the lost history of the true church, writings very much in the style of the King James Version of the Bible, which became known as the Book of Mormon. The book tells the story of a lost tribe of Israel that emigrated to America, becoming progenitors of the American Indian. Smith's followers have interpreted it and other revelations given to him as a restoration of the keys to the Aaronic and Melchizedek priesthoods as well as to Temple work.

Gaining adherents for his new church, which he organized in 1830, Smith and his sect began practicing communal living. For these and other reasons, they predictably began experiencing tensions with neighbors. Settlement in Illinois did not ultimately alleviate the troubles. Eventually a mob martyred the prophet. Brigham Young (1801–77), a former Methodist from Vermont who had been in Smith's inner circle, assumed leadership. He organized an exodus, leading most of the community, save some prominent members of Smith's own family, to a more isolated, safer territory in Utah. The settlement soon became an autonomous state. In Utah, the Mormons began practicing polygamy and resisting U.S. government claims to the land. Gradually, Mormons allowed themselves to be shaped by the rest of the society — embracing statehood for Utah and leaving aside their earlier emphasis on visions and communal living. Since 1890, polygamy has no longer been an official practice. Nevertheless, their political and social influence in Utah remains undiminished, and the church has instituted successful foreign missionary work. It has become a truly universal faith. Meanwhile during the early stages of Utah's settlement, a smaller group of the original followers gravitated to the leadership of Smith's heirs and founded the Reorganized Church of Jesus Christ of Latter Day Saints.

*Jehovah's Witnesses.* In the 1870s, the Jehovah's Witnesses grew out of independent Bible studies in western Pennsylvania that were led by Charles Taze Russell (1852–1916), a haberdasher. Apocalyptic in orientation, Russell declared that the second coming had taken place in 1872 and that the end would come in 1914. It did not.

Following the death of Russell, Joseph F. Rutherford (1869–ca. 1942) inherited leadership of the movement, organizing it brilliantly and reinterpreting Russell's apparently incorrect speculations. It was he who named the movement in 1914 and organized it into the vast, highly disciplined missionary apparatus it has become. Among its distinct teachings are denials of the Trinity and of the divinity of Jesus. Witnesses believe that Jehovah has assigned Jesus a kingdom for which the faithful should pray and that through this kingdom Christ will cleanse the earth of all wickedness and rule in righteousness.

*Church of Christ Scientist.* The fundamental stated mission of the Church of Christ Scientist is "to reinstate the primitive Christianity and its lost element of healing." Mary Baker Eddy (1821–1910), a devout, though poor, twice-widowed, and sickly Congregationalist, founded it in Boston in 1879. The turning point for her and the movement she founded transpired after she experienced healing through the teachings of P. P. Quimby and came to codify his teachings. Eddy proved to be a brilliant administrator of the movement that emerged from her own teachings. Popularly known as Christian Science, the movement is really the embodiment on American soil of the ancient tradition of Gnosticism and of spiritualism.

Christian Science holds that the material world is either imaginary or evil and that the purpose of human life is to live in harmony with the Universal Spirit. Such knowledge is available through Scripture only when spiritually interpreted. Using many of the traditional Christian concepts, the church reinterprets them with special meanings. It teaches that illness is the result of mistaken perspective. To heal, one should make use of, not physicians or drugs, but rather the spiritual "science" (knowledge) that Jesus taught. Likewise, such science produces a (middle-class) happiness and prosperity.

Eddy carefully safeguarded against doctrinal deviation in the movement. Declaring that the second coming of Christ had taken place in the divine inspiration of her major writings, she banned preaching in the church and instead prescribed assigned readings from the Bible and her own writings. Although Eddy herself died in much pain, and with medical treatment, her movement continues to thrive.

*Father Divine and his Peace Mission movement.* The most widely publicized of all twentieth-century African American religious movements, Peace Mission was originated by George Baker (ca. 1878–1965), who was originally a Baptist minister in the South. A turning point came when he met an itinerant preacher, Samuel Morris, who claimed he was the Father Eternal. Baker joined the church established by Morris in the role of the Second Person. Eventually they split, but Baker with his charismatic personality began his own churches, first in the South, but most notably in 1919 with a storefront church in Brooklyn, then in Harlem, and finally in Philadelphia. As the ministry developed, he began claiming to be God Incarnate, the father representing, not a single race, but one worldwide family. Such teachings led to his identification as "Father Divine."

The cult grew successfully with an evangelism strategy that consisted of offering free bountiful chicken dinners. No doubt this helped attract many impoverished seekers, who soon affiliated with the movement. His message of racial harmony was also most attractive to both middle-class blacks and whites.

Among other distinctive teachings held by Baker and the movement are beliefs that heaven is now here on earth, that Holy Communion is to be celebrated at banquets with God (Father Divine) present, and that the age of the Church and of water baptism is complete. In addition, there were strong ethical imperatives for peace and racial harmony as well as a kind of Holiness ethic with strictures on smoking, gambling, drinking, and sexual lust. Since the founder's death, the movement has continued under the leadership of his youngest wife (he practiced polygamy), and the continuing faithful believe that he will return in bodily form.

*Elijah Muhammad and the Nation of Islam.* A black nationalist/separatist movement, the Lost-Found Nation of Islam was established in Detroit in 1930 by Wallace Fard (ca. 1877–1934), a student of Timothy Drew's (1866–1929). Teaching Islam to African Americans in the city, Drew proclaimed the message that Islam is a religion indigenous to Africa and so is a more appropriate faith commitment for African Americans than the Christian religion of the white man. One of Fard's earliest followers was Elijah Poole, who took the name Elijah Muhammad (1897–1975). He truly organized the movement, which did not actually emerge as we know it until contention among rival elements of Fard's followers arose following Fard's death.[20] Among Poole's distinct innovations, endorsed by the new movement, were the identification of himself as Prophet and the designation of Fard as Allah incarnate.

Because the Nation of Islam endorses or reinterprets Islamic categories, the movement does not properly belong in a study of church history. However, in view of the pointed critique that Black Muslims raise to Christianity it warrants our attention. The movement clearly departs from the universal thrust of Orthodox Islam. Consequently, it has been deemed heterodox within the Islamic community. The Black Muslim movement's most controversial doctrines, in addition to its teachings of Allah's incarnation and new prophetic revelations through Elijah Muhammad, relate to its philosophy of black separatism. Among these include the doctrines that Allah is black, his people are black, and Caucasians are inferior children of the devil. Therefore, all blacks are really Moslem, and Allah dwells in each one. Christianity, by contrast, is the white man's religion, used to strip the black man of self-respect. Its rhetoric of love and peace commanded by its "white" God is simply a way of keeping the black man in his place. The hope of Islam is that Allah will put an end to the present Caucasian civilization, replacing it instead with the redemption of the black nation and its glorious rule over all the earth. Coupled with these teachings from almost the outset of the movement has been a very critical, somewhat anti-Semitic perspective towards Judaism.

---

20. Late in his life Elijah Muhammad engaged in some controversies with one of his most prominent followers, Malcolm X (1925–65). See chap. 15 for more on the life of Malcolm X and the events that have transpired since his assassination.

The movement's embracing of many of Orthodox Islam's strict life-style expectations and its emphasis on responsibility have clearly been of constructive appeal in the African American community. They tend to nurture a more positive sense of self-respect, especially among those who have known little more than systematic degradation. The importance of the Black Muslim movement in our present context makes it inadvisable for students of American religion to neglect its history.

## Summary: The Puritan Paradigm, Confessional Identity, or Ecumenism?

Consider the degree to which your own denomination is in line with or reflects the Puritan paradigm. If it is in line, is that development a good thing or a departure from your tradition? If an American reader concludes that his or her denomination does not reflect the Puritan paradigm and is really at odds with the establishment vision of religion in the nation, is that a plus or a minus for evangelism? Are those traditions, like my own Lutheran heritage for example, that historically have not shared core Puritan suppositions and so have appeared to be somehow outside the American mainstream, better served by trying to indigenize or "Americanize"?[21]

What are the implications of these theological judgments for ecumenism? Is an emphasis on confessional identity (denominational consciousness) a barrier to ecumenism? Implicit in the American Puritan paradigm is a proposal that the American Puritan combination of Reformed orthodoxy and Pietism is the best model for bringing the diversity of Christianity together. Correspondingly it could be argued, especially in light of the impact of missionary work on the formation of international ecumenism, that something like the American model of an overall Reformed-Pietist perspective provides the most promising framework for ecumenism. In contrast, the continuing existence of some traditions, such as the Lutheran, Roman Catholic, and historic African American churches, that continue stubbornly to stand outside of the prevailing paradigm of American religion suggests an alternative model for ecumenism. The continuing existence of these traditions in America's ecumenical religious ethos supports the argument that a strong confessional identity that does not understand its distinct commitments as mandating division from other churches best serves ecumenism in both

---

21. Of course, the way to "Americanize" is for these traditions to shed some of their unique characteristics in favor of practice and theology more in accord with Puritan themes.

the American and global contexts. What is the validity of both models for ecumenism? The character of religion in America poses pressing questions for denominational identity. What does it means for readers to be members of their own particular churches?

# CHAPTER 12

# INTERNATIONAL POLITICAL AND ECONOMIC DEVELOPMENTS IN THE EIGHTEENTH AND NINETEENTH CENTURIES

Developments parallel to those in the United States took place internationally in the period from the end of the colonial era to the beginning of the twentieth century. The new currents fall within the scope of five broad events or developments: (1) the secularization of Europe and the rise of the new nationalism, (2) colonial ventures by France in the Americas, (3) the economic manipulation of the Catholic Church in South and Central America, (4) colonial expansion and missionary outreach, and (5) the rise of the ecumenical movement.

## The Secularization of Europe and the Rise of the New Nationalism

The emerging secular thought embodied in the increasingly secular European state since the time of French Revolution (1789–95) has no doubt contributed to the decline of church life in Europe. In its earliest stages, the Revolution in France had included efforts to reform the Church from clerical abuses perpetrated by many clergy with aristocratic backgrounds. At the turn of the decade into the 1790s, there were some in the French National Constituent Assembly (the kingdom's representative legislative body) who hoped to see the Church disappear, as it was in their view merely a remainder of superstitious times now past and should therefore be destroyed. As the Revolution became more extreme, eventually their number and influence came to dominate.

Even at the early stage of the Revolution, the reform policies were harmful for the Church. In essence, the National Assembly had dictated to the Church without consulting the Church. After some ecclesiastical and royal resistance, the assembly decreed that all who held ecclesiastical office must swear allegiance to the "Civil Constitution of the Clergy," which it had established. Those who refused assent to this document of the assembly prescribing certain ecclesiastical reforms would be deposed. The outcome was that the Church became divided. Those who swore such allegiance continued to receive the support of the state. Those who did not could only continue in ministry with the support of their followers in a sort of "free-church" arrangement.

The final stages of the Revolution and the execution of King Louis XVI in 1793 also had significant implications for the Church. It resulted in a state officially hostile to Christianity. Believing that they were harbingers of a new age, revolutionary leaders in France created the cult of reason and proceeded to persecute the Church. Christian clergy, both Catholic and Protestant, were put to death if they refused to practice idolatry before the altars of freedom of the new cult.[1]

Military conquests by the French of Switzerland, Italy, and the Netherlands further extended these policies. In 1798, the French even captured Pope Pius VI (1717–99) in retaliation for his resistance to the various policies of the Revolution regarding the Church. When Napoléon Bonaparte (1769–1821) came to power in 1799, he toned down the persecution, for he became convinced that the best policy politically was to seek reconciliation with the Church. He decreed religious freedom for Protestants and also gave the pope more authority over French ecclesiastical affairs, though in such a way that ecclesiastical appointments would not be detrimental to French interests. In essence, Napoléon had ceded the papacy such authority that the old "Gallican liberties" precluding papal intervention in the affairs of the French Church were compromised. This concordat did not long last, as the pope was again made a French prisoner.

After Napoléon's defeat, most of the European monarchies that he had conquered were restored. Germany and Italy proceeded to construct a national unity. After some of the leaders of the Italian nationalist movement had unsuccessfully sought to convince the powerful pope Pius IX (1792–1878) to function as leader of the movement, the newly formed kingdom of Italy even offered the pope certain territory, including the Vatican, over which he could rule as papal states, after taking all of Rome from him. The offer was made in 1870, but subsequent popes, determined not to become a vassal of Italian government, refused to accept the offer until the Fascist ruler Benito Mussolini (1883–

---

1. Generally speaking, French Protestants more readily capitulated to these pressures than Catholics.

1945) prevailed on Pope Pius XI (Achille Ambrogio Damiano Ratti; 1857–1939) to do so in 1929.

### Revivals in European Protestantism

A combination of the increased impact of rationalism and the industrial revolution coupled with laissez-faire governmental economic policies had increasingly deleterious effects on the Protestant churches of western Europe. These dynamics did not just pose a direct challenge to the spirituality of the Church and the faith commitments of its members. As the century wore on, they created social dislocations and poverty with which the Church would need to deal.[2] These developments effectively marginalized the churches of Europe. As they had increasingly less impact on the cultures of western Europe, these cultures in turn became more secularized. These developments had at least one other direct impact on western European Protestantism. They stimulated the same sort of response by reformers that had characterized the seventeenth and eighteenth centuries; that is, Pietism truly took root in some nations and moved in new directions in others.

The nineteenth century was the first period of the emergence of free churches (unsupported by government funds). Largely Pietist in orientation, they were often comprised of Lutherans or Reformed Christians seceding from the state church in their land. One particularly notable example is a Pietist-inspired secession that plagued the State Reformed Church in the Netherlands. Its impact was greatly enhanced by a revival that originated within the state church, one occasioned in large part by the emergence of a theological movement called "Neo-Calvinism" (see below, pp. 285–86, for details).

Some Methodist and Baptist growth on the continent occurred with this dynamic of pietistically inspired revivals culminating in the creation of free churches. In Sweden, the formation of bodies today associated with the Conservative Evangelical movement — the Evangelical Free Church and the Swedish Mission Covenant Church (whose American sister church is incorporated as the Evangelical Covenant Church) — emerged. Most European free churches continue to this day to maintain such a theologically conservative profile.

Most of these churches did not exhibit the sort of social concern that typified the early Pietists and many nineteenth-century Pietists. Their focus on individual piety is most suggestive of the sort of later revivalism that had its origins in America in the nineteenth century with Dwight Moody and others. It is reasonable to assume that there was

---

2. See chap. 13 for more details on the precise nature of these dislocations.

some early American influence on these European ecclesiastical movements and that the influence clearly continues on these free churches
and related movements to this day.

With regard to Sweden and Finland, the nineteenth century was the
first time that the Pietist movement really became fully indigenized there.
In Finland, the movement was somewhat fractured into three distinct
revival currents, each in competition with the other, which somewhat
diluted Pietism's impact on the Church. This dynamic along with the
increased impact of rationalism on the upper class did have the effect
in Finland as in other Scandinavian nations of rendering its national
church more dependent on the peasant population.

In Sweden, although there had been earlier theological protests
against the encroachments of rationalism in the life of the church,
Pietism became fully indigenized in the nineteenth century largely
through the work of its greatest revivalist, the lay preacher Carl Olof
Rosenius (1816–68). Much like other Pietists in this era and earlier, he
remained loyal to the state church. More of a theologian than his earlier
Norwegian counterpart Hans Nielsen Hauge, Rosenius did emphasize
the role of the law in shaping the way a Christian is to live (third use
of the law) and did not emphasize the sacraments. Since he relied on a
portrait of justification as purely forensic in character, that is, having no
impact on sanctification, his emphasis on sanctification logically follows.
However, much more like orthodox theologians than the earlier Pietists,
he stressed the assurance that Christ's sacrificial work (a satisfaction
theory of the atonement) provided without regard to our experience of
it (*Faithful Guide to Peace with God*). This strong Lutheran doctrinal
emphasis continued to characterize Swedish Pietism and Swedish Lutheran piety in general. Rosenius's influence extended beyond Sweden
into parts of Norway. In the 1850s Rosenius established a domestic
mission organization within the state church that paralleled a similar
organization established by Danish Lutheran Pietists, the Inner Mission
movement. These organizations typify the Pietist movement's work in
the nineteenth century, as it inspired the formation of missionary societies and domestic missions to encourage both local evangelism and to
deal with social ills. Women played a leading role in these developments,
often, but not exclusively, through the formation of deaconess societies,
wherein they functioned with a status not unlike "Protestant nuns."

## The Oxford Movement

In Great Britain, the socioeconomic turmoil of the new era led to turmoil
in the Church of England, whose practice and piety were falling on hard
times. Two distinct reform-oriented parties formed that compete with

each other for the soul of the Anglican Church to this day. One group, the Evangelicals, were largely Pietist-influenced Anglicans, who were also influenced as Wesley was by some of the Puritan piety that had not been totally eradicated. They sought to stress the Church of England's alignment with Protestantism and have these commitments reflected in the life of the church. Along with Methodists, Quakers, Reformed Congregationalists, and Baptists, they attempted to address the social ills of the time created by the industrial revolution (see chap. 13). Together they formed a coalition that succeeded in freeing the slaves in the British Commonwealth by 1833. One of the chief movers in this development was the Anglican Evangelical William Wilberforce (1759–1833).

The other distinct party within the Church of England that began to form in this period emerged from the Oxford Movement. Led by John Henry Newman (1801–90) and John Keble (1792–1866), it sought to emphasize the Catholic elements of the Anglican heritage, such as its maintenance of apostolic succession and the central role for the Eucharist. Its aim was to renew the devotional and liturgical life of the church and its teaching office as well as to upgrade the authority of tradition. Its proponents have come to be known as Anglo-Catholics.[3]

## French Colonial Ventures in the Americas

The French initiated colonial ventures in the New World in the same period as the British (see chap. 11). The first permanent settlement in Canada was made in Quebec in 1608. The colony of Louisiana was established in 1699 but was ceded to Spain in 1762.

The Jesuits initiated missionary work among Native Americans in present-day Maine in 1680 (after Capuchin missionaries had begun their missions in 1632). More so than in the earlier established Spanish colonies, Jesuits shaped the ethos of New France. A fervent piety combined with a passionate desire to Christianize Canada's Indians was plainly evident in the first churches. There are indications that the missionaries sought to live with the Indians and learn their language. Love for the kindness of the Indians while realistically assessing their primitive lifestyle was reflected in the life and writings of one of the great missionaries, Jean de Brébeuf (1593–1649). The sincere efforts did not achieve great success, due to the hostility of the Indians to evangelistic efforts and the resistance of the English and the Dutch to French and Catholic expansion.

---

3. A fuller analysis of their theological commitments follows in the next chapter.

In the late seventeenth century with the appointment of a bishop to the region, ecclesiastical power and influence were gradually transferred away from the Jesuits, and the missionary mandate was given to the episcopacy and ecclesiastical institutions. What followed was an unmistakable waning of religious fervor in the colony and support for missions from the French motherland. Interest in certain Native American tribes was now more and more politically motivated, as the Indians effectively functioned as a buffer zone between the French and the growing British Empire.

The tensions between French colonization and the English colonial enterprise had implications for the Catholic Church in New France. It effectively solidified French Canadian loyalty to the Catholic Church, particularly after the French and Indian War and the ceding of all of Canada by the French to the British in 1763. Such loyalty came to be equated with a determination to preserve French Canadian cultural integrity against the politically dominant British. The dynamics of contemporary Quebec nationalism are closely tied to these developments.

The lasting impact of New France on religious life in the Americas has been slight. The only real legacy, save in Quebec and in Haiti among the ancestors of former slaves whose forebears were evangelized (while not totally eradicating certain vestiges of their indigenous African spirituality), has been in the region of New Orleans and along the Louisiana bayou where Cajun culture has not been totally eradicated. The rich legacy of outreach to the Native American community did not survive.

Like the French in the Atlantic colonies of Canada, the British had very few settlers in Canada, even after their conquest of the whole region. After conquering the Atlantic colonies in 1713, it had been a simple matter of Anglicizing them and their religious life. English-speaking Protestants from New England were encouraged to immigrate. The Church of England (today the Anglican Church of Canada) in these provinces dates from 1700. Quebec and the bulk of Canada presented a different problem. Catholics vastly outnumbered Protestants. There seemed to be no choice but to make as little change in the life and structures of Canada as possible. This included granting freedom of religion to the Catholics (as well as to non-Anglican Protestants), which was not characteristic of British law at home or in the colonies in this era. Such religious toleration was a landmark in North American religious history.

The religious ethos changed somewhat as a result of the American Revolution. Nearly forty thousand British loyalists — all of them Protestant and largely members of the Church of England — relocated in Canada. Most settled in the Atlantic provinces; the rest, in the southwestern region of Quebec. Quebec was then divided, with the predominantly Protestant section becoming Ontario. With its newfound strength and sense that a hierarchical society could best thwart anti-British sentiments, the Church of England in Canada became unquestionably the established church in English-speaking environs. This development spelled the end to the ethos of religious toleration. As a result, other Protestant bodies were drawn more closely together in a kind of sectarian consciousness.

Religious life in Ontario and in the western provinces has largely paralleled that of America insofar as some of the key movements, such as revivalism, reactions to urbanization, liberal theology, and Fundamentalism, emerged in Canada. Many of the Protestant denominations of Canada have their origins in missions of American denominations. There has been, however, a significant difference in the Canadian ethos. Perhaps because Protestantism had its origins in Canada as a countercultural movement to the French Catholics, there has been historically less rivalry and more a sense of unity among the various Protestant denominations in Canada than in the United States.

The unity has been particularly true among those Protestant bodies that most thoroughly indigenized, broke ties with the "Old World" or with their American parenting bodies. The Anglican Church of Canada, maintaining its ties to English leadership, and the various Lutheran churches that have continued to be linked to their founding American bodies are two notable exceptions. The unifying dynamics seem to account for why so many Protestant denominations, save the Anglican Church and the Lutheran bodies, merged into a united church, the United Church of Canada, in 1925. It was the first of the union churches, transcending Protestant denominationalism, that have been so characteristic in the second half of the century, especially in the Southern Hemisphere.

## Economic Manipulation of the Catholic Church in South and Central America

The key to understanding Latin America and its church is the relation between recent European immigrants (the *peninsulares*), descendants of early immigrants to the region (the *crillos*), its indigenous peoples, and the impoverished heirs of former slaves. The wealthy longtime immigrants resented the European powers' tendency to place recent immigrants in positions of civic and ecclesiastical power. Their discontent led to revolutions. Real power largely remained in the hands of the *crillos*, to the neglect and detriment of the masses.

In order to retain both political and economic control over their colonies, colonial rulers insisted on appointing their own countrymen as bishops. Longtime residents have rarely been able to go beyond the ranks of local clergy. Even after colonialism ended, the papacy could not easily get the Spanish government to waive authority over episcopal appointments. The whole affair has caused cynicism among the Latin American elite. It has also led to perennial tensions between the episcopacy and the local priesthood. As a result of these dynamics, calls for the creation of a national church or outright anti-Catholicism have been frequently expressed. Although some clergy descended from the longtime immigrants did play a role in the independence movements in Mexico, Argentina, and Central America, after the establishment of independent nations in the nineteenth and early twentieth centuries, one of the first acts of the new governments, such as in Mexico, Colombia, and Argentina, was to establish the separation of church and state, even confiscating and secularizing church properties, as the Catholic Church continued to be perceived as the advocate of the old colonial order. The process was wrenching for the church.

The influx of many European and Chinese immigrants to increase the labor force in the second half of the nineteenth century has made the situation even more complex. Since many of these immigrants have been Protestant, Protestantism gained religious freedom in the new nations. The immigration also created a large glut of Catholics for whom the Catholic Church has never been able to provide adequate ministry. The Catholic hierarchy did not respond well to the new situation, becoming progressively more reactionary in its attitudes and practice, often aligning itself with the interests of the wealthy and their repressive governments, and thereby further alienating the Catholic Church from the masses. Even when the Catholic Church began to concern itself in the 1950s with Latin American economic development, its agenda tended to be governed by the interests of the bourgeoisie and their North American allies. These dynamics have made the field ripe for Protestant missionary efforts in the late twentieth century. In this light, the recent phenomenal success of Protestantism in Latin America is more readily understood.

## Colonial Expansion and Missionary Outreach

The nineteenth century was a period of geographic expansion in colonial ventures, not unlike what transpired in the sixteenth century. This time the colonial ventures were undertaken by Protestant nations, not by those that were predominantly Catholic. As a result, the nineteenth century was an era during which the Protestant Church truly became universal. As earlier explorations did, the whole endeavor took place in the context of economic imperialism, which left its mark on the Church. The new Protestant nations needed new markets, and longtime residents of Latin America as well as the people of Asia and Africa welcomed investment.

In Latin America, the consequences of these developments led to the emergence of a neocolonialism in newly independent lands. Britain, France, and the United States competed for the new markets. The new investments of these powers in fact increased the wealth of the already wealthy families of longtime immigrants at the expense of almost everybody else. In Asia, the capitalist ventures were enhanced by conquest and eventual colonization. China and Japan, though never fully conquered, were forced to open trade to the West. Colonization also increased markedly in Africa as a result of these economic dynamics. The impact of such colonizing efforts both in Africa and other regions was similar. Though increasing wealth in many areas, it led to great social dislocation and the destruction of cultural patterns. By the mid-twentieth century an anticolonial reaction set in.

The missionary enterprise of the nineteenth century was ambiguously related to colonialism, sometimes reaching beyond regions never colonized. Though undertaken without state backing, the enterprise was supported by the public at large through voluntary missionary societies like the Particular Baptist Society for Propagating the Gospel and the London Missionary Society. Women played and still play a significant role in connection with these missionary societies, not just in raising funds but in exercising pastoral roles. Concern to reach out to enlightened heathen extended to the African American Christian community (Elias Morris *1899 Presidential Address to the National Baptist Convention*). In general, though there were some notable exceptions, both Protestant and Catholic missionaries of the era tended to identify Christianity with Western culture, so that conversion to the gospel also entailed renouncing the mores and values of the converts' culture.

One of the low points in the nineteenth-century enterprise was Roman Catholic missionary efforts to bring African Orthodox Christians and others in the Near East into obedience to the pope. The creation of small Eastern-rite (Uniat) Catholic churches that retained the language, ancient liturgies, and church law indigenous to their homeland was the result of these evangelism endeavors. Protestants sought merely to cooperate with the ancient Orthodox churches in these regions. The net result, though, was that a number of progressives in these churches become Protestant. In nineteenth-century missionary work, a general pattern emerged: Catholics gained more adherents in colonies established by predominantly Catholic nations, and Protestants were more successful in British and German territories.

## The Church in the Orient and the Pacific

*India.* The Church has existed in India since perhaps as early as the fourth century, with the planting of *Malabar Christianity* (an early Christian community, certainly established by the seventh century in India by Nestorian Christians of the Assyrian Church, but claiming to have been established by Saint Thomas in the first century). At least until the late sixteenth century, the Malabars maintained the *Nestorian* position (a heresy rooted in the early Church — condemned by the Council of Ephesus in 431 — that so stressed the distinction of Christ's two natures as to claim that he was comprised of two persons, as a marriage is composed of a husband and a wife). The Malabar Christians renounced this position in 1599 at the Synod of Diamper. Subsequently about two-thirds joined the Roman Catholic Church as an Eastern-rite church and the remainder associated with the Syrian Orthodox Church — one of the ancient churches still in existence that is said to hold a *Monophysite Christology* (an ancient heresy condemned by the Council of Chalcedon in 451). The Syrian Church and its sister churches — the Coptic Church, the Ethiopian Orthodox Church, and the Armenian Apostolic Church — have been identified with this heresy. While not denying that Christ was originally composed of two natures, they have, like the ancient Monophysite/Eutychian teachings, maintained that Christ only had one nature. Nineteenth-century Protestant missions, especially the Church Missionary Society (an Anglican Evangelical mission), influenced the Syrian Orthodox Church in India. They inspired a significant number of reformers within the church to withdraw and form a Protestant Mar Thoma Church.

The Portuguese were the first to bring Western Christianity to India in 1498. In this period, the Jesuits were engaged in creative evangelistic efforts. Indigenous leadership was installed as early as 1637, but it was not until 1886 that Pope Leo XIII (1810–1903) regularized the policy. Protestant missionary work began in 1660 when the English and the Dutch established settlements; however, no outreach to the indigenous people was undertaken until 1706 when King Frederick IV of Denmark founded a mission in his territory in South India.

The real turning point — in many ways the birth of the modern missionary movement — came with the founding in 1792 of the Particular Baptist Society for Propagating the Gospel amongst the Heathen by the British Baptist William Carey (1761–1834). The next year he landed in India. His influence was widespread back home, stimulating the creation of numerous other missionary societies. A talented linguist, he succeeded in translating the Bible into many of the local dialects. Although Carey himself did not enjoy great success in numbers of converts, his work planted a solid church.

Subsequent missionaries from other denominations emphasized education, which made a deep impact on the people.[4] As it had been in the Middle Ages, the Church was a most attractive alternative for those belonging to lower castes and to women, who were largely disenfranchised by the caste system. One of the most remarkable women converts was Pandita Ramabai (1858–1922). A Brahman orphan, she devoted her life to the education of women, especially of the lower castes.

Protestantism in India was clearly a religion of "liberation." Native Indians have been ordained in these churches since the mid-nineteenth century. Cooperation among the various Protestant churches was a way of life at least since 1855. An ecumenical body, the South India United Church, was formed in 1908. It was the earliest nondenominational union church. Similar movements have led to the establishment of other union churches later in the century, the largest being the Church of South India, which was formed in 1947 as a merger of the earlier body of Anglicans and Methodists. Roughly 3 percent of India's population and less than 1 percent of the Pakistani people have become Christian.

*Southeast Asia.* In Southeast Asia, the churches planted in the nineteenth and early twentieth centuries followed the colonial pattern. In French colonies (present-day Vietnam), the Catholic Church was organized in separate (exclusively Catholic) villages. In British territories (present-day Burma), Protestant missions were planted, and an indigenous leadership — notably, the ministry of Ko Tha Byu (d. 1840) — was successfully cultivated. In Siam (present-day Thailand), which retained its independence, both Protestant and Catholic missionaries planted churches. Although their work was hindered by some periods of persecutions, the missionaries succeeded in planting strong congregations.

*China.* As early as the Assyrian Nestorian outreach of the seventh century and later Catholic missions, China had been the site of missionary work, but Chinese suspicion of foreigners repeatedly threatened and on some occasions decimated these churches. The culturally sensitive missionary work of the Jesuit Matteo Ricci (see p. 127) had succeeded in founding a church, but it too was wiped out. The next opening for missions came in the nineteenth century. The Scotsman Robert Morrison (1782–1834), working under the auspices of the London Missionary Society, succeeded in preparing the first Chinese translation of the Bible.[5] Although Morrison did not succeed in gaining many converts, his work raised great hopes and proved to be of later incalculable significance.

---

4. Many of the leaders of the independence movement and the new nation in the next century were educated in schools established by the Church.

5. This missionary organization had been founded in 1795 with a largely congregationalist theological profile.

The Treaty of Nanking in 1842 between the British and the Chinese opened the Chinese mainland to foreigners and effectively protected Chinese Christians. In the new climate of religious toleration created by the treaty, a Christian rebellion (the Taiping Rebellion) that aimed to bring in the kingdom of God (in a movement not unlike that of the sixteenth-century revolutionary Anabaptists) was initiated and eventually crushed.

In 1865, the British medical missionary J. Hudson Taylor (1832–1905) founded the China Inland Mission (today called the "Overseas Missionary Fellowship"). The organization emerged from a Holiness revival in England called the "Keswick movement" (a theologically conservative endeavor to reemphasize the Methodist concern with sanctification and the "empowering" work of the Spirit, without necessary reference to perfection as a goal for which to strive). It functioned as a faith mission (with each missionary required to raise his or her own funding). It was interdenominational — committed to evangelizing China without introducing it to European and American denominationalism. Another commitment of the organization was to the missionaries' identifying with the host culture, dressing in indigenous ways.

The China Inland Mission had a great impact. It inspired the establishment of various other missionary societies, which worked in both Asia and Africa. In China itself, the society had marked success. In the final years of the nineteenth century, the Church in China endured harsh persecution as a result of antiforeign sentiments in a movement called the "Boxer Rebellion." However, by the time the Chinese Empire fell in 1911 and a republic took its place, the door was open to thousands of Protestant missionaries, and an indigenous leadership was established. Cooperation among Protestants was widely practiced, and in 1927 a Church of Christ in China (composed of Reformed, Congregationalist, Methodist, and Baptist churches) formed. The Communist takeover in 1949 marked the beginning of harsh persecution of the Church. However, it has emerged after the Cultural Revolution of the 1960s still thriving remarkably.

*Japan.* From the time of the Catholic Church's planting on the island in the sixteenth century through the work of the Spanish Jesuit Francis Xavier, Japan persecuted Christians. Miraculously a small remnant of this community seems to have survived, as Russian Orthodox and Protestant missionaries discovered after an 1864 agreement with the West put an end to Japanese strictures against foreign influence. Orthodox, Anglican, and American Presbyterian missions have been successfully planted. As in the case of China, smooth cooperation largely characterized missionary work.

*Korea.* The history of the Church in Korea (esp. today's South Korea) is especially interesting. Early in the history of Protestant missionary activity in the late nineteenth century, decisions were made that the founded churches be self-supporting and that indigenous leadership be encouraged. The creation of such indigenous churches may help account for the phenomenal growth of the Church in this region. Catholics had been present on a permanent basis in Korea since 1784, a century before the Protestant missionaries arrived. In 1866, Korean rulers' efforts to outlaw Christianity led to many martyrs. Under pressure from the United States, the land's rulers signed a treaty opening the way to foreign trade, which in turn enabled the arrival of American Methodist and Presbyterian missionaries. Eastern Orthodox churches, fully indigenized, have been established in Korea, as well as in Japan and other Far Eastern nations. They were planted in these nations largely by outreach of the Russian Orthodox Church.

Lucious Foote was the first of the Presbyterian missionaries, and he had a significant impact, which was no doubt related to the whole-hearted welcome he received from the Korean king. Horace N. Allen made an important contribution as a medical missionary. The Methodist mission in Korea was conducted by both the Northern and Southern Methodist churches. The churches they founded merged in 1930, nearly a decade before the American parent denominations managed such a union. As noted, the earliest American missionaries committed themselves to indigenizing the Church in Korea. The first native-born Korean presiding elder of the Southern Methodist Church in Korea prior to the merger, J. S. Ryang, had a notable effect on the ethos of Korean Methodism. He urged the church to assume a significant social concern, particularly to undertake a ministry to care for the poor. Other Korean Christians have assumed his spiritual mantel, more recently in working against the Communist regime in North Korea by means of criticism or economic activity.

The mission strategy in Korea has yielded resounding success. To this day, Korea has the highest percentage of Christians of any nation in the Far East except the Philippines. Presbyterianism has been particularly successful, both in terms of numbers (half of Korea's Christians are Presbyterian) and ecumenical impact, for many Methodist and Baptist churches have adopted a presbyterian polity. Some observers attribute the success of Presbyterianism in Korea to the convergence between this particular polity and Korean culture — a democratic culture coupled with a respect for elders.

The marked success of the Church in Korea and its commitment to indigenization suggests that the Korean mission strategy may be worth examination for its wider application. The Korean church teaches that missionary success in traditional cultures seems to depend on winning the trust of the royal court and encouraging the full participation of indigenous people in the mission. A no-less-noteworthy factor helps account for the mission's success: the American missionaries on the scene largely shared the indigenous culture's belief in spirits and (Confucian) importance of right conduct. When the traditions of the local culture are respected and incorporated into the Church's ministry, the Church is more than likely on the right track!

*The Philippines.* In the sixteenth century, the Philippines was colonized by the Spanish, and thereafter Catholicism was firmly established. During the struggle for independence in the nineteenth century, the Catholic Church was largely an instrument of the colonial government. Consequently there was a genuine openness to Protestant missionary work, though to this day Catholicism is still the largest religious body. Discontent with Catholicism's links to the colonial agenda did lead to discontent among some reformers. In 1902, they formed the Filipino Independent Church, which, though largely Catholic in its teachings, finally broke with the papacy. It is today the second largest Christian denomination in the Philippines.

*Indonesia.* The first exposure to Christianity came to Indonesia through Portuguese missionary work early in the 1500s. Used largely as a political weapon against Christian traders, Islam gained support among indigenous people. Matters improved for the Church somewhat after the Dutch gained control in the late eighteenth century. Under the auspices of the Dutch East India Company, there had been some Protestant control of the region in the previous century; however, missions were discouraged. Only in the nineteenth century were strong missionary efforts directed towards the indigenous population launched. The earliest missionaries were Portuguese Catholics.

On one of the Indonesian islands, Borneo, colonial rulers encouraged the immigration of Chinese, and although most were Confucian, many were Christians. To this day, Islam continues to dominate the religious life of the islands. Catholicism is still the largest Christian body, though great Protestant missionary success was achieved on the Batak plateau of the island of Sumatra. Batak Christianity has the world's most thriving churches, sending its own missionaries to surrounding islands.

*Australia and New Zealand.* Missionary work in Australia and New Zealand clearly followed the colonization of these islands by the British. In each case, the first church established among the immigrants was the Church of England. The immigrants and their diseases largely decimated Aboriginal and Maorist inhabitants of these regions. The churches, including Methodists and later-established Wesleyans, began to protest against such mistreatment. In both regions, the Church of England continued to be composed of the upper class. In New Zealand, independent churches like the Hau Hau and the Ringatu, which combined ancient Maori traditions with Christian teachings and a concern for justice and vindication, successfully emerged. In Africa, independent churches that weave together indigenous tradition and Christian teaching have likewise emerged as a most influential paradigm.

### The Emergence of Protestantism in South and Central America

Emerging discontent with the Catholic Church in Central and South America opened the door to the increasing impact of Protestantism on the region. As early as the seventeenth century, the French had planted small Protestant missions in Brazil, and the Dutch had done the same in the West Indies; however, the specifics of Protestant missions are almost exclusively nineteenth- and twentieth-century phenomena.

With independence for most of Latin America in the nineteenth and early twentieth centuries, the new governments encouraged immigration from European nations other than Spain. The purpose was both to enhance economic development and to introduce new ways of thinking that would erode Spanish ideas, which were still being propagated by the Catholic Church in their lands. Thus large numbers of Scots settled in Argentina, Uruguay, and Chile; the Presbyterian Church was thereby planted in these nations. A significant number of German Lutherans settled in Brazil. A group of over one hundred African American Episcopalians, led by James Theodore Holly, settled in Haiti after America's Civil War. Though few in the original party survived and remained in Haiti, the episode did lead finally to the founding of the Apostolic Orthodox Church of Haiti (now called the "Episcopal Church of Haiti").

Most early Protestant missions tended to neglect missionary outreach among Native Americans and African slaves in the Caribbean as well as in Central and South America, effectively accommodating to slavery. Moravian Brethren worked among the slaves in Suriname as early as 1735. The British and Foreign Bible Society established mission outreach at the dawn of the nineteenth century. In 1867, the Presbyterian Church was established in Chile. After that time, a number of missionary agencies in the United States began taking an active interest in South and Central America.

One reason for hesitation and delay among Protestants in reaching out to Latin America had to do with hesitancy about undertaking missionary work in a region already heavily Roman Catholic. Concern was expressed that missionary work in such a context would effectively deny the Christianity of Roman Catholicism. By the beginning of the twentieth century, Protestant missions were in full stride in Latin America. These missions wisely concerned themselves not just with conversion but also with the physical well-being and education of the citizens.

Protestants soon became known for their work in education and medicine. Given the identification of the Roman Catholic Church in the region with the elite, such Protestant ministries have had great resonance with the masses. In addition, the Protestant call for recognition in a predominantly Catholic context has necessitated advocacy of religious toleration, which suggested to its critics and subsequent allies a kind of post-Enlightenment liberalism. As a result of these dynamics and perceptions, from the early eighteenth century on, the perception that Protestantism was a threat to the established order was common among much of the elite in colonial Latin America as well as in the largely authoritarian republics that emerged from nineteenth-century independence movements. In fact, Protestants played leadership roles in several early-twentieth-century democratic revolutions in the region, notably in Brazil and Mexico.[6]

Another dynamic to consider in the success of Protestant missions in Latin America since the nineteenth century is the growing prestige of the United States. Consequently missionaries associated with large U.S. denominations have had increasing success. More recently, though, churches associated with the conservative Evangelical movement (esp. Pentecostalism) have experienced notable growth. With these developments, the tendency of much earlier Latin American Protestantism to align itself with revolutionary causes has been somewhat domesticated by assimilating itself to the authoritarianism that still characterizes most Latin American nations. In any case, South and Central America is in transition from a region that was once virtually entirely Catholic to a group of nations in which up to one-third of the citizens are Protestant.

## The Church in the Caribbean

Different colonial patterns have produced a rich diversity of Christian experience in the Caribbean, and yet a number of commonalities emerge. On islands colonized by Spain and France beginning in the sixteenth century, notably Cuba, Puerto Rico, the Dominicans, and Haiti, Roman Catholicism has dominated. Its original mission on these islands was closely linked to the use of civil power to dominate the indigenous people, which is not a formula designed to nurture strong and orthodox

---

6. Fidel Castro's 1959 Cuban Revolution even had Protestant support until he declared it to be a Marxist revolution.

piety. As we have already noted in the case of Haiti, Protestantism was only planted on these islands when the colonial dominance of Spain, Portugal, and France ebbed.

On islands colonized by Protestant powers, notably Bermuda, Jamaica, and the Bahamas, the dominant church of the colonial power emerged. Thus the Anglican Church has been planted in Bermuda since 1619, functioning as a kind of state church there and in the Bahamas much as it did in the colonial era in Virginia. As in Catholic colonies in the region, the church was in its origins a church for the European colonizers, not for indigenous people.

Similar attitudes towards slavery characterized both Catholic and Protestant colonies during the first centuries of its introduction (1505 until the late eighteenth century). As in North America, the European colonizers in the region were initially ambivalent about seeking to convert the slaves. More openness to evangelization of people of African descent began developing in the mid-nineteenth century as many of the colonies became independent. However, Christianizing slaves and those liberated became a means of "civilizing" them in the eyes of European church members. It should come as no surprise, then, that new Christians of African descent in the region did not unambiguously appropriate their new faith but retained many vestiges of their indigenous African beliefs. This may be a factor, in tandem with the lack of a "melting-pot" cultural ethos in the Caribbean, that helps explain why people of African descent on these islands are often more in touch with African customs than their American counterparts.

Given these dynamics it is hardly surprising that the Church in the Caribbean was not an early advocate of independence and not in the forefront of criticizing subsequent American economic dominance in the region and American-supported dictators. Of course, some of the first liberated slaves of the late eighteenth and nineteenth centuries saw Christianity as a liberating word. That awareness remains today in pockets of the Caribbean in which a kind of liberation theology (not unlike what has emerged in Latin America; see pp. 364–65) can be identified. But whenever the Church has been too critical of the government, as in Castro's Cuba or in Haiti under the Duvaliers, it has been repressed.

Uniquely native appropriations of Christianity have developed in the Caribbean during the twentieth century, as they have in Africa. The best known of these is Rastafarianism. Originating in the early 1930s, inspired by Ethiopian Christianity, it teaches that God is black, that black people are the people of God and are marching to the true Ethiopia, where they will never be oppressed. Has the Church's ministry succeeded or failed in the Caribbean and in Latin America?

## The Church in Africa

Contrary to popular belief, nineteenth-century missionaries were not the ones to plant the Church in Africa (at least not in North Africa). There is evidence of African Monophysite Orthodox churches and of a vibrant Catholic church in North Africa prior to the Islamic invasions of the seventh and eighth centuries. Nevertheless, it is during the last two centuries that the Church on this continent has experienced significant growth.

At the beginning of the nineteenth century, Northern Africa as well as the Middle East belonged to the Ottoman Empire. As such, the empire's Islamic commitments dominated in these regions. This changed by the time of World War I, when Great Britain, France, and Italy controlled the northern coast. Likewise there were few European enclaves in central and southern Africa at the beginning of the nineteenth century.[7] The British founded Sierra Leone as a land for freed slaves in 1799, and freed American slaves founded Liberia in 1820. The Netherlands planted a colony at Cape Town on the southern tip of the continent in 1652, thereby introducing Christianity in the region. By the early nineteenth century, the colony was in British hands.

Roman Catholics undertook missionary work in colonies established by predominantly Roman Catholic nations and attempted to evangelize Orthodox Christians in North Africa. Undue Roman Catholic commitments to Western cultural suppositions as well as ecclesiastical jurisdictional problems impeded these efforts. These jurisdictional problems were not unlike the quarrels observed in the Americas between colonial powers and the Catholic episcopacy. The Portuguese tried to claim ancient rights of patronage (the power to appoint bishops) over the whole African church, based on the argument that it had first planted Christianity on the continent.

Meanwhile France and Belgium disputed over the Kongo, including patronage over the centuries-old Catholic Church in that region. The increasing internal problems of the Catholic Church in Africa coupled with a decline in the fortunes of the Kongo seem negatively to have affected Catholic life there from the seventeenth century on. Visitors to the region noted the emergence of a kind of syncretism, which quite likely was a function of a shortage of priests and a sense among the masses that Christianity was only the religion of the king (and its European missionaries). These dynamics eventually manifested in the emergence of African independent churches in the region.

---

7. The western coast had been settled centuries earlier; the Spanish and Portuguese initiated the slave trade. The Kongo had been reached for Christ with permanent success as early as the late fifteenth to early sixteenth centuries.

A forerunner of African independent churches (church bodies formed largely in reaction to white domination in the mission churches, particularly the ceiling they imposed on clerical advancement) is evident in the emergence of several female prophets in the Kongo in the late seventeenth or eighteenth centuries. Most notable among these were Appolonia Mafuta and Vita Kimpa. The latter, a member of the nobility, claimed to be a medium of the patriarch of monasticism, Saint Anthony. Both Mafuta and Kimpa claimed to be possessed by the Spirit, an idea with links to traditional Kongolese religion. Kimpa destroyed the symbols of both Christianity and traditional religion, claiming that they were powerless to save. Most interestingly, she also taught that Jesus was black, a native of the Kongo; thus, the idea of a black Jesus is not really so new after all. These prophets had widespread support but were eventually condemned as heretics and executed.

In their modern manifestation, as in the Kongo, some African independent churches emerged as a result of the founding of "Christian villages," which largely forced converts to renounce traditional culture in favor of a Westernized Christianity. In the Kongo and especially in Zaire (formerly the Belgian Congo), the earliest and subsequently the largest of these movements was founded by Simon Kimbangu (1889–1951) early in the twentieth century. He initiated a prophetic and healing movement that stressed monogamy, obedience to authority, and the unity of humankind. After his imprisonment by Belgian colonial authorities, the movement gradually "mainstreamed" (according to Western Christian standards) and is today officially recognized by the World Council of Churches as the Church of Jesus Christ on Earth by the Prophet Simon Kimbangu. Though renounced by this church, other indigenous prophetic movements that recognize Kimbangu as the messiah (at least of Africans) subsequently emerged in the region.

Despite these developments and inroads made by Protestantism in the area of the old kingdom of the Kongo in the late nineteenth century, Roman Catholic church life has enjoyed striking vitality in Zaire in the twentieth century, as reflected in its numerous clerical professions and indigenization practices. In the Republic of the Congo, 92 percent of the population is Christian. Nevertheless, although there are these indications of the success of Roman Catholicism on the African continent, Protestant work in the mission field generally exerted the greater impact on Africa, albeit with no fewer ambiguities.

*Significant early Protestant missions.* Several different starting points for telling the story of Protestant mission work in Africa suggest themselves. One obvious point of departure is the western coast, where European missionaries first established African churches in the fifteenth century. South Africa qualifies as the site of the first planting of the

Church on African soil in the modern period (in the mid-seventeenth century). Protestantism was planted in both of these regions as well as on the eastern coast. However, two missions to central Africa in the nineteenth century and early twentieth centuries, neither unambiguously successful, form an even more logical starting point since they stimulated great popular interest in Africa and African missions — the ministries of David Livingstone (1813–73) and Albert Schweitzer (1875–1965).

A Scottish factory worker, Livingstone studied medicine and was determined to serve as a missionary. He arrived first in South Africa, which by then was a British colony already staffed with a number of medical missionaries. After some discouragement about the small number of conversions his ministry had produced, Livingstone undertook an exploration north towards present-day Angola. He ventured on other journeys in central Africa, through regions that today comprise the nations of Zimbabwe and Zambia. Livingstone's expeditions — funded by the government and led by High Church Anglicans, were also motivated by commercial and social-justice agendas. The first, the Zambezi expedition in 1853, had much in common with an earlier expedition of the Niger River. With blazes of publicity, both sought a river transport through the African continent that would hold the key to legitimate trade, which could in turn put an end to the slave trade. Livingstone overestimated the commercial potential of the region, and overall his mission failed (save the controversial liberation of a number of slaves). In a subsequent expedition begun in 1866, Livingstone was met by Henry Morton Stanley (1841–1904), the Welsh American journalist who led a rescue mission to find the presumably lost Livingstone. Their famous 1871 encounter ("Dr. Livingstone, I presume") did much to publicize African exploration and missions, shaping popular Western images of the continent for generations.

Though Livingstone and Stanley did not make a direct impact on missionary work in Africa, Livingstone's fame inspired the foundation of two Presbyterian missions in the region. One of these, Livingstonia, established in 1875, produced thousands of educated (and Christianized) African people for Nyasaland (present-day Malawi) and South Africa as well as for Rhodesia (present-day Zimbabwe and Zambia). The impact of this mission and others that resulted in these regions has been pronounced. In the 1990s, for example, virtually all political leaders in Zimbabwe were church members, and many were clergy. Daily prayers are broadcast on state-owned television. The mission in Livingstonia is also significant in another way — the way in which it illustrates racial tensions in missionary work in Africa. The mission was staffed by both black and white missionaries, who initially were compensated at a similar rate. In time, however, resentment arose among the Scottish missionaries, and the salaries paid to the Africans and those ethnically related to them gradually eroded. Oftentimes they were placed under the supervision of whites who were far less experienced. In the same connection, it was typical that qualified African Christians were not ordained or their ordination was interminably delayed.

In connection with the role of black missionaries in Africa, it should be noted that at least 115 African American missionaries served on the continent in the last quarter of the nineteenth century. Many of them served in Liberia and elsewhere in West Africa. Predominantly white American denominations, notably Presbyterians and Baptists, recruited black missionaries to serve where health conditions were worst, ostensibly believing (often mistakenly) that they had great resistance to tropical diseases. Among the most well known were William and Lucy Sheppard, who worked for more than twenty years in Presbyterian missions in the Congo, and Alexander Fuller, who worked at a Baptist mission in Cameroon. Though not numerous on the African continent, due to restricted financial resources, historic African American denominations such as the African Methodist Episcopal Church, the African Methodist Episcopal Zion Church, and the National Baptist Convention did send missionaries to the "homeland" and have successfully established churches in these lands.

Albert Schweitzer's renown as a scholar of theology, accomplished musician, and doctor is widely known.[8] The liberal theology he embraced led him to understand his medical missionary work in establishing a hospital in Lambaréné (present-day Gabon) as a humanitarian effort, not a work of saving souls. Giving up as much as he did (the fame and fortune his international acclaim as a scholar and musician had afforded him) for the life of self-denial in isolated Africa won Schweitzer more acclaim and admiration, culminating in his receiving the 1952 Nobel Peace Prize. Nevertheless, there was an unseemly side to the ministry of this brilliant, arrogant man. The standards of his hospital left much to be desired, and he apparently had racist attitudes towards Africans, failing to appreciate the value of their cultural traditions and often describing them as "unreliable children."

Given such imperialistic attitudes, it is not surprising that the Church in Gabon has not thrived and succeeded in indigenizing itself. As a result, a large independent church — the Bwiti — has formed among the same people of Gabon as those with whom Schweitzer worked. Today almost 20 percent of the population are members. Beginning at the turn of the nineteenth century, but expanding markedly during the period of Schweitzer's ministry, the movement grew out of an indigenous ances-

---

8. See pp. 280–81 for a discussion of his thought.

tral and initiation cult. Its members induce mystical experiences by the use of indigenous drugs. One branch of the movement emphasizes the Holy Spirit, another arises from a vision of the Virgin Mary dripping with blood, and a third considers the Christian God as the "great god." The cult conducts twelve-hour services (Saturday night until Sunday morning), permits women to exercise liturgical leadership, and promises health and fertility.

When the Church has failed to affirm the cultural traditions of indigenous people, the Christianity endorsed by Africans has tended to be superficial, a kind of veneer to qualify them for Western education and its technology. As a result, these indigenous African traditions have continued to make their presence felt, even among Christians, in some cases resulting in the establishment of independent churches like the Bwiti.

*The church in West Africa.* From the medieval period through the sixteenth century, there had been largely unsuccessful Catholic missionary efforts on Africa's west coast. Outreach to Nigeria and Ghana occurred in the eighteenth and nineteenth centuries. These efforts are especially noteworthy since large portions of the African American community have genetic roots in these regions.

More so than perhaps in any other African land, Christianity was linked with colonization in Liberia and Sierra Leone. Nineteenth-century liberated slaves from America (in the case of Liberia) and London's impoverished blacks (and other liberated slaves in the case of Sierra Leone) generally speaking brought the Christianity that they had learned abroad with them. On the whole, save in the case of some of the liberated slaves, these repatriated Africans had been thoroughly Westernized and Christianized. Throughout much of the century, they made little effort to reach out to the indigenous inhabitants of the region and generally did not throughout much of a century generally seek to establish their own self-governing churches. As a result, less than a third of Liberians and less than a tenth of Sierra Leoneans are Christian today. Elsewhere in West Africa, one finds more characteristic and successful missionary stories to tell.

*Ghana.* Known as the Gold Coast in colonial times, Ghana was of great interest very early to Portugal and later colonial powers due to its lure of gold and the slaves that could be obtained through trade and force. By the mid-eighteenth century, at least thirty European forts had been established along the coast by Portugal as well as predominantly Protestant powers like England, the Netherlands, and Denmark. Chaplains in these forts were primarily concerned, not with the conversions of Africans, but with the spiritual welfare of Europeans and Eur-Africans in these enclaves.

Two Protestant missionary endeavors were launched in the eighteenth century. One by Moravians failed due to missionary deaths. The other launched by the British Society for the Propagation of the Gospel was led by the first Anglican missionary to the Gold Coast, Thomas Thompson (ca. 1708–1773). Having previously worked among slaves in the Americas, his work in West Africa among indigenous people was a natural outcome of his earlier commitments. Unfortunately, illness forced him to return home after four years, but he did recruit three young African men to travel with him in order to be educated. One of these, Philip Quaque (d. 1816), was ordained an Anglican priest. He returned to the coast to work for fifty years, well into the second decade of the nineteenth century. Though he needed to relearn his native language when he first returned, Quaque laid the foundation for many important educational initiatives in the region.

The Methodist Church in Ghana owed its initiative to one of Quaque's schools, which inspired the formation of a Christian study group in 1831. When the bishop of London did not respond to a request for a teacher, Methodists did. The movement spread as a result of the work of indigenous Africans who traveled inland on trading missions.

Four missionaries commissioned by the Basel Mission came to the region in 1828. Founded in 1815, this missionary society was ecumenical in its origins, a work of both Lutheran and Reformed churches. Initially its impact was minimal, drawing its first converts from ex-slaves. As the mission further developed, younger sons of the nobility and indigenous women of all stations responded. By the time of World War I, this mission was assumed into the United Free Church of Scotland, which accounts for the planting of the Presbyterian Church in the region.

Christianity spread farther in Ghana after Britain formally declared the Gold Coast a colony in 1874. Improvements in communication and the value indigenous peoples came to place on Western education facilitated Christianity's growth. The process was also aided by the expansion of Catholic and Anglican missions early in the twentieth century as well as the initiation of American Pentecostal missions.

Growth in these missions was closely related to the work of indigenous leadership. From earliest times, an emphasis on educating indigenous leadership characterized Ghanian church life; however, this has not prevented the development of indigenous African churches. One of the crucial disputes within the Presbyterian Church among the Ewe has been over whether evil spirits are real (as taught by the indigenous religion) or merely symbolic imagery to describe evil as a force. The majority of the membership clearly affirms belief in the reality of traditional spirits, and much indigenous Christian spirituality continues to be centered on healing and exorcism.[9]

Among the most prominent and best organized of the indigenous churches on Ghanaian soil has been the Musama Disco Christo, founded in 1922 by Joseph Appiah (d. 1948) as an outgrowth of a Methodist prayer group. After the fashion of many African independent churches, this movement is "prophetic"; that is, it believes that its leaders have a special gift of divination and can discern people's hearts. In addition, faith healing is emphasized along with a rich doctrine of demons. The church has retained many Methodist elements of its origins, combining them with rosaries, an ark of the covenant, and burnt offerings. Another interesting aspect of this church is that its members founded a new city, the Holy City of Mozano, and its prophetic leader functions as its king.

An important influence on the founders of the Musama Disco Christo was perhaps the most influential African evangelist of the twentieth century, William Wade Harris (1865–1929). A member of the Grebo tribe, though heavily influenced by American Liberian culture, Harris had originally been a political activist. A vision (typical of much indigenous African spirituality) moved him to take up a ministry as the last prophet of God. It enjoyed phenomenal success and impact among the coastal regions of West Africa, including Ghana.[10] A dynamic preacher with a striking appearance and a ministry surrounded by numerous miracles, Harris demanded the destruction of the traditional icons of indigenous religion but tolerated plural marriages and allowed for the use of traditional songs that were "Christianized" by inserting God's name in them. His militancy against some traditional practices like sexual intercourse in the open and witchcraft led him to avoid Communion services, which might connote these practices. Harris's influence goes far beyond the churches directly founded through his ministry. He indirectly brought many indigenous people into already established Protestant churches and influenced others, like Appiah in Ghana, to take up similar ministries.

Even apart from indigenous African Christian movements, perhaps because of the earliest Ghanaian churches' commitments to the cultivation of indigenous leadership, Christianity has quite thoroughly assimilated itself into Ghanaian culture. Thus Christian images even permeated the politics of the champion of African nationalism, Kwame Nkrumah (1909–72), though he was not himself a practicing Christian.

---

9. These beliefs would have not have been foreign to the experience of most Europeans prior to the Enlightenment and to European missionaries not yet schooled in Enlightenment sophistication.

10. Over one hundred thousand per year were baptized.

*Nigeria.* Presenting a different situation is Nigeria, insofar as Christians encountered particularly strong religious alternatives to Christianity in view of the dominance of Islam in the north and a continuing vibrancy of indigenous religion. There is early evidence of Islam in the region. It was likely planted by A.D. 1000, only four centuries after Muhammad himself. More Moslems are in Nigeria than in any other country except Islam's birthplace, Saudi Arabia. The enormous size of the nation (it is the most populous country in Africa) and the polyglot character of its population (including more than three hundred spoken languages) further diminish the likelihood of the Church's full domination of the land.

The first contact Nigerians had with the Church was, as is typical of much of western Africa, through the Portuguese in the 1500s, although they largely remained on the southern coast. Though much of this first work waned, the beginnings of British colonialism in the mid-nineteenth century opened new possibilities and opportunities to explore the inland, which have endured. The key organization in promoting such mission work was the Niger Mission, which began in 1841 and intended to undermine the slave trade that had opened up the African interior to commerce as well as to Christianity. The mission was inextricably linked with Samuel Ajayi Crowther (1806–91), a member of Nigeria's Yoruba tribe. Captured as a slave, he resettled in Sierra Leone and was ordained as an Anglican priest. He headed the mission in 1857 and was consecrated as bishop in 1864. The mission succeeded in planting only a few churches in towns along the Niger River before a decline, which began in 1879 when a European replaced Crowther and its African-led character changed. Native African missionaries have experienced much pain and resentment from their European sponsors and colleagues.

The churches founded by the Niger Mission were small, with membership largely drawn from slaves and other outcasts. Relatively little interest was shown in the educational institutions that they provided. Not until the twentieth century did widespread interest in Western education permeate the Igbo tribe. However, as a result of this educational ministry, it has become the most Christianized of all the Nigerian tribes. Religious differences in Nigeria are to a great extent tribally related. Nigerian Islam tends to comprise members of the Housa and Fulani tribes. Many of the Yoruba tribe continue to practice their indigenous religion. Those who have become Moslems typically continue to have integrated their faith with the old cultural suppositions concerning such practices as sacrificing to the gods.

The work of the Niger Mission in founding Anglican churches was not the first of the modern missions in Nigeria. In 1842, a few years prior to the Niger Mission's outreach, a Methodist mission was founded.

Four years later the Church Missionary Society established a work in the region. The same year a group of black and white Presbyterians from Jamaica likewise settled. American Baptists arrived in 1855.

The obviously ecumenical composition of mission work in Nigeria has been made even more complex by the emergence of a significant number of African independent churches. The process of secession from mission churches perceived as white-dominated began as early as 1888, when a group of Baptists withdrew over matters of congregational polity. Two years earlier, stirrings for autonomy emerged in the Nigerian Church of England, largely in reaction to the racial controversies and trials within the Niger Mission. Among those formed include the United Native African Church and the African Church (Bethel). A key distinguishing issue in their formation was their openness to polygamy, a painful issue in Africa, where the early Protestant missions characteristically forbade the practice. One of the most intriguing of these sects is the Cherubim and Seraphim Society/Church, which formed in 1925 after withdrawing from the Anglican Church. Late in the twentieth century, its membership was estimated in the millions. The society's prophetic church emphasizes the gifts of the Spirit, including healing, prayer (for prosperity, healing, and fertility), and fasting. African customs such as the use of drums in worship are characteristic, and prayer garments are typical liturgical attire. The church practices all seven sacraments.

Divided as they have been, Christians have remained in a minority position in the Moslem-dominated country and government of Nigeria. However, a growing sense of unity, at least among the missionary-founded churches, and an increase in Christian population suggest that Nigeria could be on the verge of a new chapter in its history. Its increasing Christian presence has fueled more tensions in Islamic-Christian relations, a topic to be addressed in the chapter 15.

*The church in South Africa: Ally or critic of apartheid?* The sordid racial relationships that marred South African history are best understood in light of the history of its colonization and its religious implications. The Dutch established the first European settlement in the region near present-day Cape Town in 1652. The settlement was originally intended only as a halfway station for ships traveling to the Dutch West Indies. Finally some Dutch and French Huguenot settlers began to establish permanent residences. They brought slaves from the Dutch East Indies with them. Few of these slaves were baptized, as it was feared that this might qualify them for liberation. In time, many slaves took up Islam.

The Dutch settlers were of Reformed background, though largely of a theologically conservative and unsophisticated genre. This character of the Dutch Reformed Church (South Africa) has perdured into the present, despite significant theological modifications/distortions that the church has experienced. Reformed Christians undertook some missionary work among the indigenous tribes in the region; some affiliated with the church, even through intermarriage.[11] On the whole, though, the indigenous Africans were placed in subjection to the Afrikaners, even after the abolition of the slave trade.

Moravians under the leadership of George Schmidt undertook the first self-conscious missionary effort in South Africa in 1737. His work was hampered both by problems with Dutch clergy regarding his right to baptize converts and by his failure to master indigenous languages. As a result of the latter difficulty, Christianity was identified with European (particularly Dutch) culture, becoming an unattractive alternative for most indigenous South Africans in this period, for conversion would entail a break from their culture. Consequently the Church had its greatest impact among Africans who had previously been Westernized, through intermarriage or though enslavement.

The Moravian missionary strategy was to found Christian villages. By 1850, thirty-two such mission sites had been established. Another crucial chapter in the missionary outreach to native people occurred in 1799 with the arrival of the Dutch missionary Johannes Van der Kemp (1747–1811), who was sponsored by the London Missionary Society. He combined the Christian village tradition of the Moravians with a concern about justice for the indigenous peoples as well as with a firm commitment to the need for ecumenical cooperation on the mission field.

Van der Kemp's identification with the native culture (he married a South African woman of mixed race) and outspoken criticism of white injustice became a commitment typical of many of the other English-speaking (and later other non-Dutch) churches planted in the region. Part of the reason for the concern of these churches with defending the rights of indigenous people in the region was, as we shall note, tied up in political/colonial dynamics. Nevertheless, the planting of the Church among the various indigenous peoples was a painfully slow and often unsuccessful venture until the twentieth century.[12] Most of the earliest success was among those peoples who had been most uprooted from their traditional way of life. In reaching out to this constituency, missionaries aplenty descended on South Africa, sponsored by mis-

---

11. Racial purity was not a concern of the settlers, the forebears of the Afrikaners, until later centuries.

12. David Livingstone's explorations were largely occasioned by the despair he felt in South Africa over the failure of his missionary work in the region to bear much visible fruit.

sion societies from many Western nations, including France, Scotland, Germany, and Scandinavia.

Because of these dynamics — the propensities of most missionaries to identify Christianity with Western culture, their failure to abdicate leadership in these churches to indigenous people, and increasing segregation in the region — various African independent churches began developing late in the nineteenth century. One group of such churches is usually designated "Ethiopian Churches" (so named with reference to the African-administered Ethiopian Orthodox Church). To a great extent, these churches retained the belief structure and ethos of the mission churches to which their membership (largely drawn from the urban Westernized elite of the region) had originally belonged. They were particularly distinct in their being organized and led exclusively by Africans. At present, these churches are languishing; they have never really had the resources to develop and as such are less and less appealing to the African elite in the region. More profound has been the impact of so-called Zion Churches, which are prophetic. These movements embrace many practices emerging from self-conscious attempts to relate Christianity to indigenous culture, which are also evident in the African independent churches of Ghana and Nigeria. With membership in the millions, these churches have tended especially to flourish among the tribes that were most dislocated by the European invasions.

Crucial to the history of South Africa and its church was Britain's conquest of the original Dutch colony in 1795. Struggles for this territory ensued for the next decades between British forces and the Dutch. In 1820, the first substantial English-speaking colony was established. As increasing numbers of British immigrants arrived in the colony and the laws of the land became color-blind (following the abolition of slavery), the heirs of the early Dutch settlers, who had come to be known as Boers, came to bitterly resent British control.[13] Their discontent led them to embark on a series of migrations inland, where they could be free of British control. Subsequent national mythology has come to speak of these various waves of migration as the Great Trek, a people in search of a new home not unlike the Hebraic exodus.

The experience of inland migration was significant in that it has effectively forged among these Dutch and their heirs a sense of national unity as a people created by a religious experience of exodus. Also of long-term significance was the many conflicts with the Zulu people on these migrations.[14] As a result of these conflicts, existing prejudice against in-

---

13. The Boers subsequently became identified as *Afrikaners*, from a dialect of Dutch that they had developed known as Afrikaans.

14. Both the Afrikaners and the Zulus endured horrifying losses.

digenous African people was further hardened among the Afrikaners. No less significant was the Zulus' hardened opposition to Christianity and missionary efforts. To this day, those who have been Christianized largely belong to African independent churches.

The Vortrekkers (Afrikaners who had participated in the Great Trek) did succeed in establishing their own independent nation, the Republic of Natal, in 1840. It did not survive the proclamation of Natal as a British colony three years later. Tensions between English-speakers and the Afrikaners were further exacerbated. These tensions continue to persist among the heirs of these groups to this day. Other Vortrekkers traveled north and created two independent republics, the Transvaal in 1852 and the Orange Free State in 1854. Friction between the British and these Afrikaner republics dominated the latter part of the nineteenth century. The discovery of gold, which brought more English (and Asian) immigrants, further exacerbated the friction.

The Anglo-Boer War erupted during the turn of the century (1899–1902) when Britain demanded that Transvaal enfranchise British immigrants, who felt persecuted under Afrikaner rule. However, because the English outnumbered the Afrikaners, they refused this request. The outcome of the war was that both Afrikaner republics were brought under British control, though England did give self-government to the two new colonies. The Afrikaner leaders of both of these formerly self-governing republics and those remaining in the British-dominated Cape Colony began to cooperate, eventually establishing the basis for a union of all the colonies in the region. Finally in 1910 the British Parliament granted the Union of South Africa independence. To this day, Afrikaans-speaking and English-speaking peoples live in very different cultural worlds and distrust each other. Afrikaners tend to be more nationalistic and local oriented; English-speakers tend to be more internationalistic. Such characteristic worldviews have contributed to existing prejudices on each side. English-speakers as early as the nineteenth century viewed Afrikaners as lazy and dirty.

Afrikaners dominated the first government of the independent union. However, in 1920 a coalition was built with the English-speaking party to address the poor-white problem (the majority of whom were Afrikaners). Convinced that the equality of English and Afrikaners had been assured, the merged party (the United Party) supported an Afrikaner plan to place Afrikaners in Cape Province on a separate roll electing whites to Parliament. To facilitate this plan, a constitutional amendment was passed that changed the voting rights of non-European people on the soil of the Union. These developments set the stage for the formation in 1934 of the National Party, which opposed the pro-Western stance of the United Party. The new party preached a more extreme Afrikaner nationalism than had been previously propounded and planned a more rigorous separation of the races than the conventional segregation already existing.

Taking power in 1948, the new party first moved to further Afrikaner nationalism, which economic disparities among the people jeopardized. It sought to deal with this problem by seeking to increase investments in Afrikaner businesses. A kind of *Volkskapitalisme* developed with the state heavily involved in economic life. These political actions have had much to do with establishing the high standard of living that Afrikaners enjoy in contemporary South Africa.

At the same time, the government also enshrined in law the racism that had existed as a matter of custom since the nineteenth century. The centerpiece of this legalistic agenda was *apartheid* (meaning "separateness") and its program for the separate development of the races. Among the characteristics of this infamous mode of social construction were the creation of institutions that established white social privilege, segregated and unequal education, job discrimination, and finally residential segregation. In the space of a few years, mixed marriages were prohibited by law. An African Homelands policy was established early in the twentieth century to reinforce white insistence on territorial segregation.

In the development of this virulent, legislated nationalism, the Afrikaners' church, the Dutch Reformed Church (South Africa), played a crucial role. Virtually all of the early Dutch settlers belonged to the Reformed Church in their motherland. From its very origins, this church functioned as it had in the motherland as a kind of "state church."[15] To be sure, adaptations of the faith that the immigrants brought from their motherland did transpire, if for no other reason than that adaptation was necessitated by the transplanting from a Western urban setting to a rural African ethos centered on the family. In any case, Dutch/Boer identity in South Africa came to be intimately related, notably in the period of British dominance, with being a member of this church. To be Reformed in this setting increasingly came to be an ethnic designation.

Prior to the Great Trek, tensions did exist between the Dutch Reformed Church (South Africa) and the majority of the Boers. The government's subsidy of clergy salaries tended to create a distance between the church's clergy (who were born and trained in the Netherlands or Scotland) and the Boer masses. The church also opposed the Great Trek and resisted the Afrikaans language movement. However,

---

15. It assumed this status even under British administration, for its ministers received state stipends.

in subsequent interpretations of the Great Trek and of a covenant oath made by the Vortrekkers, Reformed/Calvinist theological themes were increasingly regarded as the inspiration of these nation-building events.

There is much scholarly debate regarding the degree to which the Vortrekkers were in fact self-consciously Reformed in their actions or the degree to which apartheid is a product of Reformed theology. Nineteenth-century Boer/Afrikaner culture did not see itself as chosen people, had largely not received trained leadership, and did not emphasize the theme of "covenant" as much as the Puritans (Westminster Confession VII) or even Calvin (*Institutes* 2.10ff.) had. In fact, even the Dutch Reformed Church in the motherland made very little of the theme of covenant; nothing in the liturgy of either church was pertinent to covenant renewal. On the other hand, the Dutch Reformed Church (South Africa) did take a leading role in the twentieth century through its preaching and teaching in linking the Trekker Covenant to the national consciousness. This was a crucial step in institutionalizing the links between this particular church and Afrikaner nationality. That process had truly begun in the 1870s when the British instituted the separation of church and state. In these changed circumstances, the Dutch Reformed Church (South Africa) became more clearly a "people's church," as manifested in its concern about Afrikaner "poor whites" and preserving cultural purity through separate/segregated educational systems. Given these new dynamics, it is not surprising that ministers of the Reformed Church became active in politics. In the best traditions of the Reformed heritage, which manifested themselves in the Netherlands, politics came to be seen as one segment of the Church's sphere of moral influence.

The Dutch Reformed Church's role as interpreter of the Afrikaner heritage began as early in the 1870s as the Vortrekkers were compared to the Lord's chosen people. In time, this comparison (much in the tradition of Calvin's narrative approach to Scripture, which included identifying present readers with biblical characters) became a direct equation of the Afrikaners and the chosen people. Certainly such an identification seemed to fit quite logically with the Calvinist stress on election (*Institutes* 3.21.1–4). Nevertheless, this theme, which had so readily contributed to the development of apartheid (for as chosen, the Afrikaners, it is argued, justifiably separate themselves from other people and legitimately exercise lordship over them), was quite minor in South African Dutch Reformed circles prior to 1948 (*Human Relations in South Africa*). Indeed, some have argued that its impact on the Dutch Reformed Church (South Africa) is less a function of the impact of Reformed theology on the church and more a mark of the influence of the ideology of British imperialism's ideology and self-understanding as taking up a "civilizing mission" in Africa. Is apartheid truly a product of Reformed theology?

The early Afrikaners never constituted a total community articulating independent intellectual traditions. Afrikaner culture long lacked a native intellectual class and depended on immigrants (usually from the Netherlands) to function as its ministers, lawyers, or other spokespersons. It is hardly surprising, then, that Afrikaner nationalism was closely intertwined with the rise of Dutch nationalism in the nineteenth century, as this nationalism was closely related to the leadership of the Neo-Calvinism of the great Dutch theologian and statesman Abraham Kuyper (1837–1920).

Neo-Calvinism was a self-conscious recovery of the Reformed confessional theological heritage by Kuyper and his allies in order to combat theological liberalism and, to some extent, a dead orthodoxy, which had succumbed to a dualistic separation of sacred and secular. Kuyper and Neo-Calvinism did so by endeavoring in good Calvinist fashion to establish God's ordinances in every sphere of social life (*Lectures on Calvinism* 11, 24, 101). By no means, however, was Neo-Calvinism a politically conservative movement (Kuyper *Christianity and Class Struggle* 25–32, 34–36).

In the twentieth century, Neo-Calvinism has become a most congenial theological perspective in Dutch Reformed Church (South Africa) circles, in part because of the positive response of South Africans to Neo-Calvinism's theological conservatism. To this day, the Dutch Reformed Church (South Africa) is quite theologically conservative, almost Fundamentalistic (*Dutch Reformed Church in South Africa* 2.1). Another factor in the attractiveness of Neo-Calvinism may have been Kuyper's own praise of the South African church's fidelity to the Reformed tradition in constructing a society apparently governed by its principles (*Lectures on Calvinism* 40). A third factor in the South African church's endorsement of Neo-Calvinism was Kuyper's concept of *common grace*, that is, the idea that God's grace is not just bestowed upon the elect but touches all human beings through creation (*De Gemeene Gratie*). Although it was by no means Kuyper's intention, Afrikaner appropriations of this concept became authorization in the twentieth century for the argument that God had created two realms, the sphere of creation and of redemption. The next move was to distinguish between and separate these realms (the two kingdoms of Luther and Augustine). In a manner that Kuyper and the Reformers would never have countenanced, the Afrikaner church has argued that "it is not part of the Church's calling to dictate to authorities, for instance, how they should regulate intercourse and relationships between the various groups in a multinational or multiracial situation" (Dutch Reformed

Church (South Africa) *Human Relations and the South African Scene in the Light of Scripture* 49.1).[16]

The separation of the spheres of church and state (gospel and created order) was most consistent with the sacred-profane distinctions that had characterized Afrikaner culture at least as early as 1910. Another way of describing what transpired as a result of this misappropriation of Kuyper's insights is that the convenantal emphases of the church were removed from all christological orientation; thus, the covenant theme was embodied in a manner not unlike the separatist tendencies of the ancient Hebrews. Of course, this sort of "Old Testament-like piety" had roots to some extent in the popular piety of the Boers even prior to the Great Trek.

The separation of the spheres was exploited even further by the Dutch Reformed Church (South Africa) for justifying apartheid. At least by the 1970s the church argued that since the differentiation of peoples is implicit in creation, it is appropriate to practice separation in society and in the Church (*Human Relations and the South African Scene in the Light of Scripture* 9.3, 9; 14.5; 29–30; 60). Separation in the Church provided authorization for the missionary strategy of the Dutch Reformed Church — ensuring "that each man could hear and preach in his own language, the great deeds of God" (5) — and for the development of racially segregated congregations. The combination of these commitments and practices both historically and logically gave rise to the system of segregated education and apartheid. Is the Reformed tradition's theological heritage ultimately to blame, or does the data exonerate it as the cause of these developments?

The religious landscape of South Africa in the middle of the twentieth century on the eve of the struggle against apartheid was largely divided along ethnic lines (a reality that perdures to this day). Among Whites, a close relationship to the Church characterized Afrikaners more than English-speakers. The vast majority of Afrikaners belonged to the Dutch Reformed Church (South Africa). Most English-speakers were and continue to be Anglicans, or else they affiliate in lesser numbers with Methodist, Roman Catholic, and Presbyterian churches. All of these English-speaking church bodies include more members of the other two South African racial groups (Blacks and Coloureds) than does the Dutch Reformed Church. The latter, though, does include some Coloured (those of mixed-race ethnic background) members, usually in segregated congregations.

---

16. The logic is most reminiscent of that of Southern Presbyterians in America when they sought to justify slavery with their concept of the *spirituality of the Church* (the idea that the Church is only to concern itself with spiritual affairs) or of the German Christians who unequivocally supported Hitler's policies in the 1930s and 1940s.

In South Africa there are three distinct Reformed churches, though two are much smaller than the Dutch Reformed Church (South Africa). They and others that have vanished were the result of nineteenth-century schisms occasioned by regionalism or doctrinal disputes. One is the Nederduits Hervormde Kerk, which formed in 1843 in the Transvaal. Of late, it has even taken a harder-line stance than did the Dutch Reformed Church (South Africa). As the latter had until 1974, it continued to regard apartheid as divinely instituted as the Will of God. The other Afrikaner Reformed church, the Gereformeerde Kerk, has come to be known as the Dopper Church. With particularly significant influence, it was the first of the Afrikaner churches to advocate and institute segregated education in interests of preserving "cultural purity." It was also the first of these churches to reject apartheid.

The English-speaking churches' openness to and concern for the state of blacks and black leadership bespeaks the general historically rooted cultural disposition of English speakers to function in opposition to Afrikaner-dominated culture. Other elements of the religious landscape of the republic include smaller Hindu and Moslem communities composed of Asian immigrants. Among blacks, many have retained tribal loyalties. Some formed African independent churches. Others belong to traditional mission-developed churches that have totally indigenized their leadership, such as the Evangelical Lutheran Church in Southern Africa.[17] These indigenized churches and the English-speaking churches were in the vanguard of the successful struggle against apartheid (see chap. 15).

*The church in East Africa.* Though there has been startling growth of the Church in eastern Africa in the second half of the twentieth century, the growth was discouragingly slow in the eighteenth and nineteenth centuries. For example, by 1938 Christians formed only 8 percent of the population of Kenya and 10 percent of Tanganyika (present-day Tanzania). Today 60 percent of Kenyans are Christian, and 33 percent of Tanzanians belong to the Church.

*Kenya.* Although there had been Arab and Portuguese settlements in Kenya as early as the Middle Ages, colonialism really began with the rule of the Chartered Company of England in 1887. By 1905, the British established a colony. The European settlers soon came to possess a disproportionate share of the wealth and political influence in the region. As was typical of other regions in Africa, the first missions were established among these settlers.

The Kikuyu are the largest ethnolinguistic group in Kenya. The first

---

17. Other Lutheran churches in South Africa are composed of German immigrants, and at least one of them refused to the bitter end to condemn apartheid.

missionary outreach to them was initiated in 1898. The first converts were poor workers of the land on the fringes of Kikuyu settlements. After British colonization, that land was occupied by settlers to their exclusion. In time, some Kikuyu notables embraced Christianity as a way of facilitating the adoption of modern technology. Nevertheless, there was much resistance to the adoption of Christianity out of fear of alienating the people from their way of life. Before World War II, proto-nationalist leaders were especially critical of the Church and how it divided the people.

Much controversy developed in the Kenyan churches in 1919 in a dispute over female circumcision. Though some churches, influenced by Western missionary suppositions, rejected the practice, most continued it (considered a rite of passage to adulthood) and started their own churches. In the midst of this controversy, some Kikuyu tried to re-claim land that the churches held, and there was much unhappiness with Christianity. The mission churches to this juncture in history had done little to indigenize. Were they correct not to indigenize on the matter of female circumcision?

The colonial government was certainly no friend of indigenization. It barred entry of African American missionaries and forbade entry to certain African independent churches that had formed elsewhere. After World War II, a number of independent, prophetic churches (stressing healing and taking indigenous witchcraft seriously) have grown dramatically. About 14.6 percent of Kenyans belong to such churches. The missionary-founded churches have likewise begun to take seriously the mandate to indigenize and have grown phenomenally, notably the Presbyterian Church. The Roman Catholic Church is even larger, composing 25 percent of the population.

*Tanzania.* A fast-growing Lutheran church, the Evangelical Lutheran Church, has developed in Tanzania (formerly Tanganyika). Germans (opening the door to both Lutheran and Catholic missionaries) were the original colonizers. They often exploited the indigenous people and permitted slavery. A 1905 rebellion failed but did lead the Germans to abolish slavery. Germany lost the territory to British and French troops during World War I, and Tanganyika became a British colony. Scandinavian and American missionaries assumed the role Germans had in Lutheran churches. Predictably, growth was minimal until after World War II, when self-conscious indigenization programs were instituted. Church growth since that time has been phenomenal.

In Tanzania and Kenya, missionary-founded churches lacked success until self-conscious indigenization efforts were undertaken. Is church growth only possible when the gospel is indigenized?

## The Rise of the Ecumenical Movement

International ecumenism, the work of the World Council of Churches, is not really understood apart from its original context — the mission field. The missionary movement created a spirit of cooperation among various missionaries. In fact, a number of the early missionary societies were interdenominational. Efforts were made to offer a common witness on the mission field. Converts too began taking steps to lower denominational barriers.

The first forerunner of the ecumenical movement may be traced to 1810 with the efforts of the great missionary in South Africa Johannes Van der Kemp to convene an international missionary conference. This call fell on deaf ears. However, one century later, the World Missionary Conference was held, organizing the International Missionary Council. The council's decision to exclude attention to potentially divisive theological issues in its work led to the formation of a complementary Faith and Order movement (organized in 1927 to explore whether differences in beliefs of the churches could be overcome). In 1925, another ecumenical organization, the Life and Work movement, organized with the express intention of seeking common responses to contemporary social problems.[18] These organizations would have a major role as predecessor bodies in the formation of the World Council of Churches in 1948.

## Are the Modern Missionary and Ecumenical Movements Inextricably Bound to Capitalist Dynamics?

A relationship between the modern missionary movement, the ecumenical movement, and European colonialism is indisputable. Clearly many of the first modern missionaries linked their evangelism efforts with a belief in Western cultural hegemony. Does that fact negate the validity of their work and of the ecumenical movement that sprang from such efforts? Is foreign missionary and ecumenical work inextricably mixed in Western cultural suppositions and its capitalist economy, so as ultimately not to be serviceable to the Church catholic?

---

18. Its major leader was the Swedish Lutheran archbishop Nathan Söderblom (1866–1931).

# CHAPTER 13

# THEOLOGICAL AND SOCIOCULTURAL DEVELOPMENTS IN THE EARLY MODERN PERIOD

The nature of the modern worldview (confidence in reason and determination to apply its insights to understanding the world) posed challenges for Christian faith. In the nineteenth and early twentieth centuries, these challenges to faith became even more difficult, as the industrial revolution spread throughout western Europe and eventually to North America. Various responses to the challenges and sociocultural developments emerged in the bastions of high culture. With regards to the Church's response, Catholic authorities generally condemned these developments. Protestants were more open to interpret faith in light of the new modern frame of mind. Since these sociocultural developments transpired in the West, the Eastern Orthodox churches were largely untouched by them in the nineteenth century. As such, it was a century of both theological diversity and significant uniformity.

## The Modern Worldview and the Church's Reactions to It

To say that the nineteenth century was a time of great socioeconomic changes with significant cultural impact in the West would be an understatement. Becoming more and more pronounced as the century wore on, the industrial revolution's impact was not merely limited to the economic and technological spheres. The revolution put more pressures on the nuclear family, for the traditional extended family effectively broke down as the younger generations sold their land and often left the elders and flocked to the cities, where the jobs and finer things in life were to be found. As the old community, family base broke down, more and more did the themes of private responsibility, individualism, and preoccupation with self-fulfillment become prevalent in the wider culture and in the academy.

Another significant impact of the industrial revolution was its contribution to the evolution of Western society's confidence in progress. While prior to the revolution Westerners were still inclined to draw inspiration from the past, the new technology seemed to render ancient insights increasingly irrelevant. More and more, the new scientific insights, not the traditions of the past, were regarded as the way to truth and the better life. Even the masses gradually came to accept such assumptions. Are these sociocultural assumptions and beliefs not still prevalent in Western society?

The nineteenth century was also the era when Charles Darwin's (1809–82) theory of evolution was introduced. It simply seemed to undergird the new sense that scientific progress, unencumbered by traditions of the past, was the wave of the future. In fact, this consideration was part of the reason why the theory of evolution was (and still is) so controversial. It is not just an implicit challenge to the biblical accounts of creation; the theory also implicitly calls into question the value of all traditions. Is that perhaps what is ultimately at stake in supporting the theory of evolution — that it indirectly leads to the conclusion that nothing lasts forever, and so our past wisdom must be challenged? Increasingly since Darwin, Western society has sought truth in the natural sciences. No longer is theology regarded with much academic seriousness as a resource in the quest for such truth.

In addition to these other challenges, the industrial revolution created displacement of the population in its drive towards urbanization. This in turn led to various social upheavals, all of them related to the exploitation of the working class and the dissolution of the old premodern worldview. Institutionally, the Church (esp. Protestantism) responded in at least four very significant ways.

## The Church's Programmatic Response

The Sunday school movement was one of the new programs that emerged during the century in response to the urban crisis. Essentially it was a movement framed as an attempt to reach those who no longer had much connection with traditional means of religious instruction. It was largely initiated by the socially concerned dissident churches of the British Isles (esp. Puritans, Baptists, and Methodists). Not unlike the situation today, the modern city of the nineteenth century did not encourage participation of the masses in church life. After all, most were urban immigrants who either felt themselves displaced from their former agrarian way of life and its (religious) certainties, or else they were too busy enjoying all the sensual pleasures of the city to have time for the Church.

Two other significant programs to develop in the century were the Salvation Army, which was founded in 1865 by the Methodist revivalist preacher William Booth, and the Young Men's Christian Association (YMCA), which was founded in London in 1844 by a young British layman, George Williams (1821–1905). Both were movements aimed at reaching out to the urban masses and alleviating the economic and spiritual misery that had resulted from their exploitation by the new urban factories. Both of these movements quickly spread to the United States, where they have and continue to play significant roles.

Another response to the new economic circumstances was the Cooperative movement of the renowned Danish Lutheran church leader, theologian, and hymn writer N. F. S. Grundtvig (1783–1872). This reform movement was not planted in the United States except among Danish immigrants, though it did have marked impact on the Danish motherland. Concerned about the plight of the rural poor, Grundtvig advocated and through his considerable influence instituted programs of sharing resources among the poor.[1] Closely associated with Grundtvig's Cooperative movement was his passion for providing educational opportunities for the poor. To that end, he succeeded in establishing a system of *Folk Schools* (institutions providing postprimary education for all). Clearly, the commitment of Danish Americans to establishing educational institutions that are open to all and function to keep alive the Danish cultural heritage among the immigrants was in the tradition of the Folk School system.

Were these effective responses? Is the Church's ministry still promoted by its reliance on these institutions, or are they so much bound to the circumstances of their founding that they have become more anachronistic than helpful?

Grundtvig's contributions extend also to his provocative theological orientation. It is most suggestive of parallel contemporary theological movements. Grundtvig himself was very concerned to combat the growing rationalism in the Denmark of his day. His response was to highlight the theological themes of the Reformation, which is known as "confessionalism" in Lutheran circles (Grundtvig *What Constitutes Authentic Christianity?* 35, 62–63). However, in several important ways Grundtvig broke with Lutheran orthodox theology. He was willing to accept the results of something like a historical-critical reading of the Bible, distinguishing its historical reliability from its reliability as a valid testimony concerning authentic Christianity. This emphasis on a common confession of faith as the clearest expression of God's Word meant

---

1. In many ways, these developments brought Denmark into the industrial revolution, and its Socialist Democratic ideals are rightful heirs of the Grundtvigian program.

a marked liturgical consciousness and emphasis on the sacraments for the eminent Danish theologian (109ff.). He combined these themes along with his emphasis on grace and an affirmation of Danish cultural life into a joyous, celebrative vision of Christian faith, which was reflected in his lifestyle and is evident in the numerous hymns he wrote.

Perhaps even more timely for the contemporary context is Grundtvig's passionate interest in the culture of his beloved Danish people. In fact, he insisted that we must start our reflections with the human situation before proceeding to understand Christianity, for if Christianity is true, it must have been fashioned to meet the needs of the whole human race (Grundtvig *What Constitutes Authentic Christianity?* 95). These interests led Grundtvig to undertake careful study of Danish folklife and pre-Christian mythology. He concluded that early Danish culture was compatible with Christianity and that differences between churches are related to the distinct cultures from which they emerge. These insights certainly suggest observations offered by a number of contemporary theologians concerned to articulate indigenous theologies for their own "Third World" contexts or contexts in which they are a minority. Could Grundtvig be a potentially helpful ally for African, African American, and Asian theology?

## Nineteenth-Century Intellectual Currents

Among the intellectual developments of the nineteenth century were the emergence of Marxism and of psychoanalysis, which was developed by Sigmund Freud (1856–1939); however, these movements had their greatest cultural impact on the West in the twentieth century (for a consideration of these, see pp. 302–3). Other intellectual developments had a more immediate impact on the nineteenth century.

### Immanuel Kant

Though most of his work was done in the preceding century, this renowned German Enlightenment scholar is the obvious figure with whom to begin any analysis of nineteenth-century intellectual developments. After all, it was he who mediated earlier developments in rationalism to the social context of his time.

Through his epistemology, especially the distinction between the *noumenon* (the thing-in-itself, which can never be known) and the *phenomenon* (one's perception of the noumenon), Kant insisted that one can only obtain phenomenal knowledge of the thing. The mind orders the data in accord with certain categories (synthetic a priori judgments), such as existence, space, and time (Kant *Critique of Pure Reason* 194–95). A kind of relativism emerges from such suppositions, for they imply that the real content of knowledge is, not objective data about which we can agree or disagree, but the thought processes of each individual. We are still living with the relativistic consequences of Kant's theory of knowledge.[2] His suppositions are potentially problematic in the challenges they pose for faith, for they lead to the conclusion that reason cannot prove the existence of God or any other spiritual reality. Of course, Kant conceded that all human beings possess a practical reason, one that knows the existence of a God who judges (*Critique of Practical Reason* esp. 91). This practical reason recognizes a categorical imperative — the principle that humans are to act in such a manner that the rule for one's action can be made a universal law (109, 118, 124–33, 137–39).

Late in his life Kant developed these insights, interpreting Christianity in light of morality. In fact, he translated its concepts irreducibly into moral categories. To the extent that ethics could be regarded as an academically credible exercise, Kant's endeavor can be deemed as fully consistent with his Enlightenment commitment to interpreting the whole of reality (including religion) in light of reason (*An Answer to the Question, What Is Enlightenment?*). This paradigm for interpreting Christianity in light of some intellectually credible categories of the day is most reminiscent of the correlationist method of the early Christian Apologists (like Justin Martyr and Clement of Alexandria). This theological method has been enormously influential in shaping the way most Protestants have tried to come to terms with modern intellectual developments (Kant, *Religion within the Limits of Reason Alone*).

Examples of Kant's reinterpretation of Christianity are noteworthy, as they illustrate what happens to the classical Christian doctrines when they are considered with a method of correlation. In a manner typical of this method, Kant begins his treatment of Christianity with a consideration of the human condition, especially noting the struggle between good and evil in humanity (*Religion within the Limits of Reason Alone*, bk. 1). Also typical of his theological agenda, the prior analysis of the human condition (the categories into which Christianity is translated) provides the language in which the classical Christian doctrines are articulated. Thus Kant's prior ethical analysis determined how Christ's work is understood. Christ is presented as the archetype of moral perfection. He is regarded as providing the perfect example; in so doing, Christ spreads good. To support this view of Christ as an example, it is

---

2. To this day he remains *the* philosopher of modern Protestantism — including of liberation theology.

better if he is not deemed divine, for then we could not as readily adopt him as an example to imitate (2.1A, 1B).

Another significant outcome of these sets of commitments and the methodology that underlies them is the devaluation of historical revelation. Since the biblical miracles are a source of some intellectual embarrassment, this outcome is most congenial to the task of rendering an intellectually credible version of faith (*Religion within the Limits of Reason Alone* 2. Gen.Ob.). Of course, such a devaluation of historical revelation was evident in the premodern appropriations of Kant's correlationist approach, even among the Apologists, for it is a consequence of this theological model's characteristic reliance on an allegorical approach to Scripture.[3]

The position of Kant and the great number of modern theologians who share his methodological concerns to liberate the credibility of Christian faith from judgments regarding the historical accuracy of the biblical accounts is likely a reaction to the observations of another great German Enlightenment scholar, Gotthold Ephraim Lessing (1729–81). He had maintained that the new historical consciousness developing in the Enlightenment had driven a wedge between historical reality and the eternal truths of mind and spirit. In this connection, Lessing spoke of an "ugly ditch" between history and matters of reason/spirit: "Accidental truths of history can never become the proof of necessary truths of reason" (*On the Proof of the Spirit and of Power*). The widespread acceptance of this point by the vast majority of Western scholars since Lessing has pretty well separated historical and religious truth. Kant and much modern theology have observed this "ditch," effectively agreeing that the truth of Christianity cannot be located in its history.[4]

Though Kant may have found an intellectually credible means of dealing with the hard academic questions raised by the emerging historical-critical consciousness, he and many other proponents of the correlationist method paid a price for the other strengths of their approach. The equation of Christianity with morality led him to endorse a nominalist, semi-Pelagian-like view of salvation, as he insisted on preparing for grace, making oneself worthy to receive it (*Religion within the Limits of Reason Alone* 1.IV. Gen.Ob.). Could it be that a correlationist approach, because it initiates theological anal-

---

3. Allegory locates the meaning of the biblical text, not in what it says literally (in its historical claims), but in its deeper, spiritual meaning. This depth meaning is to be expressed in concepts drawn from the prior analysis of the human condition (in Kant's case, from ethics), which is correlated with the Word.

4. Though with some notable exceptions, the endorsement of this supposition will reappear again and again in the scholars we consider in the remainder of this volume.

ysis from the viewpoint of the human situation, logically necessitates that humans determine God, that all divine actions come to be understood as necessarily correlated with human actions? Correspondingly, does a correlationist approach adequately affirm the transcendence of God?

## Georg Wilhelm Friedrich Hegel

The thought of the renowned, influential German Idealist philosopher Georg Wilhelm Friedrich Hegel (1770–1831) is best understood as a reaction to Kant. Hegel conceded the Kantian claim that the mind stamps its seal on all reality (*Phenomenology*, pref. II.2–3). However, he moved beyond Kant in positing an ontology whereby reason is reality itself. Such belief in the rational character of reality means that when one thinks, one is in touch with reality itself, being-itself. It follows, then, that one best knows the other objectively by becoming subjective, for the other is essentially related to the one (pref. III.1). As is well known, Hegel spoke of reasoning as a *dialectic* (a process, ever moving, from thesis to antithesis to synthesis). Consequently, he proceeded also to assert that likewise universal reason (being or the Spirit) is a dialectic process. The whole of reality is in process, moving towards ultimate divine-human identity (Hegel *Lectures on the History of Philosophy*).

As a religious thinker, Hegel interpreted Christian faith in light of his philosophical suppositions, as did Kant. He regarded Christianity as the absolute religion. God is thus conceived as the absolute, eternal Idea (*Lectures on the Philosophy of Religion* III.C.I). In view of the fact that rationality in Hegel's scheme is dialectic in three forms, God as Idea must unfold in three forms. This also entailed that human beings as part of the rational process of history must be seen as related to God. But in creation humans have become separate from God, that is, have become the antithesis of the Idea (III.C.II.3). However, as thesis and antithesis blend into synthesis, so the separation of God and humanity is overcome in Christ. Humans are coming home. As such, Christology is a "picture" of the absolute history of the divine Idea (III.C.II.3).

Given Hegel's philosophical suppositions, the past is never lost in his view. Likewise, the present includes past and future. Hegel's system took history with utmost seriousness, for it is no longer a secondary matter concerned only with phenomena not essentially related to the substance of reality. In fact, on Hegel's grounds, history is intimately related to understanding eternal realities. As such, Hegel created an intellectual climate in which new interest in church history and in historical-critical biblical interpretation was opened.

## Post-Hegelian Historical Criticism

Among the forerunners of modern biblical criticism in eighteenth-century Germany were the radical rationalists Hermann Reimarus and Johann Semler. Hegel's historicizing orientation gave rise to a new wave of interest in applying historical tools to the Bible. Among the most famous of these scholars was F. C. Baur (1792–1860). Having become interested in expounding the historical development of the New Testament, Baur found Hegel's dialectic helpful in relating Peter's Judaizing Christianity to Paul's universal perspective, identifying their "synthesis" in the Gospel of John (*Christianity and the Christian Church during the First Three Centuries*).

David Friedrich Strauss (1808–74) was one of the first to apply the tools of historical criticism to Gospel accounts concerning Jesus. Concluding that there is little to be found that is of historical substance, he argued that the Gospels are myths. For Strauss, the "Jesus" of the Gospels is a dialectical formula, a principal illustrating the eternal truth of essential divine-human unity. The Gospel writers, Strauss alleged, fabricated what they wrote. In a manner most suggestive of the thought of the greatest theologian of his era, Friedrich Schleiermacher (1768–1834), Strauss maintained that myths about Jesus were in fact descriptions of the subjective experiences of the faithful clothed in the language of a premodern ontology (*Life of Jesus, Critically Examined* 69–70, 892–96). In a later work (*Life of Jesus for the German People*), Strauss presented a Jesus who was a bit more palatable to the public, as he focused on the historical Jesus' self-consciousness, presenting him as a teacher of spiritual peace whose miracles pertained to spiritual healing.

## The Rise and Fall of the Quest for the Historical Jesus

Numerous other "lives of Jesus" (presenting "historical data" about him that seemed to portray him as holding views compatible with nineteenth-century Western thinking) were written by early biblical critics. These efforts were effectively put to an end by the Nobel Prize–winning great humanitarian, talented musician, and renowned scholar Albert Schweitzer (1875–1965). This multitalented Alsatian Lutheran began his career in theology. His dissertation, *The Quest of the Historical Jesus*, brought him international acclaim and became a turning point in the history of theology.

Essentially Schweitzer argued, contrary to many of his contemporaries, that the historical Jesus is not recoverable. We do not have sufficient historically credible evidence to reconstruct a biography of Jesus. Most efforts in the nineteenth century (and perhaps those making claims regarding the historical Jesus in the twentieth century) presented a Jesus who was little more than an affirmer of contemporary values. In fact, Schweitzer argued, in the New Testament, history is inextricably mixed with eschatological expectations; thus, about all we can conclude regarding the historical Jesus is that a thoroughgoing eschatology was at the heart of his message. According to Schweitzer, this message makes Jesus appropriate for every era because it lifts hearers out of their world and so conveys a world-negating spirit. In emphasizing the eschatological core of Jesus' message and dearth of biographical information concerning him, Schweitzer merely summarized at this point, then, what New Testament critical scholarship has been saying almost since the dawn of the twentieth century. At least implicitly he was an early proponent of the distinction between the "historical Jesus" and the "Christ of faith" (*Quest of the Historical Jesus*, esp. 398).

Schweitzer's observations seem commonplace to church leaders trained in modern historical criticism, but to make such points at the beginning of the twentieth century was startling. So devastating was Schweitzer's critique of efforts to reconstruct the historical Jesus that he effectively rendered such endeavors intellectually suspect until a brief revival commenced in the latter half of the twentieth century.

### Ernst Troeltsch

The examination of Christianity in relation to the new historical consciousness was perhaps undertaken by no one with more rigor and academic excellence than the renowned German scholar Ernst Troeltsch (1865–1923). Troeltsch proceeded in at least two related ways. First, he undertook sociological analysis of Christian institutions and teachings. In some respects, Troeltsch might be regarded as the founder of the discipline of the sociology of religion. Second, his commitment to interpreting Christianity as a social phenomenon led him to become one of the first Western scholars to forfeit the idea of a true "essence" of Christianity underlying all the distinct historical developments ("Das Wesen des Christentum," in *Die Christliche Welt* [1903]). This was a radical stance, since even the liberal Enlightenment scholars did maintain that there was something rational and true about Christianity that was not subject to the vagaries of history. Were these scholars or Troeltsch correct? Does Christianity have an ahistorical, unchanging essence?

Troeltsch's legacy is very much alive whenever analysis of Christian developments is conducted with an eye towards their interaction with their cultural contexts and political trends. Much of the kind of analysis of Christianity and other religions that transpires in the West's universities and seminaries is indebted to Troeltsch's insights.

*Church-type versus sect-type Christianity.* Perhaps the most well-known of Troeltsch's sociological observations was the distinction he claimed to observe among Christian communities between the church-type and the sect-type of Christianity (*Social Teaching of the Christian Churches* 1:331–37). The social structures of these two communities were thought to nurture two significantly different "religions." In making this claim, Troeltsch essentially rejected the idea that Christianity had an ahistorical essence. According to the great German scholar, the sort of Christianity that aligns itself with the powers that be in society, the church-type dominates the masses, emerging in contexts where being a Christian is perceived as virtually identical with being a good citizen. Consequently, its welfare is intimately interconnected with the state and the upper classes. As such, the church-type version of Christianity is characteristically conservative and inclined to universalize its particular values and beliefs.

By contrast, sect-type Christianity is a countercultural version of the faith. Usually comprising members drawn from the lower classes or at least those not at the center of power, sect-type Christianity tends to appeal to primitive Christianity as its paradigm. In turn, it tends to focus more on lay Christianity than hierarchical organization, to be more local than universalistic in its thinking.

Readers should consider whether their particular religious community is more church-type or sectarian in orientation. Which of these two versions of Christianity is more in accord with the gospel?

*The essence of the historical consciousness.* The other way in which Troeltsch's interests in the historical method emerged was in his study of the presuppositions of historical consciousness. He identified three principles with which historians operate, each of them posing challenges to the veracity of Christian faith (*Gesammelte Schriften* 2:729–53): criticism, correlation, and analogy.

The principle of criticism is the commitment to accept no ancient text as authoritative just because it is ancient. This challenge to the Bible's authority at the very least claims that the Bible cannot be deemed authoritative in principle. The principle of correlation is to understand all events of the past in terms of their contexts, causes, and outcomes. This principle renders the concept of miracles intellectually untenable, for it maintains that all reported events must be capable of exposition in light of these factors or else its veracity must be challenged. The principle of analogy is to identify a correspondence between a reported past event and present experience in order for the account to be deemed historically verifiable. Since one would not have experienced a resurrection in present experience, this principle effectively challenges the veracity of the Resurrection accounts.

Contemporary hesitancy about the Bible's literal sense seems to verify the validity of the analysis of the historical consciousness offered by Troeltsch. Although in the final decades of the twentieth century this analysis of the modern historical consciousness has been challenged, it still seems to have validity in describing the way in which modern Western people make historical judgments. For example, the claim of a healthy heterosexual couple who have lived together a number of years that their relationship is purely platonic would likely be met with some skepticism (principle of criticism). In evaluating the truth of their claim, we would proceed to assess the circumstances that brought about their living arrangements and to take into account their reputation for truthfulness and observe their ways of relating to each other in our presence (principle of correlation). Our skepticism about their claim is no doubt also related to the fact that most of us have little present experience with cohabiting heterosexual couples who are purely platonic in their relationships (principle of analogy). Are Troeltsch's three principles of historical judgment not regularly employed by most citizens of Western society? If so, is it little wonder why there is so much discomfort in Western pews as well as in the theological academy with the Bible's literal sense?

### The Emergence of Church History as a Distinct Discipline

Historical methods came to be applied to Scripture in the nineteenth century and also began to be applied to a new course of study — *church history*. Christian doctrines increasingly became regarded as the product of historical evolution, rather than as given in their final form in the New Testament. This observation coupled with the growing demand for specialization, which the Enlightenment and the new scientific ethos encouraged, led to the gradual evolution of church history as a distinct discipline in the curriculum of Western theological education. Two of the intellectual leaders of this new development were the eminent German scholars Albrecht Ritschl (1822–89) and Adolf von Harnack (1851–1930).

In a manner not unlike Kant, Ritschl translated the gospel into moral categories. For example, in his view, Christ is Son of God because we recognize him to have the value of God by the ethical work he does in us (Ritschl *Christian Doctrine of Justification and Reconciliation*). Harnack identified important differences between the Christianity of the Gospels and the effect of the Greek point of view on Christianity in the early Church. Many of the core suppositions of modern biblical criticism and the history of the early Church reflect Harnack's insights. Unlike Troeltsch, though much like his teacher Ritschl, Harnack did believe that there was an essence of Christianity that was construed as a moral version of Christianity — Christianity interpreted in categories of ethics. Such commitments very much set the theological agenda for early-twentieth-century theological liberalism (Harnack *What Is Christianity?* 6ff.). No matter how radically Christianity is reconstrued in interest of rendering it more intellectually respectable, such endeavors, it was argued by Harnack, were valid as long as the new conceptualization communicated Christianity's essence. In this debate between Harnack and Troeltsch over whether Christianity has an essence, who is correct? Harnack's moral reinterpretation of the Christian faith produced at least one provocative constructive proposal in addition to the profound historical insights his work offered. Seeming to prefigure theological trends of the second half of the twentieth century (esp. liberation theology), Harnack claimed that the gospel is a social message, a proclamation of solidarity, in favor of the poor (*What Is Christianity?* 101). The influence of Harnack's and Ritschl's work was in time reflected in the curriculum, in the perceived desirability of theological institutions to develop separate courses of study in the field of church history, instead of as an appendage of theology. It is evident how their theological proposals set the agenda for theology in the next century — not just for liberals who followed their agenda but also for those who reacted against it.

The new historical consciousness also contributed to the emergence of rekindled interest in the theology of the sixteenth-century Reformers, especially Luther. In a sense, this was nothing new. Committed Lutherans and Reformed/Presbyterian Christians had venerated Luther and Calvin respectively since the Reformation. However, the actual thought of these Reformers increasingly received consideration from the time of the seventeenth century, and when it was considered, it was interpreted in light of the suppositions of the dominant orthodox theology of the day. The new historical consciousness called these "orthodox" versions of Luther and Calvin into question. It also affirmed the value of studying the Reformers on their own terms in their own contexts.

Ritschl is usually credited with initiating the renewed interest in the study of Luther. Clearly the propagation of this new scholarly field was enhanced by publication of the collection of Luther's works (the so-called *Weimarer Ausgabe*). The outcome of these developments came to fruition in the 1920s with the so-called Luther renaissance. Even Catholics and other Protestants began serious study of Luther's works. In trying to make Luther relevant to the contemporary situation, scholars experienced some of the same problems that beset the quest for the historical Jesus. From time to time, notably in the work of Troeltsch on Luther, the scholarly community was reminded not to forget Luther's medieval background, that he was not a modern man.

Doubtless inspired by the new interest in the Reformation and its themes, at least two distinct reactions to the Enlightenment's theological liberalism began to develop on German soil. A revival of Lutheran orthodox theology combined with Pietism's preoccupation with spirituality, one reaction is identified as Neo-Lutheranism. Among its most prominent proponents were Ernst Hengstenberg (1802–69) and Wilhelm Loehe (1808–72). The coalition with orthodox theology altered the character of Pietism. It rendered segments of Pietism more doctrinally rigid and also, like its orthodox coalition partner, more open to the use of reason and philosophical dialogue. It is common to refer to this development as Neo-Pietism. Its ethos began to influence those segments of Pietism that have established and continue to nurture the European free churches and their American sister denominations. Correspondingly, the Neo-Pietist (orthodox) preoccupation with doctrinal purity accounts for why segments of American Pietism (including revivalism) have become associated with Fundamentalism and subsequently with the Evangelical movement.

The other German reaction to Enlightenment theological liberalism in light of the recovery of interest in Luther centered at Erlangen University in Germany. Led by J. C. K. von Hofmann (1810–77), the so-called Erlangen school of theology (also sometimes called "Neo-Lutheranism") was thoroughly post-Enlightenment in its commitment to the use of the new historical consciousness as well as to the Kantian supposition that truth is relative to the interpreter's presuppositions. However, its proponents were convinced that a historical approach would lead to a vindication of the core insights of the Reformation. Of course, they could not make these points if limited to the tools of historical criticism alone. Thus Scripture was construed as an outcome of, and so a witness to, a salvation history (*Heilsgeschichte*). This history, which is the subject matter of theology, is accessible, not to objective proof, but only to those who share presuppositions regarding its witness to Christ (Hofmann *Interpreting the Bible* 128). In this way, the Bible's authority seemed protected from negative conclusions of historical critics about its claims. Though little known in America, this school of theology would become tremendously influential on theologians of the twentieth century concerned about the undue optimism of liberal theology.

The Luther renaissance and appreciation of the Reformation theological traditions extended to the Reformed heritage as well. In the nineteenth-century Netherlands arose a Neo-Calvinism that saw in the heritage of Calvin an understanding of every sphere of social life as having religious roots. Thus, each could be evaluated by Christian criteria. With regard to hermeneutics, Neo-Calvinism had some similarities to the Erlangen school. As did the latter, these Dutch scholars, notably Abraham Kuyper (1837–1920) and Herman Bavinck (1854–1921), claimed that only with certain presuppositions (i.e., faith) could Scripture be properly understood (Kuyper *Principles of Sacred Theology* 248–56). Neo-Calvinism differed from the Luther renaissance, though, in the sense of the national impact it was able to achieve. Despite his role as a member of the Dutch legislature and as prime minister, Kuyper succeeded in framing legislation to implement his reform. Earlier he had led a secession from the state-supported Netherlands Reformed Church. The resulting free body, the Reformed Churches in the Netherlands, has become the largest free church in the nation.[5]

Despite Kuyper, a revival of interest in Calvin has not had the impact in the Reformed-Presbyterian heritage that the renewed interest in Luther has had in Lutheranism. By the mid-twentieth century, it had become virtually impossible to do Lutheran theology apart from a dialogue with Luther. That has not been the case with regard to Calvin when one does Reformed theology. The question of whether fidelity to the theology of Luther or Calvin is good for the Church in our modern context warrants critical reflection.

## Rudolf Otto

Without question, the discipline of the *history of religion* (the examination of what the religions of the world have in common) owes its origin to the great German scholar Rudolf Otto (1869–1937). In Otto's view, at the essence of all religion is the experience of the holy, the *numinous*. It is an experience so awesome that it defies reason, so bewildering that it overwhelms us. The numinous allures us with potent charm. This analysis was Otto's way of breaking out of a rationalistic interpretation of the essence of Christianity typical of many of the nineteenth-century scholars. His work also set the stage for the modern tendency to regard all religions as equally valid, to talk about religion as a field to be studied and then particular religions as species of this genus (*Idea of the Holy* 1–7, 12, 28). Such a perspective represented a radical break with the past. Premodern Western people knew no general category of religion, just their own tradition distinct from all others. Do premodern people have it right in their views on things religious, or has Otto and the history of religion more properly represented this reality?

---

5. One reason for this church's growth was the result of its merger with an early secession that was planted in the United States as the Christian Reformed Church.

# Roman Catholic Responses
## to the New Intellectual Environment

It is fair to speak of a general Roman Catholic rejection of the new historical consciousness, optimism about science and inevitability of progress, and the increasingly individualistic focus and propensity to relativism. What was ultimately at stake for the Roman Church was its authority.

The hesitancy to embrace the new order was rooted in the Roman Catholic Church's critical attitude toward the eighteenth-century French Revolution. The reigning pope at the time, Pius VI, had tried to impede the Revolution. The French republicans retaliated, successfully weakening the papacy by establishing an atheistic "cult of reason" at home and in 1798 by capturing Rome, placing the pope under arrest. After Napoléon came to power, tensions with France eased, affording the papacy an opportunity to lead the Italian nationalist movement, which eventually culminated in the creation of a united kingdom of Italy. Nevertheless, the popes of this era, perhaps with the memory of the abuses of the French Revolution in mind, generally were inclined towards political and theological conservatism, including the discouragement of Catholics who would support democratic ideas. A particularly notable and influential example of these trends was the 1864 Syllabus of Errors of Pius IX (1792–1878). This encyclical criticized the freedom of religion, the establishment of public schools, and the separation of church and state. Pius also took the occasion to affirm the right of the papacy to hold political power. There is a sense in which the widespread perception into the second half of the twentieth century of an anti-Americanism in Catholicism stems from this document and the controversy it stirred.

### The Dogma of the Immaculate Conception

As the papacy was losing temporal power, Pius IX tried to reassert its power in the religious realm. In 1854, he proclaimed the dogma of the immaculate conception of Mary (*Ineffabilis Deus*). It proclaimed that the Virgin Mary had not been conceived in sin. The question of whether Mary had been kept free from original sin in the sex act that conceived her had been debated for centuries (at least since the Middle Ages), but this was the first time that a dogma was proclaimed by the pope without support of a council.[6] Most historians believe that Pius was

---

6. It could be argued that the immaculate conception is a logically necessary affirmation that the Church must make, for how could Christ be sinless if his Mother was not?

endeavoring to test the waters to see if the world would accept papal infallibility.

## Papal Infallibility and the First Vatican Council

The dogma of papal infallibility was actually proclaimed by the Catholic Church at the First Vatican Council in 1870 (*Collectio Lacensis* VIII), which was convoked by Pius IX the previous December. The precise nature of the dogma demands clarification. It does not claim that the pope is always infallible.[7] The council merely proclaimed that the pope is infallible when he speaks *ex cathedra* (from the chair). In other words, the pope is only infallible when he speaks on faith and morals in his official capacity of defining a doctrine to be held by the universal Church. On only one other occasion has this dogma been invoked — in 1950, when Pope Pius XII (Eugenio Pacelli; 1876–1958) promulgated the dogma of the assumption of Mary into heaven (*Munificentissimus Deus* I).

Is papal infallibility an issue that must necessarily divide the Church? Like the Roman Catholic Church (the dogma of its so-called *ordinary magisterium*), the Eastern Orthodox Church has affirmed the indefectibility of the Church's teachings on issues on which the bishops have concurred over time. Luther and other Reformation traditions that rely on a strong confessional tradition of authoritative teachings that achieve consensus among the community of believers virtually affirm the same point. Can Christianity thrive and survive if it is uncertain about the Church's authoritative teachings? Indeed, the idea of an authoritative teaching office located in Rome is no new teaching. At least since the time of Irenaeus (ca. 130–ca. 200), the primacy of the church of Rome's teachings has been affirmed (*Against Heresies* III.III.1).

Granted, papal infallibility did cause a small schism in the late nineteenth century after Vatican I. Some Catholics in the Netherlands, Austria, and Germany withdrew in protest to form the Old Catholic Church, a small body that continues to exist.

## Progressive Social Initiatives

Following the Vatican Council, Pope Leo XIII (Vincenzo Gioacchino Pecci; 1810–1903) made some important modifications in the overall conservative Catholic profile. Though hardline in resistance to Italian nationalism and its dominance of the papal states, and even though at one point in his career he declared democracy incompatible with

---

7. One pope, Zosimus (d. 418), actually supported Pelagius for a time during the Pelagian controversy, though he did eventually recant the position.

the authority of the Church (*Immortale Dei*), Leo sought reconciliation with France. He went so far as to advise the French clergy to abandon opposition to the Republic.

In the sphere of social ethics, perhaps the most important Catholic intervention in the nineteenth century was Leo's 1891 bull titled *Rerum Novarum*. It clearly represented Catholicism's first reaction to the socioeconomic consequences of the industrial revolution, and it is indeed a most progressive document. The subject of the bull was the proper relation between laborers and employers, the perennial concern of capitalism that was especially prominent among social reformers in the early stages of Western industrialization. The document demonstrates an awareness of the contrast between the enormous fortunes being accumulated by the rich and the poverty of the masses. Leo proceeded to assert that there must be mutual rights and obligations between the two classes. Laws need to guarantee the rights of the poor.[8]

The bull did affirm private property. It then proceeded to authorize Catholic labor unions and advocate sufficient wages by appeal to the *natural law* (the structures of the cosmos, the way things are intended to be in the world, which are known by all). We have with the document, then, the beginning of the modern Catholic trade union movement. *Rerum Novarum* clearly made possible the significant involvement of Catholics in American labor unions of the first half of the twentieth century. Of course, this development and the bull did give conservatives something too. They could argue that the only valid union involvement by Catholics was in distinct Catholic unions.

Leo's concern to provide something for all his constituents is evident in a later bull that admitted the value of historical studies of the Bible but warned against its use to weaken the Bible's and the Church's authority (*Providentissimus Deus*). The conservatism of Leo and the Catholic Church was also reflected in another significant way. In the 1896 encyclical *Apostolicae curae*, which was based on the report of a papal commission, Catholicism officially declared that apostolic succession, and so a valid ministry, had not in fact been preserved in the Church of England. As such, from the Roman point of view the Anglican tradition's claim to a ministry that has preserved apostolic succession does it no good. This judgment remains to this day a serious ecumenical barrier.

Leo's successor, Pius X (Giuseppe Melchior Sarto; 1835–1914), was even more conservative. He condemned the so-called Modernists, who

---

8. One might say that the bull foreshadows themes of twentieth-century liberation theology. Can we say that *Rerum Novarum* establishes legitimate precedents in Catholicism for liberation theology?

had been employing biblical criticism (*Pascendi dominici gregis*). The most famous of these condemned scholars were A. F. Loisy (1857–1940), George Tyrrell (1861–1901), and Hermann Schell (1850–1906). Never again, until the Second Vatican Council of the 1960s, would Modernists be inclined to view the papacy as an ally. Although some avant-garde Catholic theologians would continue to employ biblical criticism, it was not until after Vatican II that its use would be officially acceptable in Catholic circles. Was this theological conservatism good for the Catholic Church or bad for it?

# Protestant Reactions
# to the New Intellectual Environment

By the end of the nineteenth century, the gap between Protestants and Catholics was wider than in previous centuries. While old doctrinal and ethnic divisions between the parties remained, the uniformly conservative reaction of the Roman Catholic Church to the inroads of Modernism in contrast to the relative openness of Protestant leaders to the new intellectual currents led Protestants increasingly to view Catholicism as a relic of a bygone age and led Catholics to view Protestants as heretical capitulators to challenges of the modern world.

In order to understand how constructively Protestants came to terms with the new challenges, it is necessary to reconsider the positive spiritual developments that occurred during this period in England and to consider the work of the great nineteenth-century German Reformed/United theologian Friedrich Schleiermacher. He has been called the "father of *liberal theology*" (a theology that aims to incorporate the insights of the Enlightenment in its portrayal of the Christian faith). Though Kant foreshadowed aspects of Schleiermacher's basic theological (correlationist) orientation, Schleiermacher himself has effectively functioned as the paradigm for modern theology.

## The Oxford Movement: Theological Commitments

Within the Church of England, Anglican Evangelicalism and the Oxford Movement (Anglo-Catholicism) emerged as distinct responses to the new circumstances of the nineteenth century. The industrial revolution had come to England earlier than elsewhere, and in many respects Wesley's Methodist revival in the previous century can also be understood as a kind of reaction to it and the inroads of the Enlightenment on the British Isles.

The Oxford Movement was not merely a repristination of the Catholic tradition, for the reform of spiritual life and church practice, not aesthetics nor nostalgia, were the motivating causes of the movement. This point was clearly articulated by one of the movement's leaders, John Keble, in his famed 1833 assize sermon, wherein he lamented that under the guise of toleration, we have become indifferent to religious practice. It is interesting to reflect on whether this might still be a problem for post-Enlightenment twenty-first-century Christians. Is this not still a problem in our "anything goes" ethos?

As is evident from its conflicts with the Evangelical party within the Anglican Church, the Oxford Movement produced significant controversy. The movement had its origins in the endeavor of a number of Oxford University scholars to counteract the influence of Enlightenment rationalism, theological liberalism, and Evangelicalism, and their collective emphasis on individual judgment over the authority of tradition. However, controversy over the British Parliament's reduction of the number of Anglican bishoprics in Ireland occasioned its emergence. Keble's previously noted 1833 sermon spoke against this move and led to the publication of a significant number of tracts that aimed to show the value of the Catholic tradition for the Church of England. As a result of this means of disseminating information, the members of the movement also became known as Tractarians.

As years went by, the tracts issued by the group became more and more Catholic in their orientation until 1841, when the bishop of Oxford ordered them discontinued. Feeling that all hope of genuine reform in the Church of England had been quashed, the movement's most visible spokesman, John Henry Newman (1801–90), and several other members converted to Catholicism. In fact, Newman eventually became a Catholic cardinal. The vast majority of the movement's leaders remained Anglican, and their influence has continued to be felt in the Anglican community through liturgical reform and the preservation of the Catholic elements within this community of churches.

The Oxford Movement raises several issues that continue to be relevant. One thinks of Newman's claim that the Catholic system could not have endured so long had it been a corruption of the Christian faith and that revivals change no one (*Essay on the Development of Christian Doctrine*). Were proponents of the movement, Newman in particular, correct in claiming that the Thirty-nine Articles of the Anglican Reformation could be endorsed by those who still aimed to be Catholic and that appeals to tradition, belief in purgatory, and *Masses* (celebrations of the Eucharist) said for the dead are valid (*Remarks on Certain Passages in the Thirty-nine Articles*). Is it true, as Newman claimed, that the Anglican Reformation really changed nothing, that the reform never intended to exclude Catholics?

The Oxford Movement asks us if we might need this kind of Catholicism in the Protestant context. At any rate, the Church of England (as well as the entire Anglican family, including the Episcopal Church in the U.S.A.) remains marked to the present by this sort of dialogue between Anglo-Catholics and Evangelicals. It is perhaps the genius of the Anglican tradition that it continues to hold together these distinct theological emphases.

### Friedrich Schleiermacher

Although the open-minded Catholic approach of the Oxford Movement was and continues to be one way of dealing with new challenges posed by modernity, most interpreters agree that Schleiermacher offered the paradigmatic Protestant approach to these challenges. Of a German (Prussian) Reformed background, Schleiermacher was influenced by Moravians, much as Wesley had been. Besides his work as a great modern apologist for the Christian faith and his role in providing the paradigm for modern theology, Schleiermacher was also a churchman and social commentator. Living during Napoléon's conquest of German territory, Schleiermacher preached to rally Prussian sentiment against the French; he succeeded in this and in bringing about a more liberal, democratic consciousness to his native region. When the king of Prussia mandated the union of Lutheran and Reformed churches in the region ostensibly in order to solidify unity of both Protestantism and Prussia from French and Austrian Catholic threats, he called on Schleiermacher to draw up the constitution for the new church. The existence of this Evangelical (Union) Church in Germany clearly bears the mark of this great theologian.

Schleiermacher's theological conviction is Kantian in the sense that he believed we must interpret Christian faith in light of some generally accepted conceptual framework. Influenced by *romanticism* (a philosophical movement emphasizing feeling, individuality, and the personality of the artist), Schleiermacher undertook a project of interpreting theological concepts in terms of feeling — specifically in terms of the feeling of absolute dependence, which he identified with faith. For Schleiermacher, then, doctrines assume the status of being merely formal descriptions of subjective states of faith (*Christian Faith* 4, 15–16). For example, in his view the divine attributes of eternality, omnipresence, and the like are, not something in God himself, but merely descriptions of the faithful's experience of the feeling of absolute dependence (50). In a similar manner, Schleiermacher views Christ as divine in virtue of his potent God-consciousness (94). Note the reliance on Kantian suppo-sitions at this point — that we do not know God as he is in himself (the noumenon) but only can speak of how we experience him (the phenomena of God).

In Schleiermacher's thought is a definite Christocentric, anthropocen-tric focus (*Christian Faith* 11), which has come to characterize much modern theology since his lifetime. At least two other commitments of his have also come to characterize Western theology since the time of this great German theologian. Schleiermacher deemphasized the doc-trine of the Trinity, treating it only at the very end of his dogmatics, as if it were an afterthought. In his view, the Trinity is not an utter-ance of Christian self-consciousness (feelings), for it is essential only with regard to its christological implications (170). Only very recently has subsequent Western theology begun to reconsider the Trinity doc-trine, after over 150 years of neglect. In like manner, Schleiermacher's treatment of the doctrine of the *atonement* (the work of Christ) es-tablished a trend in contemporary theology. He was critical of views of the atonement that emphasized the atoning power of Christ's sac-rifice (esp. the satisfaction theory). Rather, Schleiermacher construed Christ's atoning work as inspiring believers to acquire the power of his God-consciousness (the so-called moral influence theory of the atone-ment; 100–101). This emphasis on Christ's exemplary role continues to characterize post-Schleiermachian theology.

Although there is a certain drift in the direction of Pelagianism (works righteousness) associated with Schleiermacher's depiction of Christ's work, the German theologian expressly rejected this heresy (*Christian Faith* 80). Indeed, he insisted that the Christian's work in receiving Christ is really God's production in us of the will to assume Christ and his benefits. The faithful are attracted to Christ's person and work (100).

The paradigmatic character for subsequent Western theology of Schleiermacher's methodology is readily apparent. He attempted to cor-relate the Word of God and human experience, as did Kant, his heirs, and proponents of the correlationist approach in the early Church, such as Justin Martyr and the Alexandrian school of theology. Like them, Schleiermacher correlated Word and experience in such a way that his philosophical scheme for depicting human experience functioned as the framework for conceptualizing the Word of God.

Schleiermacher's method does not mandate that faith needs to be translated into language of feeling. It would allow for the translation of the core Christian doctrines into any conceptual system — psychology, socialism, the language of feminism, whatever. Such translation has been the prevailing theological approach in the West. Like the approach of the Apologists of the early Church, Schleiermacher's approach seems to guarantee the proclamation of a relevant, intellectually respectable version of the gospel. Schleiermacher's model also has the virtue of negating the importance of history for those portions of the Bible that are not historically accurate and scientifically credible. On his grounds, the real meaning of the Bible is, not what it says literally, but its deeper experiential meaning or the experience/feelings of the biblical authors (*Christian Faith* 103, 130).

The possible weaknesses of Schleiermacher's approach are identical with the ones noted in the dialogue between correlationist Apologists of the early Church and the Orthodox approach of the great North African theologian Tertullian (ca. 160–ca. 225). He rejected all efforts to correlate the Word of God and the prevailing conceptuality of the social context. Instead he opted for a "christocentric orthodoxy," insisting that the context be interpreted by the Word, and not vice versa as the correlationist approach endeavors to do. Will the correlationist approach inevitably construe Christian faith in a heretical manner as Tertullian alleged?

Another set of challenges to Schleiermacher and other correlationists was implicitly posed by the German nineteenth-century philosopher Ludwig Feuerbach (1804–72).[9] Feuerbach — a radical, materialistic interpreter of Hegel, after the fashion of Karl Marx — claimed that ultimately all religion is anthropology. The deities of religion, he claimed at least early in his career, are nothing but the essential projections of human nature (*Essence of Christianity* I.2). Later in his career, he attributed this religious propensity to our desire to render our dependence on nature less mysterious by conceiving its forces in a personal way (*Essence of Religion*). To the extent that Schleiermacher and other correlationists initiate their analysis of Christian faith from the perspective of human experience and reinterpret faith's claims in that light, the concern is that they cannot refute Feuerbach's conclusions. For example, even if they assert that God transcends human experience, on their own grounds, does it not follow that even the concept of God and his transcendence must be construed as an expression of human experience? Is there any way to refute Feuerbach's critique with a correlationist approach to theology? Is Tertullian's theological model (also that of the Protestant Reformers and seventeenth-century orthodox theology) the only way to respond to Feuerbach's critique?

Schleiermacher's theological approach is thoroughly Kantian in another way. Just as Kant insisted epistemologically that the interpreter cannot get to the thing-in-itself, so Schleiermacher implicitly claimed

---

9. Feuerbach's implicit challenge was explicitly formulated in the next century by the great Swiss Reformed theologian Karl Barth (*Protestant Thought* 358).

that our understanding of Christian faith is a matter of one's perspective. Faith, after all, is always to be interpreted from the perspective of the interpretive questions one brings to the text and the categories into which the theologian intends to translate the classical Christian doctrines. As Kant's philosophy has helped to undergird the emergence of relativism in Western society, does Schleiermacher's correlationist approach contribute to such an ethos, effectively negating any role that Christian faith might play in critiquing such a worldview? A number, but not all, of the other prominent religious thinkers of his own century share some of Schleiermacher's methodological characteristics.

## William James

The founder of the philosophy of *Pragmatism* (an antimetaphysical philosophy teaching that truth is to be determined solely according to the criterion of whether an idea "works," that is, whether it enhances life), William James (1842–1910) was also a religious thinker. In this connection, this famed American scholar is best known for advocating a kind of correlationist approach that translated religion into the categories of psychology. For example, he suggested that the unconscious, the development of the subliminal self, might be deemed the point of linkage between divine power and human experience (*Varieties of Religious Experience*).

James essentially employed the same method as Schleiermacher. The sole difference was the distinct categories into which each scholar translated Christian/religious concepts. This theological method has tended to dominate much psychology of religion and pastoral psychology that has been produced since James.

## Horace Bushnell

The career of Horace Bushnell (1802–76), a great nineteenth-century theologian, was devoted to mediation. His agenda was to find a way to mediate between liberal Unitarians and orthodox Calvinists, such as Jonathan Edwards. Among Bushnell's points was a criticism of an emphasis on conversion, rather than education, in the Christian nurture of children (*Christian Nurture*). In tension with the orthodox theology prevailing in his day, Bushnell rejected the idea of Christ's atonement as a sacrifice paid to God. Much like Schleiermacher and other proponents of the moral influence theory of the atonement, he preferred to speak of Christ's work as a witness to an external and divine principle of love (*Vicarious Sacrifice*). This love is expressed, he maintained, much as poetry expresses emotions (*God in Christ*).

A most interesting aspect of Bushnell's thought, one that prefigures recent theological trends, is his view of biblical language. Science and the supernatural are not in opposition in his view, for he deemed religious language to be rooted in the creative imagination. Biblical language is metaphoric and so cannot be properly evaluated by scientific means (*God in Christ; Vicarious Sacrifice; Nature and the Supernatural; Building Eras in Religion* 272ff.). Science does not challenge the Bible because the Bible is poetry. Is this an intellectually credible way of dealing with the challenges posed to faith by historical criticism and science?[10] Another most contemporary point is Bushnell's pregnant observation that because the Bible is rich in metaphor, with meaning that can never be pinned down definitively, Christians disagree. Each group's imagination is considered to be inspired differently by the gift of Scripture (*Building Eras in Religion* 263ff.).

### Fannie Barrier Williams

One of the prominent religious thinkers of the late nineteenth to early twentieth century was the African American woman scholar Fannie Barrier Williams (1855–1944). She articulated the close link between her own heritage and the moral-social influences of religion.

Lecturing to the World's Parliament of Religions in 1893, Williams insisted that African Americans are part of the American church. Emphasizing this point, she proceeded to argue that all vestiges of African culture have been stripped. By no means a blind apologist for American Christianity, she proceeded to lament how religion had been illicitly used to authorize slavery. Such religion, she asserted, had been stripped of moral instruction. At this point, she turned to praise African American churches like the African Methodist Episcopal Church as evidences of religious heroism, of the righteous protest of the black church as a whole.

In another 1893 lecture, the one given to the World's Congress of Representative Women, Williams turned to the present state of the African American community. In her view, at the heart of every social evil among African Americans is the lack of inherent moral potencies of family and home that are wellsprings of all good in human society. Slavery aimed to destroy family instincts, she claimed.

---

10. A reading of the Bible's literal sense, in a manner not unlike Bushnell's proposal, can present a most relevant gospel. Apparently one does not necessarily need to employ Schleiermacher's correlationist method in order to offer a relevant version of the Word. It is not entirely clear how Fannie Williams, Elizabeth Cady Stanton, and Walter Rauschenbusch addressed the challenges posed by historical criticism and science; however, there is at least some indication that two of them simply embraced the literal sense of Scripture.

Many late-twentieth-century analysts shared Williams's idea that slavery had destroyed African American family instincts. Such an observation, though, seems to overlook the extended-family ethos (perhaps rooted in African vestiges) exhibited in many segments of the African American community. Are Williams's observations on target, or is she guilty here and elsewhere of overlooking the perdurance of African roots in the African American community?

Williams also considered notions that were especially timely with regard to women's issues. She insisted that, despite enduring the degradation of slavery, the African American woman retains all the moral instincts necessary to teachableness, that is, an inspiring ability to rise above her condition. In pointing to the moral capabilities and leadership of African American women, does Williams have her finger on a formula of profound importance for grappling with the inner-city and rural poverty Americans face as they enter the twenty-first century?

### Elizabeth Cady Stanton

Williams's celebration of the leadership and moral capacities of women emerged in a context already ripe for such reflections in virtue of the woman suffrage movement of America. Among its most renown leaders was the theologically trained Presbyterian Elizabeth Cady Stanton (1815–1902). She was also notably active in the antislavery movement.

An examination of Stanton's theology makes it quite evident that the American suffrage movement cannot be understood apart from her Christian theological commitments. For example, in her work *The Woman's Bible* (14–16), she argued that the creation account in Genesis affirms equality of male and female, for both are created in the image of God. Male and female as the image of God has implications for understanding God. If God's image can be male and female, it follows that God is Mother as well as Father. Such an affirmation is crucial to elevating woman to her true position as an equal partner. *Elohim* is thus identified as a divine plurality. Of course, Stanton recognized that there are references to woman's subordination in the second creation account. Her conclusion that these texts are mere allegory was consistent with her rejection of the divine inspiration of Scripture, which she coupled with her apparent rejection of special revelation and insistence that "no man ever saw or talked with God" (*Woman's Bible*, Int.).

Stanton's treatment of the parable of the wise and foolish bridesmaids (Matt. 25:1–12) sheds interesting light on her views and her role as a prophet for contemporary feminism (*Woman's Bible* 124–26). She claimed that the wise women were those who continued to burn oil for their own use, not just for the men in their lives, seeking instead education and other advantages for themselves in order to be fitted to respond to the responsibilities of life. In this connection, Stanton also expressed concern that women were not permitted to occupy pulpits. Obviously, the ordination of women was a commitment of the women's liberation movement in its earliest stages.

## Walter Rauschenbusch and the Social Gospel

The concern to relate faith to the social conditions of the day, which is reflected in Williams and Stanton, was perhaps nowhere more prominent in Christian theology than in the life and thought of the German American Baptist theologian Walter Rauschenbusch (1861–1918). He was the prime proponent of the *social gospel* (a set of beliefs holding that there must be a relationship between the gospel and the misery in which the urban masses lived, that the social and economic life of America must conform to the gospel). The movement and Rauschenbusch in particular sought to break out of the otherworldliness to which his Pietist tradition had succumbed, largely as a result of its co-option by modern revivalism. The social concern of the social gospel was also a threat to the proponents of Protestant orthodox theology, which still prevailed in the denominations of the American power structure at the turn of the century. Given its doctrinal, university-based orientation, orthodox theology tended to be a theology of the educated elite, who generally speaking were less likely to have a vested interest in social reform.

Most proponents of orthodox theology regarded proponents of the social gospel as in the same camp as their other nemesis — liberal theology. However, there is good reason to distinguish the social-gospel movement and liberal theology. As implied by their general silence on the social issues of their day, nineteenth-century liberal theologians did not really have a social-gospel concern with the poor and a critical perspective on the capitalist system. The two theological movements do share an optimism, however, regarding human capabilities and the progress of society. They also shared a common belief that the Bible must be interpreted in such a way as to address the issues of the day. In the case of the social-gospel movement, the Bible was understood to embody a social concern that must be reflected in modern theology.

The distinction between liberal theology and Rauschenbusch is readily apparent in his more conservative approach to Scripture. He did not employ anything like Schleiermacher's theological model. On the contrary, Rauschenbusch simply read the Bible literally to discern that its dominant testimony is to the kingdom of God (*Christianity and the Social Crisis*). In seeing this emphasis in the New Testament, Rauschenbusch seems to have linked himself to critical biblical scholarship, as liberal theology did (insofar as nineteenth-century biblical criticism, continuing into the twentieth century, identified eschatology as the heart of the New Testament proclamation). Also like the liberals, Rauschenbusch conceded that attention to the concerns of the day, in his case social concern, does throw new light on all elements of the gospel (339).

For Rauschenbusch, all theological commitments must articulate organically with the kingdom of God theme (*Theology for the Social Gospel* 131). His agenda was that economic life conform to gospel principles (*Christianity and the Social Crisis* 340–42), which in his view entailed a concern about the welfare of the poor and oppressed (41–42) and an opposition to private property and economic monopolies. This political and economic agenda, he claimed, is necessitated because the reign of love in human affairs is the norm for the kingdom of God (*Theology for the Social Gospel* 139ff.).[11] A kind of naivete (or Enlightenment confidence in progress) seems to be reflected in Rauschenbusch's thought. At the very least, he stood in the tradition of Puritanism and Calvin with regard to his views on the relation of church and society. He clearly identified the kingdom of God with his socialist social program of abolishing private property and monopolies (*Theology for the Social Gospel* 142–45).

In the twentieth century, a number of theologians and movements emerged that worked self-consciously to relate the gospel to the social injustices of the day. An important issue to consider is the degree to which they embody the theological commitments of the social gospel. To what degree is the social-gospel movement still relevant for the contemporary Church?

## Did the Church Respond Well to the Development of Post-Enlightenment Modernity?

In the nineteenth century were two distinct responses by the Western church to post-Enlightenment modernity. The Catholic Church and some theological conservative segments of Protestantism totally rejected these new developments. Some Protestants reacting in this way in America came to form the vanguard of Fundamentalism. A middle ground is identifiable in some segments of Protestantism. Protestants largely drawn from the impoverished, less-educated classes in both western Europe and the Americas continued to embody a piety shaped by

---

11. In the tradition of Puritanism and his own Baptist heritage, Rauschenbusch apparently endorsed something like a third use of the law.

unreflected forms of Pietism or in the premodern forms of the Reformation and its oral storytelling ethos. The African American church and other ethnic and immigrant churches in America certainly continued to embody the latter. Other segments of Protestantism embraced the post-Enlightenment ethos and tried to correlate the Christian faith with these new insights (so-called Protestant liberalism).

Were the Church's various nineteenth-century responses to the crises posed by post-Enlightenment modernity adequate? Are they still adequate? In the following century, these models of response continued to prevail in the Western church, though several additional theological models responding to the challenges of modernity did develop.

# CHAPTER 14

# THE TWENTIETH CENTURY
## THE DAY BEFORE YESTERDAY

As did Western society as a whole, the tone of church life in the West changed quite markedly in the twentieth century; in fact, church life changed almost as drastically as the new technology of the millennium's final century changed lifestyles and cultures. Once again, the Church's diversity has been enriched by its encounter with new historical and social contexts.

Among western Europeans and European Americans, the nineteenth century had been an age of unambiguous optimism about the future and what technology or the industrial revolution could provide. In view of the extraordinary advances in technology — the modern conveniences that gradually came into the possession of the middle class — and the generally higher standards of living enjoyed by turn-of-the-century denizens of Western society, how could such optimism not emerge within their ranks? If life had gotten so much better in one's own lifetime, how could there be any doubt that, thanks to the new science and technology, better days were inevitably on the horizon for one's progeny?

This sort of optimism was reflected in Protestant liberal theology, which did not typically affirm a strong doctrine of sin. (It, like Schleiermacher, focused theology more on the human person and the experience of the faithful, instead of on God's act.) Such optimism was also manifested in the social gospel of Rauschenbusch with its belief that the faithful could change the world. Even missionary efforts seemed to blossom in the European colonies and other mission stations, as the native populations of Asia, Africa, and Latin America appeared most interested in adopting the "wisdom," ways, and technology of Western culture. With such Westernization, the adoption of Christianity by these populations became more attractive. Some Western observers at the beginning of the century came to express the hope that the whole world might become Christian!

Well before the 1950s, however, such optimism had been shattered. The combination of severe economic upheavals (the depressions) and international wars spelled an end to optimism. In face of this new situation, theology and church life eventually changed too.

301

# The Turmoils of Modern Western Society

Nineteenth-century Europe enjoyed relative peace, made possible by the fact that competition among its powers took the form of colonial expansion. Consequently, territorial wars in Europe did not need to be fought. New markets required for the further expansion of the West's capitalist economies were available in the colonies.

By the twentieth century, though, the most attractive regions had been colonized. There seemed to remain no place for expansion overseas. As a result, western European powers began fixing their gaze on the Balkans for expansion. It was over this territory that World War I was originally fought. Provoked by a Serbian student's assassination of the heir to the Austrian throne, the ensuing tensions between the two nations provoked their allies, Germany (the ally of Austria) and Russia (the ally of Serbia), to aggression. As a Russian ally and in defense of Belgium, France soon entered against the Germans. Emerging hostilities, largely the fruit of economic competition and the German desire for an empire (since it had been the last of these major European powers to create a national government), brought England and eventually a reluctant America into the fray.

The war (1914–18) was the bloodiest ever fought to that point in history, superseded only by the world war that would follow it. Over five million lives were lost, and over twenty-two million suffered casualties. It was to have been the war to end all wars, American president Woodrow Wilson promised. It proved to be one of the many broken promises of the new century.

## Marxism and the Communist Revolution

Russia was another region where developments raised alarm after the war. The 1917 Communist Revolution brought to power a regime at least nominally committed to the philosophy of nineteenth-century German scholar, student of Hegel, Karl Marx. In many ways, this former monarchy was the least likely and prepared of European states to adopt the most radical of Enlightenment ideologies. It had not been a fertile field for the adoption of the new liberal ideas and had not readily embraced industrialization. Nevertheless, the existence of this Communist state and its subsequent allies stood as a challenge to much of the Western establishment, causing anxiety lest Communism thrive in Russia and eventually overturn the West's laissez-faire capitalist economics.

Marx taught that workers had been alienated from their labor by the industrial revolution. His Hegelian dialectic, shorn of Hegel's spirituality with a healthy dose of materialism, demanded synthesis — that all things come back to the worker, which entailed the abolition of private property so that laborers could be liberated to own (in common) all that they produce (Marx *Second Manuscript* XL; *Third Manuscript* XXXIXff.; *Manifesto of the Communist Party* II).

Marx's materialistic view of the world was related to his critical view of religion. For him, religion is the product of man, a tool of oppression (Marx *Contribution to the Critique of Hegel's Philosophy of Right*, Int.). Marx's views on religion were heavily indebted to another German philosopher of the period, Ludwig Feuerbach, who held religion and its claims as nothing more than anthropology, just human experience.

In Russia and after World War II in Eastern Europe, the Church at first was viewed as the enemy. In 1918, the Russian Orthodox Church was officially liberated from the state, representing a radical departure from the characteristic Eastern Orthodox vision of an intimate relation between church and state. After confiscating church property, the Communists adopted a policy that eventually became one of benign neglect in hope that the Russian (and other Eastern European) churches would wither away. Obviously they did not.

## The Impact of Psychotherapy and Nihilism

The period of social turbulence occasioned by nineteenth-century Europe's confrontation with the popularization of Enlightenment ideals and the industrial revolution produced at least two other intellectual movements with which the Church would need to grapple in the twentieth century — psychology and nihilism. Modern psychology is of course intimately connected with the career of Sigmund Freud (1856–1939), who was the product of a first-rate education in the humanities. Freud's interests in the human mind led him to conclude that the psyche (energies and processes of the mind) is moved by factors that never consciously emerge. The foundational user of psychic energy (the id) is chaotic and must be ordered by the ego, which is rooted at the subconscious level by the socialization process that represses these impulses (*Outline of Psychoanalysis*). A sense of powerlessness and victimization is implicit in this view of human nature. Hardly surprisingly, other analysts of the century shared this view: for example, Marx and others who observed the wrenching social upheavals and exploitation that seemed implicit in the emerging international industrial conglomerate of the time.

Even more cynical about the alienation and oppressive character of Western technological society was Friedrich Nietzsche (1844–1900), the famed German nihilist philosopher who also lived and worked in this period. He called for the emergence of the *Obermann*, who declares oneself over-against society and the masses. Only by the negation of all that is can one truly be oneself (*Will to Power* 854, 861, 866, 881), for according to Nietzsche, society aims to suppress such salubrious egoism, and in so doing it undercuts the striving for excellence in favor of mediocrity (373). A primary means of achieving this sort of suppression is to sanctify social structures that deny the ego by means of religion. Consequently, in the interest of making possible the *Obermann*'s quest for self-fulfillment, religion must be transcended; it must be proclaimed that "God is dead!" (*Thus Spoke Zarathustra* 2). This early modern affirmation of atheism and its associated nihilism would have profound impact on the intellectual life of the West as the new century continued.

   Though Marx, Nietzsche, and to some extent Freud were nineteenth-century figures, their greatest impact has been in the twentieth century. Their thought was even later arriving in America, probably not having significant impact on its universities until just after World War II. Since then, ideas associated or implied in their thought and in the philosophy of Kant, such as relativism (for all truth is a matter of personal preference), therapy, and socialism, have gradually permeated popular culture in America.

## The Great Depressions

Challenges posed by the various new philosophies (social sciences) became all the more serious when Western capitalist economies showed vulnerability in the economic depressions during the decades between the two World Wars. It was not just the United States that experienced such depressions; the severe economic recession was an international phenomenon. In consequence of the stock market crash of 1929, the drying up of foreign markets, and the closing of banks, almost one-third of the American labor force became unemployed. Times were harsh; food and hope, sometimes scarce. Such international dynamics contributed further to shattering the optimism that characterized the nineteenth century and its theology.

## Fascism and World War II

In western Europe, fascism developed largely as an alternative to Marxism. To some extent, it was itself a reaction to the individualism associated with Enlightenment thought, for fascism is a philosophy in which the individual subordinates the self to the greater good of social order (Mussolini "Doctrine of Fascism"). The movement logically entails strong nationalistic loyalties, as the good of one's people is said to be greater than one's own personal welfare.

It is hardly surprising that fascist ideology took root in a country whose national spirit had been wounded by its defeat in World War I — in Germany under Adolf Hitler (1889–1945). It also took root in Spain, which was led by Francisco Franco (1892–1975), and Italy, under Benito Mussolini (1883–1945). Each fascist leader had a different attitude towards the Church. The Catholic Church was Franco's closest ally. Mussolini was inconsistent in his attitude. Hitler felt that the Church's teachings of universal love and turning the other cheek were antagonistic to his program, but he sought to gain support from the Church. Part of his agenda was to bring it under his control.

Hitler's strategy was to co-opt the German Church to his side by offering a religious ideology that would view his government's policies as having a legitimate claim on its obedience. By reinterpreting (distorting) Luther's two-kingdom ethic, Hitler and his Christian supporters (who came to be known as German Christians) argued that any legitimate political authority in accord with the natural law, such as the Nazi policies, was God's Will. After all, it could be argued, Luther's two-kingdom ethic (and most German Christians were Lutheran) did not authorize a role for the gospel in the affairs of state. Besides, Romans 13 teaches submission to the authority of the state.[1]

No doubt the predominance of liberal theology among the leadership of the German churches was a factor in the acceptance of Hitler's line of argumentation. His appeal for seeking to perfect his race accorded nicely with liberal theology's optimism about human nature. The liberals' Enlightenment preoccupation with the individual also tended to influence them in reinterpreting a version of Christianity that was not so sensitive to social concerns. Furthermore, the propensity of much German liberal theology to construct a "Jesus" who looked like the modern man whom these theologians addressed (recall, this was Albert Schweitzer's critique of the quest for the historical Jesus) made it quite easy to identify Christian faith with the interests of the German people and so, correspondingly, to regard the Jews as somehow removed from the divine plan in Jesus.[2]

In 1933, Hitler directed the unification of all the various Protestant Church bodies in Germany into a united German Evangelical Church. Such a move was in the spirit of the fascist insistence that the welfare of the (German) people is more important than that of the individual or a community of individuals (such as the Church). Given these fascist com-

---

1. Luther's own version of church-state relations did have a tendency to this line of thinking, but recall his openness to nonviolent resistance when governmental authorities cause us to sin or are in violation of the second table of the Decalogue.

2. Of course, such attitudes towards Judaism had been deeply ingrained in the German Christian ethos at least since the Middle Ages.

mitments, now sanctified by German Christian leaders' reinterpretations of the Bible and Luther, and in view of the gratitude the German people felt towards Hitler for ostensibly helping them find their way out of the depression, it is a bit easier to understand how Hitler could command such obedience from the German people for his maniacal projects.

Of course, some Christians living in Germany reacted negatively to these developments. Karl Barth and Dietrich Bonhoeffer along with a Lutheran pastor from Berlin, Martin Niemöller (1892–1984), who was placed in a concentration camp for his actions, were among the leaders of a group of Christians in Germany critical of Nazi policies. So named because they "confessed" the gospel in face of the apostasy of Hitler and the sympathizers who supported his policies, the Confessing Church prepared a formal protest in 1934, known as the Barmen Declaration. This statement and Bonhoeffer's involvement in a plot to assassinate Hitler were watershed moments in the resistance (see chap. 15).

All of these developments ignited further cynicism in Europe, and it, along with the continuing impact of Enlightenment thought on the masses, led to a growing spirit of skepticism and secularism on the continent. As a result, church life inevitably suffered. Analysts of the contemporary religious scene commonly note the empty churches in western Europe and observe that Christianity in that region no longer sets the agenda for society. It seems evident that these realities are related to the developments of the nineteenth and twentieth centuries. To this juncture in history, things had not yet gotten quite as bad in the American church. Its relative well-being may be related to the fact that the Enlightenment and post-Enlightenment sociointellectual trends that took hold in Europe became embedded in American society only more recently, more than 150 years after they had already become embedded in the western European psyche.

The war that followed from the conflict resulting from German and Italian nationalism and territorial designs and the rise to power in Japan of a militaristically oriented government was the costliest war ever fought in the history of humankind. Military losses ran about fifteen million, which translates into 1 out of every 450 inhabitants of the United States, 1 out of 150 inhabitants of the United Kingdom, 1 out of every 150 Italians, 1 out of every 22 for the Soviet Union, 1 out of every 25 Germans, and 1 out of every 46 for Japan. Another casualty of the war was that it truly put an end to the optimism, a kind of naive belief in the inevitability of human progress, that the Enlightenment and the industrial revolution had been nurturing among much of the elite in Western society. Replacing it was a kind of cynicism, which had already made inroads in the European psyche after World War I and during the depression. These cultural dynamics seem related to the development of new theological options, and other consequences of the war had impact on the Church and global society.

## Immediate Postwar Aftermath

A direct consequence of the war was a worldwide revolt against colonialism. As the European colonial powers had been weakened or lost confidence as a result of World War II, nationalist movements in Asia and Africa were set free, changing the political map as we know it today. A kind of idealism also crept back into the western European and American psyche as a result of the war (for the Allies perceived themselves as having been the defenders of freedom against the forces of oppression). Political independence did not put an end to economic colonialism, as with the exception of Japan, South Africa, and the newly founded modern state of Israel, the new nations of Asia and Africa continued to find themselves dominated/exploited by Western-based industries and banks.

The new anticolonial drive towards independence had pronounced implications for church life. Just as African independent churches have enjoyed marked growth since World War II, some African church leaders called for a moratorium on mission work to all African churches in the 1970s. Though by no means endorsed by all, and totally rejected by mission societies of the Evangelical movement, most of the largest Western churches have notably reduced their missionary work since the 1950s. In America, the idealism of the postwar era had significant religious significance, manifesting itself in the 1950s in a visible religiosity, if not a trivial church life.[3] The Cold War would eventually take its toll or at least affect the "revival."

Following World War II, the Cold War fractured the Allied coalition between the capitalist nations and Communist Russia, which brought all of Eastern Europe under its hegemony. At times such as in the Korean and Vietnam Wars, this tension between Western capitalism and Communist nations flared into open military confrontation. The Cold War is also the story of further exploitation of lands in the Southern Hemisphere, as the Eastern and Western blocs engaged in propaganda jousts. Now that the Cold War is over, will the result be Western and Eastern societies' neglect of the oppressed in the Southern Hemisphere?

---

3. Returning GIs and their families prospered economically, left the cities for the suburbs, and built churches, where they could return thanks (or have the appearance of being good, decent Americans). The civil rights movement in America was also not unrelated to the new worlds opened to African Americans during the war as well as the new idealism that many white American GIs and their leaders had appropriated in fighting the Nazis. This story as well as the development of new indigenous theologies, such as liberation theology in the Southern Hemisphere and other theologies of oppressed peoples, like black theology and feminist theology, will be told in the next chapter.

Also a factor to be reckoned with is the psychological impact that the threat of a nuclear holocaust has had on post–World War II generations. Has it created cynicism? It is not clear what its implications for an appropriate theology might be. At the very least, one can conclude that these global sociopolitical dynamics are one more indication that the ethos of the present generation precludes the validity of optimistic viewpoints as espoused by liberal theology. The real story of the generations of the Cold War seems to be cynicism towards all institutions, including religion. Perhaps such cynicism explains the lower percentage of involvement of the post–World War II baby-boomer generations in the Church in the West.

## Eastern Orthodoxy in the Modern Era

The core theological commitments and polity of Eastern Orthodoxy (outlined in chap. 1 of the companion volume) remained intact from the time of the Protestant Reformation in Europe through most of the twentieth century. Since the Islamic conquests in the seventh and eighth centuries, Eastern churches, including the indigenous African Oriental Orthodox churches, had been largely under siege or isolated. The Turks' conquest of Constantinople in 1453 exacerbated such perceptions and realities. After all, the archdiocese of Constantinople and its bishop/metropolitan has played a special role in the Orthodox tradition since the sixth century. The bishop of Constantinople is "the first among equals" in the Orthodox tradition, the ecumenical patriarch who functions as the fulcrum of Orthodox unity.

It is tempting to make comparisons between the role of the bishop of Constantinople for the Orthodox Church and the role of the bishop of Rome (the papacy) for the Roman Catholic Church. However, there are important differences, not only in terms of ecclesiology (the relationship between the bishop of Constantinople and other Orthodox bishops is collegial, not hierarchical) but also in terms of the role the pope and the ecumenical patriarch played in relation to the state. Since the Middle Ages, though with some exceptions, the papacy exercised an independence from political rulers in the tradition of Pope Gregory the Great (ca. 540–604). By contrast, the intimate relation that Orthodoxy posits between church and state led the ecumenical patriarchate to be co-opted by the Eastern emperor from time to time. Such commitments have in turn rendered the Orthodox tradition less inclined than the West to engage in social action on behalf of the disenfranchised.

Constantinople's conquest by Moslem Turks in 1453 meant the end of the Constantinian ideal of a Christian state, which had such an impact on Eastern Orthodoxy.[4] The conquest's impact on the Orthodox Church was not immediately catastrophic. Initially the Ottoman (Turkish) regime granted some freedom to it. The new patriarch was granted civil and ecclesiastical authority over Christians in the region. Some church buildings were co-opted as Islamic mosques, but those that were allowed to remain in possession of Christians were permitted to operate with full freedom of worship. When the Ottomans conquered Syria and Palestine in the early sixteenth century, Christians in those regions were placed under the authority of the bishop of Constantinople. Likewise, a similarly benevolent attitude towards the Oriental Orthodox Church and the patriarch of Alexandria prevailed after the Turkish conquest of that city in 1517.

The next development in Eastern Orthodoxy (especially its Greek-speaking segments) was occasioned by the influence of Western Christian thought.[5] This created a debate in the church about whether the influence of Western thought, especially of Calvinist theology, polluted Orthodoxy. One seventeenth-century patriarch of Constantinople, Cyril Lucaris (1572–1638), seemed so friendly to Calvinism (*Confession of Faith*) that he was condemned by an Orthodox synod nearly four decades after his death "if indeed he was a Calvinist heretic."

When the Ottoman Empire broke down in the nineteenth and early twentieth centuries, and individual eastern European nations like Greece, Serbia, and Bulgaria started to form, the churches on their soil became established as national Orthodox churches. Similar churches formed in more northern regions that were not previously dominated by the Ottoman Empire, such as in Estonia, Latvia, and Czechoslovakia. This dynamic created a poignant and vigorous tension between the nationalism that these churches embodied and the transnational self-identity of Orthodoxy. Eventually after much soul-searching, a weakened patriarchate in Constantinople recognized the independence of such churches during the decades between the world wars. The subsequent emergence of the Communist empire in Russia, especially after

---

4. The existence of a church in a hostile state in this region was a foretaste of what would happen elsewhere in Orthodox churches in the twentieth century.

5. Keep in mind the Lutheran Reformer Philip Melanchthon's overture to the ecumenical patriarchate (*Epistles* 65825), requesting his support in the form of a theological reaction to the orthodoxy of the Lutheran Augsburg Confession during the early stages of the Reformation. During most of the sixteenth century, the Orthodox side made little response to these Lutheran efforts to establish formal fellowship. Only later in the century was there some response from the patriarch of Constantinople, Jeremias II (1536–94), who praised the confession's trinitarian orthodoxy but raised questions both about the Roman Catholic liturgical orientation of its teaching of the Eucharist and its emphasis on justification by grace through faith. The concern was that the Orthodox witness to free will and a faith that gives witness through works did not receive sufficient testimony (Jeremias II *Epistle to the Lutheran Theologians at Tübingen* I).

the Second World War, placed these churches as well as the Russian
Orthodox Church under strict government supervision and harassment.

There are parallels between the situation of these Orthodox bodies
and that of the Orthodox Church in the ancient patriarchates of Jerusalem, Antioch, and Alexandria. They found themselves under Arab rule
in regions where Christians were a clear minority. Towards the end of
the nineteenth century, these regions came under the influence or rule
of Western powers, which began to propagate their own versions of
Christianity among the masses. In some of these regions, the Catholic
Church had undertaken these efforts as early as the sixteenth century,
culminating in the planting in the nineteenth century of the Eastern
Rite (Uniat) Catholic Church (a branch of the Catholic Church that retains its indigenous liturgy and canon/church law). However, a growing
Arab nationalism later in the twentieth century curbed the growth of
Protestantism and Catholicism in these regions.

### Russian Orthodoxy

The conquest of Constantinople in 1453 had special significance for
the identity of the Russian Orthodox Church. Many Russians interpreted the conquest as divine retribution for the reconciliation with
a "heretical" Roman Catholic tradition that the Byzantine emperor
and the church's patriarch had proclaimed in 1439 while under duress
from the imminent Ottoman Turkish invasion. Discredited by this perceived sellout, the city and its patriarch began to lose authority in the
eyes of Russian Orthodox Church leaders. As a result, Russian Orthodox leaders increasingly came to see it as their vocation, as part
of a great Christian nation, to assume the role previously reserved for
Constantinople as the true defender of Orthodoxy.

Leaders of Russia were also pleased to assume this mantle, regarding themselves as successors of the Eastern Empire. Ivan IV (1530–84),
grand duke of Moscow, took the title "czar," which translates "emperor," in order to undergird the autocratic power he was trying to seize
from the older nobility with which he and his predecessors had shared
power. He also took the title in order to make clear that he regarded his
empire as the true successor of the Roman Empire and the Eastern Empire based in Constantinople (Philotheus of Pskov *Message*). As a result
of this new self-identity, church leaders of the rest of the century and
into the next undertook very polemical writings against not just Catholics and Protestants but even against Greek Orthodoxy and its base in
Constantinople.[6] These attitudes, blending no doubt with nationalistic

---

6. German immigrants (especially Moravians) and Swedish Lutherans had planted

pride, filtered down to the masses. They became problematic when in the seventeenth century efforts were made to affect rapprochement with the Greeks.

No doubt there were political motives for the attempted rapprochement. Initiated by Czar Alexis I Mikhailovich (1629–76), who seemed to regard such rapprochement as a preparatory move to gain the support of the Greeks for an invasion of Constantinople, the Russian Orthodox Church revised its liturgy to bring it in accord with Greek practices.[7] Significant unrest, especially among the lower classes, resulted from these changes, which were perceived as aristocratic tampering with beloved native traditions. These dynamics led to the emergence of a group that came to be known as the Old Believers, as they rejected all of these reforms and the spirit of reconciliation that went with them. Led by a monk, Petrovich Avvakum (ca. 1620–82), the movement was harshly persecuted and soon turned to a fervid eschatological perspective to the point that some committed suicide through self-immolation inasmuch as conditions had so deteriorated into apostasy that reform was deemed impossible. Only Christ's return could set things right. Obviously, this movement would not endure in large numbers, but it did continue until the twentieth century.

The next crisis to be faced by the Russian Orthodox Church transpired over a debate about the validity of Western theological influences on the Orthodox Church. Although the church had earlier confronted this issue, it was faced with it even more intensely in the late seventeenth and early eighteenth centuries when Czar Peter the Great (Pyotr Alekseyevich; 1672–1725) tried to open Russia to European influences, particularly to European science. This new openness to Western influences had its impact on the Russian Church. A theological school in Kiev led by Peter Mogila (1597–1646) had always shown friendliness towards Roman Catholic teachings such as the immaculate conception of Mary (which, though not-yet-official Roman Catholic teaching, was becoming increasingly part of its piety) and the doctrine of purgatory. However, in the new pro-Western climate another school led by Theophanes Prokopovic was more influenced by Protestantism, particularly its use of Scripture as a critical principle for determining what is authentic and what is inauthentic in the tradition. Subsequently in the nineteenth century even Enlightenment ideas began to permeate the Rus-

---

some Protestant churches in Russia as early as the sixteenth century. A synod of the Russian church meeting in 1620 affirmed that both Catholic and Protestant baptisms were invalid.

7. Of course, the initiation of ecclesiastical reform by the political realm is in the best traditions of the Eastern Orthodox tradition and its belief that deification has rendered the political realm of a "Christian nation" a true agent of the Will of God.

sian Church. During this period of confrontation with Western thought, especially late in the eighteenth century, two sects with spiritualist propensities and a reputation for morality and industry, the Dukhobors (Doukhobors) and the Molokans, emerged. The revolution of 1917 effectively put an end to this debate, as the Russian Orthodox Church was now faced with a hostile government. Its major theological contributions since that time tended to concern itself with the relationship between Christianity and Marxism, though at times this preoccupation, coupled with the historic Orthodox commitment to the cooperation of church and state, lent itself to the specter of Christianity's co-option by the Marxist state.

In the century before the Communist Revolution, the Russian Orthodox Church's confidence in its mission led it to undertake successful mission ventures in Japan, China, and Korea. As noted in a previous chapter, the Orthodox churches in these lands are totally indigenized both in terms of leadership and liturgy.

### Oriental Orthodoxy and Other Eastern Churches

The Assyrian Church, a Nestorian body claiming to be in the apostolic line with the early Christians of Nineveh and supposedly converted by Saint Thomas, had fallen on harder and harder times ever since the conversion of the Persian royal house to Islam late in the thirteenth century. In more recent centuries, the church endured harsh persecution from Moslems, and its membership had been widely dispersed in exile and shrunk to only about 150,000 members. Nevertheless, it has endured and survived.

The so-called Monophysite churches, such as the Coptic Church, the Ethiopian Orthodox Church, the Armenian Apostolic Church, and the Syrian Orthodox Church, have played an important role in preserving national identity in face of exile or Moslem pressure, which they have endured for centuries. Yet their isolation as a result of Moslem persecution has permitted little theological development since the period of the early Church, save two exceptions. The Armenian Church, in exile as a result of Persian invasions in the fifth and sixteenth centuries and the Turkish massacres of the nineteenth and twentieth centuries, was exposed to modern Western ideas and in turn established theological centers that produced significant apologetic and systematic works.

Other noteworthy theological developments within these churches are identifiable in Ethiopian Orthodoxy. In the fourteenth and fifteenth centuries the Ethiopian Church was engaged in disputes (largely between clergy attached to the royal court and regular clergy) over the observance of Christmas and other feasts. A dispute between two powerful monastic orders over when to observe the Sabbath was not resolved until the mid-fifteenth century, establishing the present practice of worshiping on Sundays but still observing the Hebrew Sabbath. During these centuries the Ethiopian Church also contended with two heresies. The Mikaelites taught a Gnostic dualism contending that God cannot be known and so only can be approached by degrees under the guidance of certain teachers who can interpret the secret meaning of Scripture. Stephanites did not venerate the Cross or the Virgin Mary. Although repressed by Ethiopian kings, these heresies persisted in some monasteries through the end of the sixteenth century. We should consider whether the church made a good move in condemning these movements.

Also in the sixteenth century, largely prompted by Portuguese Catholic missionary endeavors in the region, renewed attention to the unique Monophysite Christology of the Ethiopian Church culminated in the evolution of two distinct schools of Monophysite Christology in Ethiopia (the Sons of Unction and the Sons of Grace schools). This development created a controversy that persisted in dividing the church until well into the nineteenth century. The Sons of Unction (*Walda-qeb*) teach a radical unification of Christ's two natures. In eternity, they maintain, the divine nature has absorbed the human natures to such an extent that Christ's humanity is sometimes portrayed as a phantasm, just as when water is poured into wine, the wine remains wine. The Sons of Grace (*Walda-saga*) teach that the unification of Christ's divinity and humanity takes place through the redemptive birth of Christ, which happened when the Father anointed the Son with the Spirit (Mark 1:8–11). This unity, proponents held, renders the nature of Christ a special nature; they rejected both absorption and distinction of the two natures.

A synod called by the Ethiopian monarchs at Berru Meda in 1878 finally settled the controversy between these two schools of Christology. The synod largely endorsed the suppositions of the Sons of Unction, though partly inspired by political considerations to unify contending parties, it urged them to submit to the common faith and under those suppositions effectively conceded the validity of both schools. The decisions of the synod on this point account in large part for the continuing impact of both schools in the Ethiopian Church. In this ongoing debate, is either one of these alternatives preferable to the other?

Ethiopian exposure to Western influence in the late sixteenth and seventeenth century even resulted in a 1622 conversion of an Ethiopian king to Catholicism and consequent reunion of the Ethiopian Orthodox and Roman Catholic churches. Much resistance to the reunion emerged from Ethiopian quarters, and the independence of its church was reaffirmed in the next decade when the converted king died.

Another important development in the Ethiopian Orthodox Church was its declaring itself autocephalous in 1952, maintaining its longtime sisterly relation with the Coptic Orthodox Church while becoming independent. The ties between these two church bodies were long-standing, dating back to the fourth century. Essentially the Ethiopian Church had functioned as a Coptic diocese, with all its bishops (usually Egyptian) appointed by the patriarch of Alexandria. Ethiopian monastic clergy had likewise been placed under Egyptian abbots until the fourteenth century. The growing nationalism in Ethiopia in the first half of the twentieth century clearly facilitated this ecclesiastical "declaration of independence."

## The Secrets to Orthodoxy's Success: Lessons for the Western Church?

Under terrible conditions for church life, either persecuted by Arabs or Communists or with too much "intimate friendliness" by a Christian ruler who historically tends to dominate Eastern Church life, cut off from theological enrichment by other sources, the Eastern Church has maintained itself. Indeed, one might say that it has flourished. Why? The three constants of the Orthodox Church perduring in all historical periods and in distinct national contexts have been the historic episcopacy (contending that apostolic succession had been maintained), its commitment to the historic liturgy, and its fidelity to historic tradition. In a sense, these three characteristics have held the Orthodox churches together. Must it not be these factors that have made it possible for the Orthodox Church to thrive under difficult circumstances? This in turn raises a challenge to Protestant churches, suggesting that biblicism and a style of worship not dependent on the historic Eastern or Western liturgies may not be the one historic way to church growth. The Orthodox experience raises the question of whether liturgy, episcopacy, and tradition might be what it takes to make church growth happen.

## Cutting-Edge Theology: Nikolai Berdyaev

The son of Russian aristocrats, exiled to Paris on account of his critique of the czar and later of Communism, Nikolai Berdyaev (1874–1948) is perhaps the most renown Orthodox theologian of the twentieth century. His theological Christocentric critique of the Renaissance and its impact on the West suggests the work of several Protestant thinkers, notably Karl Barth (*Freedom and the Spirit*). The heart of Berdyaev's thought is the Incarnation and its implied affirmation that God and humanity are not wholly alien. In Christ the human spirit is liberated. (The Orthodox concept of deification is suggested at this point.)

The fault of the Renaissance (and so presumably its Enlightenment heritage) in the eminent Russian Orthodox thinker's view was that it had so exalted reason as to ignore the link between God and humanity that gave people their freedom. The result was that in an industrial age the Renaissance had led to the denial of humanism, rendering humans captive to their machines. Only Christ's second coming could give history significance. Is this an Eastern Orthodox theology with contemporary relevance for the West?

## Roman Catholicism in the First Half of the Century

Not much changed for the Roman Catholic Church from the nineteenth to the first half of the twentieth century. It continued taking a negative position on modern intellectual developments. Of course, there were some leaders within the church yearning for reform. These aspirations came to fruition in mid-century with the convening of the Second Vatican Council (see pp. 332–39).

## Protestant Developments

The upheavals of the first half of the century undercut nineteenth-century optimism, rendering Protestant liberalism and its optimistic view of human nature and the like no longer viable. Increasingly, the perception came to be that what was needed was a theology with deeper moorings — one more realistic/pessimistic about human nature and more inclined to stress God's act, rather than our own ethical strivings or feelings (as liberals like Ritschl, Kant, Harnack, Rauschenbusch, and Schleiermacher had).

Some scholars recognized that such a view might be found in the Reformation. The early twentieth century was a period of profound revival of scholarship on Luther, drawing upon the previously described beginnings made earlier in the nineteenth century. Developments that made this possible include the discovery of a number of previously unknown early manuscripts of Luther and the new Enlightenment critical historiographical mind-set that set the study of the Reformer free from mere ecclesiastical apologetics. There has not yet been a comparable movement for the study of Calvin.

The German historian Karl Holl (1866–1926) is generally recognized as the initiator of this Luther renaissance. Interestingly enough, he was a liberal theologian after the fashion of Harnack and Ritschl, interpreting Luther in light of ethical suppositions (*Gesammelte Aufsatze zur*

*Kirchengeschichte* 1:111ff.). Subsequent giants in the modern study of the Reformer would radically break with these suppositions, stressing unconditional grace in Luther's thought by organizing the analysis of his theology in dialectical categories (in terms of polar opposites like law and gospel, faith and works, reason and faith, or hidden God and revealed God.) The impetus for these insights was provided by a combination of the rediscovery of Luther's theology of the Cross and the breakthroughs of a young Swiss Reformed pastor, Karl Barth (see his theology analyzed below). Among the most prominent figures in this new interest in Luther's thought include continental European scholars like Paul Althaus (1888–1966), Werner Elert (1885–1954), Gustaf Aulen (1879–1977), Anders Nygren (1890–1978), and Regin Prenter (1907–90). All the major theologians considered below represent this kind of Reformation tradition (though some like Rudolf Bultmann and Paul Tillich try to synthesize it with the liberal method of Schleiermacher).

Another significant contributor to this new interest in Luther was the Catholic scholar Joseph Lortz (1887–1975). His significance is that in contrast to Catholic research on Luther since the Reformation, which had been polemically critical of the Reformer, he called for a more positive/sympathetic assessment of Luther's reform by Catholics. His work has in fact made that contribution to Roman Catholic theological scholarship, significantly contributing to increasing Catholicism's ecumenical openness.

Reaction against liberal theology as not right for the time took another form in America in the development of the Fundamentalist movement (see pp. 227–31 for a description of its history and theological commitments). Upper-class in origin, the movement had an impressive impact on the media and the American social psyche in the first years of the century. After its decline at the Scopes trial, the movement maintained itself, indeed thriving in the decades before, during, and after World War II.

### Denominational Mergers

Another twentieth-century development of note was probably a consequence of the impact that the new spirit of ecumenism was already having on the missions fields of the Southern Hemisphere. A push towards denominational mergers began to make itself known in North America and would come to a feverish pitch after World War II (see pp. 352–54 for details). Prior to the war was the merger of two bodies; the Christian Churches, a branch of the Restorationist movement that had never become part of the Christian Church (Disciples of Christ), and the Congregational Churches (the heirs of American Puritanism) merged in 1931 to form the Congregational Christian Churches. In 1934, the Reformed Church in the U.S. (the heirs of German Reformed settlers) and the German Evangelical Synod of North America (heirs of the Evangelical merger of Lutheran and Reformed churches in Prussia in the previous century) merged to create the Evangelical and Reformed Church. Both of these bodies would eventually become partners in a merger in 1957 that created the United Church of Christ.

The North and South in Methodism merged in 1939. In 1946, another predecessor body of today's United Methodist Church was formed: the Evangelical United Brethren Church, a merger of two distinct, though Pietistic, almost Methodist-like movements formed by German settlers in America's East Coast in the eighteenth and nineteenth centuries. Likewise Lutherans in North America, for the most part divided by ethnic and geographical factors though sometimes by theology, caught the merger fever. The United Lutheran Church was formed in 1918 from the largely German predecessor bodies in the East. Different denominations founded by Norwegian immigrants formed the Evangelical Lutheran Church in 1917. In 1930, the American Lutheran Church was formed from a merger of four predominantly midwestern synods with roots in earlier German immigration to the region.

The fruits of all of these developments will be dealt with more fully in the final chapter. It is preferable to close at this point with a review of the Protestant theological heavyweights of the first half of the century.

### Søren Kierkegaard

The nineteenth-century Danish Christian philosopher Søren Kierkegaard (1813–55), a younger contemporary of Nikolai Grundtvig, reacted to the stilted Lutheran orthodox theology and church life of his day. During his lifetime, he never received much attention, except local derision. The son of a moderately successful father who was both strict and tortured with guilt, Kierkegaard grew to be a highly talented, though frail and sensitive, figure cursed with melancholy (*Point of View for My Work as an Author* 76–77).[8] His contemporaries seem to have regarded him as a talented, though very peculiar, figure who was ruining his life. Besides being an object of derision for his peculiar lifestyle and virulent attacks on the Church of his day (*Present Moment*), Kierkegaard contributed further to his image as a rather "strange sort" by his decision to break an engagement with the love of his life, presumably in order to protect her from his melancholy and because he came to conceive

---

8. Should we say that Kierkegaard embodied a classical Lutheran piety? However, he does not seem to have been quite as life-affirming as Luther.

of marriage as an obstacle to his increasingly fervent religious preoccupations (*Journal*). Given these interpersonal dynamics, it is hardly
surprising that Kierkegaard's project did not make a profound impact
on the Danish Church in his lifetime. Only in the twentieth century was
his work discovered and appreciated by the rest of the theological world.
It has had profound impact.

Many scholars regard Kierkegaard as the father of *existentialism* (a
philosophical movement that holds that human beings are totally free
and responsible for making themselves who they are and that this responsibility is the source of dread and anguish in face of the finite
meaninglessness in which we exist). Certainly Kierkegaard's thought
inspired the development of this philosophy, but in fact he is more
properly regarded as a Pietist, concerned with enhancing the spirituality and practice of Christian life. His overriding agenda was how
to become a Christian, an undertaking rendered especially difficult
by living in "Christendom" (*Journal* 5–6, 13, 42). To accomplish
these aims, Kierkegaard tried to get readers to become self-concerned,
more concerned about their existence, their subjectivity, than the objective givenness of life — their essence. Such emphases amount to a
break with all attempts to systematize life as Hegel had sought to
do, and his philosophy was quite influential among the Danish population in Kierkegaard's day (*Concluding Unscientific Postscript* esp.
99–108, 270–72). These Kierkegaardian commitments are also a key
to identifying his influence on existentialist philosophy.

In a context in which being a Christian was no big deal, Kierkegaard
was concerned to get people to take faith, becoming Christian, seriously (*Concluding Unscientific Postscript* 49ff.). The way to do that,
he maintained, was to arouse self-concern, or subjectivity, among readers (116ff.). Indeed, we must become subjective in order to understand
Christianity, for it is only understood through subjectivity. Because passionate interest in eternal happiness is the extremity of subjectivity,
Christianity intensifies subjectivity to the utmost (51, 116).

*The method of indirect communication and the stages.* Kierkegaard's
strategy for accomplishing his aims was to seek to move the mass of
people to subjectivity because in his view many were existing in the
mode of existence of objectivity. Kierkegaard decided to accomplish this
indirectly (called his "method of indirect communication") by luring
them with clever aesthetic writing that he undertook under assumed
names. The strategy was that after having accumulated a readership for
his books, he could gradually lure readers to think subjectively and then
expose them to the religious dimension in subsequent books (*Point of
View for My Work as an Author* 25–26). Kierkegaard's strategy presupposes three possible modes, or stages, of human existence — aesthetic,

ethical, and religious. No rational justification for any of these ways of living can be given. Like a twentieth-century existentialist philosopher, Kierkegaard claims that life lived in each stage is absurd, paradoxical (*Concluding Unscientific Postscript* 261ff.).

The aesthetic stage is the living of life as a turning back to sensuality. Aesthetic people are mere spectators — acting in an unthinking, uncommitted manner. They do what is most readily apparent. Such persons are eminently adaptable to circumstances, seeking enjoyment in order to avoid boredom. They evaluate all things on the basis of whether it is interesting.[9] Aesthetic people do what is natural, avoid commitment, but are ultimately prone to despair. They lack identity because none of their acts define who they as individuals are. In the interest of evangelism, Kierkegaard advocated trying to move people off the aesthetic plane to the more ethically oriented mode of existence, as only then will they be ready to hear the gospel (*Either/Or* II:223).

The ethical stage is a life lived in commitment to a course of action and assuming responsibility for one's actions. Ethical individuals are no longer mere spectators. Such individuals make free decisions, defining who they are. Subjectivity or self-concern is more intense at this stage (*Either/Or* II:196, 233–34).[10] Ethical people come to despair over living a morally perfect life, over oneself and the tension between what one is and what one should be (199, 212–14, 222–23). Kierkegaard calls such despair the "sickness unto death." Religious life becomes an attractive alternative to such people, a way of coping with this despair. Insofar as ethical demands condemn one as a sinner and religion provides comfort from despair, it is evident that the Lutheran law-gospel dialectic seems operative in Kierkegaard's strategy at this point.

The religious stage allows the individual more intense individuality through its sense of immediate relationship to God. The God relationship is so all-consuming that it renders believers oblivious to the finite (and its trials). The ethical is suspended at the religious stage. Kierkegaard clearly reflects his Lutheran heritage at this point; such commitments embody Luther's concept of freedom from the law (*Concluding Unscientific Postscript* 433–41).

*The paradoxical character of faith.* Kierkegaard's method of indirect communication through his use of anonymous, nonreligious works to attract an audience explains another of his core insights, his emphasis on the paradoxical character of Christianity. If Christianity is not a paradox, contrary to reason, one could become a believer objec-

---

9. Such a lifestyle certainly seems to resonate with attitudes associated with the contemporary "New Age" ethos.

10. Indeed, subjectivity does not exist at all at the aesthetic stage.

tively through reason. In Kierkegaard's view, this is the problem with Hegel's system. The greatest possible infinitely qualitative contradiction is affirmed by Christian faith, Kierkegaard maintained. God became an individual man (*Training in Christianity* 123, 132; *Point of View for My Work as an Author* 97). The Incarnation is an offense (a contradiction of all that is rational)! As such, it cannot but heighten one's subjectivity to its most intense heights. This is the nature of faith (*Training in Christianity* 83ff.).

The aim of Kierkegaard's commitments is to ensure that Christians have become so existentially involved in their faith commitments that they are never disciples-at-second-hand but always contemporaneous with the offense of Christ (*Philosophical Fragments* 135–37). Along with this commitments, so suggestive of Erlangen theology and the later development of neoorthodoxy, Kierkegaard embraces another conception most suggestive of these two movements. He refers to the Bible as a "sacred history" (*Training in Christianity* 33). The paradoxical character of Christian faith quickens the faith of modern disciples like us.

**An assessment of doctrinal commitments.** Some possibly troubling conclusions, at least from Kierkegaard's own Lutheran perspective, must be noted. His focus on becoming inward or subjective may have led him to neglect attention to social issues. Like other Pietists, he opted for something like the third use of the law (*Training in Christianity* 174). The language employed by the great Danish thinker sometimes suggests a deemphasis on grace, as if it were earned by following Christ (71). This fits his apparent reliance on a moral influence theory of the atonement, much like Schleiermacher and other liberal theologians. For Kierkegaard, Christ's Passion was an instance of his pattern of life; his suffering was its prime exemplification. The Passion only has meaning, Kierkegaard asserts, when the believer also suffers (171, 168, 108). On the other hand, Kierkegaard does endeavor to assert the primacy of grace and the divine initiative (*Training in Christianity* 13). In fact, he went so far as to assert that Christ gives us the condition for understanding truth, gives faith (*Philosophical Fragments* 17–18).

In characteristic Pietist fashion, Kierkegaard tended to deemphasize the sacraments. He was critical of the Lutheran conception of the ubiquity of Christ's body (that it is everywhere present), which logically follows the Lutheran claim that Christ is really present in every celebration of the sacrament. Kierkegaard believed that such ideas undermine the offense of faith (*Training in Christianity* 101). Likewise, though not repudiating infant baptism, he found it a foolish practice that seems to make it more difficult to become a Christian, for the practice makes one think that he or she is already Christian (*Concluding Unscientific Postscript* 327; *Present Moment* VII, 6).

Regardless of one's reaction to the question of his fidelity to his Lutheran heritage, are Kierkegaard's characteristic themes, notably his strategy for proclaiming the gospel to people who are living (aesthetically) only for the moment, useful models for ministry in the twenty-first century?

## Karl Barth

The greatest countervoice to liberalism, perhaps the greatest theologian of the century, may well be the German Swiss Reformed pastor Karl Barth (1886–1968). He never earned a doctorate; in fact, one of his formative intellectual experiences was his service in parish ministry to a working-class congregation that seemed to be exploited in their struggle to obtain better living conditions. In that context, Karl Barth came to believe that the liberal theology he had learned at the university was bankrupt in addressing the people. A far more relevant resource, he concluded, was the classical themes of his Reformed tradition. The experience also soured Barth on free-market capitalism and directed him to the socialist agenda, at least in a qualified sense (*Church Dogmatics* III/4:543ff.). His concern about the poor and outcast was also embodied in his reported weekly trips to the local prison during his years of teaching.[11]

Another landmark event in Barth's life was the heroism he exhibited during his years teaching at a German university. He stood up to the Nazis and Hitler's sympathizers in German Protestantism. In response, Hitler exiled him; he spent the remainder of his career in his native Switzerland. Before and during the war, Barth was part of the resistance movement (the Confessing Church). In fact, he was the primary author/ drafter of the Barmen Declaration.

***Divine transcendence and its theological consequences.*** Barth is credited with being the founder of a theological movement that protested against liberal theology. The movement Barth initiated has come to be called "neoorthodoxy" because it tried to vivify categories of Protestant orthodox theology in a *new*, modern setting. For Barth, the major problem with liberal theology was that it had compromised the transcendence of God by reducing theology to human experience — to anthropology. Such theology had fallen prey to the critique of religion formulated by the nineteenth-century German philosopher Ludwig Feuerbach, who claimed that all language about God is really objectification of human nature (*Essence of Christianity* II–III). The only way

---

11. Barth's personal life has more recently been the subject of attention as a result of revelations about a long-term affair with a research assistant.

to refute the Feuerbachian critique, Barth argued, was to be sure that the relation between God and humans is one way, always initiated from God's side (*Die Theologie und die Kirche* II:212–39).

These commitments to the transcendence of God, the objectivity of revelation, and the priority of God's action are reflected throughout the corpus of Barth's writings. They are clearly suggestive of Calvin's priorities and so highlight Barth's indebtedness to his Reformed roots. Of course, these commitments also manifested themselves in a strong Reformation emphasis on justification and sin. Barth assumed a Christocentric, almost Christomonist, perspective that entailed a special emphasis on the primacy of God's act. In his view, one cannot even know the self apart from Christ, for he is true Man. We are only humans in a reflected sense (Barth *Die Theologie und die Kirche* II:212–39).

Because of sin, Barth insisted, we cannot know anything of ourselves. We must look to the man Jesus Christ to know ourselves. These commitments are unambiguous affirmations of the primacy of God's act. There is no innate spiritual knowledge in humanity. Collectively such commitments ensure that in no way can theological affirmations made on such grounds be confused with human experience. Such a theological model is just the opposite from the approach of Schleiermacher and the liberal Protestant establishment. Instead of interpreting theological concepts in light of human experience, Barth would have us interpret human experience in terms of traditional theological concepts. In many ways, Barth's challenge to liberal theology is simply a recapitulation of the classical controversy of the early Church between correlationists like Justin Martyr and Christocentric orthodox theologians like Tertullian.

Barth's commitments logically entailed his rejection of the natural knowledge of God (*Church Dogmatics* II/1:85ff.). Such a natural knowledge essentially connects God-talk with human experience, as Feuerbach did. Barth's position on this point led him into a controversy with one of his earliest supporters, another Swiss Reformed theologian, Emil Brunner (1889–1966). Brunner wanted to insist that a "point of contact" between God and human nature existed (*Theologie und Ontologie* 112). Barth responded with an emphatic "No" (*Church Dogmatics* I/1:29ff.)! Contrary to his intentions, Brunner had correlated the Word of God and human experience, much as liberal theology had done. Readers need to assess where they stand in this debate.

The challenge Barth posed to liberal theology surfaces not just methodologically but also in the renewed attention he gave to the doctrine of the Trinity, in contrast to its neglect by liberals like Schleiermacher. Barth's emphasis on the doctrine (*Church Dogmatics* I/1:339ff.) manifested itself in a fresh treatment of the mystery. Breaking with static Greek philosophical assumptions, Barth employed a philosophical ontology that takes into account the role of action in shaping the structures of reality (commitments most in line with his narrative-like view of Scripture). A being is what it does, Barth claimed (IV/1:492). Thus, God is three in essence because he does three distinct works (creation, reconciliation, redemption), yet is one insofar as the three works are one in Christ (I/1:340, 426–29). Likewise, this ontology offers a fresh treatment of Christology. Christ's two natures are affirmed as Jesus is said to have a human nature insofar as he does what humans do and has a divine nature insofar as he does works that only God can do (IV/3:39ff.).

***Theological consequences of Barth's Christocentrism.*** Given Barth's radical Christocentrism, his claim that we can only know ourselves in Christ entails, at least by implication, that redemption is logically prior to creation. In contrast to the Reformers, who in accord with the Catholic tradition regarded creation as preceding redemption, for Barth the gospel precedes the law. If Christ, the agent of redemption, is the first and true man by whom we know ourselves, then in that sense redemption does precede creation (*Church Dogmatics* II/2:7–8). This treatment of law and gospel, the subordination of the former to the latter, helps explain Barth's Reformed views on the relation between church and state. Government, the realities of the law and creation, is to be subordinated to (have its laws judged by) Christ and the principles of the gospel. This was a crucial commitment of the Barmen Declaration (II), which Barth drafted.

Regarding predestination, Barth modified his mentor's teaching by claiming that all creation is elect in Christ (*Church Dogmatics* II/2:59–60, 94ff.), which would entail a kind of universal salvation. Barth neither endorses nor rules it out, arguing that there is no reason not to hope that all might be saved (IV/3:477–78). However, in faithfulness to his Reformed roots, Barth still maintained something like double predestination, claiming that God has rejected Satan, who is the sum and substance of not being chosen by God, the shadowy, nonbeing aspects of creation (II/2:122, 171, 174f.). With this majestic portrayal of God's love, is Barth still sufficiently in touch with his Calvinist roots? Or, contrary to his intentions, is he not more in touch with Luther's notion of single predestination?

***View of Scripture.*** Barth's emphasis on the primacy of God's act and on biblical authority is evident in his view of Scripture. Indeed, he conceded affinities between his own view and the old doctrine of verbal inspiration (Barth *Epistle to the Romans* 12, 16–19). He was committed to the authority of the Bible's literal sense, which in turn implied endorsement of the historicity of the biblical accounts, at least in some sense. Barth did this by claiming, in accord with the nineteenth-century

Erlangen school of theology, that the Bible gives testimony to God's salvation history, which is a history distinct from verifiable historical events and so only accessible to faith. Scripture might be considered to provide historical accounts (in the sense of this special "salvation history") even when its accounts cannot be substantiated by critical historiography, for the tools of historical criticism are inadequate for dealing with the majesty of God in history, which is what Scripture reports. Scripture gives testimony to such "salvation-events," Barth argues, when it becomes the Word of God (*Church Dogmatics* I/1:373–78). Does the concept of salvation history solve the problems raised by historical criticism? Until the 1960s, and still in some theological circles, it was a most popular view.

In a related dimension, because Scripture narrates salvation history only when it becomes the Word of God (*Church Dogmatics* I/1:124–25), there is no direct identification of the Word and the Bible (127). As the Word is identical with Christ, so Christology functions for Barth as the governing norm for reading the Bible (121, 134). This idea that the Bible is not the Word in itself, but only becomes it from time to time by God's grace, is intended as another way of affirming the primacy of God's act in face of Feuerbach's critique (131–33). Affinities are obvious between these Barthian commitments and the spirit-letter distinction of Luther and Calvin.

A related point pertaining to Barth's hermeneutics should be noted. When Scripture functions as the Word, it does not just provide information in his view. Jesus Christ himself and the event of reconciliation are actually made present to the hearer (*Church Dogmatics* I/1:134, 125). When the Word is proclaimed, salvation is given. Affinities between Barth's reflections and the Reformers' narrative approach to biblical interpretation and homiletics as well as with characteristic African American theology seem evident. This is interesting in view of the favorable notice he paid to the African American community during his one visit to America (Barth *Evangelical Theology* vii-ix). In a number of ways, Barth called the Church back to its roots. Are his agenda and execution still helpful for the Church today?

## Reinhold Niebuhr

Probably the greatest, most renowned American theologian of the first half of the twentieth century, Reinhold Niebuhr (1892–1971) had a German American Reformed background. Like Barth, he also had a significant and life-transforming parish experience in the inner city early in his career. It awakened him to the exploitation of the workers by the capitalist elites and also to the evils of racism (*Leaves from the Notebook of a Tamed Cynic*). His brother, H. Richard Niebuhr (1894–1962), was also a renowned American theologian.

Concerning his influence, Niebuhr became one of America's most prominent social analysts. After some experimentation with more politically radical alternatives, he aligned himself with the left wing of the Democratic Party. His prominence was displayed not only in his numerous publications in opinion-making periodicals; indeed, so great was his influence that John Kennedy is said to have sought out Niebuhr's advice concerning his running mate in 1960. Largely because of Niebuhr's advice, Lyndon B. Johnson found himself on the ticket.

**Theological orientation.** Although Niebuhr did not totally identify himself with neoorthodoxy, as he found its proponents too inclined to fit life into a dogmatic mold and not sufficiently concerned about sociopolitical problems, he largely followed Barth's neoorthodox perspective in the sense of using traditional Reformation concepts to interpret contemporary experience, rather than interpreting these concepts in light of our experience (*Nature and Destiny of Man* 1:4–5, 12–14, 16–18, 227). Granted, he may have had a bit more theologically liberal propensities, as he was not always inclined to interpret biblical images literally (2:290ff.).

One of Niebuhr's primary theological commitments was his focus on the doctrine of sin, which he employed to explain the human situation and its political dynamics. Given his Augustinian-Calvinist predispositions, it is not surprising that he found sin at the center of human personality (*Nature and Destiny of Man* 1:14). Self-interest underlies all humanity activity, he claimed; as soon as a group gains power, it will inevitably go about exercising it arrogantly (186ff.). These are the theological roots of Niebuhr's famous political "realism," which he sometimes called "cynicism." In view of the "group egoism" inevitably surfacing in politics, all relations among groups of people must be political, not ethical, that is, based on powers and coercion. Justice, not love, is what we must aim for in society, but the nature of humankind makes it a mere approximate justice for which we need to strive. When it comes to justice, we never can get to the real thing (253–58; *Moral Man and Immoral Society* xi–xii, 172–92; *Faith and Politics* 134–37).

Such appreciation of the need to curb the power of special interests, even if they constitute a majority, makes the connections between Niebuhr's reflections and American constitutional assumptions (especially those of James Madison) readily apparent (Madison *Federalist Papers* 10; cf. Niebuhr *Moral Man and Immoral Society* 163–64, 201–2). One of the reasons Niebuhr exerted so much influence on the politicians of his day was because his thought is so much in touch with core assumptions of the American political system. Consequently, these leaders came to perceive him as someone who was, not a mere religious idealist, but one who understood them and what it takes to get things done. Crucial at this point is Niebuhr's insistence that even though all are equally sinners, we must still make judgments concerning relative degrees of guilty actions. With these assumptions, Niebuhr demonstrates special concern for the poor that they not be exploited by the rich (Isa. 3:14–15; *Nature and Destiny of Man* 1:219ff.)

*The quest for racial justice: a prophetic voice before his time.* At numerous points throughout his career, Niebuhr's concern for the poor and oppressed surfaced in his concern about the exploitation and suffering inflicted on African Americans and Africans. Such concern about racial justice was a core commitment of Niebuhr's, dating back to the 1930s. He suggested at that time a program of nonviolent resistance, such as economic boycotts by the "Negro" community in order to attain full equality. Such power politics must be employed, he argued, because no matter how many good-hearted whites there are in America, the white race as a class will not admit Negroes unless forced to do so (*Moral Man and Immoral Society* 252).

Niebuhr was not just a civil rights advocate; his vision of equality was holistic. Consequently, he recognized as early as 1968 that racism was not just a matter of civil rights and the vote. It must also be recognized as tied up in economics. Thus, he claimed that America could only end racism by providing necessary economic clout to the African American community so that it might be no longer dependent on government aid or European American classes (*Faith and Politics* 265–66). In a similar connection, it is interesting to note how he voiced appreciation of the development of twentieth-century black theology (see chap. 15) and of the appointment of its prime advocate, James Cone (b. 1938), to the Union Seminary faculty, where Niebuhr taught for over thirty years.

*Is this really a Calvinist social ethic?* One would expect Niebuhr, committed Reformed theologian that he was, to have operated with the characteristically Calvinist gospel-oriented approach to authorizing his social ethical proposals. He often took delight in critiquing the shortcomings of the Lutheran two-kingdom ethic (Niebuhr *Moral Man and Immoral Society* 75–77). His endorsement of this Calvinist orientation, however, is not always clear. For instance, it might be hard to reconcile an insistence that the gospel should function as a norm for political engagements with the old-fashioned power politics that he advocated. Also, a more law-oriented version of social ethics, typical of Luther and only implicit in Calvin, does appear in Niebuhr's thought at points. He spoke of a distinction between church and state and also insisted that the decisions of the state must proceed under the jurisdiction of reason, not of revelation (38, 259–60; *Love and Justice* 51–54).

To be sure, Niebuhr did concede a significant role for the gospel in helping us live together while in the midst of political struggle. If love does not seek something more than justice, he writes, we will not have justice. In his view, religion provides a sublime madness to help us see the common human frailties and transcendent worth of those with whom we are contesting (*Moral Man and Immoral Society* 254–55, 266). Insofar as Luther did not rule out a role for the gospel and Christian love in leavening or motivating justice (Luther *Temporal Authority: To What Extent It Should Be Obeyed*, in LW 45:121), are Niebuhr's commitments more characteristic of Luther or of Calvin? An even more practical question is raised from these considerations: Is Niebuhr a resource for the contemporary liberation agenda?

### Georgia Harkness

Perhaps the most prominent American female theologian at midcentury, Georgia Harkness (1891–1974) was also a leader in the struggle against segregation as well as in the women's rights and ecumenical movements. She characterized herself much like a liberal theologian and was concerned to try to demonstrate that faith can be intellectually respectable. Like Schleiermacher and other liberals, she described faith in relation to human experience. In the tradition of liberal theology, she minimized the doctrine of original sin, claiming only that we are born with a biological tendency to self-centeredness, a propensity, she claimed, that is natural but can easily pass over into sinful selfishness. Harkness's Methodist commitments also surfaced in apparently Arminian claims that God delivers only those who will accept (*Understanding the Christian Faith* 16–23, 114–20). In all of these commitments, can we say that she is truly a forerunner of contemporary feminist and womanist theology? Are her thought and these movements then privy to the Barthian critique of liberal theology?

### Rudolf Bultmann

Generally recognized as the greatest New Testament scholar of the twentieth century, Rudolf Bultmann (1884–1976) was a German Lutheran. His skilled and fearless use of the methods of historical criticism led him to reach radical conclusions regarding how little of the New Testament is historically verifiable. The question then to be faced was how to make faith believable to the modern world in view of what we know of science and historical research.

**Demythologization.** In Bultmann's view, the problem is that New Testament cosmology is essentially mythical. Thinking today is shaped by modern science and a different view of what would be persuasive to modern people. As a result, the mythical worldview is obsolete. Unless the *kerygma* (the proclamation of the gospel) is stripped from its New Testament mythological framework, it will seem untenable. The New Testament must be demythologized (Bultmann *Kerygma and Myth* 1–11).

Bultmann assumed a decidedly anthropocentric orientation. His method is most consistent with Schleiermacher's, and just the opposite from Barth's emphasis on God's transcendence. Bultmann's methodology is evident in his claim that the real purpose of myth is, not to present an objective picture of the world, but to express a person's understanding of oneself in the world. Myths, he argued, should be interpreted anthropologically. Faith claims that the understanding of existence enshrined by New Testament mythology is true (10–11). In order to express this understanding of existence in intelligible categories, Bultmann turned to the thought of Martin Heidegger (1889–1976), an existentialist philosopher who greatly influenced him (*Kerygma and Myth* 24–25; *Jesus Christ and Mythology* 56–57). The key issue of existence for Heidegger, and so for the New Testament kerygma in Bultmann's view, is authentic Being — being in touch with one's nature. In fact, the dilemma of human existence is that we are alienated from ourselves. This is what Christians mean by *sin*, Bultmann claims (*Kerygma and Myth* 26–31).

*Eschatological existence.* A chief characteristic of the human condition, according to Bultmann and Heidegger, is that we exist in a permanent tension between past and future (because in their view we are Being-in-history). In the state of alienation in which we currently exist, we are bound by the past. Tangled up in such bondage, we have no real future. Sharing the consensus of the New Testament scholarly community of his day that the kerygma is primarily an eschatological message, Bultmann reinterpreted it in light of the categories of Heidegger's existentialist analysis of the human condition. This eschatological message, he claimed, is a proclamation of freedom, a promise that gives us a future (*Kerygma and Myth* 24–25; *Jesus Christ and Mythology* 11, 77). With this emphasis on freedom, there are obviously some clear affinities between Bultmann's version of the kerygma and classical Lutheran themes. But is it precisely the same?

*Assessment.* Bultmann seems to compromise divine transcendence, at least to the degree that this was true of Schleiermacher's similar method.[12] Scripture, the biblical accounts, have been ultimately

---

12. Just as Schleiermacher translated Christian concepts into Romantic philosophy, so Bultmann did the same with regard to the categories of existentialism.

relegated to the status of nothing more than an expression of the biblical authors' experience (Bultmann *Theology of the New Testament* 2:238–39). Has the critique of religion mounted by Ludwig Feuerbach been confirmed? Has Bultmann (and others who employ his correlationist method) not reduced theology to anthropology? On the other hand, it seems difficult to avoid his conclusions regarding the incomprehensibility of the biblical worldview in our modern scientific context.

Bultmann's treatment of Christology also warrants an assessment. The generally accepted verities of historical criticism made Bultmann, in the spirit of Albert Schweitzer, exceedingly cautious of the credibility of any claims regarding the historical Jesus. Given this meager data, he concluded that Christ functions as Savior only when he meets us in the kerygma (in proclamation). The historical Jesus, then, is not essential for faith. He is only a presupposition for the theology of New Testament, not part of that theology (*Theology of the New Testament* 1:3). Only *that* Jesus existed is significant (Bultmann *Historical Jesus and the Kerygmatic Christ* 20). Is this bare "that" enough for faith?

*The post-Bultmannian new quest for the historical Jesus.* After World War II, a number of Bultmann's students, notably Gerhard Ebeling (b. 1912) and Ernst Fuchs (b. 1930), responded negatively to the supposition of Jesus' existence being enough for faith. They initiated a new quest for the historical Jesus, which is sometimes called the "new hermeneutic." As was their teacher, these German theologians were indebted to the philosophy of Martin Heidegger. Late in his career, though, Heidegger had made a shift in his thinking. He spoke of the linguistic character of Being. Since reality itself is structured by linguistic patterns, language does not just express the thoughts of the speaker but in some events actually lets Being be expressed (Heidegger *Unterwegs zur Sprache* 255ff.) Theologians appropriating these insights could proceed to argue that the language event of the Word of God in Christ brought to expression the very being of the historical Jesus. The faith that comes to expression in the Word is Jesus' faith, for Jesus' Word and person are one. In that sense the Word, by bringing Jesus' faith to expression, puts us in touch with his person, with the "historical Jesus" (Ebeling *Word and Faith* 288ff.; Fuchs *Studies of the Historical Jesus* 28–31).

Has this new quest succeeded in recovering the historical Jesus? Or has it merely reduced the "historical Jesus" to a few glimpses of his spiritual psyche? The failure of this movement to affect the life of the Church late in the second half of the twentieth century as much as other movements may provide some insight in answering these questions.

## Paul Tillich

Next to Niebuhr, Paul Tillich (1886–1965) was probably the most influential American theologian of the first half of the century. A German immigrant who belonged to the Evangelical and Reformed Church (a body composed of Lutheran and Reformed congregations in Germany), he spent his most productive years in America at Union Theological Seminary (where Niebuhr had a hand in bringing him to America) and later at Harvard. An intellectual who loved the finer things in life, Tillich also engaged in a rather avant-garde sexual lifestyle.[13]

*The method of correlation.* Tillich was self-consciously committed to doing apologetic theology. He sought to accomplish this by employing the correlationist approach of the early Apologists (as well as of Schleiermacher, other Enlightenment scholars, and Bultmann). He even referred to this approach as the "method of correlation," correlating questions posed by the human situation with answers drawn from theology, which are themselves formulated in the language of the questions originally posed. Because in Tillich's view such questions are existential, the philosophy of existentialism functions in his system as concepts in which original questions are posed and in turn as the concepts into which theological themes are translated (*Systematic Theology* 1:3–8, 59–66).

*Christology and hermeneutics.* As typical of modern Protestant theology, Tillich's system is Christocentric. The man Jesus called the Christ is identified as the material norm of theology, our ultimate concern (*Systematic Theology* 1:49–50). However, in the spirit of earlier liberal theology and of Bultmann, Tillich claimed that the Bible is, not an accurate account of God's works in history, but the witness of those participating in revelatory events. The Bible, he asserted, is a symbolic (mythological) expression of biblical authors' experience (1:35). The biblical picture of Jesus as the Christ is not accurate history; it is merely the result of the disciples' picture of what happened. Tillich proceeded to develop the logic of the analogy further. The relation between what the Gospels say about Jesus and the historical facts are like the relation between a painting and the actual event. Tillich speaks at this point of an *analogia imaginis* (2:114–16). The biblical Jesus is like an impressionistic portrait of the historical Jesus. Has Tillich's proposal solved the dilemma faced by modern theology in trying to take seriously the challenges of historical criticism?

*The Christian life.* In accord with his method of correlation, Tillich described the human condition and the nature of the Christian faith in terms of the categories of existentialist philosophy. According to him,

---

13. He and his wife reportedly practiced open marriage.

the fundamental problem of human existence is estrangement. We are estranged from our essence (our Being). Likewise, if we are estranged from our Being, we must also be estranged from the Ground of Being (whom Tillich identified as God). This estrangement is the essence of sin (*Systematic Theology* 2:44ff.; 1:155–57). Since estrangement happens when essence (pure potential) is actualized (2:43–44), creation (the actualization of potential) and the Fall seem to be one for Tillich. Is it appropriate to so identify creation and the Fall into sin?

Humans need the New Being, which overcomes the estrangement of essence and existence. We have this in Jesus the Christ. He takes on the negatives of finite existence into Being-itself and transcends them (*Systematic Theology* 2:134–35).[14] All individuals in Christ are taken up into Being-itself. For Tillich, much as for Hegel, when we are in touch with our essence, we are in touch with the whole (3:406–7).

*Assessment.* In Tillich's thought is a majestic, cosmological vision of the whole, which is lacking in Bultmann's view.[15] The essence of all that has or will exist is *in* God. Tillich's holistic, ontological vision, subsuming all reality in God, is reminiscent not just of Hegel but also of the Apologists of the early Church, like Origen and Gregory of Nyssa. However, Tillich's reliance on the method of correlation, which begins our theologizing with human experience, itself entails that even his references to transcendent Being-itself are ultimately only descriptions of the speaker's experience. Has Tillich really been successful in affirming the transcendence of God, or has he too, in the vein of Schleiermacher and Bultmann, reduced theology to anthropology?

## Is There an Early-Twentieth-Century Theologian Who Can Still Speak for Us?

What we should make of the plethora of theological alternatives that emerged in the first half of the twentieth century? Are any of the alternatives a helpful resource for addressing our contemporary situation? Why does a particular theologian seem more promising than others, and how is he or she an improvement on the others? To what extent are the answers to these questions related to a modern version of the classical debate in the early Church between correlationists, like Justin Martyr, and orthodox theologians, like Tertullian?

---

14. Note how in accord with Tillich's method, the categories employed in the prior philosophical analysis of the human condition are in turn employed to describe the key doctrines of the Christian faith.

15. For Bultmann, God seems little more than the one who gives authentic existence.

# CHAPTER 15

# TODAY AND TOMORROW

## A LIBERATING CHURCH
## OR A CHURCH IN DECAY?

From the aftermath of World War II until the turn of the twenty-first century have been years of ecclesiastical and theological change — years of great hope (esp. the 1950s), of ferment (the 1960s), of startling realignments, and at least in the West of seemingly meandering decline (since the 1970s). The theological ethos of this era in the West can be characterized most readily by the failure of a consensus to develop. One might call it an aimless diversity. There have been no dominant movements or theologians in these years by which or by whom the era can be characterized. The main trends or theological preoccupations of these years, though, might be summarized in terms of ecumenism, hermeneutics, indigenization, and liberation.

## The Way to and from Vatican II

In the years immediately following World War II, the Roman Catholic Church became increasingly isolated. During the war and immediately prior to it, the papacy was in the hands of Pius XII (Eugenio Pacelli; 1876–1958), an experienced diplomat, a man of prayer and personal magnetism, but with a pronounced authoritarian streak. He tried to prevent the war and remained neutral, presumably so he could function as a mediator. One cannot but wonder if relations with Mussolini in Italy were an issue, as Pius's predecessor had signed an agreement with the Fascist dictator in 1929 finally recognizing Italy but gaining official sanction to rule Vatican City. In any case, Pius XII remained silent about Nazi atrocities to Jews but defended Catholics in Poland.[1] The centuries of strained Jewish-Catholic relations in western Europe were further exacerbated by these twentieth-century developments.

---

1. This is not one of Catholicism's greatest moments!

After the war, Pius was preoccupied with anti-Communism and with centralizing church government. In 1950, he proclaimed the second church doctrine based on papal infallibility (the first having been the doctrine of the immaculate conception): the assumption of Mary into heaven, which maintains that the Virgin Mary went directly into heaven without experiencing bodily decay. At least since the Middle Ages, this article of faith had been a part of popular Catholic devotion. Pius formalized its status as dogma with this ex cathedra pronouncement that the devoted Son would not fail to honor Mary by keeping her safe from the corruption of the tomb (*Munificentissimus Deus*).

Pius's theological conservatism surfaced in other ways. In a 1950 bull (*Humani generis*), he reiterated earlier warnings against innovations in theology. Five years later, he repudiated the involvement of Catholic priests in a French labor movement with socialist orientations. However, Pius did, perhaps unwittingly, open the door to reform in several ways. (1) He encouraged the use of biblical criticism (*Divino Afflante Spiritu*). (2) He initiated reform of the liturgy. (3) He encouraged an end of colonialism, which was related to his advocacy of the formation of truly indigenous churches with native leadership. And (4) he helped make the Catholic Church become truly international, by bringing non-Italians to the *curia* (the Vatican's administrative hierarchy) and by internationalizing the college of cardinals with more indigenous bishops.

### The Reign of John XXIII

The election of Pius's immediate successor in 1958, John XXIII (Angelo Giuseppe Roncalli; 1881–1963), was the beginning of a new day. The new pope, an aged man but young in heart and spirit, one thought by some critics to be too simple a man to assume such an awesome responsibility, changed both the papacy and the Catholic Church forever.

The new pope had lived in Istanbul under Islamic rule and in thoroughly secularized Paris. In these contexts, he had come to appreciate the marked degree to which the Catholic Church had cut itself off from dialogue with the world. Another aspect of his thought was the absence of hierarchicalism. He frequently referred to other bishops as his "brothers." These commitments came together very quickly in his reign.

Only three months after taking office, John XXIII announced his intention to call a council to "update" the Catholic Church, for which he claimed to need the wisdom of all the bishops that only a council could provide. This decision produced no little controversy. The Vatican hierarchy, since Vatican I, had grown accustomed to thinking of the Catholic Church's polity as unilateral and centralized in decision making. Furthermore, John's council would be the first ever convened to address issues that were not expressly heretical. John's dream came to fruition in late 1962 with the convening of the council, the second one to be held in Vatican City (thus it is known as Vatican II). It did not adjourn until three years later, long after his death.

## Theological Precedents for the Council

If some twentieth-century theological reform movements in the Catholic Church had not laid the groundwork for reform, John XXIII would not likely have achieved his aims. Among the significant and exciting theological developments in the Roman Catholic Church during the first half of the twentieth century included the work of the French priest and trained scientist Pierre Teilhard de Chardin (1881–1955). He was the first prominent Catholic thinker to seek to open the Church to certain insights drawn from modern science and evolutionary theory. So tight did he make this synthesis that he spoke of Christ as eucharistically present in matter and the things of the world (*Hymn of the Universe*). Another French Catholic scholar, Henri de Lubac (1896–1991), spoke of Christ as the single goal of humanity and described the Church as a sacrament. The French Dominican Yves Congar (1904–95) proved to be no less a cutting-edge thinker; his thought was eventually reflected in the documents of the Vatican Council. He, like de Lubac, sought to find a way to talk about the Church apart from hierarchical, institutional, juridical models. In a manner most suggestive of the insights of certain sixteenth-century Reformers, he referred to the Church as the "people of God" and evolved a theology of the laity (*Jalons pour une théologie du laicat*).

Of all the cutting-edge theological influences that inspired John XXIII and the council, none was perhaps more profound than the German Jesuit theologian Karl Rahner (1904–84), a former student of the eminent German existentialist philosopher Martin Heidegger.[2] Influenced by Rudolf Bultmann and other Protestant theologians, Rahner developed his own distinct method and cosmology. His overall agenda was to affirm both tradition and the modern world (*Theological Investigations* 20:128). His development of the *transcendental method* aimed to serve

---

2. Another cutting-edge Catholic theological movement of the era was Neo-Thomism, which sought to reinterpret Aquinas's theology in such a way that it would be in dialogue with existentialist philosophy. Although its primary representatives like Jacques Maritain (1882–1973) and Étienne Gilson (1884–1978) did not perhaps influence the Vatican Council as directly as those movements noted in the text, the Neo-Thomist concern to engage the Catholic theological heritage in dialogue with contemporary philosophy was most compatible with the council's agenda to enter into dialogue with the modern world (*Gaudium et Spes*).

that agenda. Many of the prominent post–Vatican II theologians, both Catholics and Protestants, have come to embrace commitments akin to this method.

Rahner's method presupposes that theology is about human experience (*Theological Investigations* 9:28). In this sense, he embraces a method something like that of Schleiermacher and liberal theology. Rahner tried to show that to claim that theology needs to be anthropology is not a compromise of theocentricity, as Thomas Aquinas or Karl Barth maintained. Man is absolutely transcendent with respect to God. Human experience can take in the whole of reality because grace is everywhere; that is to say, the object of theology is given in the believer's experience because this object (grace) already subsists in the structures of human being. The experience of grace is the foundation of knowing grace (28ff.). In a manner somewhat reminiscent of Paul Tillich, Rahner refers to God as "the ground of the individual's existence, involved in perception and action." This also entails for Rahner that persons in touch with their own being through conscience are seeking God; in that sense, all such human beings are at least "anonymous Christians" (*Pastoral Approach to Atheism* 75ff.).

A strong affirmation of the *sola gratia* is implicit in Rahner's approach. All we know is by grace. In this sense, we might regard the transcendental method as a middle ground between Barth and Schleiermacher, between Justin Martyr and Tertullian. For Rahner, as for the liberal theologians and the Apologists, theology begins with human experience. However, for Rahner, Barth, and the Christocentric orthodox theologians, God can be said at least implicitly to initiate theological reflection insofar as grace permeates the whole of human experience such that to begin with human experience is to begin with grace (and so with God). The question is whether such a mediating position between the Christocentric orthodox and the correlationist theological methods has in fact been achieved. Or is it the case that if one initiates theological reflection with anthropology, all theological assertions, even those pertaining to the primacy of God's work (grace) and divine transcendence, are logically reduced to mere descriptions of human experience? The question posed by Karl Barth to liberal theology must be raised anew: Have Rahner and those who share his methodological commitments ultimately overcome Ludwig Feuerbach's contention that all religion is ultimately anthropology?

Among Rahner's other important theological contributions was his plea for more collegiality among the bishops and for less emphasis on the centralization of power in Rome, though he did not reject Roman primacy. No less significant was his endorsement of the priesthood of all believers (*Theological Investigations* 20:128, 130). This theme was very much on the agenda of Pope John XXIII and the Vatican Council.

A younger contemporary of Rahner's, the Swiss Catholic theologian Hans Küng (b. 1928), also participated in the Vatican Council, though without the kind of influence exerted by Rahner and the others. A student of Barth's and a brilliant theologian in his own right, Küng has proven to be a controversial figure in the theological world. In 1957, he wrote a book on the compatibility between Barth's view of the doctrine of justification and the historic Catholic position (*Rechtfertigung: Die Lehre Karl Barths und eine katholische Besinnung*). More controversial has been his subsequent criticism of the doctrine of infallibility (*Unfehlbar?*).

## The Teachings of Vatican II

Most of the commitments of the older cutting-edge theologians emerged in John's XXIII's encyclicals, culminating in Vatican II. One encyclical issued in 1963, *Pacem in Terris* (157ff.), addressed concerns of peace, justice, and disarmament, arguing that such positions were intelligible to all people of good will. The argument was authorized by appeal to the *natural law* (the commonsense belief in right and wrong accessible to all human beings because these values are structured in the created order). The document asserts that human resources alone cannot achieve justice and peace; God's assistance is required. With this, the pope seems to endorse a Reformation-like emphasis on *sola gratia*. This document and an earlier encyclical dealing with contemporary social issues (*Mater et Magistra*, issued in 1961) undergird Pope John's overall commitment to address the concerns of the modern world.

The concern to build bridges between the Church and the modern world was precisely the agenda of the council as described by John's successor, Pope Paul VI (Giovanni Battista Montini; 1897–1978), who completed the council (*Mater et Magistra* 352–55). Among the council's progressive decisions were:

1. An affirmation of the validity of the ministry of the sacraments of Eastern Orthodox churches (*Orientalium Ecclesiarum* 24ff.).

2. A further opening of the way to ecumenism, recognizing members of Protestant churches as "separated brethren" and the "truly Christian endowments" that can function as a means of salvation as found in these communities (*Unitatis Redintegratio* 3–4). With this statement, it is no longer official Catholic teaching that all Protestants are damned as heretics. Ecumenism was identified as a principal concern of the council (1).

3. A countenancing of the use of the vernacular, instead of Latin, in worship (*Sacrosanctum Concilium* 36, 54). Prior to the council, the Mass was always in Latin. By contrast, the council even expressed openness to indigenizing the liturgy to adopt it to particular cultures (40).

4. An affirmation of lay ministry, urging its promotion (*Lumen Gentium* 37).

5. An assertion that the magisterium is to be in service of the Word, not to dominate the Word (*Dei Verbum* 10).

6. A decree, in the spirit of Congar, that the Church is not a mere institution identified with hierarchy but is rather a mystery. The council made a Protestant-like distinction between the visible and the invisible Church, even portraying it as a sacrament. Further, the council did not unequivocally identify the Church with the Roman Catholic Church, saying merely that it "subsists" in the Catholic Church (*Lumen Gentium* 1–3, 8).

7. A condemnation of racism (*Nostra Aetate* 5) and an expression of concern about the poor (*Gaudium et Spes* 27, 69), most suggestive of the preferential option for the poor espoused by liberation theology (see below). The latter document made its argument by appeal to the natural law, much as John XXIII did in his 1963 encyclical. On the other hand, much like Calvin, this conciliar document claims that church and state interpenetrate, construing the former as the soul for human society. In fact, the created order is even subordinated to grace insofar as grace is said to be invisibly active in all men (40, 22). With these affirmations the council aligned itself with the theocratic orientation of the Catholic Church's medieval heritage. It did break with earlier positions in endorsing religious freedom (21). As such, a strict theocracy is thereby rejected. This is much more a Catholicism suited for contemporary democratic societies.

8. A recognition of non-Christians sincerely seeking to do God's Will with their actions, though they do not know him (actions always moved by grace), as numbered among the people of God (*Lumen Gentium* 16). Much in the spirit of Chardin, de Lubac, and Rahner, the council noted the occasional subordination of creation to grace. Such language also seems to endorse the concept of the righteous unbeliever as an "anonymous Christian."

9. An affirmation of justification by faith as the doctrine that constitutes a Christian (*Unitatis Redintegratio* 3). Such an affirmation

is most consistent with the Lutheran emphasis on centrality of this doctrine. The council also used language compatible with the concept of justification as conformity to Christ (*Gaudium et Spes* 22) and affirmed supralapsarian election, that is, the belief that the divine decision about election was made before the Fall (*Lumen Gentium* 3). Such commitments are most consistent with good Reformed theology. On the basis of these affirmations, it seems difficult to accuse Vatican II and the Catholic Church of legalism.

Elsewhere in the documents of Vatican II are references to theological commitments compatible with the emphases of other traditions. At points, the documents mention the mandate to strive for perfection, much in the spirit of Methodism and Eastern Orthodoxy (*Lumen Gentium* 11, 39). Ideas compatible with the Eastern Orthodox concept of salvation as deification are also reflected in at least one document of the council (17). However, the council did not overlook traditional Roman Catholic ways of referring to the process of salvation. Sometimes the council spoke of justification more in line with Aquinas's model of justification as a function of cooperating with grace. The bishops claimed that grace only "helps" or "aids" us (*Gaudium et Spes* 17, 77) and that the good done apart from Christ by unbelievers, albeit itself a work of grace, is a preparation for the gospel (*Lumen Gentium* 16). If one questions how all this conceptual diversity can be held together, could the answer perhaps be that the Roman tradition is indeed a "catholic" heritage?

### Has the Vatican Council Negated the Justification for Protestantism?

An important story to be told about the council was the participation of a number of prominent Protestants in the role of advisors. Although these advisors were already sympathetic to the prospect of bridging the schism between Protestants and Catholics, the council spurred a number of them to initiate a new theological movement, which might be termed "evangelical Catholicism." From the Protestant side, this movement has played a crucial role. Not only has it spurred Protestant initiatives for dialogue with the Roman Catholic Church, but it has also called Protestant traditions to a recovery of their Catholic roots, including a fresh appreciation of the historic (Catholic) liturgy and a high, episcopal view of the ordained ministry.

The significant number of convergencies between the statements of the Second Vatican Council and core Protestant commitments like justification by faith and the priesthood of all believers, not to mention a largely progressive social agenda, raises the question whether the justification for Protestantism has been negated by Vatican II. In view of all these convergencies, is the Reformation a mistake insofar as its heirs maintain their separation from the Roman Catholic Church?

## The Roman Catholic Church since Vatican II

Paul VI and subsequent popes have been somewhat more conservative than John XXIII (perhaps in order to placate their conservative constituency and keep it from splitting the Catholic Church). This has been the strategy for implementing the council's decisions, most of which have in fact been incorporated into Catholic practice. Paul's 1968 encyclical *Humanae Vitae* endorsed the long-standing Catholic opposition to abortion but added to it strictures on the use of artificial birth control.[3] Needless to say, the papal position has been most controversial.

The present pope, John Paul II (Karol Wojtyla; b. 1920), the first non-Italian pope since the sixteenth century, has a strong social conscience pertaining to justice and poverty. His work in the Polish Catholic resistance to Communist abuses testifies to this. However, he is conservative on personal morality and theological issues (the latter commitment accounting for his opposition to liberation theology). Having worked in the former Eastern bloc, where his conservative church thrived largely as a countercultural protest against the Communist regime, the pope sees more liberalism in the church in the West and observes that it is not thriving in that context. His conclusion has been the obvious one: conservatism is the way to make the Church thrive, which is why John Paul II and his premier theological consultant, Cardinal Joseph Ratzinger (b. 1927), at times seem so conservative.

Regardless of one's assessment of the present papal administration, we must concede that the Catholic Church has come a long way since the sixteenth century, indeed in the last century. Are the days in which negative Protestant assessments of this church were justifiable forever gone? As the Roman Catholic Church was changed by Vatican II, so the postwar Protestant ethos became dramatically altered (albeit with significant continuities to the post-Enlightenment era). A crucial, though sometimes unwitting, figure in the development of this new ethos was a young German theologian who died as a martyr before the end of the war.

---

3. Vatican II had outlawed it (*Gaudium et Spes* 27).

# Dietrich Bonhoeffer

The young German Lutheran Dietrich Bonhoeffer (1906–45) was a hero in the context of the German Church struggle, but the international impact of his life and theology was not fully felt until after World War II. Born of a well-to-do, highly educated family, Bonhoeffer had established the reputation of a young phenom under the tutelage of Adolf von Harnack and later under the influence of Karl Barth. Indeed, his dissertation, completed while he was still in his early twenties, was described by Barth as a "theological miracle."

Bonhoeffer had an opportunity to avoid direct involvement in the German Church struggle. He had become acquainted with Reinhold Niebuhr and the Union Seminary faculty when he had earlier studied in America before World War II. They urged him to return to the United States and the Union faculty in order to save himself from the turmoils that were developing in his native Germany. But feeling that he had a mission back home that he could not forgo, Bonhoeffer returned to Germany to resist Hitler, both through teaching in a clandestine seminary organized in protest of the Fuhrer's policy and later through involvement in a plot to assassinate him. When it failed, he was jailed and eventually executed as a martyr just a few days before the Allies liberated the region.

## The Impact of the African American Church

A little-known fact of Bonhoeffer's biography is that while in America, he became immersed in the life of the black church. He taught confirmation and preached at Abyssinian Baptist Church in Harlem, whose pastor at the time of his first visit in America (1930–31) was Adam Clayton Powell Sr. (1865–1953), whose son would become the premier congressional spokesperson for black Americans for decades.

Bonhoeffer's encounters in the United States left him deeply disturbed by racism. He reported that the black church profoundly affected him; he deeply appreciated its resistance to racism, the power and passion of its preaching, and the joy mixed with sober melancholy reflected in its music (*Gesammelte Schriften* 1:97). His experience with the black church so moved him that upon his return to teach at his alternative seminary in Germany, he taught African American spirituals to his students. Is it not clear that Bonhoeffer's experience with the black church nurtured his sense of righteous protest against injustice, which he so bravely undertook?

## Costly Grace: Is This a Lutheran Theology?

A key concept for understanding Bonhoeffer's theology that he developed early in his career was the distinction between cheap grace and costly grace. Cheap grace, as defined by Bonhoeffer, is when justification is a mere doctrine, not leading to repentance or church discipline. Costly grace, by contrast, is defined as obedience to the command of Christ (*Cost of Discipleship* 36ff.). In essence, Bonhoeffer appealed to a third use of the law in a manner more like Calvin than Luther. In fact, he expressly seems to have endorsed a third use (*Ethics* 318–19).

The context for the development of Bonhoeffer's reflections on these issues is important to note. Though he had achieved impressive heights as a scholar at an early age, he had come to fear that he might become so caught up in the careerism that affects most young scholars of religion that he would forget the real purpose of theological studies. Additionally he lamented, not unlike Kierkegaard had, that the Christendom of his day had become overlaid with so much ballast that it was extremely difficult to be a disciple (*Cost of Discipleship* 37). In this regard, his reliance on theological emphases not unlike those of Kierkegaard (esp. utilization of the third use of the law) is hardly surprising.

Though he invokes Luther, Bonhoeffer did concede that the Reformer treated discipleship as a spontaneous response to the gospel, not always requiring express attention (*Cost of Discipleship* 38–41). Of course, even this aspect of Luther's thought could be reconciled with Bonhoeffer's thinking in another work (*Communio Sanctorum* 22–23, 44, 46, 50), where he says that the social nature of human beings entails that the Church spontaneously nurtures the Christian and discipleship into being.

Also worth noting in connection with the question of the Lutheran identity of Bonhoeffer's theology is his engagement in the plot to assassinate Hitler. His willingness to be involved in a plot to murder another human being for the sake of justice is also suggestive of a perspective that emphasizes freedom from the law (a kind of situational ethic), entailing rejection of a third use of the law. Bonhoeffer theoretically affirmed such a view in the 1929 sermon "What Is a Christian Ethic?"[4]

Likewise with regard to his view of church-state relations and the two-kingdom ethic, Bonhoeffer's commitments are not entirely clear. In the spirit of Barth and other leaders of the Confessing Church in the struggle against Hitler, he was critical of Luther's views, especially of the "two-spheres" that characterized the German Christians (*Ethics* 197–99). But at other points, he insisted that a distinction must be

---

4. Bonhoeffer's lesson at this point seems to be that Christians should employ the third use of the law wherever they encounter sloth but not in other contexts.

made between what is Christian and what is of the world. He also defended Luther from what he perceived to be distortions of his thought by Hitler and his loyalists, arguing that Luther intended that the two kingdoms exist in a polemical unity, with Christians at times opposing the secular realm. To what extent did Bonhoeffer continue to maintain a confessional Lutheran perspective?

### Religionless Christianity

Bonhoeffer's development of the concept of "religionless Christianity" and his meaning of it has been a hotly debated theological issue since the end of World War II. Some have claimed that it opened the door to the "God-is-dead" movement (see below for details), and its proponents generally did interpret Bonhoeffer as an ally (Paul van Buren *Secular Meaning of the Gospel* 1–3). In fact, though, it seems more appropriate to interpret Bonhoeffer at this point as merely developing Karl Barth's critique of religion as a human effort with which we hide God or undermine the divine initiative (*Letters and Papers from Prison* 139–45; cf. Barth *Church Dogmatics* I/2:280ff.). In this regard, Bonhoeffer has also endorsed Barth's emphasis on God's transcendence.[5]

Bonhoeffer contended that we must respond with religionless Christianity, which means that we can no longer interpret God as a deus ex machina, as an answer to life's problems (*Letters and Papers from Prison* 179, 142). Liberal theologians like Tillich had fallen prey to this approach, presenting God as an answer to questions raised by human experience. However, Bonhoeffer insisted, Barth's positivist doctrine of revelation is not the answer. Barth's view, he argued, does not drive us sufficiently into the world, for it makes us become content merely with the Church (144–45).

Religionless Christianity in a world come of age means living fully in the world as if there were no God. One might say that for Bonhoeffer God is to be conceived as the wise parent who recedes in the background as one's child matures. These theological commitments entail immersing oneself fully in the world, concerning oneself with the state of creation, not personal salvation (*Letters and Papers from Prison* 144). Such this-worldliness (forgetting about spiritual matters for the sake of worldly affairs) is a renunciation of religious accomplishment, a throwing of oneself into God's arms, into the arms of a weak God who wins power and space in the world by his weakness (188). Is the

---

5. By contrast, the method of liberal theology tends to interpret Christianity in light of religion as its foundation, finding an intellectually credible religious realm into which Christian doctrines are interpreted.

concept of religionless Christianity ultimately compatible with modern versions of Luther's theology of the Cross, or has Bonhoeffer sold out the Reformation/Catholic heritage, thus clearing the way with Friedrich Nietzsche for the death of God?

## The German Church Struggle: Was It Luther's Fault? Is a Calvinist Social Ethic the Only Way to Have Liberation?

The events surrounding Bonhoeffer's involvement in the German Church struggle and Hitler's invocation of Luther's two-kingdom ethic to support his program of church-state relations have led most Western Christians since World War II to become wary of Luther's thinking. The debate touched off by the theological implications of the struggle did not become an object of international theological preoccupation until after the war. Since that time most prominent church leaders (even some Lutherans) have rejected the two-kingdom ethic for fear that it might authorize the kind of reactionary Christian social ethic that typified the so-called German Christians' response to Hitler's agenda. In general, the Western theological community and most Southern Hemisphere theologians have preferred the vision of church-state relations characteristic of Calvin and the Reformed tradition. The Reformed insistence that the gospel must govern all realms, including the political sphere, has found broad consensus.

The reason for this preference is not merely denominational loyalty. The events of the German Church struggle seem to have authorized this preference, for the Confessing Church, which protested against Hitler, and its most famed protest statement, the 1934 Barmen Declaration (II), drafted by Barth, reflected his Christomonism (a rejection of the two-kingdom ethic) and his corresponding insistence that all areas of life, like politics, are subject to Christ. Given such suppositions, no political power may claim to be God's revelation (through natural knowledge). There is only the Word.

Is such a Calvinist ethic, in which the gospel prevails in all realms, including politics, the only way to ensure that government operates properly? Will the two-kingdom ethic, as an ethic rooted in the concept of the natural law, inevitably lead to total obedience to the state, giving one no alternative to unjust practices like those that characterized Hitler's regime (Rom. 13)? Must Christian social ethics always be done from the perspective of the gospel?

In assessing these questions, one must consider the history of Christianity in order to discern whether some socially progressive Christians might have operated with theological suppositions compatible with a two-kingdom ethic. Theologians covered in this and in previous chapters need to be considered with regard to this question. Certainly Bonhoeffer's qualified endorsement of this characteristic Lutheran social ethic warrants attention. Also worth noting in connection with this question is the Norwegian nonviolent resistance to the Nazis during World War II, a resistance led by Bishop Einvind Berggrav (1884–1959). This was a resistance undertaken with the express invocation of Luther's two-kingdom ethic and openness to nonviolent resistance (Berggrav *Man and State* 300–319). At least in the case of Norway and Denmark during World War II, the two-kingdom ethic did not entail political passivity. Luther himself at points in his career did not advocate political passivity. In that connection, one should not overlook that he recognized the corruptibility of reason (Luther *Disputation concerning Man*, in *LW* 34:137–38) and so like proponents of the Barmen Declaration claimed that not all governments were good and just, that is, by implication, not always deserving respect (*Commentary on Psalm 101*, in *LW* 13:193–94).

Does this additional data exonerate the two-kingdom ethic from charges that it will invariably nurture political passivity or reactionary politics? Is it as inherently capable of functioning to provide theological authorization/motivation for the cause of liberation and social justice as the more Reformed Christocentric model? Indeed the Reformed model, one might argue, is less tolerant of minorities than the two-kingdom ethic. That is, if the state is to be run in accord with gospel principles, the non-Christian is effectively disenfranchised. He or she does not possess the same political wisdom as the Christian. On the other hand, the two-kingdom ethic, by rooting political institutions in the realm of the universally accessible natural law, seems more inclusive. But if the two-kingdom ethic has such virtues, how does one explain its vulnerability to co-option by Hitler and the reactionary position Luther himself took against the peasants?

## Ecclesiastical Developments in Europe after World War II

After the war, Russia's building of the Communist empire in Eastern Europe had an impact on Protestant and Catholic churches in these regions not unlike the impact that it had on Orthodox churches (see chap. 14). Though harassed, churches in these regions were formidable enough to endure, forcing the Communist regimes to cooperate. State support for the church was in fact maintained in Czechoslovakia and Hungary. Some Communist-Christian dialogue was undertaken. Like the Orthodox churches, which historically have capitulated to the state, these Protestant and Catholic churches similarly capitulated to some extent. At international meetings they often sent leaders functioning as Communist spies. In the waning days of the Communist regimes, these churches did become centers of protest, attracting many. However, attendance and interest have waned since the Communist era ended.

Elsewhere in Europe, Christianity's social contribution has been more mixed or ambiguous. National churches in virtually all western European nations have progressively lost membership and influence since World War II, to the point that in some nations only 10 percent of the population has any significant contact with the Church. In at least two other politically sensitive regions — Yugoslavia and Northern Ireland — Christianity has even exacerbated existing ethnic conflicts.

## Yugoslavia: Serbia, Croatia, Bosnia, Kosovo

Tensions in the former Yugoslavia, a twentieth-century political entity dissolved after the death of the man who had almost single-handedly kept Yugoslavia together, Marshal Tito (Josip Broz; 1892–1980), and the subsequent breakdown of the Communist stranglehold on the nation are not unrelated to religious differences among residents in the region. Republics, which had been progressively gaining more and more autonomy under Tito's successors, especially Slovenia, Croatia, and Kosovo, seceded in 1990. Though largely dominated by Serbs, Yugoslavia seemed to be dissolving.

When war broke out in Bosnia in 1991, it was originally a conflict about whether to preserve the Yugoslav union or grant republics the right to secede. Serbs of course favored preservation of the union. The federal army had already succeeded in retaining Kosovo but failed to hold Slovenia. Battles followed in Croatia between Croats and Serbs. The union died. The war that followed concerned how to partition the region that was Yugoslavia, especially Bosnia and Herzegovina (regions in west central Yugoslavia near, but not bordering on, the Adriatic Sea). Each side tried to control as much territory as possible in order to establish legal possession. The Serbs had the better of this struggle. Armed conflict broke out in Bosnia in April 1992 when the minority Serbs (about 32 percent of population) rebelled against a vote by Bosnia's Moslems (39.5 percent of the Bosnian population) and Croats (18.3 percent of the population) to secede from Serb-dominated Yugoslavia. The new state had a Moslem government aligned with a Croat minority.

An Albanian Moslem majority dominates over a Serbian minority (only about 20 percent of the population) in Kosovo.

One school of thought maintains that the three major groups involved in the conflict in Bosnia — Serbs, Croats, and Moslems — are ethnically related; that is, all are Slavic. However, it is undeniable that each group has a long tradition of separate autonomous states and distinct cultures. Only in 1918, after World War I, were they brought together to form the Yugoslav state. There had been such an empire led by Serbs in the twelfth to fourteenth centuries until it was conquered and destroyed in 1389 by the Turks.

The Serbs have a strong historical tradition of independent existence. As a result of the division of the old Roman Empire in A.D. 395, the Eastern (Byzantine) Empire strongly influenced the Serbs' premedieval history and culture. The line of territorial demarcation between East and West placed the Serbs in the East. Consequently the Serbs came to be Eastern Orthodox in spiritual orientation. During the period of domination by the Islamic Ottoman Empire, many Serbs emigrated to regions that the Austrian Empire ruled. These centuries made Serbian commitment to the Eastern Orthodox tradition even more staunch, as it was the Serbian Orthodox Church that kept the people together during the period of Ottoman hegemony.

Croatians have a similar history of autonomous existence. They organized as an independent kingdom in the ninth century and are clearly the most politically and culturally Western of the ethnic groups in the region, which is partly a function of their unification with Hungary from 1102 to 1526. However, this Western orientation of the Croats has had more ancient roots, owing to the fact that the A.D. 395 division of the Roman Empire located Croatia in the Western Empire centered in Rome. Not surprisingly, Croats tend to be Roman Catholic.

Moslems live primarily in Bosnia (and are Slavic peoples) or are Albanians living in Kosovo. They are the descendants of those who conformed under Ottoman rule, though such conforming was rarely out of deep conviction. One school of thought claims that Moslems in Bosnia are not a distinct nationality (ethnic group) at all. In fact, some Bosnians go so far as to claim that the people of Bosnia are a single ethnic group divided only by religion, those who are Catholic calling themselves Croats and those who are Orthodox calling themselves Serbian. Moslems have been least inclined to identify themselves as a distinct nationality/ethnic group, it is argued, partly because they have no other nearby nationality with which to identify. This is not so clearly the case in Kosovo, where the Moslems are Albanian, and so of non-Slavic ethnicity distinct from the Serbs with whom they live.

Regardless of the question of whether Bosnian Serbs, Croats, and

Moslems are genetically distinct and despite the fact that these people have at points in history lived together, there is a long history of not just cultural and religious differences but also of mutual suspicions and betrayal.[6] Croats (with Moslems generally as their allies) tended to resent Serb dominance in periods when the three groups formed one nation. The Axis powers' invasion of the region further exacerbated tensions as they tried to divide the groups by placing Croats in charge, who responded, ostensibly endeavoring to settle old scores, by launching a campaign to "Croatize" the Serbs. In a sense, the war of the 1990s in Bosnia may be understood as a Serbian attempt to retaliate against a perceived fascist Croatia.

Although the Bosnian War has obviously developed because of historical and cultural factors, religious overtones have clearly surfaced insofar as the Serbian-Croatian conflict is also an Orthodox-Catholic conflict. This is all the more pronounced when it comes to Bosnia and Herzegovina (the most ethnically mixed of the former Yugoslav republics) with the added Islamic ingredient. The war has become a kind of "religious war," but it is one fought by people who, because of the forced circumstances of their conversion (in the case of Islam) or the primitive and ineffective quality of its community life (in the case of the Serbian Orthodox Church), have only the vaguest notions of what their religion is all about. However, because of the role the respective religious bodies play in defining and nurturing ethnicity, the clashes have clearly taken on a religious overtone.

Some of this same ambiguity about the degree to which religion has occasioned conflict is evident in the war in Kosovo. In one sense it appears to be an Orthodox-Moslem clash, as the Albanian majority has attacked Serbian Orthodox Church property. The actions of Albanian rebels in the late 1990s in hope of liberating Kosovo from Serbia were initiated as early as 1981. In a sense the Serbian reaction might be construed as a defense not just of their ethnicity but also of their faith. However, the situation's complexity is exacerbated by an awareness that at least 10 percent of the Albanians in Kosovo are not Moslem, but are mostly Catholic with some Orthodox. The impact of this Christian minority on the Moslem community is pronounced, for as in the case of Bosnian Moslems the Islamic community in Kosovo often commemorates certain Christian rituals along with their (on the surface) Islamic faith. When one also considers that in the war in Kosovo there have been instances of Christian (Orthodox) Albanians fighting Chris-

---

6. Other smaller groups in the region (esp. Slovenes, Macedonians, and Montenegrins) seem not to have played as major a role in the conflict, partly because they are aligned with one of the larger ethnic groups, partly through shared religious convictions — the first being Catholic and the other two belonging to Eastern Orthodox churches.

tian (Orthodox) Serbs, it seems apparent that this conflict is more about Albanian ethnicity than about religion.

The role of religion in fostering turmoil in Croatia is equally complex. The Catholic Church practiced triumphalism by refusing to recognize full Serb cultural autonomy in traditional Serbian regions of Croatia. The Serbian Orthodox Church in its classical role as defender of Serbian nationalism was the first Serbian institution to warn about the welfare of Serbs in regions where they were minorities and has advocated restoring the Yugoslav monarchy, which would be Serbian and Orthodox. The Church has certainly seen finer hours than the role it has played in the Yugoslav conflict.

## Northern Ireland

The Church's role in the conflict in Northern Ireland has been no less problematic. The distinct character of Northern Ireland owes much to the plantation (colonization) scheme of the early seventeenth century. The special relationship between England and Northern Ireland dates to 1603, when the last great Celtic prince of the region surrendered to the English. This ensured that the Anglican Reformation could proceed without fear of interference from the Counter-Reformation mediated through a Catholic Northern Ireland. The British responded by allowing the prince and his allies to keep the land, but now in accord with British laws. It was the beginning of a strategy of Anglicizing the island.

Humiliated by the continuing decline of their influence, Irish leaders left Ireland to live on continental Europe. The British quickly ceded land to colonize (for the plantation of) the region. A relatively small amount of land in Northern Ireland was reserved for Irish who could be trusted and promised to adopt English social and agricultural customs. Most of the remaining land went to those British subjects willing to build villages and fortified enclosures. It was found economically advantageous to allow large numbers of Irish to remain on the land as tenants, intermixed with English and Scottish colonizers. British colonizers were predominant in the region surrounding Ulster and tended to make up the upper class of the region. Scottish colonizers arrived independently and came to dominate in regions closest to Scotland.

In the eighteenth and nineteenth centuries, the Scotch-Irish population, largely but not exclusively through further waves of immigration, far surpassed the population growth of native Irish in the region. The percentage of land owned by Roman Catholics correspondingly dropped dramatically as anti-Catholic legislation (originally instituted during the period of Puritan rule in England) progressively made it illegal for Catholics to purchase freehold lands or to pass on family holdings. In this period developed a distinct Scotch-Irish culture and a sense among these Scottish immigrants that Ireland was indeed their new homeland, that they were an indigenous culture, not just Scots. Another crucial development was that from 1800 those born in Ireland provided the culture's religious (cultural) leadership in its Presbyterian Church (the national faith they had brought with them from their Scottish motherland).

Just before Great Britain granted the bulk of Ireland independence, the North was granted semiautonomous rule in 1920 to be led by the Scotch-Irish majority. This came after some struggle against factions seeking a reunion of the whole of Ireland under home rule. As this would have made the Scotch-Irish Presbyterian majority in the North a minority under Roman Catholic rule on the island as a whole, the Presbyterian faction worked hard to discourage reunion. A turning point came in 1912 when virtually the entire male population of the North's largest city, Ulster, signed Ulster's Solemn League and Covenant. This covenant was a mutual pledge before God, consciously based on earlier Scottish Protestant covenants to stand against Catholic persecution during the Reformation period (see p. 118), to resist Irish home rule of their region. Having succeeded in keeping the North out of the new Irish Free State, the new semiautonomous government in the North that was subsequently created tended to be regarded as a semisacralized entity, having divine sanction. To this day, many Scotch-Irish believe that avoiding the Irish has divine sanction.

The new government had a rigged system against Catholics. Many were effectively excluded from the right to vote because most Catholics were not landowners and only such persons were given the franchise. These policies effectively exacerbated tensions even more between the majority Scotch-Irish and the ethnic Irish in the region. Terrorism launched by the Irish and their liberation organization, the Irish Republican Army (I.R.A.), with help from the republic, has been a way of life in the North for decades.

A Catholic civil rights movement begun in the 1960s led to a Protestant backlash early in the 1970s. A more stringent radicalism emerged in the I.R.A. with Bernadette Devlin (b. 1947) as its primary spokesperson. The whole affair and the quandaries it raised for the Protestant community about how to respond effectively fractured the unity that had characterized the Protestant (particularly Scotch-Irish) community. Some of that unity had been compromised as early as 1960, as most members of the Church of England in the North had come to see themselves as connected to the Republic of Ireland. Further fracturing of Protestant unity has transpired as a result of the emergence of serious social-class differences among Protestants. The middle class became increasingly less politically active, while militant groups drew their principal support from the working class. Even at the outbreak of the civil rights movement, Protestant authorities in Northern Ireland had begun to investigate liberalizing policies, and some Protestants had even joined the movement for civil rights. A backlash among Protestant militants, for whom the Fundamentalist Presbyterian Ian Paisley (b. 1926) has been the main spokesman, ensued.

Ever since the outbreak of terrorism in the early 1970s, Britain has been compelled to intervene, at times instituting direct rule. The British themselves have not welcomed these interventions. A significant fork in the road occurred in 1985, when an Anglo-Irish agreement gave the Republic of Ireland a consultative role in Northern Ireland's affairs. Needless to say, strong protests emanated from the Protestant community for fear that this might be a first step towards reunification of Ireland. Negotiations between Protestants and Catholics did result in a cease-fire in 1994, and a 1998 peace agreement has raised further hopes, but tensions remain.

In view of these and other dynamics, the Protestant community encounters bleak prospects at the end of the twentieth century, despite its continuing socioeconomic dominance of the region. Polls show that most Ulster Protestants favor complete integration into the United Kingdom. They have presumably given up hope of preserving a distinct cultural identity. Yet such loyalty to the British seems contingent on Britain leaving them alone. Another potential problem for Protestants is the increasing birthrate of Catholics, which is much higher than that of Protestants. If rates since 1924 continue, Catholics could become the majority in Northern Ireland by the middle of the twenty-first century. The implications for possible reunion with the Republic of Ireland are obvious.

As in Yugoslavia, although the conflicts have been cultural and ethnic (indigenous Irish vs. Scotch-Irish), religion has played a role, at least insofar as the respective churches have functioned as enclaves for preserving the respective cultures. This is especially evident in the case of Scotch-Irish culture, whose leaders may regard themselves as on a holy mission. The heritage of Ulster's Solemn League and Covenant with its Calvinist/Presbyterian theocratic orientation mandates that their politics be regarded in this manner. A certain shrill intolerance in the positions taken is inevitable given such suppositions. In that sense there is some validity in blaming the Church for the conflict. However, it should be noted that since the 1950s the theologically conservative Presbyterian Church in Ireland and its main ally, the Methodist Church in Ireland, have officially begun to distance themselves from the covenant and have called for peace. Paisley's Free Presbyterian Church, a secessionist movement balking at such liberalization, continues to espouse the old nationalist covenant in a Fundamentalist way. In this connection, it is also significant that Catholics are generally not supportive of terrorist tactics. Is the Church to blame for the conflicts in Northern Ireland and the former Yugoslavia any more than it played a role in earlier western European "religious" struggles like the Thirty Years' War?

## The Modern Ecumenical Movement and Its Impact

In 1948, immediately following World War II, the ecumenical movement, especially the World Council of Churches (WCC), came to fruition after decades of preparatory work. The WCC is a merger of the Faith and Order movement (concerned with common doctrinal teaching), the Life and Work movement (concerned to have Christians cooperate on social issues), and the International Missionary Council. In the WCC's earliest stages, the theology of Karl Barth and the ethical orientation of Reinhold Niebuhr tended strongly to influence the theological posture of the council and its social-ethical interventions. More recently, with the affiliation of increasing numbers of denominations from the Southern Hemisphere, primary influences on the theological-ethical tone of conciliar work has shifted more towards liberation theology (see pp. 364–65) and liberal theology (esp. with regard to theological method and relations between Christianity and other religions).

Helped by Vatican II's ecumenical impulses, the WCC has overseen some exciting strides to unity, most notably the so-called Lima Text (a 1982 consensus statement of representatives of the member churches on baptism, Eucharist, and ministry). All the member churches of the council were asked to prepare formal responses on the degree to which this statement adequately represented the faith of the Church through the ages and its implications for new relations with other churches that might recognize the text. Numerous responses, many of them favorable, were received, and work continues in incorporating suggestions.

In the United States in 1985, the Consultation on Church Union (COCU), which formed in 1962, drew up a theological consensus statement among representatives of its member denominations (all of them Protestant), which has been put forth as a basis for bringing the churches into full communion with each other. Over the years, the vision of unity of the ecumenical movement has been modified, become more realistic. Some of the early participants in the movement may have envisaged the end of denominationalism, after the fashion of the union churches that developed in Canada and the Southern Hemisphere (see chap. 12). However, as the twenty-first century dawned, it was generally agreed by most ecumenical organizations that the vision of unity that should be pursued is *interdenominational* (a situation in which denominations would preserve their distinct characteristics but their differences would be understood as reconciled). As such, these distinctions are to be seen as, not divisive, but as a witness to the diversity of the biblical witness. Given this new ecumenical vision of unity, it would be possible for the denominations to make binding decisions together.

*Bilateral dialogues* (theological dialogues between two denominational traditions) have also made exciting progress. Dialogues between Lutherans and Reformed denominations as well as between Lutheran churches and the Anglican heritage have led to the establishment of *full communion* (the sharing of the Eucharist, mutual recognition of each other's ordained ministries, and promises to collaborate at the denominational level to the point of making binding decisions together) in western European nations. Similar decisions by the American counterparts of these traditions are in the process of implementation.

Bilateral dialogues have also transpired between Protestant bodies and Roman Catholics. The international Lutheran-Catholic conversations have perhaps progressed the furthest: on the basis of points of consensus, both churches are currently considering the mutual withdrawal of formal condemnations that each issued against the other regarding the doctrine of justification during the Reformation. Such a decision would effectively overcome the schism between these traditions, for inasmuch as they no longer condemn each other's view as heretical, there would no longer be a rationale for their continuing separation.

Another bilateral dialogue offering impressive results has been one on Christology between the Eastern Orthodox churches and the so-called Oriental Orthodox (Monophysite) churches. Intriguingly this dialogue has concluded that perhaps the more-than-a-millennium-long schism over the two natures doctrine of Christ as formulated by the Council of Chalcedon need not divide the churches.[7] The dialogue team asserts that both sides do in fact continue to affirm both the divinity and humanity of Christ. Their differences are only over the language employed in order to make this affirmation.

### Denominational Mergers

A series of mergers of American churches creating larger denominations within confessional families after the war also helped to prepare

---

7. The implications of this emerging convergence are truly catholic inasmuch as the churches of the West also subscribe to the Eastern Orthodox position on this matter.

for the present ecumenical climate. These mergers were the completion/
continuation of a process begun in the first half of the century, a process that has continued to the end of the century. An earlier postwar
example is the 1957 merger of the Congregational Christian Churches
and the Evangelical and Reformed Church to form the United Church
of Christ. It brought together segments of the American Puritan, American Restorationist, German American Reformed, and German American
Evangelical traditions.

Lutherans initiated a process of further mergers in the early 1960s.
The American Lutheran Church was created out of a merger of a denomination of a similar name founded by German Lutherans in the
Midwest, the Evangelical Lutheran Church (the product of a 1917
merger of various Norwegian Lutheran bodies), and the United Evangelical Lutheran Church (the body of Danish Lutheran Pietists in the
United States). Three years after the denomination formed in 1960, it
was joined by the Lutheran Free Church, a body formed by Norwegian Lutheran Pietists who had not affiliated with other Norwegians
when they merged in 1917. The Lutheran Church in America formed
in 1962 out of the United Lutheran Church (a largely eastern body
whose origins were rooted in early German immigration), the Augus-
tana Lutheran Church (first founded by Swedish immigrants), and the
American Evangelical Lutheran Church (a body formed by Danish immigrants who were influenced, not by Pietism, but by Grundtvig — the
so-called "Happy Danes").

In 1987, after years of negotiation, the American Lutheran Church
and the Lutheran Church in America merged with each other and
with the Association of Evangelical Lutheran Churches (a body created
in 1976 as a result of a highly controversial schism in the Lutheran
Church–Missouri Synod over the use of historical criticism). The merged
denomination incorporated as the Evangelical Lutheran Church in
America (ELCA). It was not, however, the fulfillment of the American
Lutheran dream — the establishment of a single American Lutheran
church that would bring together all segments of the tradition. The
Lutheran Church–Missouri Synod and other smaller theologically conservative Lutheran bodies remain separated from and quite critical
of the perceived liberalism of the new, more theologically moderate
body. The formation of this new American Lutheran denomination
was preceded by the formation in 1985 of a united body of Lutherans in Canada, the Evangelical Lutheran Church in Canada. Its
predecessor bodies were Lutheran denominations previously linked to,
but later independent from, the same American bodies that formed
the ELCA.

The United Methodist Church was founded in 1968, the result of a merger between the Methodist Church and the originally German American Pietist body the Evangelical United Brethren Church. In the same year, a denomination of the Holiness movement, the Wesleyan Church, was established; it was the product of a merger between the Wesleyan Methodist Church of America and the Pilgrim Holiness Church. The latter, smaller body had its origins in modern revivalism and was also influenced by the Bible and prophetic conferences of the Fundamentalist movement. Consequently, the merger of these two bodies was one more indication of the degree to which the Holiness movement had come thoroughly to identify itself with the heritage of Fundamentalism (esp. the Evangelical movement).

Presbyterians finally concluded decades of failed merger conversations when in 1983 the old southern body (Presbyterian Church in the United States) and the northern body (the United Presbyterian Church) merged to form the Presbyterian Church (U.S.A.). The latter predecessor denomination had itself been the result of an earlier union (in 1958) between the Presbyterian Church in the U.S.A., which was the oldest Presbyterian body in the States (the Northern Presbyterian Church) and the United Presbyterian Church of North America, which had been started by Scottish Presbyterians who had belonged to churches that had seceded from the state (Presbyterian) church in the motherland.

We have previously noted that the 1950s and early 1960s were golden years of growth for the predecessor bodies of these merged and other mainline Protestant churches in America. Returning GIs from World War II showed their thankfulness by filling the pews and initiated a baby boom, which swelled their churches' membership rolls. Underlying the growth was a vague sense of many analysts that the increased numbers in the pews and the resulting financial resources did not represent real spiritual growth. However, optimism about the opportunities that the future would provide, especially if resources could be marshaled properly, no doubt contributed along with the new economic and ecumenical ethos to the merger hysteria. In view of the short-lived character of this "revival" — the shrinking of mainline church membership and financial resources since the baby boomers began to leave the nest in the 1960s — it seems valid to ask whether these mergers, the urge to create larger denominational bodies, have in fact been in the best interests of the Church in America. It is interesting to note that predominantly African American churches have not experienced this decline and that although only the theologically conservative of these denominations have grown, the black churches in general are at least holding their own.

# The Emergence of the Evangelical Movement and the Religious Right

After the Scopes trial, Fundamentalism retreated into a kind of religio-cultural, lower-class ghetto, which had a salubrious effect of strengthening the movement. As subsequent generations of its membership increasingly came to realize the "American dream" through the Puritan work ethic, which Fundamentalist theology inspired in them, and through the increased educational opportunities afforded to younger generations, an exciting period was on the horizon. Another dynamic during Fundamentalism's "period in the wilderness" following the Scopes trial was the movement's increasing influence on the theologically conservative Holiness churches, Scandinavian American free churches, and even on Pentecostal denominations. While these groups were not originally proponents of biblical inerrancy, their general theological conservatism (in most cases including the endorsement of dispensationalism, so characteristic of Fundamentalism) gradually led them to look to Fundamentalism and its theological statements regarding biblical authority when formally articulating their own views. Some historians of these denominations have spoken of the Fundamentalist co-option of their movements.

During World War II, an important development on the American scene was the formation in 1942 of the National Association of Evangelicals. Led primarily by Harold Ockenga (1905–85) and other open Fundamentalists, this group warned about the sectarian character of Fundamentalism and its image in American culture as anti-intellectual. They had come to feel that the whole movement could profit from a new image and would have broader appeal if presented to the public in a more winsome, open manner that was able to take into account new historical and scientific data while clinging to the fundamentals of the faith. These leaders deliberately took a new name for identifying themselves: Evangelicals (originally "New Evangelicals"). Today we speak of an Evangelical movement that is distinct from the Fundamentalist movement.

Fundamentalists teach, and the history of the movement demonstrates, that if one's views are not in accord with theirs, separation must follow — a new church must be begun if the liberals are in charge of the denomination. (This has been the history of the movement.) Such liberals are not deemed Christian. By contrast, Evangelicals who were members of the mainline churches have remained within these churches and sought to infiltrate them with the "old-time religion." Are the faith commitments of Fundamentalists and Evangelicals really "modernist" versions of the faith to the extent that a concern with biblical inerrancy/infallibility only came to the fore as a pressing issue after the rise of modern science and critical historiography?

Fundamentalists are nearly always politically conservative, whereas some Evangelicals are liberal. Fundamentalists will have nothing to do with historical criticism; some Evangelicals will go so far as to say that the Bible may not be perfect on history and science but is infallible in what it teaches about God and morality (Fuller Theological Seminary, Statement of Faith 3). Although Fundamentalists suspect Evangelicals of compromising the fundamentals of the faith, Evangelicals are concerned to affirm classical Christian teaching (as both parties understand it). For this reason, and partly insofar as the movement continues to embody the ethos of Fundamentalism, until very recently Evangelicals have remained aloof from the ecumenical movement in part because of its alleged theological liberalism.

The main difference between the two movements may be summarized as follows: Fundamentalists practice separation from those with whom they do not agree. Evangelicals are more inclusive. In fact, they include Pentecostals in their movement. Fundamentalists never did.

## The Charismatic Movement

The inclusion of Pentecostalism in the Evangelical movement contributed to a new development starting in the 1960s — the outbreak of tongues in the mainline churches. In the spirit of the Evangelical movement, members of these church bodies who had such an experience generally did not leave their churches to join Pentecostal denominations. Charismatics, as they have come to be known, are to be found in virtually every Protestant denomination and in the Catholic Church as well. Essentially, then, the difference between charismatics and Pentecostals is not unlike the difference between Evangelicals and Fundamentalists: Charismatics do not separate from their churches but seek to infiltrate them. Pentecostals find themselves compelled to start their own churches in which all members speak in tongues.

## Billy Graham

Another crucial component of the Evangelical movement has been the ministry of America's (the Christian world's) most famed twentieth-century evangelist, William Franklin Graham (b. 1918). In many respects, this former Southern-Presbyterian-turned-Baptist is truly responsible for keeping the Evangelical movement together. Not surprisingly, Fundamentalists typically repudiate Graham as being too liberal and for compromising separatist commitments. His whole evangelistic strategy embodies the Evangelical commitment to infiltration, as he has fully co-operated with members of more liberal churches in his crusades while using them to propound a theologically conservative version of the gospel. Much in the tradition of Dwight Moody's (1837–99) version of modern American revivalism, unlike earlier American revivals, Graham avoids addressing social issues. He concentrates simply on the conversion of the individual believer. However, he does so with Puritan suppositions about a sovereign God (*Larry King Live*, 24 July 1999). (To some extent, then, Graham's impact on America seems related to his ability to interact with the Puritan paradigm.)

Graham's first great success — what led him to international prominence — was his 1949 Los Angeles Revival. He impressed, among other dignitaries (Richard Nixon's mother responded to an altar call), newspaper mogul William Randolph Hearst. He instructed his international communications network to "puff Graham." From then on, Billy Graham was an international phenomenon.

### The Impact of the Movement

The Evangelical movement has experienced impressive growth since its inception. Like much of American Christianity, it enjoyed numerical growth in the 1950s but has also continued to flourish since the beginning of the decline of mainline American denominations in the 1960s. This has manifested itself in the growing impact of theologically conservative voices in a number of American and German denominations, most notably in a Fundamentalist coup of the leadership of the Southern Baptist Convention and of the Lutheran Church–Missouri Synod. In recent decades, the only denominations to have gained members in America, while most were losing membership, have been those associated with the Evangelical movement. Interestingly enough, the fastest-growing American denomination in recent years has been a theologically conservative African American Pentecostal denomination, the Church of God in Christ.

A number of the Evangelical movement's *parachurch organizations* (ecumenical organizations not formally related to any of the denominations) have flourished. Among them include the movement's flagship theological institution, Fuller Seminary (which has become increasingly liberal in recent years); its premier magazine, *Christianity Today* (started with Graham's influence); its numerous media outlets (of which perhaps Pat Robertson's Christian Broadcasting Network is the flagship); relief agencies such as World Vision International; domestic mission organizations like Inter-Varsity Christian Fellowship and Campus Crusade;

and Evangelical lobbying organizations within most mainline Protestant denominations. The emergence of internationally renowned theological spokespersons like Carl Henry (b. 1913), who was also the founding editor of *Christianity Today*, and Francis Schaeffer (1912–84), who was perhaps its most significant popularizer, has further evidenced the Evangelical movement's maturity. It began to receive much media attention, coming to prominence in America in the later 1970s, notably with the rise of the so-called Religious Right and its premier lobbying organizations, the Moral Majority led by Jerry Falwell (which has tended to align itself more with a revivified Fundamentalist movement than with the Evangelical movement) and more recently Pat Robertson's Christian Coalition. This movement has become a sociopolitical force with which to be reckoned, not least of all on account of its creative and regular use of the media by televangelists.

Much has been written of the growth in the last decades of the twentieth century of *megachurches* (congregations with weekly worship attendance of above one thousand) in the United States. Many African American Christians refer to some predominantly black megachurches as "Word churches." These congregations, like their European American counterparts, are noted for employing special evangelism techniques, which include targeting their prospects with marketing devices designed to reach the target audience and structuring worship as entertainment, employing not just the music but the media devices of popular culture. The untold element is that most of these "success stories," though not affiliated with any denomination, endorse a theological profile that is conservative, if not expressly identifying with the Evangelical movement.

## The Theological-Ecclesiastical Climate in the West: The Demise of Theological Consensus, Christian Culture, and Segregation

In the years immediately following World War II, neoorthodox theology and its idea of a special salvation history to which the Bible witnesses, not discredited by science and historical criticism, were very much in control of the theological agenda. Both in America and in western Europe, though, the synthesis began to crack. One factor was a critique of the concept of salvation history on grounds of its alleged intellectual dishonesty. How can one say with any intellectual integrity that a book (the Bible) reports accurate history when it does not satisfy the evidential criteria of historical criticism?

The demise of neoorthodoxy did not seem to matter in America at first. Hand in hand with the flight to the suburbs that began in the 1950s came the religious revival (or at least the marked membership growth) we have observed. Among segments of the new idealistic American public developed a new optimism, which is best epitomized by the popularity of Norman Vincent Peale (1898–1993) and his "power of positive thinking." The development of secular theology, especially as embodied in the book *The Secular City* by the American Baptist Harvey Cox (b. 1929), represents a much-discussed, albeit short-lived, alternative to the fading influence of neoorthodoxy. He advocated employment of a kind of correlationist approach to reinterpret Christian faith in light of the opportunities for freedom and openness afforded by urban, secular society. The Church, he insisted, must become an agent for social change. A more theologically radical version of this approach developed almost concurrently.

## God Is Dead!

*Radical theology* (affirming that God is dead) emerged in the late 1950s and 1960s. Its leaders included Paul van Buren (1924–98) and Thomas Altizer (1927–98). Van Buren argued that the way most theologians speak of God renders "God" meaningless, an absurd concept (*Secular Meaning of the Gospel* 64–79). Altizer argued that God died, annihilated himself on the Cross, so that we can be set free from the guilt of having an alien lawgiver in order to be energized enough to give ourselves totally to the world for service (*Gospel of Christian Atheism* 145–57). Though the movement was short-lived, contemporary theology has not recovered from it. No real theological consensus has developed, save unquestioned adherence to a Kantian relativistic epistemology and a related insistence that the content of Christian faith, critically interpreted, must be correlated with the insights of the theologian's context. In that sense, perhaps not much has changed in Western theology since the Enlightenment.

## The Civil Rights Movement

As radical theology was flowering, the civil rights movement had already begun to make a significant social impact in the United States; by the 1960s, it was exerting international influence. Of course, the movement is deeply rooted in the yearnings and heritage of the African American church.

One factor in bringing matters to a head with regard to racial justice was the return of African American GIs from World War II and the increasing middle-class prosperity in the black community. African

Americans began to ask why they were still not free. Another factor in the stirrings for reform was the new generation of influential political leaders like Adam Clayton Powell Jr. (1908–72), the Harlem black Baptist minister who became a highly influential Democratic member of the U.S. House of Representatives. As did his father, in a manner that prefigured the strategy of the civil rights movement, Powell used the ministries of his predominantly black congregation to create interracial contacts in the church's life in order to try "to help all races understand each other better that they may love each other more" (*Upon the Rock* 39).

Crucial government responses to America's racial problem were made in 1949 when President Harry Truman integrated the armed forces and in 1952 when the U.S. Supreme Court ruled against school segregation (*Brown v. Board of Education*). Historic European American churches, except for those denominations headquartered in the South, lent their support by officially speaking out against segregation. This was all part of the new idealism that the experience of "fighting for freedom" had instilled in white GIs and their families. Such idealism was more or less an international phenomenon among the Allies of World War II, as they began to renounce colonialism after the war. Of course, the coincidence, perhaps the impact, of the American civil rights movement on the renewed quest for freedom by Africans and other colonized peoples should not be overlooked. Was the new idealism of the European powers really such a definitive factor in the end of colonialism?

To be sure, the critical event of the civil rights movement was the stand taken by the well-respected African American working woman Rosa Parks in 1955 on a segregated bus in Montgomery, Alabama. She was arrested for refusing to give up her seat to a white customer, as per the law. In response to her arrest, a movement of protest began in the city's black community. A young African American Baptist pastor with a recently received Ph.D., Martin Luther King Jr. (1929–68), was cast into the leadership of an eventually successful bus boycott by African Americans in the community. Later sit-ins and marches in Montgomery, Birmingham, Selma, Greensboro (involving students of North Carolina A & T), and finally Washington succeeded in exerting enough political pressure to bring about a civil rights bill and the eventual end of legalized segregation. On the way, King's vigorous advocacy of nonviolent resistance led to his receiving the coveted Nobel Peace Prize.

A number of controversies besides the obvious confrontation with segregation and virulent racism were associated with the movement. King became disappointed with the white church for its relative lack of support. He responded in a very Augustinian/Niebuhrian way, insisting that the nature of sin and racism was such that tension in society must be created in order to coerce a response of justice ("Letter from a Birmingham Jail"). Another debate that engaged King transpired within his own black Baptist denomination; it concerned the most appropriate strategy for the black church. The conservative leader of his National Baptist Convention, Joseph Jackson (1900–1982), advocated less protest and more individual responsibility on the part of African Americans (*Story of Christian Activism* 270–76). In a tone not unlike some themes of later African American separatism, such as the Nation of Islam, Jackson insisted that the Negro must do for himself, not merely receive help from whites. His call was for "production, not protest." Is this a strategy ahead of its times, a valid contemporary model for the cause of liberation?

Those friendly with King's agenda perceived Jackson's call as a preoccupation with spiritual mission over activism. Personal animosities between him and the King family and its supporters had previously existed, largely the result of a 1957 controversy over the validity of Jackson's continuing to hold the convention's presidency in a contested election. These animosities, exacerbated by another dispute about the next election of the convention's president, as well as the conflicts over the best civil rights strategy, led King and many of his admirers to leave the convention and form the Progressive National Baptist Convention in 1961.

Late in his life, King and his supporters also needed to deal with the question of what to make of the *Black Power movement* (an African American nationalist movement that advocated that civil rights were not sufficient, that racism must be confronted with power). It was to some extent associated with the life and work of Stokely Carmichael (1941–98) of the Student Nonviolent Coordinating Committee (SNCC) and of Malcolm X of the Lost-Found Nation of Islam (see pp. 234-35). King refused to endorse the movement to the extent that it advocated black separatism and the use of violence. Yet he did concede that the next stage of the civil rights movement must be for "Negroes" to learn how to grasp power, including the exercise of economic power, in order to influence the course of events ("Black Power Defined," *New York Times Magazine*, 11 June 1967). Which model, King's integrationist dream achieved through nonviolence or the more separatist vision of Black Power, will best serve the cause of liberation? It is perhaps significant that late in his life Malcolm X moved away from the separatist orientation to a more inclusive viewpoint. As a result, he came into conflict with the leadership of the Lost-Found Nation of Islam, which may have been a factor in his assassination in 1965.

Unfortunately the tragedy of King's assassination did not allow him sufficient opportunity to work out in detail his reactions to the Black

:ment. That task would be left to the development of black ⌐gy. Nevertheless, that new theological perspective and several others seem to owe their emergence or some of their impact to King. Clearly, his life was a glorious chapter.

Since King's death, there has been much debate regarding his personal life. This much is clear: he was the progeny of African American "royalty," the son of the pastor of *the* African American Baptist church in Atlanta, Georgia, in *the* elite black neighborhood of the South. Originally named Michael, he was renamed in 1934 by his father, who also took the name, after Martin Luther, with whose courage in face of oppression the father had become so impressed.

## The Theology of Martin Luther King Jr.

King's role as a public theologian, not unlike the role of Reinhold Niebuhr, has been too much overlooked. In fact, one may better understand his and the movement's long-term aims in light of his core theological commitments. King himself sketched his influences in a way that provides helpful insights about his commitments (*Christian Century*, 13 April 1960, 439–41). His black Baptist background had been theologically conservative and literalistic. King never forfeited its narrative/storytelling homiletical style. He endorsed liberal theology for a time and never ceased to cherish its devotion to search for truth with an open mind. In a manner like Schleiermacher, he referred to Jesus' "unique God-consciousness" ("Letter from a Birmingham Jail"). However, King became too much influenced by Reinhold Niebuhr's political realism and the Augustinian understanding of sin to endorse liberalism's optimistic view of persons. Evil, he insisted, is collective. Just as Niebuhr's thought found so much resonance with American politicians in view of the convergence between his thinking about human nature and the Constitution's realistic assessment of human nature, so we can account in part for the resonance of King's views with the American public. His realistic views of human nature and the vision of justice he upheld clearly echo themes consistent with the American Constitution. In a similar vein, King noted an appreciation of the social-gospel movement but found Walter Rauschenbusch wrong to identify the kingdom of God with a socioeconomic system. In the best tradition of the black church, though, King did share with Rauschenbusch a kingdom-oriented eschatological perspective on hope for the future. His famed 1963 "I Have a Dream" speech in the march on Washington clearly illustrates this emphasis.

King also found the theology of Paul Tillich helpful, particularly his use of existentialism, which King believed well portrays the human condition as Niebuhr had sought to describe our sinful state. Also like Tillich, King spoke of God as if Being-itself were given in experience.

Despite his strong doctrine of sin, elsewhere King referred to our being coworkers with God (*Christian Century*, 13 April 1960, 439–41; "Letter from a Birmingham Jail"). On the other hand, this theme stands alongside references in his thought to images suggesting a Reformed conception of divine sovereignty. King's God was "toughminded and tenderhearted," not incapable of controlling what he has made (*Strength to Love*, chap. 1).

The influence of the great Indian leader Mohandas Gandhi (1869–1948) on King's method of nonviolence is well known. Less known and appreciated is the impact of the black church in this regard. King believed that it furnished the spirit for such a method. He also seems to have been aware of Niebuhr's advocacy of "Negro" boycotts as early as 1932 (*Where Do We Go from Here?* chap. 5).

In this connection, it is interesting to consider King's theological rationale for seeking social justice and his views on the proper relation of church and state. As a Baptist, one would expect him to endorse the Puritan vision of a state governed by gospel principles, which is the way he has characteristically been interpreted. After all, at some points he claimed to identify an overlap between Christian faith and the American dream ("Letter from a Birmingham Jail"). On the other hand, at other points King seems to have operated with something like the two-kingdom ethic. He cited Augustine's idea that an unjust law is no law at all and that a law is just only if it squares with the moral law. Note that the law, not the gospel, functions to provide the criteria for sociopolitical judgments in these remarks. Another observation relevant to suggesting King's reliance on the two-kingdom ethic is the involvement of secular humanists and Jews in the civil rights movement, notably the Atlanta rabbi Jacob Rothschild (1911–74), who was a close King family confidante. Was King more in the heritage of Augustine and his namesake or of Calvin and the Puritan Baptists? Like other important theological movements, the civil rights movement of Martin Luther King is so rich in its insights as to leave us with some significant open questions calling for further exploration.

### The Theological and International Heritage of the Civil Rights Movement in the Post-King Era

The civil rights movement and its commitment to freedom seems to have generated at least two, if not three or four, distinct theological perspectives with similar agendas. They have also effectively sought to fill the gap left by neoorthodoxy's demise. The ones most clearly inspired by movement include liberation theology, feminist and womanist theology, indigenous African theology, and black theology.

*Liberation theology.* A Latin American movement, liberation theology was born of the oppression and exploitation that the poor in the region suffered and the Church's failure to address it. Proponents seek to relate the gospel to communism as the only way to achieve liberation from the bondage that capitalism has imposed on the poor and oppressed.[8] Among its primary spokespersons are Gustavo Gutiérrez (b. 1928), Leonardo Boff (b. 1938), Rubem Alves (b. 1933), and Juan Luis Segundo (1925–96).

The Peruvian Catholic Gutiérrez's views are typical of the liberation theologians. A key commitment for Gutiérrez and his colleagues is a concern for the poor and oppressed. One cannot be Christian without a concern about social justice, he claims ("Liberation Praxis and Christian Faith," in *Frontiers of Theology in Latin America* 1–4).[9] He affirms something like a "preferential option for the poor, which is the belief in a divine propensity to advocate the interests of the poor, necessitating a similar ethic for Christians (8–9). Such views are clearly in line with the teachings of Vatican II.

Elsewhere Gutiérrez and like-minded colleagues speak of collective evil, that is, social sin by which those in control of the system and those profiting from it oppress the poor. A revolutionary struggle is thus necessary, and private ownership will need to be eliminated (*Frontiers of Theology in Latin America* 1). A socialist agenda is quite evident in such theologizing. What will happen to Latin American liberation theology in light of the decline of socialism? Indications are, however, that the Latin American intelligentsia has not yet given up on socialism. Will this ensure the continuing relevance of liberation theology?

Though by no means completely setting the agenda at the local level for the church in Latin America, liberation theology has increasingly made its presence felt in church and society. Not only does it reflect certain teachings of Vatican II and call the Vatican hierarchy to accountability to these commitments, but various Latin American Catholic bishops and Protestant church leaders have become its advocates. An influential 1968 conference paper prepared by the Latin American Catholic bishops meeting in Medellín, Colombia, reflects liberation theology's influence in church life. In practice, church leaders have advocated for the poor, criticized oppressive governments (notably, if not always consistently, in Brazil, Uruguay, Nicaragua, and Haiti), and implemented the formation of "base communities" working locally for justice. Some leaders, such as Archbishop Oscar Romero (1917–80) and

---

8. Note that some kind of "correlation" of Word of God and philosophical/economic conceptions is advocated.

9. Note the presence of a third use of the law at this point.

Bishop Enrique Angelelli (d. 1976), have been martyred for the cause. In addition, liberation theology has affected not only theological education but has also occupied the attention of the Vatican hierarchy. Pope John Paul II has been very critical of it, in part due to its "uncritical appropriation of Marxism," but primarily on account of its liberal (correlationist) theological method (Congregation for the Doctrine of the Faith *Instruction on Christian Freedom and Liberation* 70). In view of these dynamics, is the impact of liberation theology likely to be of long duration? Is the Vatican correct in linking it to the prevailing currents of theology since the Enlightenment? At least some proponents of liberation theology have opted for a method of relating the Word of God and experience more in line with Karl Rahner's transcendental method (Alves *Theology of Human Hope* 4–5, 72–74). But does that necessarily negate the Vatican's critique of the movement?

*Feminist and womanist theology.* The decision after World War II of a number of mainline Protestant denominations, which had not previously done so, to ordain women and the emerging feminist movement were accompanied by the development of feminist and womanist theology. The struggle for the acceptance of women's leadership in theology and ecclesiastical affairs continues in these denominations as well as in those that still reject it, such as the Roman Catholic and Eastern Orthodox churches and various Fundamentalist churches. In fact, disagreements between these bodies and the rest of the Christian world over the ordination of women remain one of the most contentious issues in the modern ecumenical movement, even threatening to fracture the WCC. Feminist theology is an endeavor to interpret Christian faith (using a liberal theological method akin to that of Schleiermacher) into the categories of feminism. Rosemary Radford Ruether (b. 1936) is one of the primary figures, along with Mary Daly (b. 1928) and Jane D. Douglas (b. 1933).

Typical of other feminists, Ruether notes that the history of the domination of women is related to world-negating dualisms that Christianity has endorsed. Women, she argues, need to be spokespersons for a new humanity that reconciles spirit and body, which will overcome the dualisms with a positive doctrine of creation and incarnation. In this way, she can contribute to reinstating old myths of a virgin-mother goddess (*Christianity and Crisis*, 13 December 1971, 267–72).

The critical perspective Ruether and most of her colleagues implicitly take on Scripture and its patriarchal tenets (1 Cor. 11:2–16; 1 Tim. 2:9–15) is readily apparent.[10] In addition, she and they also propose a distinct Christian feminist ethic that nurtures community and shuns

---

10. In many respects, Ruether employs a characteristic post-Enlightenment critical hermeneutic.

male competitiveness and the propensity to manipulate nature techno-
logically. Note the implied affirmation of a third use of the law at this
point. Hers is a theology aiming to remain ecologically sensitive as well
as concerned for the poor and oppressed. But does such a focus on the
feminist agenda unwittingly lead to a preoccupation that would become
forgetful of these other social agendas? Might the critical perspective
on Scripture and insistence on accounting for women's experience by
feminist theology fall prey to Feuerbach's critique of Christianity for
reducing God-talk to woman-talk?

A unique version of these commitments known as "womanist theology" has been very recently developed by a number of African American
women. These theologians, while appreciating both feminist theology
and black theology, contend that the former is too focused on white
women's experience and the latter too centered on the experience of
African American men. Besides, womanists argue, the latter is also too
focused on the struggle for liberation. A more womanist approach portrays Christology, not so much in relation to the atonement on the
Cross, but in terms of a ministerial vision concerned about righting relations between various contending forces (Delores Williams *Sisters in
the Wilderness* 158–59, 164–65). Has womanist theology truly broken
with the kind of patriarchal theology that has dominated in the West
since the Enlightenment (201–2)?

**Indigenous African theology.** Another theological model that developed very much in line with the King heritage is indigenous African
theology. The eminent Kenyan theologian John Mbiti (b. 1931) is perhaps its best representative. The overall agenda of Mbiti and those who
share his thinking is to relate Christian faith to indigenous African religion. God has been active among African people, he insists. A key point
is Mbiti's rejection of a "Western" distinction between general (natural)
revelation and special revelation (*Christian Century*, 27 August–3 Sep-
tember 1980), which means that indigenous pre-Christian African religion is as authoritative as the revelation in Christ. Is such a relativizing
of the revelation in Christ really characteristic of African thinking, or is
it more in line with the post-Enlightenment correlationist approach?

**Black theology.** Developing at a time when the Black Power movement was issuing a challenge to African American Christians regarding
the relevance of Christian faith for the liberation cause, black theology
to some extent might be understood as a dialogue between the Christian
faith and Black Power (*Journal of the American Academy of Religion*
[December 1985]: 768–69). It is most clearly identified with the African
Methodist Episcopal theologian James Cone (b. 1938), though it is increasingly espoused by many African American theologians. Whether it
is in fact embodying the historic popular theology of the black church

is a question that should be considered. Sometimes it is called "liberation theology," though the Latin American version of that theology seems to predate it (at least in its use of the term "liberation"). It is certainly a theology of liberation, as Cone construes the true meaning of the gospel to be God's liberation of the oppressed from bondage (755–56).

Cone is concerned to relate the Christian faith as practiced by the African American church to African religion but not in a "precise correlation" (*Journal of the American Academy of Religion* [December 1985]: 755–56). Are there similarities between Cone's method and liberal theology's method of correlation that interprets the gospel in light of human experience? Has he really broken as much with European assumptions as he thinks? An attempt by a number of prominent black church leaders in 1969 to work out their own definition of black theology opted for a critical correlation of black experience and the Word of God akin to Rahner's transcendental method (National Committee of Black Churchmen *Why Black Theology?*). At times Cone himself embraces this theological method (*God of the Oppressed* 30–31, 34), but is this approach any freer from Enlightenment influence than the method of correlation?

Cone's major agenda is to avoid white distortions of the gospel. He argues that the African inheritance helps African Americans see the gospel's true meaning: God's liberation of the oppressed from bondage. The gospel story concerns God's suffering with victims (*Journal of the American Academy of Religion* [December 1985]: 755–56, 768–69). In addition to this theme, so suggestive of ancient Alexandrian Christology, proponents of black theology seem to have a general, though not exclusive, disposition to embrace something like the Calvinist-Puritan model of a social ethic oriented by gospel principles (*Cross Currents* [summer 1977]: 147ff.).

Implicit in black theology is a critique of King, not least of all for accepting white theology too uncritically (*Cross Currents* [summer 1977]: 147ff.). Should we say that the black theology Cone represents has truly broken with all European and European American theological allies? In any case, can we agree that black theology, like Black Power, would not have been possible apart from the civil rights movement?

The King movement was also deeply and indubitably influential in South Africa's struggle against apartheid. Around the time of "updating" (enforcing) the Homelands Policy of restricting certain land to African ownership in order further to codify segregation, the primary South African freedom organization, the African National Congress (ANC), launched a Defiance Against Unjust Laws Campaign in 1952. Nonviolent breaking of apartheid laws was advocated, though violence broke out against its nonviolent campaign. Among the later champions of nonviolent approaches was the Anglican bishop, eventual winner of a Nobel Peace Prize, Desmond Tutu (b. 1931), who has acknowledged the impact Martin Luther King had on him. Likewise a black consciousness movement in the 1970s was influenced by Black Power in the United States and African socialism.

The international ecumenical community and the WCC in particular advocated international economic sanctions, and they began making an impact on South Africa in the 1980s. Another significant, to some extent problematic, matter in this connection was that several church bodies issued statements condemning apartheid that, inspired by the Barmen Declaration, claimed the issue to be a *status confessionis*, that is, a matter over which the nature of the faith was at stake such that to support apartheid would be a heresy (World Alliance of Reformed Churches *Racism in South Africa* I; South African Council of Churches *Theological Rationale and a Call for Prayer for the End to Unjust Rule*). Was the issuing of such statements valid? Should Christian fellowship be fractured by ethical disagreements? The impact of the Barthian/Calvinist perspective on the broader ecumenical movement is apparent at this point, for that perspective would affirm that the gospel (and faith) is at stake in social-ethical decisions. Can a two-kingdom ethic legitimately make such an affirmation?

A turning point in the struggle occurred in 1989 when P. W. Botha assumed political leadership in South Africa. His government permitted antiapartheid demonstrations and selectively engaged in desegregation. In 1990, the leader of the antiapartheid movement, Nelson Mandela, was released from prison, and the ANC was legalized. These actions represented a way of dealing with South Africa's economic crisis, which the sanctions had created. The strategy seems to have been to try to stop violence in order to put an end to economic paralysis.

As these events transpired, the Dutch Reformed Church and the smaller Dopper (Reformed) Church began to soften their support of apartheid. In part, this may have been a consequence of the banishment from ecumenical bodies and the resulting isolation of churches supporting apartheid. In 1990, the Dutch Reformed Church did proclaim apartheid to be a sin when it functions to oppress parts of the population, but the church did not in principle condemn the apartheid structures of South Africa (*Church and Society* 97, 109–10, 130–47, 280–85, 303). The Dopper Church, by contrast, abandoned the belief in apartheid decades earlier as well as the idea of a covenant that designated Afrikaners as chosen people. In fact, this church came to include a number of black members by the mid-1980s. These developments were either related to or a consequence of the fragmentation of Afrikaner culture and its former social solidarity in favor of preoccupation with one's own economic advancement.

The elections of 1993 finally achieved without violence the black majority government. Mandela has been under great pressure to bring economic equality to the country more rapidly while not alienating the white population, but the peaceful ethos of the republic to date has been nothing short of miraculous.

## Other Major Theological Options

A survey of the plethora of modern theological options receiving significant international attention since World War II remains incomplete unless several more major alternatives are considered. Like the theological approaches already considered, all of these additional options have roots in earlier movements.

**Theology of hope.** The roots of this influential theological alternative are found in Germany, among the generation too young to have fought in World War II but who nonetheless experienced the suffering and despair wrought by the Allies' victory. Its premier representatives have been the Reformed theologian Jürgen Moltmann (b. 1926) and, to a lesser extent, his countryman Wolfhart Pannenberg (b. 1928), both of whom are directly indebted to the experience of hope they as youth had in the midst of the despair that characterized Germany after the war. Moltmann in particular has had some fruitful dialogue with Latin American liberation theology.

For Moltmann and Pannenberg, eschatology (in a realized sense) is at the heart of the gospel (Moltmann *Theology of Hope* 37). Moltmann in particular has great concern that God's omnipotence not be affirmed at the cost of his loving nature. God must be transcendent but also this-worldly. The Trinity, he insists, allows us to affirm both. From this point, he proceeds to refer to the suffering of God in us when we suffer, and this suffering gives us hope and the power to continue to love (*Crucified God* 249ff.). Moltmann seems to be creating a certain distance between himself and his Reformed commitments, for the idea of a suffering God is certainly more compatible with an Alexandrian Christology than with the Antiochene suppositions of the Reformed heritage.

The eschatological emphasis of these theologians also provides a way for them to address challenges posed by historical criticism without falling prey to the weaknesses associated with the neoorthodox concept of salvation history. Proponents of the theology of hope are able to address the historical-critical demand for an analogy between reported accounts and present experience with regard to biblical accounts such as the Resurrection by maintaining that such accounts are to be read in light of their future (Moltmann *Theology of Hope* 180–82, 187–91; Pannenberg, *Jesus — God and Man* 97–108). Those who know the future of these events (the hope that they engender for the future concerning God's ongoing creative activity in the midst of despair) already have in their experience a predisposition to accept a resurrection from the dead. In accord with the historical critic's demand for an analogy between the historian's contemporary experience and a reported account of the past in order to verify its historicity, the faithful have been provided with and so have an analogy in present experience from which to assess positively the historicity of the Resurrection accounts. Jesus' Resurrection is said to make history, but we must evaluate it in light of our own subjectivity. A kind of critical correlation of Word and experience as was observed in Rahner seems evident at this point. Moltmann adds, at least by implication, an argument that Jesus' Resurrection, like all biblical accounts, pertains to Jesus' future. In that sense, his Resurrection cannot be discredited by historical criticism because it is, not a past event, but a revelation of what Christ will be in the future (*Theology of Hope* 87). Have the theologians of hope avoided the Feuerbachian critique?

**Process theology.** In the United States, this new theological perspective emerged out of the process philosophy of Alfred North Whitehead (1861–1947). A core commitment of the thought of this brilliant British-born mathematician-philosopher was that being is constituted by becoming, such that nature is always in process (*Process and Reality* 28), which means that God must also be "becoming," have his nature determined by what happens in reality (406). On the other hand, God is unlimited and transcendent in the sense of being primordial. Although not an imperial ruler, God is said to be the creator in the sense of being the presupposed actuality of every creative act, "the absolute wealth of potentiality." As such, the deity exemplifies and establishes the conditions of creation in a process that experience derived from him motivates. In that sense, God is truly *with* all creation (405–7).

Among theologians to appropriate this idea of God as transcendent yet in and affected by reality are John Cobb (b. 1925) and David Ray Griffin (b. 1939) (*Process Theology* 43, 96–97). An earlier proponent of this school of theology was Daniel Day Williams (1910–73), a colleague of Reinhold Niebuhr's at Union Theological Seminary (Williams *God's Grace and Man's Hope*). Given the essential nature of the relationship that process thought posits between God and the world, these theologians have a difficult time accounting for the world's creation out of nothing. On the other hand, their emphasis on God's work of creative transformation does open them to endorse many socially progressive positions (Cobb and Griffin *Process Theology* 128ff.). Methodologically,

Cobb relates the biblical text to the process conception much as the theologians of hope and Rahner do, envisaging a mutual correction of text and philosophical interpretive scheme (Cobb *Process Theology as Political Theology* 52–56, ix).

**Narrative theology.** Proponents of this other influential contemporary theological option, a number of whom have been influenced by Barth, initiate theological reflection with the biblical text, as Barth did. In narrative theology, the Bible interprets experience, rather than vice versa, as has been the prevailing model for theology since the Enlightenment (Hans Frei *Eclipse of Biblical Narrative*, esp. pp. 4ff.). However, these theologians view the Bible, not as a special salvation history (they have been chastened by charges of the concept's intellectual dishonesty), but as a piece of literature standing with its own integrity (like a novel), even if its accounts are not good history. Have we not in these commitments parallels to Bushnell and the classical African American approach? By subordinating human experience to the Word, the transcendence of God seems affirmed, for the concept of God apart from human experience has been presented as a meaningful concept.

Note that the approach of narrative theology subdivides into at least two distinct groups: one more Barthian in orientation and insisting that in some instances the literal meaning of Christian concepts can be identified (Frei *Eclipse of Biblical Narrative*, esp. p. viii), the other a kind of revisionist theology closely related to Rahner's transcendental method of a critical correlation between the biblical text and the interpreter's experience, with each correcting the other. Frequently proponents of this second model also relate the structures of the biblical narrative to an ontology of story and claim that reality itself is narrative in character. As do proponents of correlation, these narrative theologians portray the Word of God as more likely true because it embodies the structures and conception of our experience (Paul Ricoeur *Time and Narrative* 2:29–60, 156–60). Which of these two models of narrative theology might be most effective in facilitating the theological task in the twenty-first century?

## What Is the Most Adequate Theological Model of the Postwar Era?

Questions raised at the conclusion of the preceding chapter deserve our attention and should be considered in relation to the theologians dealt with in this chapter. Do any of the theologians dealt with in this chapter improve on the approach of the twentieth-century figures previously covered? If so, why would the reader prefer one or two of the theologians dealt with above over the others? Are the answers to these questions still related to a modern version of the classical debate in the early Church between correlationists, like Justin Martyr, and orthodox theologians, like Tertullian?

## Is the Church in Decline?

To judge whether or not the Church is in decline requires examination of international statistics regarding church membership. It is true that the Northern Hemisphere is progressively becoming de-Christianized, but the Church is growing significantly in the Southern Hemisphere. If present membership patterns continue, by early in the twenty-first century only 39.8 percent of Christians will be in the North. By contrast, in 1900, 49.9 percent of all Christians lived in Europe, while by 1985 it was only 27.2 percent.

Much, though by no means all, of this growth in the Southern Hemisphere has been the result of the emergence of African independent churches and prophetic churches, which promise new revelations.[11] Many of these fast-growing churches are Pentecostal and indigenize the gospel with an African concern for healing. Indeed, the Church in Africa, as well as in South Korea, has enjoyed phenomenal growth, even in the midst of turmoil.[12] As religion has been pressed into the service of justifying ethnic conflicts in South Africa, Northern Ireland, and the former Yugoslavia, so this has occurred in Nigeria as resentment has built between the predominantly Islamic people and the largely Christianized Igbo tribe, mostly because of the latter's earlier and greater access to Western education and its economic advantages. Such ethnic conflict has manifested itself in tensions over a 1966 civil war, which was perceived by some Moslems as a Christian revolution, and since the late 1970s in a series of clashes.

In the midst of such difficult circumstances the growth rate of Christianity in Nigeria as in the rest of Africa and in Korea remains nothing short of phenomenal. Why? What are these churches of the Southern Hemisphere doing right? What can they teach the Northern Hemisphere churches that are in decline? At the very least, such growth may be a reminder that Christian faith is truly embedded in a rich, diverse heritage. Its roots are not ultimately Western after all. That insight is very crucial for helping Christians reclaim all their roots.

---

11. The independent churches of Nigeria, noted in chap. 12, p. 262, are examples of such prophetic churches.

12. See chap. 12, pp. 64, 271, for a discussion of the amazing growth of the Church since World War II in Kenya and Tanzania.

**Appendix**   *Significant Events for the Church since the Late Middle Ages*

| | POLITICAL EVENTS | RELIGIOUS/PHILOSOPHICAL DEVELOPMENTS | THEOLOGICAL SIGNIFICANCE |
|---|---|---|---|
| 1300s | Portuguese begin exploring Africa | Jubilee Year declared by Pope Boniface VIII (1300) | Indulgences given to those making pilgrimage to Rome |
| | | William of Ockham (ca. 1285–1347) | Nominalism begins to make an impact on Western society and the Church |
| | | Robert Holcot (d. 1349) | |
| | | John Tauler (ca. 1300–61) | |
| | | Avignon papacy (1309–77) | |
| | | *German Theology* | |
| 1337–1453 | Hundred Years' War | Controversies over Christmas and other festivals in Ethiopian Orthodoxy | |
| | -Joan of Arc (1412–31) | | |
| | | Emergence of Mikaelite and Stephanite heresies in Ethiopian Orthodoxy | |
| | | Emergence of Strigolnik heresy in Russian Orthodox Church | |
| | | Papacy of Clement VI (1342–52); issues papal bull authorizing indulgences (1343) | |

| | POLITICAL EVENTS | RELIGIOUS/PHILOSOPHICAL DEVELOPMENTS | THEOLOGICAL SIGNIFICANCE |
|---|---|---|---|
| 1347–48 | Bubonic plague | Gerhard Groote (1340–84) and founding of Brethren of the Common Life | |
| | | Julian of Norwich (1342–after 1413) | Increasing impact of mysticism |
| | | Catherine of Siena (1347–80) | |
| | | Thomas à Kempis (1380–1471) | |
| | Spain and Portugal initiate settlements in Africa | Great Western Schism and rise of conciliar movement (1378–1415) | Period of rival claimants/ pretenders to papacy |
| | | -Council of Pisa fails to resolve schism (1409) | |
| | | John Wycliffe (1330–84) and the Lollards | |
| | | John Huss (1372–1415) and the Hussites and Taborites | Pre-reformers |
| | Period of Henry the Navigator's explorations | Council of Constance (1414–18) | End of Great Western Schism with election of single pope; condemns Wycliffe and Huss |

| | POLITICAL EVENTS | RELIGIOUS/PHILOSOPHICAL DEVELOPMENTS | THEOLOGICAL SIGNIFICANCE |
|---|---|---|---|
| | | Council of Basle/Ferrara-Florence (1431–45) | Designates seven as the number of sacraments; proclaims nominal reunion with Eastern Orthodox, Armenian Orthodox, and Jacobites; in early stages, council meeting in Basle defies Pope Eugenius IV and illegitimately elects Martin V as pope |
| | | Pope Eugenius IV decrees a rationale for slavery (1434) | |
| 1453 | Fall of Constantinople and Eastern Empire | Union of Brethren secede from Catholic Church in Bohemia | |
| | Renaissance begins to flower<br>-Leonardo da Vinci (1452–1519) | Settlement reached with Coptic Church in Ethiopian Orthodoxy regarding Egyptian patriarch's role of leadership of Ethiopian Church; Ethiopian monastic clergy given autonomy | |
| | -Michaelangelo (1475–1564) | | |
| | -Desiderius Erasmus (ca. 1466–1536) | Has theological controversy with Luther (1525) | |

| | POLITICAL EVENTS | RELIGIOUS/PHILOSOPHICAL DEVELOPMENTS | THEOLOGICAL SIGNIFICANCE |
|---|---|---|---|
| | | Sabbath controversy in Ethiopian Orthodox Church resolved | Both Christian and Jewish Sabbath observed |
| | | Judaizers in Russian Orthodox Church | |
| 1474–1504 | Reign of Ferdinand and Isabella in Spain | Reform in Spanish Catholic Church | |
| | | Francisco de Cisneros (1436–1517) | |
| | | Girolamo Savonarola (1452–98) | |
| | | Church planted in Kongo (1483) | |
| 1492 | Columbus lands in the Americas | Gabriel Biel (d. 1495) | Most prominent German Nominalist in Luther's lifetime |
| | | Royal patronage over Church in Americas granted by papacy to Spain and Portugal (1493ff.) | |

| | POLITICAL EVENTS | RELIGIOUS/PHILOSOPHICAL DEVELOPMENTS | THEOLOGICAL SIGNIFICANCE |
|---|---|---|---|
| 1497 | Vasco da Gama discovers route to India | Martin Luther (1483–1546) | |
| | Vasco Núñez da Balboa explores the Americas | | |
| 1509–47 | Reign of Henry VIII in England | | |
| | Pope Julius II grants Henry a dispensation to marry Catherine of Aragon (1509) | Fifth (Ecumenical) Lateran Council (1512–17) | Condemns conciliarism |
| 1516 | Ottoman Empire conquers Syria and Palestine | | |
| 1516/ 1519–56 | Reign of Charles I/V in Spain and as Holy Roman emperor | Ninety-Five Theses (1517) | Luther's criticism of sale of indulgences starts Reformation |
| | | Heidelberg Disputation (1518) | Luther develops his Theology of the Cross |

| | POLITICAL EVENTS | RELIGIOUS/PHILOSOPHICAL DEVELOPMENTS | THEOLOGICAL SIGNIFICANCE |
|---|---|---|---|
| 1518 | Diet of Augsburg | Pope Leo X approves ordination of qualified Africans and Indians (1518) | Luther's debate with Cardinal Thomas Cajetan links Reformer with conciliarism |
| 1519–21 | Ferdinand Magellan on round-the-world voyage | Leipzig Disputation (1519)<br><br>Pope Leo X excommunicates Luther (1519)<br><br>James Latomus (ca. 1475–1544)<br><br>John Oecolampadius (1482–1531)<br><br>Ulrich Zwingli (1484–1531) | Luther aligned with conciliarism by his partner in the debate—John Eck (1486–1543) |
| 1521 | Diet of Worms | Zwickau Prophets (1521) | German princes condemn Luther<br><br>Lutheranism rejects their radical charismatic orientation |

| POLITICAL EVENTS | RELIGIOUS/PHILOSOPHICAL DEVELOPMENTS | THEOLOGICAL SIGNIFICANCE |
|---|---|---|
| | Andreas von Karlstadt [Carlstadt] (ca. 1480–1541) | Opts for a more radical reform; Lutheranism embraces many elements of Catholic heritage |
| | Philip [Philipp] Melanchthon (1497–1560) | Influences Lutheranism toward a more inclusive and Renaissance humanist perspective |
| **1523** Zurich Council defies Catholic hierarchy in support of Zwingli in indulgence controversy -Sweden wins independence from Danish Empire | Martin Bucer (1491–1551) | Reformed Reformation initiated in Zurich |
| | Hans Denck (ca. 1495–1527) | Lutheranism established in Strasbourg (1523); influenced Calvin |
| **1524–25** Peasants' Revolt | Thomas Müntzer [Münzer] (ca. 1490–1525) | |
| | Anabaptist movement (Swiss Brethren) initiated in break with Zwingli -Conrad Grebel (ca. 1498–ca. 1526) -Felix Manz (ca. 1498–1527) -George Blaurock (1491–1529) | |

| POLITICAL EVENTS | RELIGIOUS/PHILOSOPHICAL DEVELOPMENTS | THEOLOGICAL SIGNIFICANCE |
|---|---|---|
| | Balthasar Hübmaier (ca. 1485–1528) | |
| | Sebastian Franck (ca. 1499–ca. 1542) | |
| 1526 Diet of Spire | Michael Sattler (ca. 1490–1527) | Withdraws condemnation of Luther by Edict of Worms |
| | Wittenberg Concord (1526) | Agreement between Luther and Bucer that their differences do not divide the Reformed churches |
| | Schleitheim Confession (1527) | Early (Swiss Brethren) Anabaptist confession |
| 1529 Second Diet of Spire | Matteo da Bascio (d. 1552); Capuchin Order founded (1529) | Affirms condemnation of Luther by Edict of Worms; labels dissenting princes as "Protestant" |
| | Marburg Colloquy (1529) | Luther and Zwingli unable to resolve differences on Eucharist |

| | POLITICAL EVENTS | RELIGIOUS/PHILOSOPHICAL DEVELOPMENTS | THEOLOGICAL SIGNIFICANCE |
|---|---|---|---|
| 1530 | Diet of Augsburg | The Augsburg Confession (1530) | Henceforth the official doctrinal standard for Lutheranism |
| 1531 | Peace of Kappel | | Swiss princes agree to recognize each other's freedom of religion within their own territories |
| 1532 | Peace of Nuremberg | Thomas Cranmer (1489–1556)<br><br>Waldensians become constituted as a Protestant Church (1532)<br><br>Melchior Hofmann (ca. 1500–43)<br><br>Revolution in Münster | German princes agree to recognize each other's freedom of religion within their own territories (as long as Lutherans promise not to seek reforms other than those espoused by The Augsburg Confession) |

| | POLITICAL EVENTS | RELIGIOUS/PHILOSOPHICAL DEVELOPMENTS | THEOLOGICAL SIGNIFICANCE |
|---|---|---|---|
| 1534–42 | Turbulence in German territories between Protestant and Catholic factions | Jacob Hutter (d. 1536) and establishment of Hutterite Brethren Church | |
| | | Establishment of Church of England (1534) | |
| | | William [Guillaume] Farel (1489–1565) | Reformation established in Geneva (1535) |
| | | John Calvin (1509–64) | |
| | | Menno Simons (1496–1561) and formation of Mennonite Church (1536) | |
| | | Lutheran Church established in Denmark and Norway (1537) | |
| | | Bartolomé de las Casas (1474–1566) | Crusades against Native American slavery |
| | | Pope Paul III condemns slavery of Native Americans (1537) | |

| POLITICAL EVENTS | RELIGIOUS/PHILOSOPHICAL DEVELOPMENTS | THEOLOGICAL SIGNIFICANCE |
|---|---|---|
| 1542–67 | | |
| Reign of Mary Stuart in Scotland | Ignatius Loyola (ca. 1491–1556) and establishment of Jesuits (1540) | |
| | Caspar Schwenkfeld (1490–1561) | |
| | Francis Xavier (1506–52); Catholic outreach to Orient initiated (1541) | |
| | Catholic mission work in India begun (1542) | |
| | Council of Trent (1545–63) | Condemns Protestants, consolidating Catholic Reformation; regulates indulgences; mandates clerical and monastic reform; affirms most theological convictions of Thomas Aquinas |
| | Anne Askew martyred in England (1546) | |

| | POLITICAL EVENTS | RELIGIOUS/PHILOSOPHICAL DEVELOPMENTS | THEOLOGICAL SIGNIFICANCE |
|---|---|---|---|
| 1547–53 | Reign of Edward VI in England | | Anglican Reformation takes Protestant turn |
| 1548 | Interim of Augsburg | | Protestant-Catholic peace treaty in Holy Roman Empire; Protestants largely dissatisfied |
| | | Catholic mission work in Japan begun (1549) | |
| | | Johann Heinrich Bullinger (1504–75) | |
| | | Faustus Socinus (1539–1604) | Framer of modern Unitarianism |
| | | Zurich Consensus (1549) | Agreement between proponents of Zwingli and Calvin that their differences do not divide the Reformed churches |
| | | Michael Servetus (1511–53) | |
| | | Lutheran Church established in Iceland (1550s) | |

| | POLITICAL EVENTS | RELIGIOUS/PHILOSOPHICAL DEVELOPMENTS | THEOLOGICAL SIGNIFICANCE |
|---|---|---|---|
| 1553–58 | Reign of Mary Tudor in England | Catholic Church planted in Brazil (1554) | Protestant sympathizers in The Church of England repressed |
| 1555 | Peace of Augsburg | | Guarantees religious freedom for Lutheran regions in Germany espousing The Augsburg Confession |
| 1556–98 | Reign of Philip II in Spain | | |
| | Dutch and Belgians begin revolt (1568); treaty established with Belgium (1578) | Regions comprising Belgium and Luxembourg remain predominantly Catholic | |
| 1558–64 | Reign of Ferdinand I as Holy Roman emperor | Relaxed policies of Ferdinand I and Maximilian II (1564–76) toward Protestantism make possible its expansion in Austria | |
| 1558–1603 | Reign of Elizabeth I in England | Elizabethan Settlement | Church of England assumes middle-ground position between Protestantism and Catholicism |

| | POLITICAL EVENTS | RELIGIOUS/PHILOSOPHICAL DEVELOPMENTS | THEOLOGICAL SIGNIFICANCE |
|---|---|---|---|
| | | John Knox (ca. 1513–72) and Reformation in Scotland | |
| | | Scottish Protestant Covenant (1557) | |
| | | Matthias Flacius (1520–75) | Development of Gnesio-Lutheranism in response to emergence of Philippists |
| | | Synergist Controversy in Lutheranism | |
| | | Teresa of Ávila (1515–82) and John of the Cross (1542–91); establishment of Discalced Carmelites | |
| 1560–74 | Reign of Charles IX in France | | |
| 1565 | Spanish establish settlement in St. Augustine and conquer Philippines | | Catholic Church planted in both regions |
| 1567–1625 | Reign of James VI in Scotland (reigned as James I in England after 1603) | Michael Baius (1513–1589) condemned by Pope Pius V for his Augustinian teachings | |

| | POLITICAL EVENTS | RELIGIOUS/PHILOSOPHICAL DEVELOPMENTS | THEOLOGICAL SIGNIFICANCE |
|---|---|---|---|
| 1572 | Massacre of St. Bartholomew's Day | | Slaughter of thousands of French Huguenots |
| | | Thomas Cartwright (1535–1603) | Prominent spokesman for Presbyterianism |
| 1576–1612 | Reign of Rudolf II as Holy Roman emperor | Martin Chemnitz (1522–86) | Resolves Philippist-Gnesio-Lutheran dispute in Lutheranism |
| | | Formula of Concord (1577) | |
| | | Jesuit mission to China commenced (1582) | |
| | | Matteo Ricci (1552–1610) | |
| | | Third Lima Council (1582–83); convened by Toribio Alfonso de Mogrovejo | Passes laws to defend liberties of Native American and African slaves |
| | | Jesuit (esp. Luis de Molina [1535–1600])-Dominican (esp. Domingo Báñez [1528–1604] dispute over predestination | Debate in Catholic Church over whether election is based on foreknowledge |

| | POLITICAL EVENTS | RELIGIOUS/PHILOSOPHICAL DEVELOPMENTS | THEOLOGICAL SIGNIFICANCE |
|---|---|---|---|
| 1589–1610 | Reign of Henry IV in France | Anna Absalon martyred in Norway (1590) in retaliation for her husband's, Absalon Beyer (d. 1574), reforming humanistic propensities | |
| | | Lutheran Church established in Sweden and Finland (1593) | |
| | | Robert Bellarmine (1542–1621) | |
| 1598–1621 | Reign of Philip III in Spain; treaty established with Netherlands (1607) | Guarantees continued existence of Reformed Church in Netherlands | |
| 1598 | Edict of Nantes | | Grants Huguenots freedom of religion in France |
| | | Malabar Christian Synod of Diamper (1599) | Renounces Nestorianism; some members forming a Uniat Church, others associating with Syrian Orthodox (Jacobite) Church |

| POLITICAL EVENTS | RELIGIOUS/PHILOSOPHICAL DEVELOPMENTS | THEOLOGICAL SIGNIFICANCE |
|---|---|---|
| | Roberto de Nobili (1577–1656) | Practices a culturally sensitive mission strategy in India |
| | Martin de Porres (1579–1639) | One of the first African monastic candidates in the Americas |
| | Mikaelite and Stephanite heresies in Ethiopian Orthodox Church crushed | Veneration of Mary and the Cross defended; gnostic conceptions of church leadership refuted |
| | John Smyth (ca. 1554–1612) | Early English Baptist leader |
| | Richard Bancroft (1544–1610) | Affirms Catholic traditions of Anglicanism against Puritanism |
| | Jakob Boehme (1575–1624) | Forerunner of modern spiritualism |
| 1607 British establish colony in Virginia | | |

| | POLITICAL EVENTS | RELIGIOUS/PHILOSOPHICAL DEVELOPMENTS | THEOLOGICAL SIGNIFICANCE |
|---|---|---|---|
| 1608 | French establish first permanent settlement in Canada | | |
| 1610–43 | Reign of Louis XIII in France | Armand Jean du Plessis Richelieu (1585–1642) | |
| | | Johann Arndt (1555–1621) | Lutheran mystic |
| | | Jacob Arminius (1560–1609) and Remonstrant movement | Teaches that predestination is based on foreknowledge |
| | | Francis Gomarus [Gomar] (1563–1641) | Chief opponent of Remonstrants |
| 1612–19 | Reign of Matthias as Holy Roman emperor | Georg Calixtus (1586–1656) and development of Syncretism | |
| | | Abraham Calovius (1612–86) | Lutheranism rejects Syncretism |
| 1618–48 | Thirty Years' War | Synod of Dort (1618–19) | Condemns Remonstrants; henceforth predestination receives more emphasis in Reformed-Presbyterian tradition |

| | POLITICAL EVENTS | RELIGIOUS/PHILOSOPHICAL DEVELOPMENTS | THEOLOGICAL SIGNIFICANCE |
|---|---|---|---|
| 1619–37 | Reign of Ferdinand as Holy Roman emperor | Emergence of Orthodox theology | |
| | | Church of England planted in Bermuda (1619) | |
| 1620 | Mayflower Pilgrims -Founding of Massachusetts Bay Company | Russian Orthodox Synod (1620) | Recognizes validity of Protestant and Catholic baptisms |
| | | René Descartes (1596–1650) First stirrings of Enlightenment | Origin of rationalism |
| | | Forced reunion of Ethiopian Orthodox and Roman Catholic churches (1622–32) | |
| | | Pedro Claver (ca. 1580–1654) | Crusader for African slaves in America |
| | | Cornelius Jansenius (1585–1638) and Jansenism | French Catholics try to recover Augustinian heritage |
| 1625–47 | Reign of Charles I in England and Scotland (until 1649 in Scotland) | Cyril Lucaris (1572–1638) | Orthodox patriarch of Constantinople attempts to relate Orthodoxy to Protestant thought (esp. Calvin) |
| | | Galileo (1564–1642) condemned by inquisition (1632) | |

| POLITICAL EVENTS | RELIGIOUS/PHILOSOPHICAL DEVELOPMENTS | THEOLOGICAL SIGNIFICANCE |
|---|---|---|
| | Peter Mogila (1596–1646) | Russian Orthodox patriarch endeavors to relate Orthodoxy to Roman Catholic thought |
| | French Catholics initiate missionary efforts among Native Americans<br>-Jean de Brébeuf (1593–1649) | |
| | William Laud (1573–1645) | Archbishop of Canterbury's policies harass Puritans |
| | Presbyterian Church established in Scotland (1638)<br>-Scotish National Covenant (1639) | Rejects efforts to impose Catholic elements of Anglican tradition on Scottish church |
| Puritan Revolution | The Solemn League and Covenant in England (1643) | Based on earlier Scottish covenant; puts an end to the episcopacy |
| | London Confession (1646) | Early English Baptist confession |
| | Westminster Assembly (1643–1647) and Confession (1648) | Official theological statement of Puritan movement; confession continues to be the theological statement of Presbyterianism |

| | POLITICAL EVENTS | RELIGIOUS/PHILOSOPHICAL DEVELOPMENTS | THEOLOGICAL SIGNIFICANCE |
|---|---|---|---|
| 1648 | Peace of Westphalia | | Peace agreement to end Thirty Years' War; gives freedom of religion to all citizens of western Europe, regardless of preference of their ruler |
| 1643–1715 | Reign of Louis XIII in France | Jean de Labadie (1610–74) | French Reformed mystic |
| 1652 | Dutch settle in South Africa | | |
| 1653–58 | Puritan Protectorate in England led by Oliver Cromwell | Antoine Arnauld (1612–94) Blaise Pascal (1623–62) Probabalism (condemned in 1713 by Pope Clement XI) Establishment of Unitarian movement in England (1658–62) | |
| 1660 | Restoration of monarchy in England to Scottish king Charles II; he and son James II (through 1701) unsuccessfully seek to restore Catholicism in both kingdoms | George Fox (1624–91) and establishment of Quakers Old Believers' schism in Russian Orthodox Church initiated (1666–67) | |

| POLITICAL EVENTS | RELIGIOUS/PHILOSOPHICAL DEVELOPMENTS | THEOLOGICAL SIGNIFICANCE |
|---|---|---|
| -Legislation against Puritans (1661-65) | Petrovich Avvakum (ca. 1620–81) | |
| | Joachim Stoll (1615–78) | Influences Spener |
| | Philipp Spener (1635–1705) · | Origins of Pietism |
| | Miguel de Molinos (ca. 1640–97), Jeanne Guyon (1648–1717), and quietism (condemned in 1685) | |
| | Benedict Spinoza (1632–77) | Post-Cartesian proponent of pantheism |
| | Nicolas Malebranche (1638–1715) | Post-Cartesian proponent of occasionalism |
| | Robert Barclay (1648–90) | Premier apologist for Quakers |
| | Second London Confession (1677) | Particular Baptist confession of faith |
| | Gallicanism | French Catholic movement that resides ecclesiastical authority, not in papacy, but in local bishops |

| POLITICAL EVENTS | RELIGIOUS/PHILOSOPHICAL DEVELOPMENTS | THEOLOGICAL SIGNIFICANCE |
| --- | --- | --- |
| | William Penn (1644–1718) and establishment of Pennsylvania | |
| | Edict of Nantes abolished (1685) | |
| | Isaac Newton (1642–1727) | Formulates theory of gravity |
| | Gottfried Leibniz (1646–1716) | Post-Cartesian proponent of "preestablished" physical-spiritual harmony |
| | Papacy accepts antislavery proposition (1686) | |
| | Policies of Toleration | |
| 1689–1702 William and Mary reign in England and Scotland | John Locke (1632–1734) | Origin of empiricism |
| | John Toland (1670–1722) | Proponent of Deism |
| | Church of England established in Canada (1700) | |
| | Alexander Mack (1679–1735) founds the Dunkers (elsewhere becoming River Brethren and Brethren in Christ) | |

| POLITICAL EVENTS | RELIGIOUS/PHILOSOPHICAL DEVELOPMENTS | THEOLOGICAL SIGNIFICANCE |
|---|---|---|
| | Danish mission in India undertaken (1706) | |
| | Heresies of Appolonia Mafuta and Vita Kimpa (d. 1706) in Kongo | Taught a black Jesus |
| | Jacob Ammann (ca. 1644–ca. 1730) and foundation of Amish communities | |
| | August Hermann Francke (1663–1727) | Focuses Pietism on evangelism and concern with the poor |
| | F. A. Lampe (1683–1729) | Leading Reformed Pietist |
| | Founding of America's first presbytery (1706) | |
| | Church of the Brethren founded in Germany under leadership of Alexander Mack (1708) | |
| | Christianity (Lutheranism) planted in Greenland (1721) | |

| POLITICAL EVENTS | RELIGIOUS/PHILOSOPHICAL DEVELOPMENTS | THEOLOGICAL SIGNIFICANCE |
|---|---|---|
| | Great Awakening in America<br>-Jonathan Edwards (1703–58)<br>-George Whitefield (1714–70) | Effectively stamped American with a "Puritan paradigm" |
| | Baron de Montesquieu (1689–1755)<br>Voltaire (1694–1778)<br>Jean-Jacques Rousseau (1712–78) | French philosophers lay foundation for French Revolution and also influence American Constitution |
| | Conrad Beissel (1691–1768); founding of Ephrata Cloister (1732) | Early American Christian cooperative community |
| | David Hume (1711–76) | Turned empiricism in direction of skepticism |
| | Nikolaus von Zinzendorf (1700–1760) and formation of Moravian Church | |
| | Schwenkfelders settle in America (1734) | |
| | Moravian Brethren undertake mission among slaves in Suriname (1735) | |

| | POLITICAL EVENTS | RELIGIOUS/PHILOSOPHICAL DEVELOPMENTS | THEOLOGICAL SIGNIFICANCE |
|---|---|---|---|
| | | Moravian mission to Gold Coast and South Africa begun (1737) | |
| | | John Wesley (1703–91) Aldersgate Experience (1738) | Founder of Methodism |
| | | Henry Melchior Muhlenberg (1711–87) | American Lutheranism's most prominent missionary |
| | | Emanuel Swedenborg (1688–1772) | |
| | | Hermann Samuel Reimarus (1694–1768) | Proponent of natural religion |
| 1750–1900 | Industrial Revolution | Society for Propagation of Gospel mission to Gold Coast, led by Thomas Thompson (ca. 1708–1773), begun (1752) | |
| 1756–63 | French and Indian War | John Woolman (1720–72) | Along with other American Quakers, rejects slavery |

| POLITICAL EVENTS | RELIGIOUS/PHILOSOPHICAL DEVELOPMENTS | THEOLOGICAL SIGNIFICANCE |
|---|---|---|
| | Febronianism | German Catholic movement like Gallicanism |
| | Thomas Reid (1710–96) | Chief proponent of Scottish Common-Sense Realism; important influence on U.S. Constitution |
| | Philip Quaque (d. 1816) begins to serve in ministry in Gold Coast (1766) | Early indigenous African Protestant clergyman |
| | Francis Asbury (1745–1816) | Leader of early American Methodism, beginning ministry in 1771 |
| Reign of Louis XIV in France | Johann Salomo Semler (1725–91) | Early proponent of use of historical criticism |
| | Gotthold Lessing (1729–81) | Helps define implications of modern historical consciousness |
| | Dukhobors and Molokan sects emerge in Russia | |

1774–92

| POLITICAL EVENTS | RELIGIOUS/PHILOSOPHICAL DEVELOPMENTS | THEOLOGICAL SIGNIFICANCE |
|---|---|---|
| 1775–83 American Revolution | Quakers and Mennonites condemn slavery (1776) | White America begins to raise its consciousness about the evils of slavery |
| | Brethren in Christ Church founded (1778) | |
| | Immanuel Kant (1724–1804) | By nineteenth century his epistemology becomes primary philosophical presupposition for Protestant theology |
| | Anglicans in America organize as Protestant Episcopal Church (1783) | |
| | American Methodists become organized (as Methodist Episcopal Church) and condemn slavery (1784) | |
| | Catholic mission work in Korea initiated (1784) | |
| | Religious toleration of Protestants in France proclaimed (1787) | |

| POLITICAL EVENTS | RELIGIOUS/PHILOSOPHICAL DEVELOPMENTS | THEOLOGICAL SIGNIFICANCE |
|---|---|---|
| | Church of New Jerusalem (today known as Swedenborgian Church) established (1787) | |
| | Richard Allen (1760–1831) and African Methodist Episcopal secession from Methodist Church in Philadelphia (1787); denomination organizes (1816) | Creation of the first independent African American denomination |
| | Church planted in Australia (1788) | |
| 1789 U.S. Constitution ratified | William Carey (1761–1834) founds Particular Baptist Society for Propagating the Gospel amongst the Heathen (1792) | Essentially initiates the modern missionary movement |
| 1789–99 French Revolution | Universalist Church organized (1793) | Catholic Church in France endures harassment from the revolutionaries |

| | POLITICAL EVENTS | RELIGIOUS/PHILOSOPHICAL DEVELOPMENTS | THEOLOGICAL SIGNIFICANCE |
|---|---|---|---|
| 1795–1820 | British settle in South Africa | African Methodist Episcopal Zion secession from Methodist Church in New York (1793); after unsuccessful efforts by Allen to associate with this body, denomination organizes (1824) | |
| 1798 | Pope Pius VI seized by French | British Methodists break with Church of England (1795)<br>London Missionary Society founded (1795) | |
| | | Henrik Schartau (1757–1826) | Forerunner of Pietism in Sweden; critic of rationalism and orthodoxy |
| | | Second Great Awakening in America begins (1797)<br>-Charles G. Finney (1792–1875) | |
| 1799 | British found Sierra Leone as land for free slaves | Johannes Van der Kamp leads London Missionary Society outreach to native South Africans (1799) | |

| | POLITICAL EVENTS | RELIGIOUS/PHILOSOPHICAL DEVELOPMENTS | THEOLOGICAL SIGNIFICANCE |
|---|---|---|---|
| 1799–1814 | Napoléon Bonaparte (1769–1821) rules over his empire<br><br>-Beginnings of independence movements in Latin America | G. W. F. Hegel (1770–1831) | Develops a post-Kantian ontology that recovers significance of history as a source of truth |
| | | First serious missionary work undertaken in Indonesia | |
| | | Sunday school movement initiated | |
| | | Friedrich Schleiermacher (1768–1834) | Provides paradigm for modern liberal theology |
| | | Church of the United Brethren in Christ established (1803) | |
| | | Robert Morrison (1782–1834) | British missionary prepares first Chinese translation of the Bible |

|  | POLITICAL EVENTS | RELIGIOUS/PHILOSOPHICAL DEVELOPMENTS | THEOLOGICAL SIGNIFICANCE |
|---|---|---|---|
| 1808–14 | Years of captivity of Pope Pius VII by Napoléon | Basel Mission founded (1815) | |
| | | American Bible Society and American Colonization Society founded (1816) | |
| | | Friedrich Wilhelm II of Saxony creates Evangelical (Union) Church (1817) | |
| | | American Presbyterians reject abolition (1818) | |
| | | British and Foreign Bible Society undertakes mission to Native Americans in Latin America | |
| 1820 | Liberia founded as land for freed American slaves | Hans Nielsen Hauge (1771–1824) | Norway's greatest revivalist |
| | | N. F. S. Grundtvig (1783–1872) | Originates Cooperative movement |
| | | Samuel Schmucker (1799–1873) | |

| POLITICAL EVENTS | RELIGIOUS/PHILOSOPHICAL DEVELOPMENTS | THEOLOGICAL SIGNIFICANCE |
|---|---|---|
| | Basel Mission begins ministry in Gold Coast (1828) | |
| | Morman Church organized under leadership of Joseph Smith (1830) | |
| | Predecessor movements of Methodist Church in Ghana begin to form (1831) | |
| | Oxford Movement<br>-John H. Newman (1801–90)<br>-John Keble (1792–1866) | Some Anglican Church leaders attempt to recover Catholic heritage |
| | Anglican Evangelicals<br>-William Wilberforce (1759–1833) | |
| | Barton Stone (1772–1844) and Alexander Campbell (1788–1866) found Christian Church (Disciples of Christ; 1832) | Embody American Christianity's nondenominational ethos |
| Abolition of slavery by British Commonwealth | Christian Reformed Church established in Netherlands (1834) | |

1833

| | POLITICAL EVENTS | RELIGIOUS/PHILOSOPHICAL DEVELOPMENTS | THEOLOGICAL SIGNIFICANCE |
|---|---|---|---|
| 1836 | Beginnings of Great Trek of Afrikaners in South Africa | F. C. Baur (1792–1860) David Friedrich Strauss (1808–74) | Leaders in applying tools of historical criticism to Scripture |
| | | Franckean (Lutheran) Synod organized in U.S. (1837) | |
| | | New School-Old School American Presbyterian division, eventually culminating in creation of different denominations (1837) | |
| | | Søren Kierkegaard (1813–55) | |
| | | Carl Olaf Rosenius (1816–68) | Sweden's greatest revivalist |
| | | Neo-Luthernism -Ernst Hengstenberg (1802–69) -Wilhelm Loehe (1808–72) | |
| | | Quest for historical Jesus undertaken by numerous scholars | |

| POLITICAL EVENTS | RELIGIOUS/PHILOSOPHICAL DEVELOPMENTS | THEOLOGICAL SIGNIFICANCE |
|---|---|---|
| | Formation of free churches and numerous missionary societies in western Europe<br>-Niger Mission founded (1841) | |
| | Ludwig Feurbach (1804–72) | Criticizes religion by reducing it to anthropology |
| | Lutherans in Prussia gradually withdraw from Union Church | |
| Treaty of Nanking | | British-Chinese treaty opens China's mainland, effectively protecting Chinese Christians |
| | Methodist mission in Nigeria founded | |
| | Samuel A. Crowther (1806–1891) leads Niger Mission | A movement encouraging Africans to evangelize Africans |
| | Holiness movement in America leads to schisms in Methodist Episcopal Church (1843; 1858) | |
| 1842 | | |

| POLITICAL EVENTS | RELIGIOUS/PHILOSOPHICAL DEVELOPMENTS | THEOLOGICAL SIGNIFICANCE |
|---|---|---|
| | Nederduitsch Hervormde Kerk in South Africa established (1843) | |
| | Joseph Smith (1805–44); Mormon Church established | |
| | George Williams (1821–1905) founds YMCA | |
| | John Nelson Darby (1880–1882) | Prime modern spokesperson for dispensational premillennialism |
| | Baptists and Methodists in America split over slavery (1845) | |
| | Church Missionary Society and Presbyterian missions begun in Nigeria (1846) | |
| | Founding of Oneida Community (1848); reorganized/terminated (1881) | Christian cooperative community |
| | Karl Marx (1818–83) | Development of Communism |
| | Horace Bushnell (1802–76) | |

1846–47

Mormon settlement in Utah led by Brigham Young (1801-77)

| POLITICAL EVENTS | RELIGIOUS/PHILOSOPHICAL DEVELOPMENTS | THEOLOGICAL SIGNIFICANCE |
|---|---|---|
| | Taiping Rebellion by Christians in China (1850–53) | |
| | Pius IX (1792–1878) proclaims dogma of immaculate conception (1854) | |
| | Daniel Payne (1811–93) | |
| | American Baptist mission in Nigeria begun (1855) | |
| | Charles Hodge (1797–1878) | Forerunner of Princeton theology |
| 1859/1871 Theory of evolution developed by Charles Darwin (1809–82) | David Livingstone (1813–73) | Biblical creation accounts and truth of Christianity challenged |
| | Old School and New School Presbyterians divide over slavery (1857; 1861) | |
| 1861–65 American Civil War | J. C. K. von Hofmann (1810–77) and origin of Erlangen theology | |

| | POLITICAL EVENTS | RELIGIOUS/PHILOSOPHICAL DEVELOPMENTS | THEOLOGICAL SIGNIFICANCE |
| --- | --- | --- | --- |
| | | American Lutheranism's General Synod divides over Civil War and slavery (1862) | |
| | | Seventh Day Adventist Church formally organized (1863); led by Ellen Harmon White (1827–1915) | |
| 1862/63 | Emancipation Proclamation | | |
| 1864 | Japanese agree to open their society to more foreign (Western) influence | Pope Pius IX propounds Syllabus of Errors (1864) | Catholic criticism of church-state separation, public education, freedom of religion |
| | | J. Hudson Taylor (1832–1905) founds China Inland Mission (1865) | Stimulus to future Protestant foreign missionary work |
| | | William Booth (1829–1912) founds Salvation Army (1865) | |
| 1866 | Korea outlaws Christianity | General Council established through secession from American Lutheranism's General Synod (1867) | Heightened awareness of Lutheranism's confessional heritage by certain (General Council) American Lutherans |

| POLITICAL EVENTS | RELIGIOUS/PHILOSOPHICAL DEVELOPMENTS | THEOLOGICAL SIGNIFICANCE |
|---|---|---|
| | Presbyterian Church established in Chile (1867) | |
| | Old School and New School Presbyterian denominations in North and South reunite | |
| | Phoebe Palmer (1807–74) | |
| | First Vatican Council (1869–70) | Affirms papal infallibility |
| Italian nationalist movement takes control of Rome from papacy, ceding Vatican to Church | Formation of Old Catholic Church | |
| | Dwight Moody (1837–99) | Develops modern revivalism |
| | Abraham Kuyper (1837–1920) Herman Bavinck (1854–1921) -Initiate movement leading to establishment of Reformed Churches in Netherlands established (1886); merged with Christian Reformed Church (1892) | Neo-Calvinism |
| | Colored Methodist Episcopal Church established (1870) | |

1870

| | POLITICAL EVENTS | RELIGIOUS/PHILOSOPHICAL DEVELOPMENTS | THEOLOGICAL SIGNIFICANCE |
|---|---|---|---|
| | | Albrecht Ritschl (1822–89) | |
| | | Charles Taze Russell (1852–1916) founds predecessor body of Jehovah's Witnesses | |
| | | Lucious Holsey (1842–1920) | |
| 1871 | Henry M. Stanley (1841-1904) meets Livingstone | | |
| 1874 | Britain declares Gold Coast a colony | Woman's Christian Temperance Union founded (1874) | |
| | | Keswick movement | |
| | | Establishment of Livingstonia in Zambia (1875) | |
| | | Apostolic Orthodox Church of Haiti founded (1876) | Church founded by African American leadership |
| | | Synod of Berru Meda (1878) | Ethiopian Orthodox Synod resolves Sons of Unction-Sons of Grace debate |

| | POLITICAL EVENTS | RELIGIOUS/PHILOSOPHICAL DEVELOPMENTS | THEOLOGICAL SIGNIFICANCE |
|---|---|---|---|
| | | Niagara Conference (1878) | Influential American Bible and prophetic conference may have influenced emergence of Fundamentalism |
| | | Mary Baker Eddy (1821–1910) founds Church of Christ, Scientist (1879) | |
| 1882 | Commercial treaty between Korea and U.S.A. opens Korea to Western influence | Protestant (esp. American) missions planted in Korea | |
| | | Friedrich Nietzsche (1844–1900) | Development of modern nihilism |
| 1884 | Germany establishes colony in East Africa | | Lutheran Church planted in territory of present-day Tanzania |
| | Increased European immigration in Latin America | Pope Leo XIII regularizes practice of installing indigenous leadership in India (1886) | Opens new opportunities for Protestant church growth in region |

| | POLITICAL EVENTS | RELIGIOUS/PHILOSOPHICAL DEVELOPMENTS | THEOLOGICAL SIGNIFICANCE |
|---|---|---|---|
| 1887 | British settlements in Kenya initiated | Alpha Synod established (1889) | |
| | | *Rerum Novarum* (1891) proclaimed by Pope Leo XIII (1810–1903) | Catholic Church rejects socioeconomic consequences of modernity |
| | | United Native African Church founded (1891) | |
| | | Fannie Barrier Williams (1855–1944) | |
| | | Elizabeth Cady Stanton (1815–1902) | Leader in woman's suffrage movement |
| | | National Baptist Convention, U.S.A., founded (1895) | |
| 1896 | Filipino Revolution | Leo XIII proclaims *Apostolicae curae* (1896) | Refuses to recognize validity of Anglican ministries |
| | | Pilgrim Holiness Church founded (1897) | |

| | POLITICAL EVENTS | RELIGIOUS/PHILOSOPHICAL DEVELOPMENTS | THEOLOGICAL SIGNIFICANCE |
|---|---|---|---|
| 1898 | Spanish-American War | Missionary outreach to Kikuyu in Ghana initiated (1898) | |
| 1899–1902 | Anglo-Boer War in South Africa | George Tyrrell (1861–1901) A. F. Loisy (1857–1940) | Roman Catholic Modernism |
| | Boxer Rebellion in China | Church in China endures harsh persecution | |
| | | William James (1842–1910) | Founder of Pragmatism and early proponent of psychology of religion |
| | | Ernst Troeltsch (1865–1923) | Initiated field of sociology of religion |
| | | Sigmund Freud (1856–1939) | Originator of Psychology |
| | | Outbreak of Pentecostal movement under leadership of Charles Parham (1901) | |
| | | African Church (Bethel) founded | |

| POLITICAL EVENTS | RELIGIOUS/PHILOSOPHICAL DEVELOPMENTS | THEOLOGICAL SIGNIFICANCE |
|---|---|---|
| | Adolf von Harnack (1851–1930) | |
| | Filipino Independent Church formed (1902) | |
| | Albert Schweitzer (1875–1965) | Theological work puts an end to quest for historical Jesus; becomes medical missionary in Gabon (1913) |
| | Bwiti movement begins in Gabon | |
| Rebellion against Germans in East Africa leads to abolition of slavery in region | Azusa Street Revival (1906) | Pentecostalism becomes an international movement |
| | C. H. Mason (1866–1961) founds Church of God in Christ as Pentecostal denomination (1907) | |
| | Church of the Nazarene founded (1907) | |

1905

| POLITICAL EVENTS | RELIGIOUS/PHILOSOPHICAL DEVELOPMENTS | THEOLOGICAL SIGNIFICANCE |
|---|---|---|
| | Walter Rauschenbusch (1861–1918) | Social gospel; recovery of a sense of the gospel's relevance to addressing social issues |
| | Church of God (Cleveland, Tenn.) established as a Pentecostal denomination (1908) | |
| | South India United Church established (1908) | |
| | T. B. Barratt (1862–1940) | |
| 1910 Union of South Africa formed | World Missionary Conference (1910) | |
| | William Wade Harris (1865–1929) | Most influential native African evangelist |
| | *The Fundamentals* published (1910–15) | |
| 1911 Fall of Chinese Empire | Ulster's Solemn League and Covenant (1912) | Protestants in Northern Ireland pledge to resist Irish home rule in their region |

| | POLITICAL EVENTS | RELIGIOUS/PHILOSOPHICAL DEVELOPMENTS | THEOLOGICAL SIGNIFICANCE |
|---|---|---|---|
| 1914–18 | World War I | Assemblies of God organized (1914)<br><br>Joseph F. Rutherford (1869–ca. 1942) reorganizes Jehovah's Witnesses (1914)<br><br>National Baptist Convention, Unincorporated (National Baptist Convention of America), established (1915) | |
| 1917 | Russian Revolution | Luther Renaissance initiated<br>-Karl Holl (1866–1926)<br>-Gustaf Aulen (1879–1977)<br>-Paul Althaus (1888–1966)<br>-Regin Prenter (1907–90)<br>-Werner Elert (1885–1954) | Repression of Russian Orthodox Church; Marxism becomes a necessary dialogue partner for the Church |

| POLITICAL EVENTS | RELIGIOUS/PHILOSOPHICAL DEVELOPMENTS | THEOLOGICAL SIGNIFICANCE |
|---|---|---|
| | Evangelical Lutheran Church formed (1917) | Brings together most Norwegian Lutherans in America |
| | Rudolf Otto (1869–1937) | Initiates modern study of history of religion |
| Russian Orthodox Church officially separated from Russian state | United Lutheran Church formed (1918) | Reunites northern and southern East Coast American Lutheranism |
| | Presbyterian Church in Ghana begins to emerge from earlier Basle Mission | |
| | Father Divine (1878–1965) founds Peace Mission movement in Brooklyn (1919) | |
| | Mission churches in Kenya divide over female circumcision controversy (1919) | |
| | Karl Barth (1886–1968) | Beginnings of neoorthodox theology; primary spokesperson for movement |

1918

| | POLITICAL EVENTS | RELIGIOUS/PHILOSOPHICAL DEVELOPMENTS | THEOLOGICAL SIGNIFICANCE |
|---|---|---|---|
| 1922 | Benito Mussolini (1883–1945) assumes power in Italy | Pierre Teilhard de Chardin (1881–1955) | Opens Catholic Church to insights of modern science |
| | | Joseph Appian (d. 1948) founds Musama Disco Christo (1922) | |
| | | Martin Heidegger (1889–1976) | Important existential philosopher whose ontology influences a number of twentieth-century theologians |
| | | Rudolf Bultmann (1884–1976) | |
| | | Paul Tillich (1886–1965) | |
| | | Simon Kimbangu (1889–1951) initiates African independent church movement; recognition given to his Church of Jesus Christ on Earth by the Prophet Simon Kimbangu (1959) | |
| | | Fundamentalist controversy in American Presbyterianism (1924–26) | |

| | POLITICAL EVENTS | RELIGIOUS/PHILOSOPHICAL DEVELOPMENTS | THEOLOGICAL SIGNIFICANCE |
|---|---|---|---|
| 1925 | Scopes trial | United Church of Canada formed (1925)<br><br>Cherubim and Seraphim Society/Church formed (1925)<br><br>Nathan Soderblom (1866–1931) organizes Life and Work movement (1925)<br><br>Emil Brunner (1889–1966)<br><br>Aimee Semple McPherson (1890–1944) founds International Church of the Foursquare Gospel (1927)<br><br>Church of Christ in China formed (1927) | Eventually serves to authorize public consensus about teaching evolution in American public schools; Fundamentalism discredited |

| | POLITICAL EVENTS | RELIGIOUS/PHILOSOPHICAL DEVELOPMENTS | THEOLOGICAL SIGNIFICANCE |
|---|---|---|---|
| | | Faith and Order movement organized (1927) | Process philosophy |
| | | Alfred N. Whitehead (1861–1947) | |
| | | Reinhold Niebuhr (1892–1971) | |
| | | H. Richard Niebuhr (1894–1962) | |
| 1929 | Depression begins | | |
| | Benito Mussolini prevails on Pope Pius IX formally to accept ceding Rome to Italian government in exchange for Vatican | American Lutheran Church formed (1930) | |
| | | Methodist Church in Korea formed (1930) | |
| | | Wallace Fard (1877–ca. 1934), influenced by Timothy Drew (1866–1929), founds Lost-Found Nation of Islam (1930) | |
| | | Rastafarionism established in Jamaica (1930s) | |

| POLITICAL EVENTS | RELIGIOUS/PHILOSOPHICAL DEVELOPMENTS | THEOLOGICAL SIGNIFICANCE |
|---|---|---|
| | Congregational Christian Churches formed (1931) | |
| | Anders Nygren (1890–1978) | |
| | Fundamentalists in Northern Baptist Convention form General Association of Regular Baptists (1932) | |
| Adolf Hitler (1889-1945) becomes ruler of Germany | German Christian movement | Initiates policies of unifying all German churches |
| | Confessing Church in Germany | |
| Adam Clayton Powell Jr. (1908–72) | Martin Niemöller (1892–1984) | Important African American voice in U.S. House of Representatives |
| | Dietrich Bonhoeffer (1906–45) | Warns against "cheap grace"; advocates religionless Christianity; criticizes and seeks to end Hitler's oppression |

1933

| | POLITICAL EVENTS | RELIGIOUS/PHILOSOPHICAL DEVELOPMENTS | THEOLOGICAL SIGNIFICANCE |
|---|---|---|---|
| | | Barmen Declaration (1934) | Barth's vision of church-state relations prevails among Christians resisting oppression |
| | | Evangelical and Reformed Church formed (1934) | |
| | | Elijah Muhammed (1897–1975) assumes leadership of Lost-Found Nation of Islam, beginning to give it its unique profile (1934) | |
| | | Fundamentalists in Northern Presbyterianism form Orthodox Presbyterian Church (1936) | |
| 1939 | Spanish Revolution ends with Francisco Franco (1892–1975) in power | Inter-Varsity Christian Fellowship established (1939) | |
| 1939–45 | World War II Holocaust | Jacques Maritain (1882–1973) Etiénne Gilson (1884–1978) Papacy of Pius XII (1939–58) | Development of Neo-Thomism |
| | | Methodist Church (U.S.A.) formed from merger of its northern and southern branches (1939) | |

| POLITICAL EVENTS | RELIGIOUS/PHILOSOPHICAL DEVELOPMENTS | THEOLOGICAL SIGNIFICANCE |
|---|---|---|
| | National Association of Evangelicals founded (1942) -Harold Ockenga (1905–85) | Luther's two-kingdom ethic authorizes the resistance |
| | Norwegian and Danish Lutheran resistance movements to Nazis -Einvind Berggrav (1884–1959) | |
| | Evangelical United Brethren Church formed (1946) | |
| | Georgia Harkness (1891–1974) | |
| | Church of South India established (1947) | |
| | Fuller Theological Seminary established (1947) | |
| | Francis Schaeffer (1912–84) | |
| 1945 Marshal Tito (1892-1980) takes control of a united Yugoslavia | | |

| | POLITICAL EVENTS | RELIGIOUS/PHILOSOPHICAL DEVELOPMENTS | THEOLOGICAL SIGNIFICANCE |
|---|---|---|---|
| 1948 | Worldwide struggle in Southern Hemisphere for independence | Mohandas Gandhi (1869–1948) | Directs Roman Catholic research on Luther in a more positive, appreciative position |
| | Apartheid policies in South Africa enacted | Yves Congar (b. 1904) | |
| | | World Council of Churches founded (1948) | |
| 1949 | Communist Revolution in China succeeds | Joseph Lortz (1887–1975) | Worldwide evangelistic crusades; brings popular credibility to Evangelical movement |
| 1950–53 | Korean War | Pope Pius XII proclaims dogma of assumption of Mary (1950) | |
| | | Norman Vincent Peale (b. 1898) | |
| | | Billy Graham (b. 1918) | |
| | | Campus Crusade founded (1951) | |
| 1952 | U.S. Supreme Court bars segregation in public schools | Ethiopian Orthodox Church becomes autocephalous (1951) | |
| | African National Congress launches Defiance against Unjust Laws Campaign (1952) | | |

| POLITICAL EVENTS | RELIGIOUS/PHILOSOPHICAL DEVELOPMENTS | THEOLOGICAL SIGNIFICANCE |
|---|---|---|
| Civil rights movement (U.S.A.) | Martin Luther King Jr. (1929–68) Jacob Rothschild (1911–74) | |
| | Joseph Jackson (1900–1982) | Longtime president of National Baptist Convention; opposes King's strategy |
| | Carl Henry (b. 1912) | Premier theologian of Evangelical movement |
| | *Christianity Today* established (1956) | |
| | United Church of Christ formed (1957) | |
| | United Presbyterian Church formed (1958) | |
| | Karl Rahner (1904–84) | |
| | Hans Küng (b. 1928) | |
| | Gerhard Ebeling (b. 1912) | Initiates new quest for historical Jesus |
| | Ernst Fuchs (b. 1930) | |

1955–64

| | POLITICAL EVENTS | RELIGIOUS/PHILOSOPHICAL DEVELOPMENTS | THEOLOGICAL SIGNIFICANCE |
|---|---|---|---|
| 1959 | Fidel Castro's Cuban Revolution | Papacy of John XXIII (1958–63) | |
| 1960s | Student movement in Western society; Catholic civil rights movement in Northern Ireland | Bernedette Devlin (b. 1947) | Primary spokesperson for radical branch of IRA |
| | | Ian Paisley (b. 1926) | Leader of militant Protestants in Northern Ireland |
| | | The American Lutheran Church formed (1960) | |
| | | Unitarian Universalist Association formed (1961) | |
| | | Progressive National Baptist Convention established (1961) | African American Baptist denomination committed to supporting Martin Luther King's strategies |
| | Cultural Revolution in China | Lutheran Church in America formed (1962) | |

| | POLITICAL EVENTS | RELIGIOUS/PHILOSOPHICAL DEVELOPMENTS | THEOLOGICAL SIGNIFICANCE |
|---|---|---|---|
| 1962–74 | | Henri du Lubac (b. 1896) | |
| | | Second Vatican Council (1962–65) | Seeks to bring Catholic Church to confront modern world; Mass to be in indigenous language; recognizes Orthodox churches and deems Protestants as "separated brethren"; teaches justification by faith and preferential option for the poor |
| | | Juan Luis Segundo (1925–96) Gustavo Gutiérrez (b. 1928) Rubem Alves (b. 1933) Leonardo Boff (b. 1938) | Latin American liberation theology |
| | Vietnam War | Consultation on Christian Union (U.S.A.) established (1962) | |
| | | Papacy of Paul VI (1963–78) | |

| POLITICAL EVENTS | RELIGIOUS/PHILOSOPHICAL DEVELOPMENTS | THEOLOGICAL SIGNIFICANCE |
|---|---|---|
| Black Power movement<br>-Stokely Carmichael (1941–98) and Student Nonviolent Coordinating Committee<br>-Malcolm X (1925–65) and Lost-Found Nation of Islam | Outbreak of tongues in mainline churches | Charismatic movement |
| | Harvey Cox (b. 1929) | Secular theology |
| | Thomas Altizer (1927–98)<br>Paul van Buren (1924–98) | God-is-dead movement |
| | Mary Daly (b. 1928)<br>Jane D. Douglas (b. 1933)<br>Rosemary R. Ruether (b. 1936) | Feminist theology |
| | Medellín Conference (1968) | Roman Catholic bishops in Latin America largely affirm liberation theology |
| | United Methodist Church formed (1968) | |
| | Wesleyan Church formed (1968) | |
| | Humanae Vitae (1968) | Pope Paul VI (1897-1968) condemns abortion and artificial birth control |

| POLITICAL EVENTS | RELIGIOUS/PHILOSOPHICAL DEVELOPMENTS | THEOLOGICAL SIGNIFICANCE |
|---|---|---|
| | Jürgen Moltmann (b. 1926) | Theology of hope |
| | Wolfhart Pannenberg (b. 1928) | |
| | John Cobb (b. 1925) David Ray Griffin (b.1939) | Process theology |
| | John Mbiti (b. 1931) | Indigenous African theology |
| | James Cone (b. 1938) | Black theology |
| | Schism in Lutheran Church-Missouri Synod (1976) | |
| | Enrique Angelelli (d. 1976) | Martyr for cause of liberation theology |
| | Papacy of John Paul II (1978–) | |
| | Controversy among Ewe Presbyterians in Ghana concerning the reality of evil spirits | |
| | Fundamentalist takeover of Southern Baptist Convention | |

| POLITICAL EVENTS | RELIGIOUS/PHILOSOPHICAL DEVELOPMENTS | THEOLOGICAL SIGNIFICANCE |
|---|---|---|
| | Moral Majority founded (1979) | |
| | Oscar Romero (1917–80) | Martyr for cause of liberation theology |
| | Joseph Ratzinger (b. 1927) | Primary theological adviser to John Paul II, advocating a more theologically conservative profile |
| | WCC Lima Text (1982) | Ecumenical document stating consensus on baptism, Eucharist, and ministry |
| | Presbyterian Church (U.S.A.) formed (1983) | |
| | Evangelical Lutheran Church in Canada formed (1985) | |
| | Evangelical Lutheran Church in America formed (1987) | |
| | National Missionary Baptist Convention of America established (1988) | |
| Anglo-Irish Agreement gives Republic of Ireland consultative role in Northern Ireland | | |

1985

| | POLITICAL EVENTS | RELIGIOUS/PHILOSOPHICAL DEVELOPMENTS | THEOLOGICAL SIGNIFICANCE |
|---|---|---|---|
| 1990 | Breakdown of Yugoslav government as result of secession of Slovenia and Croatia; war breaks out | Desmond Tutu (b. 1931) | |
| 1993 | Black majority government assumes power in South Africa | | |
| 1994 | Cease-fire in Northern Ireland | | |

# INDEX

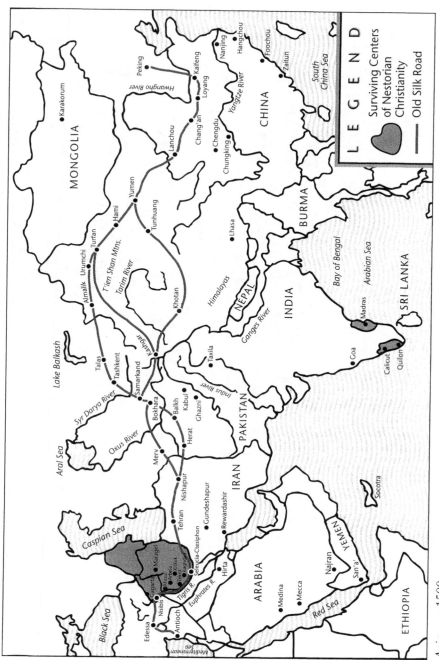

Asia, ca. 1500

*Europe at the Time of the Reformation*

PACIFIC
OCEAN

ATLANTIC
OCEAN

Florida

Cuba

Jamaica

Hispaniola

Puerto Rico

Santo Domingo

Tenochtitlan
(Mexico City)

Portobello

Panama

Cartagena

Quito

Amazon

Lima

Cuzco

Pernambuco
(Recife)

Bahia

Rio de Janiero

Asuncion

São Paulo

Buenos Aires

Straights
of Magellan

Spanish Possessions

Portuguese Possessions

Jesuit Mission Possessions

*Americas in Early Colonial Period*

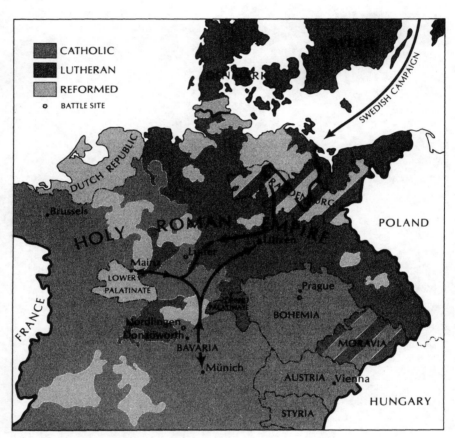

*The Thirty Years' War*

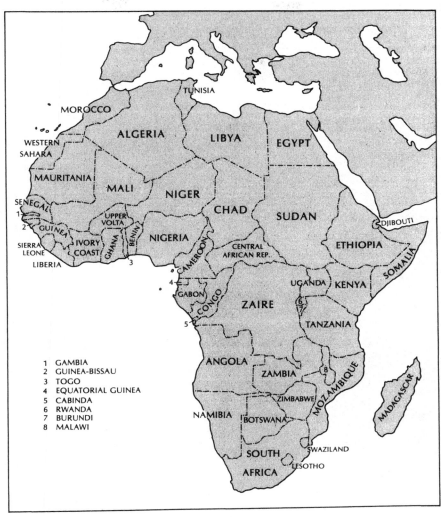

1  GAMBIA
2  GUINEA-BISSAU
3  TOGO
4  EQUATORIAL GUINEA
5  CABINDA
6  RWANDA
7  BURUNDI
8  MALAWI

*Africa 1984: The Growth of Independent Nations*